THE**GREEN**GUIDE
Delhi, Agra & Jaipur

Fresco in Ramgarh Photo: © Anurag Mallick, Priya Ganapathy/MICHELIN

THE GREEN GUIDE **Delhi, Agra & Jaipur**

Editorial Director	Cynthia Ochterbeck
Editor	Gwen Cannon
Contributing Writers	Kamini Dandapani, Priya Ganapathy, Parvati M. Krishnan, Anurag Mallick, George Michell, Élisabeth Cautru, Philippe Longin, Joseph Perrin, Catherine Pommier
Production Manager	Natasha G. George
Cartography	Peter Wrenn, Thierry Lemasson, Michèle Cana
Photo Editor	Yoshimi Kanazawa
Proofreader	Parvati M. Krishnan
Interior Design	Chris Bell, Yoshimi Kanazawa, Rachel Mills
Cover Design	Chris Bell, Christelle Le Déan
Layout	Nicole D. Jordan, Natasha G. George
Cover Layout	Michelin Travel Partner, Natasha G. George

Contact Us	Michelin India Tyres Private. Limited
	7th Floor, The Pinnacle Business Tower
	Shooting Range Road
	Surajkund
	Faridabad - 121001
	☏+91 - 129 3097777
	www.michelin.in
	Michelin Travel Partner
	Hannay House
	39 Clarendon Road
	Watford, Herts WD17 1JA
	UK
	☏01923 205240
	travelpubsales@uk.michelin.com
	www.ViaMichelin.com
Special Sales	For information regarding bulk sales, customised editions and premium sales, please contact us at: travel.lifestyle@us.michelin.com www.michelintravel.com

HOW TO USE THIS GUIDE

PLANNING YOUR TRIP

The blue-tabbed PLANNING YOUR TRIP section at the front of the guide gives you **ideas for your trip** and **practical information** to help you organise it. You'll find tours, practical information, a host of outdoor activities, a calendar of events, information on shopping, sightseeing, kids' activities, books, films and more.

INTRODUCTION

The orange-tabbed section, INTRODUCTION, explores **Delhi, Agra and Jaipur Today** focusing on religion, language, government, economy, media and cuisine. The **History** section spans early dynasties and empires to the Colonial period and post-Independence. **Architecture, Art, Literature, Cinema, Music** and **Dance** are all covered, while **Nature** delves into the natural landscape, flora and fauna.

DISCOVERING

The green-tabbed DISCOVERING section is ordered geographically, and features the most interesting local **Sights**, **Walking Tours**, nearby **Excursions**, and detailed **Driving Tours**. Admission prices shown are for a single adult.

ADDRESSES

We've selected the best hotels, restaurants, cafes, shops, nightlife and entertainment to fit all budgets. See the Legend on the cover flap for an explanation of the price categories. See the back of the book for an index of where to find hotel and restaurant listings in this guide.

Sidebars

Throughout the guide you will find blue, peach and green-coloured text boxes with lively anecdotes, detailed history and background information.

😊 A Bit of Advice 😊

Green advice boxes found in this guide contain practical tips and handy information relevant to your visit or to a sight in the Discovering section.

STAR RATINGS★★★

Michelin has given star ratings for more than 100 years. If you're pressed for time, we recommend you visit the ★★★, or ★★ sights first:

★★★   **Highly recommended**

★★   **Recommended**

★   **Interesting**

MAPS

😊 Principal Sights map.

😊 Region maps.

😊 Maps for major cities and villages.

😊 Local tour maps.

All maps in this guide are oriented north, unless otherwise indicated by a directional arrow. The term "Local Map" refers to a map within the chapter or Tourism Region. A complete list of the maps found in the guide appears at the back of this book.

© DINODIA/age fotostock

PLANNING YOUR TRIP

INTRODUCTION TO DELHI, AGRA & JAIPUR

CONTENTS

© Christian Heeb/John Warburton-Lee/Photononstop

DISCOVERING DELHI, AGRA & JAIPUR

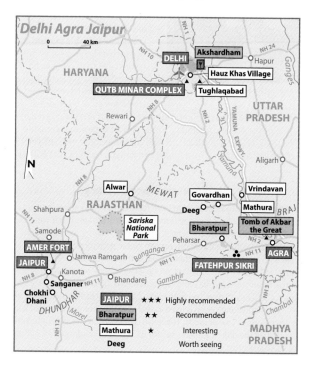

Sustainable Tourism

By far the most enticing tourist route in the country is northern India's 'Golden Triangle', beckoning travellers to the magnificent monuments of Delhi; Agra's famed Taj Mahal to the south-east; and Rajasthan's 'Pink City' of Jaipur to the south-west. The rich residue of their past—ancient mosques, ornate temples, grand palaces, imposing forts and mural-splashed mansions—enthralls and intrigues visitors. So do the people of the region, their religious rituals, colourful dress, and age-old traditions—all set before a backdrop of undulating hills, sacred rivers, dune-enfolded desert, wondrous wetlands, and forested reserves holding a wealth of flora and fauna.

© Anurag Mallick, Priya Ganapathy/MICHELIN

Women making quilts in Ranthambore

Yet the question remains: how to protect this precious architectural, cultural and natural heritage from polluted air, dwindling resources, increased waste, and burdened infrastructure—the impact of an expanding population and growing numbers of tourists.

Government efforts include conversion to compressed natural gas for Delhi's public buses, banning plastic bags in Jaipur and Delhi, adding "green lungs" to Agra and Delhi by planting trees. Rajasthan has created **sustainable tourism** opportunities such as helping rural women plant onions or till a field, working on an organic farm and learning about agricultural practices that are environmentally friendly.

NGOs and other organisations are doing their part: the **Ranthambore Foundation** (see sidebar p7) is improving socio-economic conditions by reviving traditional crafts. **Virasat Experiences** arranges walking and bicycle tours, farm stays, village trips and craft workshops in Rajasthan. The Delhi chapter of the Indian National Trust for Art and Cultural Heritage (**INTACH**) organises

Shyamota's Black Pottery

The small village of Shyamota, 25km from Ranthambore, is known for its black pottery. Craftsmen collect fine clay from the Banas riverbank, mix it with china clay and sculpt a product on the wheel. After it dries overnight, decorations are punched out with humble tools: broken metal, pens, bottle caps, etc. It is polished with pebbles from the Banas river. In the early days, the technique was used to make earthen pots, pitchers, pickle jars and cooking utensils. Today, decorative figurines, Ganesha idols, lamps, lanterns, tiles, curd bowls, etc. are produced over 12 to 15 days and fired in the *bhatti* (kiln) in one go to avoid waste of fuel. *Kande* (cowdung cakes) is used as fuel, and the chimney is stuffed with the dung of buffalo, cow or goats. The finish is done using *laal mitti* or red mud and the resin of the *doh* tree. Plates sell for Rs.300-400, lanterns for Rs.300 and figures Rs.50 upwards.

Making block-printed cotton at Dastkar Kendra, Ranthambore

© Anurag Mallick, Priya Ganapathy/MICHELIN

Dastkar's Success

Creation of the Ranthambore National Park preserved the habitat of the tiger population, but displaced local villagers. Resettled outside the park, they lost access to wood, water and land. The **Ranthambore Foundation** was founded to help improve their socio-economic condition by promoting village craftsmen and reviving dying arts. Within 5 years, Dastkar Ranthambore blossomed into a successful grass-roots social enterprise. Waste materials like rags, reed, wool waste and newsprint were converted to handcrafted products. For the block-printing, only natural colours are used: for example turmeric is used for yellow; pink is obtained from onion peels. The Kendra houses a production centre, raw materials store, sales outlet, and workshops focusing on block printing, tie-dye, embroidery and patchwork quilts and rugs. Besides centres at Sherpur and Kundera (8km away), Rawal village recycles scrap cloth into toys; cement sacks are upcycled to iPad covers at Padli. Today, many of the 300 women working at Dastkar are its directors. www.dastkarranthambhore.org.

educational walks to the city's historic and cultural attractions. The **Morarka Foundation** promotes organic products and **agri-tourism** holidays in the Shekhawati region, and has restored havelis (mansions built by nobles and merchants) in the area. In this guide the **green § symbol** calls attention to sights and activities like these, indicating their link to sustainable tourism.

Tourists can play a significant role in preserving northern India's cultural and natural resources by:

- using public transport and traveling by bicycle or foot as much as possible
- staying in homestays and farm stays
- buying products from businesses that encourage traditional practices
- buying locally produced goods
- minimizing personal trash from modern-day packaging.

For observances that respect local culture, see Tips for Travellers in Planning Your Trip.

The key to safeguarding the environment, fostering economic development and conserving the historic landmarks of northern India lies in the hands of us all. The awareness of the importance of doing so, and actually acting on that awareness, will go far in assuring that this fascinating region's assets are sustained for years to come.

Rural stay in the Shekhawati

© Anurag Mallick, Priya Ganapathy/MICHELIN

Elephant Festival Jaipur
© DINODIA/age fotostock

When and Where to Go

WHEN TO GO
SEASONS

The Indian weather can broadly be categorised into three distinct seasons: winter (November–February), summer (March–May) and monsoon (June–September). October marks the onset of the tourist season and despite fog delays, **winter** is the best time to travel, especially to Delhi and Rajasthan, where summer temperatures can skyrocket. The proximity to the Himalayas also affects the climate of North India as snowfall in Kashmir or Shimla leads to the mercury dipping in Delhi.

CLIMATE

Delhi and its adjoining areas have an extreme climate. It gets very cold in **winter** (December–January) with temperatures dropping to 3-5°C, while **summers** are scorching with temperatures varying between 25°C to 45°C. Hot winds called '*loo*' sweep through North India in peak summer and by late May, humidity rises with dust storms and thunderstorms marking the onset of **monsoon**. Adequate precautions ought to be taken in summer. Wear light cotton clothing, an SPF 30 sunscreen (or higher), a hat or sunshade while outdoors and drink plenty of liquids. In winter, wear warm or woollen clothing to protect against the cold.

WHERE TO GO
WEEKEND BREAKS

Being centrally located with excellent road and rail connections, Delhi offers quick escapes to Agra and Bharatpur (2.5-3hr by train, excellent road connection via the Yamuna Expressway) or Jaipur (4.5-6hr by train). Nearby places like Surajkund, Tughlaqabad, Sultanpur Bird Sanctuary and Pataudi are great as weekend getaway options.

ONE WEEK

For a one-week holiday, do the essential **Golden Triangle** tour. Spend two days in Delhi covering the less congested tourist spots of New Delhi on Day 1 as it helps ease you in before tackling the grit and grime of Old Delhi on the second day. Leave a day each for Agra Fort-Taj Mahal *(closed for prayer on Fridays)*, Bharatpur-Fatehpur Sikri, Mathura-Vrindavan and 2 days for Jaipur.

SECOND WEEK

For the second week, do a 2-day extension from Jaipur to Shekhawati, though even a week may be not enough for the hundreds of frescoed havelis. Spend a day each in Alwar-Sariska, Gwalior and Chambal (morning river safari) and 2 days for tiger safaris in Ranthambore National Park.

THEMED TOURS
TEMPLES AND PILGRIMAGES

Delhi has several iconic places of worship that make for a great spiritual tour – the grand temple complexes of Akshardham and Chhatarpur, the serene Lotus Temple of the Baha'i faith, the ISKCON Temple, the Laxmi Narayan Temple or Birla Mandir, nearly half a dozen historic gurdwaras (Sikh shrines) like Bangla Sahib, Rakabganj, Sisganj, Moti Bagh and Majnu ka Tila,

Safari in Ranthambore National Park

© Anurag Mallick, Priya Ganapathy/MICHELIN

colonial-era churches like St James Church, Central Baptist Church and Sacred Heart Cathedral besides mosques such as Jama Masjid in Old Delhi and dargahs of Sufi saints like Nizamuddin Auliya in Delhi, Moinuddin Chishti in Ajmer Sharif and Salim Chishti at Fatehpur Sikri. The Mathura-Vrindavan-Govardhan-Nandgaon belt is the most popular spiritual circuit around Delhi besides Pushkar and Khatu Shyamji.

WILDLIFE

Delhi has a diverse habitat with sites like the forested Delhi Ridge, marshlands of Okhla Barrage and scrub and wetlands of Sultanpur serving as great birdwatching spots within the city. Spotted deer, langurs, macaques, peacocks and nilgai can be sighted fairly easily. The proximity of Delhi to the birdwatching haven of Bharatpur and national parks such as Sariska, Ranthambore and Chambal offers tourists a rewarding wildlife experience.

CULTURAL HERITAGE

The rich cultural heritage of the region spans several millennia. Ancient sites like Kurukshetra and Indraprastha are linked to India's greatest epic, the *Mahabharata*. Architecture and history buffs can appreciate the medieval monuments of Delhi or uncover the Mughal legacy stretching from the present capital to Agra, Sikandra and Fatehpur Sikri. Discover the proud legacy of the Rajput warriors in the forts, palaces and pleasure pavilions at Jaipur, Alwar, Bharatpur and Shekhawati. Arts, crafts, cuisine and music, patronised by rulers and perfected over centuries, are part of the region's intangible heritage.

NATURAL SITES

Surrounded by small forest patches and wildlife reserves, the rugged Aravalli hill range, the riverine habitat of the Yamuna and scenic lakes such as Surajkund, Sultanpur, Siliserh and Sambhar, the region is rich in its natural bounty. Explore local flora and fauna as you uncover myths and legends behind rocks, rivers and mountains.

GREEN HOLIDAYS §

Rajasthan in particular is focused on **sustainable tourism** opportunities. Help village women plant onions, till a field, work on an organic farm, milk a cow or learn about *go-mutra kheti* (agriculture using cow urine) in the Shekhawati region. The MR Morarka Foundation promotes organic agriculture and agri-tourism holidays in and around Nawalgarh.

Planting onions in the Shekhawati

© Anurag Mallick, Priya Ganapathy/MICHELIN

11

What to See and Do

OUTDOOR FUN

CYCLING §

Cycling is a clean, green and unique way of exploring any destination. With cycling as a hobby taking off in India in recent years, many tour companies offer half-day **cycling tours** in Delhi and Jaipur, besides longer circuits in the Golden Triangle and Rajasthan.

DELHI BY BICYCLE

Started by Dutchman and former South Asia correspondent Jack Leenaars in 2009, the thematic circuits commence from Delite Cinema and include the Shah Jahan Tour (exploring Shahjahanabad), Yamuna Tour (riverside explorations), Haveli Tour (mansions of Old Delhi) and Raj Tour (recent colonial landmarks). Tours cost Rs.1,750 per person and hours are 6:30am to 10am, except for the Nizamuddin afternoon tour (October-April), which begins at 1:15pm from the Police Station on Mathura Road and ends at 5:30pm. ℘ 011 64645906, +91 9811723720. www.delhibycycle.com.

ART OF BICYCLE TRIPS

Founded by cycling enthusiasts, this company offers several pedalling adventures across India. You can choose from half-day bike trips such as the 25km Nahargarh Loop in Jaipur starting from Hawa Mahal (Rs.1,950/person). Or opt for longer 10-day trips with 50km cycling each day such as Rajasthan ($3,895/person, double occupancy) or Agra-Bharatpur-Jaipur ($4,295/person), inclusive of food and stay. Group size varies from 2 to 10 with moderate level of difficulty. ℘ +91 8129945707, 9538973506. www.artofbicycletrips.com.

JAIPUR CYCLE TOURS

Virasat Experiences, a community tourism initiative, offers bicycle trips past Jaipur's pink stucco buildings to hilltop forts, charming villages and remote shrines. Choose from the Ramgarh Lake Ride or the Nahargarh Ride (Rs.1,650/person). ℘ 0141 5109090/95, +91 9667200797. www.virasatexperiences.com.

FISHING

While most angling trips in North India start from Delhi, the majority of fishing beats lie on the Saryu, Kali Pancheshwar and Western Ramganga rivers in the Kumaon and Garhwal region of Uttarakhand and Himachal. There are few fishing options in the Golden Triangle, except small lakes and rivers like Chambal and Banas.

HIMALAYAN OUTBACK

Spend a day to a fortnight in diverse angling holidays: mahseer fishing on the Western Ramganga and Pancheshwar, tackling the goonch (giant catfish) or fly-fishing for the brown and Himalayan trout. ℘ 011 40514060. www.himalayanoutback.com.

GOLF

The colonial-era Delhi Golf Club next to the Oberoi Hotel is the capital's premiere golfing venue, though the Delhi Development Authority has developed two courses at Lado Sarai and Bhalswa. New private courses in Noida and Gurgaon (both part of the National Capital Region) designed by golfing legends match up to international standards. Golftripz organises golfing holidays around the world and has a Golden Triangle Golfing Tour. For information ℘040 40183454, +91 9849225432. www.golftripz.com.

DELHI GOLF CLUB

Located on Dr. Zakir Hussain Marg, Delhi's oldest golf club has two courses: the 18-hole Lodhi Course, part of the Asian PGA tour, and the 9-hole Peacock Course. Prior booking is required. Open all days 5am–7pm. Charges for non-members: US $50 (weekdays) $75

(weekends). ✆ 011 24360002.
www.delhigolfclub.org.

QUTAB GOLF COURSE, LADO SARAI

This course has a putting green with
clubs and golf balls on hire at nominal
charges. Open Tue–Sun 6 am–9pm
(floodlit), Monday closed. Green fee
for walk-in guests Rs.300 (weekdays),
Rs.600 (weekends/holidays).
Siri Fort Road. ✆ 011 26496657.
www.qutubgolfcourse.com.

ITC CLASSIC GOLF RESORT, GURGAON

The first South Asian Signature
Championship Golf Course designed
by Jack Nicklaus, this resort spreads
over 300 acres at the Aravalli foothills.
With 27 holes of 3 nines each (The
Ridge, The Valley and The Canyon), it
has four water bodies and more than
100 bunkers. The 18-hole Signature
Championship Course is par 72, 7,114
yards and a par 36, 9-hole course
of 3,135 yards. ✆ +91 9999996099.
www.cgronline.com.

GOLDEN GREENS GOLF CLUB, GURGAON

Spread over 275 acres against the
Aravalli hills, the 18-hole, par 72,
7,100-yard championship course has
been designed by Dr. Martin Hawtree.
Walk-in guests can just pay Rs.1,600 on
weekdays and Rs.3,200 on weekends
to play the full 18-hole course.
✆ 0124 4969708, +91 9818852200.
www.gggrl.com.

JAYPEE GREENS GOLF COURSE, GREATER NOIDA

Started by the Jaypee Group in 2000
as a 450-acre golf-centric real estate
development project in Greater Noida,
this 18-hole course is the only one
in India designed by Greg Norman.
It won the Best Golf Course award in
2011. Opposite Sector Alpha-I, Near
Pari Chowk, Jaypee Greens, Greater
Noida ✆ 0120 2326725. www.
jaypeegreens.com.

RAMBAGH GOLF CLUB, JAIPUR

One of the oldest and most prestigious
golf clubs affiliated with the Indian
Golf Union, the 18-hole championship
course (Par 70, 6,303 yards) was set
up at the behest of Rajmata Gayatri
Devi in 1944 after trying golf in
Gulmarg. While on the course, see
sites like Rambagh Palace Hotel, Moti
Doongri Fort, Nahargarh Fort and Birla
Planetarium. Bhawani Singh Road,
Rambagh. ✆ 0141 2385239, 2385482.
www.rambaghgolfclub.com.

HIKING

At 1.5 billion years, the Aravalli range
in North West India ranks among the
oldest mountain ranges on the planet.
The rugged terrain covered in scrub
forests has some exciting hikes of
easy to moderate difficulty that offer
a close look at this fascinating region.
The Delhi Ridge is a delightful place
for nature hikes, while the hill forts of
Rajasthan are also suited for day hikes.
*Check with the tourism offices in the
Discovering section of this guide.*

RAJASTHAN TREKKING

The Udaipur-based company
organises short and multi-day treks
in the Aravallis around Ghanerao,
Ranakpur and Kumbhalgarh.
✆ +91 9571981961.
www.rajasthantrekking.com

HORSE RIDING

With its fearless nature and trademark
upturned ears that curve inwards,
the Marwari horse is like no other.
Riding enthusiasts from around the
world converge on Rajasthan for
cross-country horse safaris in the
Shekhawati region as they visit animal
fairs like Balotra and Pushkar or opt for
a luxurious Forts & Palaces tour and
customised riding holidays.

ROYAL RIDING HOLIDAYS

Roop Niwas Kothi, Nawalgarh.
✆ 0141 2622949. www.royalriding
holidays.com.

ROYAL EQUESTRIAN AND POLO CENTRE

Dundlod Fort ℰ 015 94252519, 252199. www.dundlod.com.

BIRDWATCHING

Despite its dense population, Delhi does have its share of parks, gardens and green pockets like the Delhi Ridge, Okhla Barrage and Sultanpur Bird Sanctuary. Nearly 450 species can be found in Delhi and its adjoining areas. For aquatic birds, waders and winter migratories, Bharatpur is an unparalleled site, while Chambal is a great spot for the Indian skimmer.

WILD WORLD INDIA

WWI is an award-winning specialised nature/wildlife company that organises birdwatching trips and customised wildlife itineraries to parks and nature reserves across India. ℰ +91 9818130303. Email wwi@wildworldindia.com.

DELHI BIRD

The northern India network of birding enthusiasts has photos of birds and trip reports by members, besides listing of local birdwatching trips and events. ℰ +91 9810008625. www.delhibird.com

ORGANISED SIGHTSEEING TOURS
BY COACH

Delhi Tourism organises a half-day Morning Tour of **New Delhi** daily (except Monday) between 9am–1:45pm, which costs Rs.207 per person by air-conditioned (AC) Bus. It covers Laxmi Narayan Temple, Qutub Minar, Baha'i Temple and Gandhi Smriti, driving past India Gate and Parliament House. The half-day Afternoon Tour from 2:15pm–6pm costs Rs.207 per head by AC bus and covers Red Fort, Rajghat, Humayun's Tomb and drives past Shakti Sthal and Purana Qila (Old Fort). The two tours can be combined into a full-day sightseeing tour for Rs.361 per person.

For a more flexible experience, try the HOHO Hop-On/Hop-Off Dilli Dekho (*see Delhi*) Bus service (every 30min). The route showcases more than 18 sights such as Hauz Khas Village, Dilli Haat, Safdarjung's Tomb, Jantar Mantar and the National Museum, with the option of hopping on or off at any pick up/drop off point. Tickets can be booked online or onboard, with monument entry tickets also available to save time. Call ℰ 011 40940000 or visit www.hohodelhi.com.

Delhi Tourism also runs a 3-day **Golden Triangle** Tour of Delhi-Agra-Bharatpur-Jaipur (departs 7am every Tuesday and Friday) for Rs. 4,742 (adult) and Rs. 4,330 (child). The cost includes AC transport, accommodation and guide charges. RTDC organises a full-day tour of **Jaipur** between 9am–6pm for Rs.300 per person, covering Amer Fort and Palace, City Palace and Museum, Jantar Mantar, Hawa Mahal, Jal Mahal, royal cenotaphs at Gaitor, Nahargarh Fort and Palace, Jaigarh Fort, Laxmi Narayan Temple (Birla Mandir) and Kanak Vrindavan. The half-day tour costing Rs.250 runs 8am–1pm, 11:30am–4:30pm and 1:30–6:30pm, covering Amer Palace, City Palace, Hawa Mahal, Gaitor, observatory, Albert Hall, Laxmi Narayan Temple and Jal Mahal. A Pink City-By-Night Tour for Rs.375 is offered 6:30–10:30pm and includes a vegetarian dinner at Nahargarh. For more details, visit www.rtdc.in.

ON FOOT

Delhi on foot is a great way to slow down and understand the city, meet its residents, explore its parks and monuments. Several tour companies and institutions organise urban and heritage walks. Delhi Food Tours and 1,100 Walks even take you on gastronomical walks to local eateries. Areas like Chandni Chowk, Nizamuddin, Mehrauli, Lodhi Garden, Hauz Khas and the Delhi Ridge are also quite popular.

INTACH

The Delhi Chapter of **Indian National Trust for Art and Cultural Heritage** (INTACH) regularly organises heritage walks to Chandni Chowk, Nizamuddin, Mehrauli Archaeological Park, Lodhi Garden and Hauz Khas, details of which are regularly updated on their website. 71, Lodhi Estate, New Delhi 110003 ℘ 011 24632267. www.intachdelhichapter.org.

1100 WALKS

The Trail of Nizam Piya, Stepwells of Delhi, Food Walks in Paharganj, Old Delhi, Karol Bagh, Night Food Walk. Urban Village Walks such as Shahpur Jat in South Delhi. Half day walk (3-4 hrs) Rs. 11,000 for maximum 4 people or Rs. 2,750/person. ℘ 011-41671100. www.1100walks.com.

DELHI HERITAGE WALKS

Choose from historic sites such as Chandni Chowk, Old Fort, Tughlaqabad, Mehrauli, Hauz Khas and Lodhi Garden to the 1857 Uprising, the Lanes of Old Delhi and the Special Heritage Walk to Jahanpanah and Begumpur. Look out for their fixed monthly schedule or customise one as per your convenience. Rs. 2,500/person or Rs. 3,500 for groups of 2-5. B-3/97, Safdarjung Enclave, New Delhi 110029. ℘ +91 9212534868. www.delhiheritagewalks.com.

VIRASAT EXPERIENCES, RAJASTHAN

Leisurely walking tours in Jaipur meeting residents, local craftsmen and iconic shops are organised by interesting themes that will appeal to photographers, food lovers, etc. Temples & Havelis Tour, Bazaar, Crafts & Cuisine Walk, Art & Antiquities of Old Jaipur and Amer Heritage Walk. Heritage Walks in Jodhpur and Udaipur. In addition, guided tours and trekking are also offered. ℘ 0141 5109090/95, +91 9667200797. www.virasatexperiences.com.

WATER SPORTS

Lakes like Sultanpur and Siliserh near Jaipur as well as some lakes in Delhi offer boating along with water parks like Splash and Just Chill.

SPLASH WATER PARK

This amusement water park in North Delhi has water slides, rides, wave pool and other aquatic attractions. Entry Fee: Rs.300 children, Rs.400 adults. Main GT Karnal Road, Near Palla Mod, Alipur Delhi 110036. ℘ 011 27708503-04, +91 9250059678, 9250055222. www.splashwaterpark.co.in.

JUST CHILL WATER PARK

Main GT Karnal Road, Near GTB Memorial, Delhi 110040. Entry Fee: Rs. 300 children, Rs. 400 adults (Rs.100 surcharge on weekends and public holidays) ℘ +91 9910499774, 8285111565. www.justchillwaterpark.com.

INDOOR FUN
SPAS

Ayurveda, detox and rejuvenation have become high on the travel agenda of visitors to India. Skin treatments to massages and relaxing therapies such as reflexology, hydrotherapy, meditation and aromatherapies are available. Among the many spas in Delhi are **NeoVeda Spa** at the Metropolitan Hotel, **The Four Fountains** in South Ex2 and Aman Resorts, with its private plunge pool in every room. **Hammam Spa** facilities are great places to luxuriate in New Delhi. **Amatrra Spa** is another true-blue metropolitan lifestyle spa that combines Ayurveda and Astrology in its treatments. In Agra, visit ITC WelcomGroup's **Kaya Kalp**. The Royal Spa and Oberoi's **Amarvilas Spa** offer regal lavishness. Besides the traditional **Kerala Ayurveda Kendra**, Jaipur has **Aura Thai Spa** and **Ziva Thai Spa** that offer Asian-style treatments and therapies.

COURSES
COOKERY

Besides long-term diploma and certificate courses, the Asian Academy of Culinary Art (www.aaca.co.in) organises hobby classes for salads, soups, snacks, baking, desserts, Indian, Chinese and International cuisines at its culinary academy at E-9 Kalkaji (Rs.2,000 for 1-day, Rs.3,000 for 2 days). Several leading chefs run cooking institutes as well.

NITA MEHTA COOKING CLASSES

A wide range of Gourmet Certificate courses by one of India's most celebrated cookbook authors, Nita Mehta, Asaf Ali Road, Amar Colony, Vivek Vihar. ✆ 011 29221645, +91 9873937670. www.nitamehta.com.

MADHU GUPTA COOKING CLASSES

Some 29 thematic courses for tourists with a simple to cook approach by homemaker-cook Madhu Gupta. Hours are 10am–2pm. ✆ 011 23843675, +91 9968053589. www.madhugupta.com.

MUM'S KITCHEN

Cooking Classes with Mrs. Kalra for Rs.5,000/person (minimum 2 people) besides lunch, dinner and Dhaba Discovery Tours for Rs.4,000 (groups of 2-8). ✆ +91 9560002222. Email ayesha@delhifoodtours.com.

MEDITATION

Experiences from Vipassana meditation to Swami Kriyananda's Kriya Yoga meditation, Sadhguru's Shambhavi Maha Mudra for Inner Engineering, Sri Sri Ravishankar's Sudarshan Kriya & Art of Living or Osho's Vigyana Bhairava Tantra or 112 methods of meditation given by Shiva to his consort Sati; these are many paths leading to the same goal. Listed here are a few of the centres that offer meditation courses.

ANANDA SANGHA

Founded in 1968 based on the teachings of Paramhansa Yogananda by his disciple Swami Kriyananda, the sangha teaches meditation, kriya yoga, hatha yoga at meditation groups and yoga retreats at its centres in Rajouri Garden, Uday Park and Delhi Kannada School. ✆ +91 9810276511. www.anandadelhi.org.

ISHA YOGA CENTRE

The Inner Engineering or Isha Yoga Program helps in guided meditations and transmission of the Shambhavi Maha Mudra at its centres in Chennai and Coimbatore. New Delhi ✆ +91 9971800069, 9958844887. www.ishafoundation.org.

ART OF LIVING

The Sahaj Samadhi Meditation program teaches an effortless meditation technique in just three sessions of 2hr each. Temple of Knowledge B182A, Sector 48, Noida 201301. ✆ +91 9958934488. Opposite B6/98 Safderjung Enclave, New Delhi 110029. ✆ 011 43232201-19, 9810078867. www.artofliving.org.

OSHO DHYAN MANDIR

Besides the Osho Rajyoga Meditation Centre in Safdarjung, the secluded wooded campus of Osha Dham near Najafgarh (30km from Delhi) is ideal for meditation camps that can range from three days to three weeks. 44 Jhatikra Road, Pandwala Khurd, Near Najafgarh, New Delhi 110043. ✆ 011 25319026, 25319027, +91 9717490340. www.oshoworld.com.

DHAMMA THALI VIPASSANA MEDITATION CENTRE

Run by a charitable trust, Vipassana Samiti, the 10-day residential meditation courses are held throughout the year at its centres in Jaipur, Pushkar and Jodhpur. The courses run solely on a donation basis, with no charges for food and stay either. ✆ 0141 2680220, 2680311. www.thali.dhamma.org.

YOGA

From introductory classes over a few weeks for beginners to different levels for intermediate yoga practitioners and advanced level teacher training classes, Yoga schools in Delhi provide wide-ranging courses in various yoga disciplines. Institutions like Morarji Desai National Institute of Yoga (www.yogamdniy.nic.in), Bhartiya Vidya Bhavan (www.bvbdelhi.org/yoga.html) and Srima International School of Transformational Integral Hatha Yoga (www.srimayoga.com) offer long duration certificate courses for serious enthusiasts.

IYENGAR YOGA CENTRE

Plot No.65-67, Deendayal Upadhyay Marg, Rouse Avenue, New Delhi 110002. ℰ 011 23234356, 23234357. www.iyengaryogakshema.org.

SIVANANDA YOGA

Vedanta Nataraja Centre, A-41, Kailash Colony, New Delhi 110048. ℰ 011 32069070, 2923 0962. www.sivananda.org/delhi.

VOLUNTEERING

There are many ways in which travellers can aid others while enriching themselves. Work at an orphanage, join a women's empowerment program, help people with disabilities or enlist yourself in a volunteer program for educating street children. Of the 100 million street children in India, 175,000 are estimated to be in Delhi alone.

VOLUNTEERING INDIA

A Mini Break Program is offered from 1 to 24 weeks that starts every first and third Monday. A one-week Starting Program costs US $249 (separate $180 application fee) and a three-week Summer Volunteer Program costs $1,100 and includes pre-departure info, airport pickup, orientation, stay, food and in-country support, besides add-on travel extensions at extra cost. ℰ +91 9716235166. www.volunteeringindia.com.

SANKALP VOLUNTEER

Offered are a three-week summer program with two weeks of volunteer work in Jaipur and a week of travel to Agra, Amritsar, McLeodganj and a three-day trekking adventure in the Himalayas. Application Fee $210/person, Program Fee $1,255/person, Extra week $132/person. ℰ 0141 6454422. www.volunteersindia.org

MISSIONARIES OF CHARITY

Headquartered in Kolkata, this charity offers a chance to volunteer in its regional centres in North India. Commissioner's Lane, Civil Lines, Delhi 110054. ℰ 011 23831080. Mother Teresa Orphanage, Agra. ℰ 0562 2269722.

ACTIVITIES FOR KIDS 👫

Delhi is full of parks and open spaces where kids can play. Besides Lodhi Garden, Garden of Five Senses and Leisure Valley Park in Gurgaon, the 10-acre Children's Park near India Gate has play equipment, musical fountain and illumination at sunset. Purana Qila (Old Fort), with its lake and paddle boats, is also a popular choice. There are Bal Bhavan, National Science Centre, Dilli Haat, International Doll Museum, National Rail Museum with a toy train and a profusion of malls, amusement parks and water rides to keep them occupied all summer. Listed below are a few special places.

KINGDOM OF DREAMS

This fantastic land with a carnival-like atmosphere blends India's art, culture, heritage, craft, cuisine and performing arts with tech wizardry. Catch cinema, theatre and musicals in Nautanki Mahal, craft and food boulevard Culture Gully, Indian mytho dramas in Showshaa Theatre, great Indian talent circus, a Bollywood themed cafe and for the first time in India, a Reverse Bungee. Hours 11:30am–2:30pm, 4pm–9pm, Auditorium Complex, Sector 29, Gurgaon, Haryana 122001. ℰ 0124 4528000. www.kingdomofdreams.in.

WORLDS OF WONDER

Great India Place, Noida. ✆ 0120 4015011/2. www.worldsofwonder.co.in. Road Show zone, La fiesta zone with rides and Games Zone Amusement Park. Hours noon–8pm, Water park 10am–6pm. Children Rs.450, Adults Rs.500.

FUN N' FOOD VILLAGE

Old Delhi Gurgaon Road, Kapashera Estate, New Delhi 110 037. ✆ 011 43260000. www.funnfood.com. Amusement Park 9:30am–5pm, Water park closed in winter. Children Rs.300, Adults Rs.400.

ADVENTURE ISLAND ROHINI

Unitech Amusement Parks, Opp Rithala Metro Station, Sector-10, Rohini, New Delhi 110085. ✆ 011-47041111. www.adventure islandrohini.com. Children Rs.450, Adults Rs.500.

Shopping

The Delhi-Agra-Jaipur triangle is a virtual souk for the avid shopper. For fashion clothing, jewellery, footwear, objet d'art and home accessories, travellers and locals make a beeline to Janpath, Connaught Place, Palika Bazaar and Paharganj in Central Delhi, Sarojini Nagar, Dilli Haat, Hauz Khas, Lajpat Nagar and South Extension in South Delhi, Karol Bagh in West Delhi and Chandni Chowk in Old Delhi. Boutiques like India Crafts in Okhla and Sharma Farm in Chhatarpur stock replicas and antiques in large warehouses. Choose from a motley collection of curios, ceramics, treasure chests, painted cupboards, and even camel saddles in addition to Colonial and Art Deco furniture. Flush with designer boutiques for fashion, home décor and art galleries, Hauz Khas Village and Meherchand Market in Lodhi Colony have emerged as major shopping hubs. Jaipur in Rajasthan is a storehouse of exquisite handicrafts, stunning blue pottery, gemstones, silver, pearl and minakari jewellery and leather footwear. In Gwalior the MP state government-run emporium Mrignayanee is a good place to shop, besides Bada Chowk and Sarafa Bazaar.

OPENING HOURS

Most shopping areas are open daily, running a brisk business from around 10am to 10pm. However, many shops in markets like Chandni Chowk, Old Delhi and Khan Market down their shutters on Sundays. Paharganj, Sarojini Nagar and Lajpat Nagar are officially closed on Mondays, though some outlets remain open.

WHAT TO BUY
CRAFTS

India has been the birthplace for a sizable number of handicrafts, many of which have flourished for centuries. Unique traditions like stone and metal work, clay sculpture, miniature painting, inlay work in marble and woodcarving thrived under the royal patronage in the past. Today, several craft traditions like embroidery, block printing, lacquerware and pottery have been revived and encouraged under government schemes, aid from NGOs and tourism. Brass and bronze sculptures, tribal and folk crafts like *dokra* and blackmetal curios hold as much appeal as classical crafts. Weavers, metalsmiths and woodcraftsmen showcase furniture made of cane, reed and rattan or *sheesham* wood with wrought iron and tile inlays, intricately carved walnut wood sofa sets and screens, Gujarati and Rajasthani-style painted seats.

Many artists have upscaled old artefacts into contemporary and distressed furniture.

Dilli Haat and Haryana's annual Surajkund Mela act as great curtain-raisers to the world of Indian handicrafts, set in a rustic fair ambience. Badi Chaupar near Hawa Mahal and MI Road in Jaipur are popular with travellers for the sheer range of items for sale.

LEATHERWORK

From jackets and ladies bags to delicately designed *chappals* and sandals, saddles, belts, wallets, stuffed dolls and exquisitely painted lampshades and fashionably embroidered bags and satchels, leather crafts have come a long way. Delhi, Agra, Rajasthan and Gwalior are great places to buy leather. Travellers find it hard to resist the lure of Rajasthan's and Gwalior's vibrant *mojris* and *jootis* (closed shoes), typically embellished with threads, beads and mirrors or cutwork designs. Boutique fashion shops display leather garments such as funky tasselled tops, bustiers and corsets, skirts and pants. Leather furniture like sofa sets and stools are also very popular.

JEWELLERY

Indians possess a great love for adornment, which translates into a huge range of fascinating jewellery from antique ornaments to contemporary designs; shoppers are spoilt for choice. Using age-old techniques dating to Mughal times like Jadau and Kundan, the stunning enamel and inlay work of minakari and the 300-year-old *theva* tradition (embossing gold sheets on glass), jewellers craft gold, silver and precious gems and pearls into fine ornaments. Dedicated jewellery streets in South Extension, Karol Bagh, Old Delhi and Jaipur's Johri Bazaar dazzle with glittering chains, necklaces, bracelets and rings, earrings, anklets and more. One can strike great bargains on chains and bracelets made of pearls,

lapis lazuli, amethyst, garnet, agate and carnelian. Often, craftsmen can customize designs to your taste. In addition, wayside stalls, gypsies and street vendors hawk chunky beaded chains; old silver; and tribal, shell and junk jewellery.

TEXTILES

Delhi is a hub for fashion and textiles. People flock to buy silks, cotton, crepes, muslin, satin and lace, trousseau saris, heavy wedding wear and *zardozi* garments at wholesale prices. In this shopping haven, one can find handwoven fabrics, block printed material, ikat and indigo fabric, Lucknowi chikkan work, linen, upholstery and furnishings, signature fashion brands at unimaginable rates. From the simplicity of khadi and raw silks at Khadi Gram Udyog to the shiny world of Chandni Chowk's three markets Kinari Bazaar, Cloth Market and the Katra Neel Market, which offers fine silks, traditional wear and readymade fabric and dress materials to the trendy fashion hubs of Janpath, Paharganj and Sarojini Nagar, there's a lot to redesign a home or wardrobe. Typical handloom houses and Fab India outlets stock a fine range of handwoven cotton and silk fabrics for men and women. With a rich textile tradition, Jaipur is a dream place to shop.

Rajasthani textiles ranging from age-old *bandhej* and *leheriyan* (tie-dye)

Shopping for dupattas in Jaipur

© Anurag Mallick, Priya Ganapathy/MICHELIN

19

styles to bold floral block prints of Sanganer and Bagru are the rage for wardrobes and home décor.

From *dupattas*, stoles, *kurtas*, saris, *salwar* suits, harem pants to quilted rugs, mirrorwork, patchwork appliqué bedspreads and wall-hangings, embroidered cushions and tableware, there's a lot to buy.

In Gwalior, Kothari Sons is a reputed fourth generation shop in Sarafa Bazaar, a great place to pick up a wide range of fabrics including *chanderi* cottons, silks and Madhya Pradesh's famous Bagh prints.

MUSICAL INSTRUMENTS

Music lovers will not be disappointed when they visit places like Delhi, Agra, Jaipur and Gwalior, which have nurtured musical maestros and every kind of musical genre over the years. Lajpat Nagar's **Bharat Music House** is a treasure trove of instruments and offers world-class guitars, harmoniums and keyboards. Since 1918 **Marques & Co**. at Connaught Place has been a music salon beyond compare, stocking pianos, violins, guitars, tablas, etc. Another 105 year-old institution on Parliament Street nearby is **A. Godin & Co.** that sells sitars, *tanpuras* and tablas besides hiring out pianos. However, the shop that occupies prime position among musical geniuses like Pt Ravi Shankar, Ustad Ali Akbar Khan, the Beatles and Pandit Jasraj is **Rikhiram Musical Instruments Manufacturing Company** at Connaught Place. It is considered the best outlet for Indian musical instruments in the city.

The Chandpol Bazaar area in Jaipur has a cluster of stores for musical instruments like **Vandana Music Centre** and **Shri Kalyan Music Store**. Agra's Sadar Bazaar has shops like Jhankar. A cradle of Hindustani classical music, the Gwalior *gharana* of music with emphasis on *Dhrupad* and *Khayal* styles of singing is renowned the world over. Gwalior's thriving musical tradition boasts **Sarod Ghar**, the first ever museum dedicated to musical instruments and shops like **Krishna Flutes** at Phalika Bazaar and the **Yamaha** showroom at Bada.

EMPORIUMS

Being the capital, Delhi houses official State Emporiums on Baba Kharak Singh Marg near Parliament Street showcasing affordable handicrafts and products at government-controlled prices. The emporium complex is spread across three blocks. A walk through these stores is like a virtual tour of India–Kashmiri shawls, rugs and papier-mâché, Tamil Nadu bronzeware, Karnataka's silks and sandalwood sculptures, Andhra *kalamkari*, vegetable dyed woodwork and textiles, Rajasthani miniatures and marbleware, Uttar Pradesh's marble inlays and sandstone carvings, stone carvings from Odisha, Chhattisgarh's *dokra* and black metal crafts, Bengal's saris and Shantiniketan leather bags, bamboo and cane goods from the North East. Most emporiums open at 10am and close at 6pm with an hour off for lunch between 1pm–2pm. Avail the best bargains during festivals like Diwali, stock clearance sales and end-of-year discounts.

CENTRAL COTTAGE INDUSTRIES EMPORIUM

Established in 1952, CCIE has showcased India's arts and crafts for several decades. Known simply as **Cottage Emporium**, it is a sprawling shop floor with a fine collection of pan-India handicrafts. Choose from pottery, alabaster/marble inlays with mother of pearl and semi-precious stones, wood and stone figurines, curios, lamps, traditional treasure chests, brass and bronzeware, jewellery and assorted handlooms and silks. The tasteful display and choice of items cater to discerning clientele who prefer to avoid crowded market places. CCIE is usually priced slightly higher than regular State Emporiums and has emporiums in Delhi and franchise showrooms in Gurgaon and Jaipur.

Books and Films

BOOKS

Reference/Biography

A Princess Remembers: The Memoirs of The Maharani of Jaipur
(Gayatri Devi, Santha Rama Rau, Kailash 1997) – An intimate look at the extraordinary life of Maharani Gayatri Devi, one of Vogue's most beautiful women in the world.

The Painted Towns of Shekhawati
(Ilay Cooper, Prakash Books 2009) – An insider's guide to the frescoed havelis of Rajasthan.

Rajasthan: The Painted Walls of Shekhawati
(Francis Wacziarg & Aman Nath, Croom Helm 1982) – Written by the duo who started Neemrana Hotels about the region of Shekhawati.

Trees of Delhi
(Pradip Krishen, DK Publishing 2006) – A Field Guide to the 252 tree species found in Delhi. Great photos and illustrations, with a graphical scale describing the size of each tree with respect to the average human being.

Delhi Metropolitan: The Making of an Unlikely City
(Ranjana Sengupta, Penguin 2007) – An informative book trying to make sense of New Delhi's past century, from the city the British built, to the colonies created to absorb refugees, from post-Independence to newer suburbs.

Besieged: Voices from Delhi 1857
(Mahmood Farooqi, 2010) – Historian Farooqi digs into the National Archives to translate Urdu documents from the time of the Mutiny. The book is an account of the resistance and life in Delhi during the five, harrowing months.

The Seven Cities of Delhi
(Gordon Risley Hearn, Aryan Book International 2005) - A reprint of the excellent volume first published in 1906 by W Thacker, the book dissects the history and architecture of Delhi.

New Delhi: Making of a Capital
(Malvika Singh and Rudrangshu Mukherjee, Lustre 2009) – A path-breaking book on the eighth reincarnation of this historic city with century-old telegrams, maps, letters, the signed agreement of chief architects Edwin Lutyens and Herbert Baker and even their arguments! Exclusive construction pictures and aerial shots trace New Delhi's growth.

Travel

City of Djinns
(William Dalrymple, Flamingo 1994) – Amusing accounts of the author's life in the late 1980s like visiting the MTNL telecom office interspersed with deeper forays in the past like the 1984 Sikh riots.

Delhi, Adventures in a Mega City
(Sam Miller, Penguin 2008) - A portrayal of Delhi as a walking city from Lodhi Garden and Connaught Place to the suburbs of Noida and Gurgaon between manholes, obstacles and traffic that speeds up when it spots a pedestrian, providing a visual and cultural overview of the city.

Jaipur Nama: Tales from the Pink City
(Giles Henry Rupert Tillotson, Penguin 2006) – The story of Jaipur and its rulers from the 18C to Independence, as seen through the eyes of residents and European visitors, who witnessed and recorded key moments in the city's history.

Fiction

Delhi
(Khushwant Singh, Penguin 2000) – A monumental novel that traces the checkered, romantic and terrible history of this decadent city with eunuchs, sultans and unscrupulous courtiers.

The White Tiger
(Aravind Adiga, Harper Collins 2008) – A dark humorous

perspective of India's class struggle in a globalised world as told by Balram Halwai, who moves from a village to the shallow life in the glass houses of Gurgaon and Bangalore. The debut novel won the 40th Man Booker Prize.

Twilight in Delhi
(Ahmed Ali, New Direction Paperbook 1994) – A novel set in pre-Independence Delhi that recounts the saga of a family who traces its roots to the era of the Delhi Sultanates.

The Taj Trilogy
(Indu Sundaresan, Atria Books 2010) – Historical fiction that brings to life the world of the emperors Akbar, Jehangir and Shah Jahan.

Beneath a Marble Sky
(John Shors, McPherson & Company 2013) – The story of the life and times of the daughter of the builder of the Taj Mahal, Emperor Shah Jahan.

Gastronomy

The Essential Delhi Cookbook
(Priti Narain, Penguin 2000) – Recipes drawn from Delhi's different communities – Khatris, Kayasths and Punjabis, including Mughlai dishes as well as *raan bheja, methi dal ki pakori, muthanjan pulao, mathri papri chaat* and *sharbat-e-gulab*.

Moti Mahal – Tandoori Trails
(Monish Gujral, Roli Books) – From the legendary 1920 restaurant Moti Mahal, a great introduction to tandoori cooking and North Indian staples like dal makhani, tandoori chicken and Butter Chicken.

Rajasthani Cookbook
(Tarla Dalal, Sanjay & Co 2002) – Part of the Total Health Series, the quantity of oil and ghee have been toned down without compromising the taste of Rajasthani classics like *gatte ki sabzi, pyaz ki kachori, ker sangri, dal bati churma* and Rajasthani *kadhi*.

FILMS

The historic monuments, forts, palaces and landscape of the Golden Triangle have served as a backdrop for several Indian and Hollywood movies. The 1965 Merchant Ivory production **Shakespeare Wallah** on a theatrical troupe performing Shakespeare plays in post-colonial India had the City Palace Alwar as a location. The 1972 film **Siddhartha** by Conrad Rooks, based on Herman Hesse's novel, was shot at Bharatpur. The 1984 HBO TV mini-series on MM Kaye's **The Far Pavilions** about an English officer's exploits during the British Raj was shot extensively at Samode Palace and Rajasthan. Kate Winslet's 1999 film **Holy Smoke** about a girl's journey of self-discovery through India and trysts with a charismatic religious guru was shot in Delhi and Pushkar. Julia Roberts' 2010 flick **Eat Pray Love** placed the royal bastion of Pataudi on the international tourism map. Indian classic **Mughal-e-Azam** was shot in Bharatpur and the opulent Sheesh Mahal at Amber Palace. MS Sathyu's poignant post-partition film **Garam Hawa** in 1973 on the plight of an Indian Muslim family was filmed in Agra and Fatehpur Sikri. **Karan Arjun** was largely shot at Sariska Palace and the old capital of Bhangarh. **Ghulami**, on Rajasthan's feudal system, was filmed in the haveli town of Fatehpur in Shekhawati. Jaipur has featured in films like **Ajnabee, Chor Machaaye Shor, Bade Miyan Chote Miyan** and **Bol Bachchan**. Aamir Khan's hit film **Rang De Basanti** was shot in Delhi and Agrasen ki Baoli near CP and Nahargarh Fort, Jaipur. **Fanaa**, in which he plays a Kashmiri tourist guide, featured key monuments of Delhi. The streets of Chandni Chowk and Old Delhi in the 2009 film **Delhi-6** were re-created at Sambhar near Jaipur. Several brigand movies like Sunil Dutt's iconic **Mujhe Jeene Do** and the recent **Paan Singh Tomar** about a steeplechaser-turned-dacoit were shot in the ravines of the Chambal.

Calendar of Events

FESTIVALS AND PUBLIC HOLIDAYS

JANUARY

Jaipur Literature Festival (17-21 Jan) – This festival, held at Jaipur's Diggi Palace over five days, offers panel discussions by Nobel Laureates and world-famous authors by day with folk and world music by night. www.jaipurliteraturefestival.org.

JANUARY–FEBRUARY

Gwalior Mela (1 Jan-15 Feb) – The largest trade fair in Madhya Pradesh, the historic mela was started in 1905 by Maharaj Madho Rao. Held on 104 acres of the Mela Ground on Race Course Road, the fairground stretches several blocks. Besides shopping, Ferris wheels and amusement rides, there's humorous poetry, singing competitions, music nights and even a cattle trade fair.

FEBRUARY

Delhi International Arts Festival (1-9 Feb) – Held at more than 50 locations in Delhi, DIAF is a multi-cultural festival where visual and performing arts, films, literature, poetry and cuisine from across the globe come together. www.diaf.in.

Surajkund Craft Mela (1-15 Feb) – Started in 1987, this fortnight-long ethnic fair, organised by the Surajkund Mela Authority and Haryana Tourism, is spread over 40 acres with 735 work huts showcasing artisans, weavers, jewellers, sculptors, metal workers, stone and wood carvers, embroiders, lace makers and textile printers from India. Folk performances are held at the two *chaupals* from 11am and evening recitals at Natyashala from 6pm, with an Amusement Zone and Food Court offering cuisines from India & SAARC countries.

Shekhawati Festival (12-14 Feb) – Organised jointly by the State Department of Tourism and the district administrations of Sikar, Jhunjhunu and Churu. Nawalgarh serves as the central venue with some events held in the three district headquarters. One-day tour of the region, camel and jeep safaris, farm visits, traditional and rural games, cultural programs, haveli competitions and fireworks.

FEBRUARY–MARCH

Braj Mahotsav – The Braj Festival takes place a few days before Holi (the festival of colours). Celebrating Lord Krishna, this festival has been organised at Delhi, Jaipur and Barsana, providing glimpses into Braj's rich culture. It is marked by Bihari ji's *phool bangla, shrinath ji's chhappanbhog darshans,* song and dance performances of Raas-Leela, depicting the immortal love story of Radha and Krishna besides food courts serving the cuisine of Braj.

MARCH

Lath-mar Holi (March) – While Holi is celebrated across North India, in the Braj region of Mathura-Brindavan it takes on a different hue. Lord Krishna's visit to his beloved Radha's village Barsana on Holi is re-enacted and a ceremony is held at Radha Rani temple in Barsana. On the second day, Nandgaon is the stage for a sadomasochistic Lath-mar Holi, characterised by Holi songs in Braj *bhasha* and chants of Sri Radhey and Sri Krishna.

Elephant Festival Jaipur (March) – During the annual Holi celebrations at Jaipur, tourists flock to see this festival and cultural extravaganza at Rambagh Polo Ground. A procession of painted elephants, camels and horses draped in rainbow-hued saddlecloth as well as folk dancers enthrall crowds. The most beautifully decorated elephant is awarded. Pachyderm polo, races and elephant vs humans tug-of-war are top draws.

JUNE–JULY

Delhi International Mango Festival

(30 Jun-2 Jul) – Held since 1987, this celebration of the king of fruits takes place at Talkatora Indoor Stadium. Organised by DTTDC, the National Horticultural Board and agro boards, it showcases more than 550 mango varieties for visitors to taste while chefs demonstrate mango recipes. Mango products like jams, pickles, and juice are also featured, as are mango-eating competitions, mango carving demos, magic shows and a mango quiz.

AUGUST

Teej Festival (9-10 Aug) – This

vibrant monsoon festival of Rajasthan is signaled by traditional songs, folk dances, and fanfare. Green is the predominant colour and ladies enliven the air with lilting Teej songs as they sway on garlanded swings hung from trees. Young girls don their best clothes and gather at a temple or ground to pray to Goddess Parvati for well being of their husbands or prospective beaus. Jaipur's markets are stocked with trendy fashions and fine fabrics in *leheriyan* and *bandhej* (tie-dye) styles. Sweetshops are stocked with Teej sweets like *ghevar and feeni*.

OCTOBER–NOVEMBER

Bateshwar Fair (Oct-Nov) – Touted

to be over 2000 years old, this fair is one of the biggest and oldest in India. Spread across 4 sq km, the fair begins 5 days prior to Diwali, climaxes around the full moon on the last day of Kartik (Oct-Nov) before continuing for 5 days in Aghan (Nov-Dec). Trading of buffaloes, cows, horses, camels, donkeys and goats goes on for 3 weeks. After a fortnight, the religious fair starts at the main Bateshwarnath temple with rituals and ceremonies held at its ghat.

On Puranmasi (full moon), pilgrims bathe in the Yamuna and make offerings at the temple.

NOVEMBER

Pushkar Fair (9-17 Nov) – One of the

best showcases of rural India's livestock markets, the Pushkar Mela is the only one of its kind in the world. The unique **camel fair** is held in November and draws *lakhs* of people for trade in camels, horses and cattle besides pilgrims who visit the country's only Brahma temple and take holy dips at the famous Sarovar lake. Tourists throng the area to witness brisk auctioneering of cows, sheep, goats, horses and colourful stirrups. The fair is marked by camel races, music, exhibitions and quirky competitions like 'biggest moustache', 'break the pot' and a cricket match between the local Pushkar club and foreign tourists.

India International Trade Fair

(14-27 Nov) – Organised by the India Trade Promotion Organisation (ITPO), the nodal trade promotion agency of the Government of India, IITF was started in 1980 and has now become a major tourist attraction. Held at Delhi's Pragati Maidan, the fair exhibits products from India and across the world, with cultural events, food kiosks and great bargains. www.iitf.in.

DECEMBER

Tansen Samaroh (9-12 Dec) –

Gwalior's premier four-day music festival is held near the *samadhi* (tomb) of Tansen, the 16C musical maestro in Mughal Emperor Akbar's court. The leafy neem tree providing shade to his grave is lit up at night as India's top exponents of Hindustani classical music and singers are invited to perform in the *sabhas* (musical gatherings). The event is organised by the Academy of Department of Culture, Government of Madhya Pradesh.

RELIGIOUS FESTIVALS

MARCH

Holi – Known also as the Festival of Colours, this popular Hindu festival celebrates Vasant Utsav (spring) and the *raas* (playful banter) between Lord Krishna and Radha. On the first day, bonfires (representing an ogress) are lit at night. The next day, people throw *gulaal* (coloured powder) and water at each other. Vegetarian feasts include a drink with leaves of *Cannabis sativa* and dry fruit paste in milk *(bhaang/thandai)*, making for hilarity.

Khatu Shyamji Fair – Khatu Shyamji temple draws lakhs from Phalgun Sudi Dashmi to Dwadashi. A place of pilgrimage, people also come for the *mundan* or *jadula* ceremony of their children (first time ritualistic shaving of hair).

APRIL

Mahaveer Jayanti – (Mar-Apr) Commemorates the 24th Jain *tirthankara* Mahavir, in Chandangaon *(176 km from Jaipur)*. The image of Mahavirji is washed followed by *puja* and *ashta-argha* (eight oblations) and *aarti* with evening lamps lit by ghee (clarified butter). The high point is the *Rath Yatra* (the deity is taken in a golden chariot drawn by bullocks to the river Gambhiri in a grand procession for Kalash Abhishek).

MAY

Ajmer Urs – The annual Urs (death anniversary) of Sufi saint Khwaja Moinuddin Chishti sees *lakhs* of devotees across communities gathering to pay tribute at his tomb. They give *nazrana*: floral baskets of rose and jasmine, sandal paste, perfumes and *chadar* (ornamental shrouds), besides *Ghilaph* and *neema* (votive offerings borne on their heads) to the *khadims* inside the sanctum sanctorum. Highlights include the mesmeric tunes of qawwalis, or devotional music, performed in the premises of the dargah.

JULY

Ramzan – Ramzan or **Ramadan** is the holy month of fasting, prayer and charity when Muslims observe *roza,* or daily fast from dusk to dawn. The devout refrain from smoking, drinking and all vices. Food and drink are served daily, before sunrise and after sunset with a light, pre-dawn meal called *suhoor* and a heavy meal at sunset after the fast called *iftar*. After downing their shutters all day, restaurants and food stalls open in the evening after prayers with a feast of kebabs, meat curries and sweets like *firni* and *malpua*. The month is of 29–30 days based on the visual sighting of the crescent moon. Delhi-based NGO Itihaas organises a history walk from Jama Masjid and Chandni Chowk to witness festivities.

Eid-ul-Fitr – This most important Muslim festival, or 'festivity of breaking the fast' follows Ramzan. On this day, families rise early, dress in new clothes, give alms to the needy, offer special prayers; women apply henna, children receive *eidi* (pocket money) and feasts are prepared. Non-Muslim neighbours and well-wishers offer their greetings and are treated to *sevaiyan* (sweet vermicelli).

November: Pushkar Fair

© Joel Bennett/age fotostock

AUGUST

Janmashtami – The birth anniversary of Lord Krishna is celebrated across India but on a grander scale at his birthplace, Mathura. Houses and temples are illuminated and small cradles installed with a tiny idol of infant Krishna. Raas-Leela dances depict his life. Celebrations take place at midnight to coincide with the Lord's birth in a prison cell on a stormy night. The day is marked by fasting until midnight, with prayers, songs, donating alms and preparation of *chhapan bhog* (56 sweets) dear to the Lord.

OCTOBER

Navratri – The nine nights of the celebration of the Mother Goddess, this fertility festival features fasts, song, dance and elaborate costumes. The Chaitra Navratri culminates in Ram Navami while the Sharad Navaratri culminates in Durga Puja and Dussehra.

Dussehra – After nine days of Navratri, the 10th day of victory or Dussehra coincides with Lord Rama vanquishing the demon king Ravana as well as the Goddess Durga's vanquishing of the demon Mahishasura. It is marked by Ravana *dahan* or burning effigies of Ravana, with Ram-Leela performances (Rama's story in theatre), reading of scriptures like Ram Charit Manas and fairs. Of the regional variations the Kullu Dussehra and Mysore Dasara are quite famous.

NOVEMBER

Diwali – It is believed that Deepavali or Diwali was first celebrated to mark the homecoming of Lord Rama to Ayodhya after 14 years of exile. The Festival of Lights is characterised by the lighting of *deepas* or *diyas* (earthen lamps) and bursting of *patakas* (crackers, sparklers and bombs). Celebrations are kicked off with Dhanteras on the first day, when people buy gold, new utensils and play cards, often for money. The next day, Choti Diwali, is a quiet celebration with lights. On the main day, people burst firecrackers, wear new clothes, light lamps and candles, meet friends and relatives and eat sweets.

DECEMBER

Christmas (25 Dec) – While the devout maintain the sanctity of the festival with visits to the church for midnight mass, fasts, giving of alms and lighting candles, for most others it's an opportunity to wear red caps, eat plum cake and go shopping.

November: Family celebrating Diwali at Pushkar Lake

© DINODIA/age fotostock

Know Before You Go

USEFUL WEBSITES

www.delhitourism.nic.in
The official Delhi Tourism website has valuable information on tourist places in the National Capital Region, architectural heritage, museums, shopping, eating out, transportation, accommodation, package tours besides travel tools and tips.

www.mptourism.com
The Madhya Pradesh tourism website offers tourist info on Gwalior, adjoining sites, suggested tours and itineraries and online booking of MPSTDC hotels and buses.

www.brajfoundation.org
A good resource on the developments in the Braj region of Mathura, Brindavan, Govardhan, Nandagaon and Barsana with information on festivals, heritage sites and rural tourism.

www.rajasthantourism.gov.in
The Rajasthan Tourism website is the perfect primer for destinations, package tours, upcoming events and festivals, RTDC hotels and contact information.

www.delhimetrorail.com
Delhi Metro Rail Corporation's website has information on Delhi metro routes, fares, timings and an interactive map.

www.rtdc.in
RTDC runs 33 hotels,10 motels and a restaurant across Rajasthan. Booking of RTDC hotels, city tours, package tours, bike/car rentals and Palace on Wheels train can be done online.

www.intach.org
INTACH, or Indian National Trust for Art and Cultural Heritage, is India's largest non-profit membership organisation dedicated to conservation and preservation of India's natural, cultural, living, tangible and intangible heritage. Besides information on heritage sites, the website also provides heritage alerts.

www.whc.unesco.org
Great resource on the sites in India inscribed on World Heritage List like Taj Mahal, Agra Fort, Fatehpur Sikri, Jantar Mantar, Humayun's Tomb, Red Fort complex, Keoladeo National Park and the hill forts of Rajasthan.

TOURIST OFFICES

Delhi

- **DTTDC (Delhi Tourism and Transport Development Corporation)**
  18-A, D.D.A. SCO Complex, Defence Colony, New Delhi 110024
  ✆ 011 24647005, 24698431, 24618026
- **Tourist Central Reservation Office**
  ✆ 011 23365358, 23363607
- **Booking Offices**
  New Delhi Railway Station (Paharhanj side)
  ✆ 011 23741871
- **Dilli Haat**
  INA ✆ 011 65390009
  Domestic Airport T-1 (Arrival)
  ✆ 011 25675609
  www.delhitourism.gov.in

Agra

- **UP Tourism**
  Taj Road, Agra Cantt, Idgah Colony, Agra, Uttar Pradesh 282001
  ✆ 0562 2226431

Jaipur

- **Rajasthan Tourism Development Corporation**
  Hotel Swagatam Campus, Near Railway station, Jaipur 302006 Rajasthan
  ✆ 1800 1033500

Gwalior

- **MP Tourism**
  ✆ 0751 2234557, 4056726
  www.mptourism.com
- **Tourist Office (Railway Station, Gwalior)**
  ✆ 0751 4040777

INDIA TOURIST OFFICES ABROAD

Australia

Sydney – Level 5, 135 King Street, Glasshouse Shopping Complex, Sydney, NSW 2000 ✆ +61 29221 9555. www.indiatourism.com.au

Canada

Toronto – 60 Bloor Street, West Suite 1003, Toronto, M4 W3, B8, Canada ✆ +1-416-962-3787/8 www.indiatourismcanada.ca

South Africa

P.O. Box 412542, Craighall 2024, Hyde Lane, Lancaster Gate, Johannesburg-2000, South Africa. ✆+27 113250880. www.global.co.za

United Kingdom

London – 7 Cork Street, London WIS 3LH ✆ +44-207-4373677, 7346613. www.indiatouristoffice.org

United States

East Coast
1270, Avenue of the Americas, Suite 1808, 18th Floor, New York 10020. ✆001 212 586 4901/4902/3. www.itonyc.com

West Coast
3550 Wilshire Boulevard, Suite 204, Los Angeles, California 90010 2485. ✆001 213 380 8855.

INTERNATIONAL VISITORS

EMBASSIES AND CONSULATES

Australian High Commission
1/50 G Shanti Path, Chanakyapuri, New Delhi 110021. ✆ 011 41399900. www.india.embassy.gov.au

British Deputy High Commission
Shanti Path, Chanakyapuri, New Delhi 110021.✆011 26872161. www.ukinindia.fco.gov.uk/en

High Commission of Canada
7/8, Shanti Path, Chanakyapuri, New Delhi 110021. ✆011 4178 2000/2100. www.international.gc.ca/New-delhi

Embassy of France
2/50-E Shanti Path, Chanakyapuri, New Delhi 110021. ✆011 24196100. www.france-in-india.org

New Zealand High Commission
Sir Edmund Hillary Marg, Chanakyapuri, New Delhi 110021. ✆ 011-26883170. www.nzembassy.com

High Commission of South Africa
B-18, Vasant Marg, Vasant Vihar New Delhi 110057. ✆ 011 2614941120. www.home-affairs.gov.za

Embassy of United States
Shanti Path, Chanakyapuri, New Delhi 110021. ✆011 24198000. www.newdelhi.usembassy.gov

ENTRY REQUIREMENTS

PASSPORT

Foreign Nationals coming to India are required to possess a genuine and valid national passport or any other internationally recognised travel document establishing his/her nationality and identity, bearing the photograph of the individual. US citizens must show a valid, machine-readable passport to re-enter the United States.

VISA

Starting October 2014, the Indian Government will provide Visa on Arrival for citizens of 180 countries for a period of 30 days. For more information, see www.indianvisaonline.gov.in. The fees for getting an Indian Visa vary from country to country. Foreigner's Regional Registration Offices (FRROs) in New Delhi, Mumbai and Kolkata and the Chief Immigration Officer in Madras, handle visa renewals as well as permits for Restricted Areas like Andaman Islands, Sikkim, Assam, Ladakh, Lahaul Spiti, etc.

FRRO: East Block-VIII, Level-II, Sector-1, R.K. Puram, New Delhi 110066.✆ 011-3319489 www.immigrationindia.nic.in For Visa conversions or extensions, foreigners can approach the Ministry of Home Affairs (Foreigners Division) at Jaisalmer House, 26, Man Singh Road, New Delhi Mon–Fri 10am–noon.

CUSTOMS REGULATIONS

Every passenger entering or leaving the Indian border has to pass through Customs check. One must fill up the Disembarkation Card clearly mentioning the quantity and value of goods brought. If carrying dutiable goods, one must go through the red channel and pay the required duty. Green Channel is for those who have nothing to declare. High-value items and jewellery require an export certificate from the customs. Trafficking of narcotics and psychotropic substances, wildlife articles and antiquities is a serious and punishable offence. For information on baggage rules and the latest traveler guide: Central Board of Excise and Customs at www.cbec.gov.in.

HEALTH

The quality of health care facilities is excellent in Delhi with 24hr chemist shops and good hospitals. Visit your doctor or travel clinic in advance of your departure date to receive needed **immunisations** and medications, especially with regard to malaria and hepatitis. It is advisable to carry a medical prescription while buying **medicines**. The following are reliable: Max Chemists: In Max Hospitals in Delhi. For locations, see www.maxhealthcare.in. Guardian Pharmacy: branches in Delhi and Jaipur. www.guardianlifecare.com. Religare Wellness: branches in Delhi and Jaipur. www.religarewellness.com.

North India can be hot in summer so sun block, umbrellas and sufficient water intake are advisable to prevent heat stroke. Most decent restaurants serve purified RO water, but to be safe, avoid tap water and ice, and stick to bottled **mineral water**. Traveller's Diarrhoea or Delhi Belly is the most common ailment so avoid street food and oily preparations, raw salads and cut fruits unless from a trustworthy source. Mosquitoes can be a problem in forests or riverine areas so use insect repellent.

INSURANCE

It is important to have proper travel insurance that covers theft or loss of baggage, tickets and money (cash or cheques up to a certain limit), besides cancellation or curtailment of journey. Sometimes, an additional health insurance may be required that covers medical expenses abroad. Any existing medical conditions must be declared. Insurance companies check if the problem was pre-existing, and if undeclared, they offer no cover.

VACCINATIONS

It is not mandatory to get an inoculation before visiting unless one is coming from a country infected with yellow fever. Any person, foreigner or Indian (excluding infants below six months) arriving by air without a vaccination certificate of yellow fever will be kept in quarantine isolation for a period up to 6 days if he arrives in India within 6 days of departure/transit from a yellow fever endemic area (Africa and South America). Foreign nationals residing in, or who have passed through, Yellow fever endemic countries during the preceding six days are granted visas only after the production of a vaccination certificate of Yellow Fever. After the vaccination certificate is checked, an entry of "Valid Yellow Fever Vaccination Certificate Checked" is made in the passport of the foreigner. The validity period of the international certificate of vaccination or re-vaccination against yellow fever is 10 years, beginning 10 days after vaccination.

SAFETY *See p42.*

ACCESSIBILITY

Several monuments have stepped doorways or high steps, making it difficult for the physically challenged. Some sites, hotels and restaurants described in this guide that are accessible to people of reduced mobility are indicated by the symbol ♿.

Getting There and Getting Around

BY PLANE

Delhi's Indira Gandhi International Airport is at Palam, 23km from the city and it takes 45min-1hr to travel from the airport to the city center. Terminals 1 (only budget domestic airline) and 3 (international and domestic) are 5km apart, though are connected by shuttle bus. Fog often causes flight delays at the airport in the peak winter months of December-January.

International airlines to Delhi include:

♦ **Air France**
 ℰ 0124 2720272, 1800 1800033
 www.airfrance.in

♦ **British Airways**
 ℰ 0124 2540543, 4120747,
 1800 102 3592
 www.britishairways.com

♦ **Cathay Pacific**
 ℰ 011 23353643, 43544777
 www.cathaypacific.com

♦ **Emirates**
 ℰ 011 33773377
 www.emirates.com/in

♦ **Etihad Airways**
 ℰ 011 43537300, 43537310,
 1800 2090808
 www.etihadairways.com

♦ **KLM**
 ℰ 0124 2720273, 1800 1800044,
 18001800033
 www.klm.com

♦ **Lufthansa**
 ℰ 0124 4888999
 www.lufthansa-india.com

♦ **Qatar Airways**
 ℰ 011 43636002
 www.qatarairways.com

Internal airlines to Delhi include:

♦ **Air India**
 ℰ 011 24622220 extn. 4710
 www.airindia.in

♦ **Go Air**
 ℰ 011 25671319, 25674480
 www.goair.in

♦ **IndiGo**
 ℰ 0124 4352 500, 1800 1803838
 www.indigoairlines.com

♦ **Jet Airways**
 ℰ 011 39893333
 www.jetairway.com

♦ **Kingfisher Airlines**
 ℰ 011 2331, 23730238,
 1800 1800101
 www.flykingfisher.com

♦ **Spice Jet**
 ℰ +91 9871803333, 1800 1803333
 www.spicejet.com

Between Domestic Terminals: Indigo, Spice Jet & Go Air flights departs from Terminal 1D & arrives at Terminal 1C. Air India, Indian Airlines, Jet Airways, Jet Lite, Jet Konnect & Kingfisher Airlines depart & arrive at Terminal 3.

Main international airports:

♦ **Jaipur International Airport** at Sanganer, 13 km from the city, is the only international airport in Rajasthan. Air Arabia, Air India Express, Etihad and Oman Air connect it to Middle East destinations like Sharjah, Dubai, Abu Dhabi and Muscat respectively. Airport Road, Jagatpura, Jaipur, Rajasthan, 302011. ℰ0141 2550623

♦ **Chaudhary Charan Singh International Airport**, Lucknow at Amausi, Uttar Pradesh, is the second busiest airport in North India after IGI Airport in Delhi. There are 92 domestic and 20 international flights from Lucknow every week. In peak winter, due to fog delays in Delhi, flights are often diverted to Lucknow.

Other airports in the region are:

◆ **Jodhpur Airport** is located in the southern part of town, around 5 km from the railway station. Jet Airways and Air India fly direct from Delhi and Mumbai to Jodhpur. Airport Road, Air Force Area, Jodhpur, Rajasthan 342011. ℘ 0291 2512934

◆ **Maharana Pratap Airport**, Udaipur is located 22km east of the city. Jet Airways, Jet Konnect, Air India and Spice Jet fly direct from Delhi and Mumbai to Udaipur. NH-76, Dabok, Udaipur, Rajasthan 313023. ℘ 0294 2655950

GETTING TO AND FROM THE INTERNATIONAL AIRPORT

Besides yellow-and-black taxis, there are several pre-paid, air-conditioned cab services to/from the Delhi airport like Meru Cabs (℘ 011 44224422. www.merucabs.com), Mega Cabs (℘ 011 41414141. www.megacabs. com) and Easy Cabs (℘ 011 43434343. www.easycabs.com).
Delhi Metro's superfast Airport Express runs every 13 minutes and connects Terminal 3 with New Delhi metro station. The 22km distance, with stops at Shivaji Stadium, Dhaula Kuan, Delhi AeroCity and Dwarka Sector 21, is covered in just 18 minutes. At over 100 km/hr, it's the fastest metropolitan train ride in India. The first train from T3 is at 5:15 am and from New Delhi at 5:35 am. The last train from T3 is at 11:15 pm and from New Delhi is at 11:35pm.
While traveling on a full service domestic flight in India, it's possible to check in your baggage and get your boarding pass for baggage-free travel on the Metro and avoiding two layers of security checks. Air India, Kingfisher and Jet Airways have check-in counters at New Delhi Metro station and Shivaji Stadium station on the Airport Metro Express line.
All buses for Terminal 3 arrive and depart from a 'staging area' opposite Centaur Hotel. DIAL (Delhi International Airport Ltd.) provides a shuttle bus every 15 minutes to the Airport. The State-owned Delhi Transport Corporation (DTC) runs a regular shuttle service (every 30 minutes) connecting the airport to central Delhi including Connaught Place & Interstate Bus Terminal. Inter-terminal transfer: DIAL provides a complimentary shuttle bus service for passengers, every 20 minutes between terminals T1 and T3 of the Indira Gandhi International Airport.

BY BOAT

Boat rides on the polluted Yamuna in Delhi is no ride on the Thames, though boating at Vishram Ghat in Mathura is a more pleasurable experience. Tourist sights with water bodies include the Purana Qila, Rail Museum and Boat Club at India Gate, in Delhi, which offer recreational boating. Boating facility is also available at Surajkund, Siliserh Lake near Alwar and Mansagar and Ramgarh in Jaipur. A rowboat gives closer access for observing and photographing birds at the swamplands of Keoladeo Ghana National Park in Bharatpur. For wildlife viewing of crocodiles, gharials, Gangetic dolphins and birds on the Chambal River, take one of the motorised boat safaris organised at Dholpur and Bah, the two ends of the Chambal National Park.

BY TRAIN

Catching a Superfast or Express train is a quick and economical way of getting around. Delhi has excellent rail connections to nearby tourist sites like Mathura, Bharatpur, Agra, Sawai Madhopur and Gwalior. The fast Shatabdi train now runs on all the legs of the Golden Triangle. RTDC runs the opulent Palace on Wheels $575/ person/night, double occupancy) and an improved version called The Royal Rajasthan on Wheels, India's most luxurious tourist train. It departs on a 7-night, 8 day journey from Delhi between November and March every Sunday at 6:30pm. Tickets cost $590 per person per night, plus 3.09% service tax, and can be booked at www.royalrajasthanonwheels.co.in. Normal train tickets can be booked online at the Indian Railways Catering and Tourism Corporation site (www.irctc.co.in). For train timings, routes, stations and other details, visit the Indian Railways official website www.indianrail.gov.in

CLASS

Accommodation in Indian trains is of three types: berths, seats or chair cars. The classes for long distance trains are Sleeper (non AC), AC 3-tier, AC 2-tier and AC First Class or Second Sitting (non-AC) and AC Chair Car for day trains. Premier trains like the daytime Shatabdi Express and the overnight Rajdhani Express have special fares, with meals included. A limited number of seats are released as per a special emergency quota called Tatkal (Instant) at 10am a day before the train journey for a premium of 30% of basic fare (non-refundable, non-transferable). There's also a limited Foreign Tourist Quota, which can only be booked at reservation offices through foreign currency or Indian currency by showing an encashment certificate or ATM receipt, besides the passport. Indrail passes for short-term unrestricted travel across the Indian Railways network are also sold at General Sales Agents abroad.

RESERVATIONS

Seat/berth reservations for all long-distance trains must be made well in advance as there's a lot of rush, especially during festivals and summer holidays. Bookings open 90 days before departure (30 days for short distance trains) and can be done online or at railway reservation counters. After a train is fully booked, a few tickets are sold in each class as Reservation Against Cancellation

(RAC), after which further prospective passengers are Waitlisted (WL). Often, due to cancellations, an RAC or WL ticket gets confirmed (CNF). Passengers can track the status of their RAC/WL tickets at www.indianrail.gov.in through a PNR (Passenger Name Record), a 10-digit number on the top left of the ticket or top right of an e-ticket. Passengers with WL tickets cannot board the train; those with RAC tickets are allotted shared seats and a berth is confirmed during the journey. The final chart is prepared three hours before the departure of the train.

DISCOUNTS

The Indian Railways offers a 50% discount on base fare to women over 58 years of age and a 40% discount on base fare to men over 60 years. To avail the discount, select the Senior Citizen option under Quota and carry an age proof along with the e-ticket. Children aged 0 to 4 travel free of charge, aged 5 to 11 at half the fare, aged 12 and above at full adult fare.

SCAMS

Touts outside railway stations or unauthorised persons near computerised reservation offices often sell illegally procured tickets booked on another name or false aliases, while instructing prospective passengers to use the name of the original passenger. Often such tickets are sold at a considerable premium, usually 75-100% of the original ticket fare. A person found travelling on transferred tickets is liable to be fined.

BY COACH/BUS

Delhi Transport Corporation or DTC runs Delhi Darshan or budget sightseeing tours (Rs.100 for children, Rs.200 for adults) from Scindia House in Connaught Place to popular attractions around Delhi. The newly introduced Delhi Hop on Hop Off (Ho-Ho) bus service for tourists is more value for money (Rs.150 for children, Rs.300 for adults).

BY CAR
HIRING A CAR AND DRIVER

Cabs are available on hire with an English-speaking driver at reasonable rates, making it an ideal mode to getting around and exploring the city. It is more comfortable to book an air-conditioned one as the noise and pollution in most Indian cities can be hard to handle. A basic car can be booked in Delhi for Rs.1,000 upwards (approx. 8 hours). Usually, hotels or tour operators can arrange for a driver and taxi to any address in the city. A 1-day outstation travel to Agra from Delhi would work out anywhere between Rs.4,000-4,500 and upwards, depending on the choice of car. Rates may vary anywhere between Rs.8-18/km. Minimum distance for outstation trips is 250km/day. Also account for a separate driver fee called *bata* that ranges between Rs.200-300/day. Inter-state permits, parking and toll charges are extra besides an additional Rs. 100 for a driver's night halt. Travelling at night on the highway can be dangerous as speeding trucks with exhausted or drunken drivers may cause accidents. Make sure to book a cab from a recognised or reputed car rental company in advance.

BY MOTORCYCLE
HIRE

In Delhi there's a big used-motorbike market in Karol Bagh that deals in second-hand bikes ; it is the best place to look for a bargain. Inder Motors (www.lallisingh.com) rents out 350cc and 500cc Royal Enfield Bullets for Rs.1,000 per day, with a security deposit of Rs.20,000 completely refundable after the bike is returned free of damage. There are several cheaper options in Karol Bagh as well. Though some find maintenance of used Bullets a little troublesome, modern Indo-Japanese machines like Pulsar 180cc and Karizma 223cc can be hired for Rs.250-350. One must provide an address and photo ID other than a Driving License, original Driving License and a copy, a passport-size photo, and refundable deposit at the time of renting.

PURCHASE

While buying a second-hand bike in Delhi or elsewhere, one must get original registration papers of the bike, valid insurance and a No-Objection Certificate that helps the buyer (or anybody else) transfer or sell the bike to another. The bike remains in the original owner's name, but one must get a letter from the owner saying that he/she has received all payment for the bike. To buy a new bike is a simpler procedure, and the dealers can guide one through it while agents help speed up the time for paperwork for a small fee.

INSURANCE

A comprehensive Motor Insurance policy for a two-wheeler ranges between Rs.500-2,000 per year and can offset the cost of repair for damage caused by natural or man-made calamities, including acts of terrorism. Several insurance companies offer an online all in one policy that covers Own Damage, Personal Accident and Liability, with access to some 2,700 network garages across India.

LOCAL TRANSPORT
CYCLE RICKSHAWS

The three-wheeled cycle rickshaws are a great way to cover intermediate distances in Delhi around metro stations, monuments, market areas, main roads and residential colonies. Rickshaw pullers charge Rs.10-30 for one or two passengers. Rickshaw Tours through the bylanes and markets of Old Delhi and Paharganj are quite popular with tourists (around Rs.150/hr). In Keoladeo Ghana National Park in Bharatpur, rickshaw pullers usually double up as excellent birdwatching guides (Rs.100/hr).

Ownership Papers

Owning a motorcycle requires a fair amount of paperwork and the process can take up to two weeks before you finally hit the road. When the bike is first sold, the local registration authority issues registration papers, which are required when buying a second-hand bike. Foreign nationals cannot change the name on the registration; only a change of ownership and transfer of insurance is possible. The company selling the bike does the registration for a small cost. For all bikes, registration has to be renewed every 15 years and costs around Rs.5-6,000.

AUTO RICKSHAWS

Delhi has plenty of auto rickshaws, but it's extremely difficult to get any of them to put their meters on. The base fare for short distances is Rs.30 and drivers will often quote a fixed fare for the journey, so it's important to know the correct fares from a local before you travel.

CABS

Most markets and residential colonies have local taxi stands with black-and-yellow cabs (mostly non-AC Ambassadors or Omnis) who ply as per a fixed rate. Delhi Traffic Police runs prepaid taxi counters at popular locations, including major railway stations and the airport, which helps prevent overcharging and misbehavior by taxi drivers. For more comfort, try any of the pre-paid AC cabs.

BUS

Buses in Delhi are operated by the government-owned Delhi Transport Corporation (DTC) that services 2,500 bus stops in the city between 5:30 am to 10:30pm. The frequency of buses varies from 5 to 30 minutes, depending on the route and time of day. Fares on ordinary buses range between Rs.5-15 though the new air-conditioned buses are more expensive (Rs.10-25). The private-run Blueline buses supplement the DTC services, but are often crowded, rash and erratic. The city's inter-state terminals (ISBTs) are located at Kashmere Gate in Northern Delhi, Anand Vihar in Trans-Yamuna and Sarai Kale Khan in South-East Delhi. For more details, visit http://dtc.nic.in/.

METRO

The Delhi Metro has revolutionised the way people commute in the capital. The trains operate both underground and above ground covering the length and breadth of the National Capital Region. The Red Line runs from Dilshad Garden (Trans Yamuna) to Rithala, Yellow Line from HUDA City Centre (Gurgaon) to Jahangirpuri, Blue Line from Dwarka Sector 21 to Noida City Centre/Vaishali, Green Line from Inderlok to Mundka, Violet Line from Central Secretariat to Badarpur and an Airport Metro Express Line from New Delhi to IGI Airport and Dwarka Sector-21. The metro operates on an automated ticketing system with tokens available at ticket counters at the stations for Rs.8-30. The trains run between 6 am-11pm with a frequency of 3-12 minutes. Special Tourist Cards are available for unlimited travel over short periods: Rs.100 for one day or Rs.250 for three days. A refundable deposit of Rs.50 is payable as cards must be returned at the end of travel. Delhi Metro Rail Corporation Ltd. Metro Bhawan, Fire Brigade Lane, Barakhamba Road, New Delhi 110001. ℘ 011 23417910/12. www.delhimetrorail.com. The nearest metro station to reach Metro Bhawan is Barakhamba Road on Blue line of the Dwarka-Noida city center/Vaishali corridor.

The Metro Project is currently underway at Jaipur and is being completed in two phases. The first trains began operations in April 2013. Two lines (East West Corridor and the North South Corridor) will serve the city.

Where to Stay and Eat

WHERE TO STAY

The choice of accommodation options in the Golden Triangle region covers the entire spectrum from 5-star luxury to intimate homestays. Choose from boutique hotels, service apartments, guest houses, plush resorts, palace hotels, quaint homestays and colonial bungalows to Spartan spiritual retreats. Several temple trusts run *dharamshalas* or budget accommodation options for pilgrims free of cost or at a nominal charge.

SELECTION

The Addresses in this guide provide a selection of hotels, resorts and homestays in Delhi, Agra, Jaipur, Gwalior and adjoining regions classified according to the price of a standard double room in high season. Some hotels have a lower tariff on weekdays, nearly 20% discount in the off-season *(May–Jun)* and a higher rate for peak season (around Christmas to New Year). Most hotels are air-conditioned and accept credit cards unless indicated otherwise.

BOOKING

Rack rates (published rates) are usually higher than online reservations, which offer much cheaper deals. Rates often fluctuate across the year so it's best to enquire before booking, which should be done well in advance. In most top star hotels, guests have to pay an additional luxury tax, 12.5-20% of the room tariff. Most homestays do not accept cards and prefer cash settlements with confirmation of a reservation only after receiving an advance payment through transfer to a bank account.

HOSTELS

The Youth Hostels Association of India offers budget accommodation in its International Youth Hostels at Delhi, Agra, Jaipur, Alwar and Gwalior.

- ◆ **YHAI**
  5 Nyaya Marg, Chanakyapuri, New Delhi 110021.
  ℘ 011 26116285, 24101246
  Email hostelbooking@yhaindia.org www.yhaindia.org
- ◆ **YMCA** (Young Men's Christian Association) tourist hostel in Delhi has over 100 air-conditioned double/single rooms with attached/common bath for budget travellers, besides an Internet cafe.
- ◆ Jai Singh Marg
  Connaught Place, New Delhi
  ℘ 011 43644000
  Email info@newdelhiymca.org www.newdelhiymca.in
- ◆ **YWCA** (Young Women's Christian Association) runs Blue Triangle Family Hostel with single/double rooms (Rs.1,500-3,000) with a maximum stay of one month.
- ◆ YWCA of Delhi
  Ashoka Road, New Delhi 110001
  ℘ 011 23360133, 23365014, 23743178, 23365441
  Email btfh@ywcaofdelhi.org

ECONOMY CHAIN HOTELS

- ◆ **Ginger**
  Part of the Tata Group, Ginger is India's first chain of budget hotels the first-of-its-kind category of Smart Basics™ hotel chain across the country.
  ℘ 1860 266 3333,
  +91 2261802500
  www.gingerhotels.com

- ◆ **Red Fox Hotels**
  Part of the Lemon Tree chain of boutique hotels, Red Fox Hotels is an economy chain with fresh bold interiors and crisp, clean rooms at unbeatable value. Located at Delhi and Jaipur. Business facilities include hi-speed Wi-Fi, Cyber Kiosk, Clever Fox Café, an efficient meeting room, a well-equipped gym and laundry service.
  ℘ +91 9911701701
  www.lemontreehotels.com

Some more expensive chain hotels include:

- **Park Plaza**
  Part of the global Carlson Rezidor hotel group, this upscale brand has stylish guest rooms and meeting spaces usually located in city centers. With 46 hotels operating worldwide, Park Plaza has hotels in Delhi, Gurgaon, Noida and Jaipur.
  ✆ +1800 1800700
  www.parkplaza.com

- **Fortune Hotels**
  National chain of business hotels affiliated to the ITC Group with hotels in Delhi, Jaipur & NCR (National Capital Region).
  ✆ 1 800 1022333
  www.fortunehotels.in

RAILWAY RETIRING ROOMS

Most important railway stations have AC and Non-AC retiring rooms and dormitories, which serve as transit accommodation for rail passengers at a reasonable cost. Only those holding a valid ticket for an inward/outward journey are eligible to apply.
The completed Application Form along with the journey ticket must be presented to the Station Manager/Matron-in-charge to book rooms/beds, which are allotted for a maximum of 12-24hr based on availability.

HOMESTAYS

Staying at guest houses or bed and breakfast accommodations with knowledgeable hosts is a great way to understand local culture and cuisine. Delhi has several homestays in colonial-era bungalows and boutique guest houses at South and Central Delhi.
From the cheery G49 and colonial Bed and Breakfast at Eleven in Nizamuddin to Tree of Life near Qutb to the Rose and Colaba House in Hauz Khas, Delhi can surprise you with its B&B options. Rajasthan offers several homestays in Jaipur like Jai Vilas, Giri Sadan and

Pratap Bhawan, besides frescoed havelis and fort stays in Shekhawati like Ramgarh Fresco Hotel, Alsisar, Dundlod, Mahansar and Roop Niwas Kothi. Unless specified, meals are usually included in the price, which can range from Rs.3,000 to Rs.6,000. Morarka Foundation also runs a few **agri-tourism farm stays**§ in and around Nawalgarh, with an average cost of Rs.750/night per person, including breakfast and dinner. For details,see www.morarkango.com.

HERITAGE HOTELS

- **Neemrana**
  Popular chain of 29 'non-hotel' heritage hotels across India in 14C palaces and stunning 21C properties at Neemrana, Kesroli, Pataudi, Bagar (Shekhawati), Gwalior and upcoming at Tijara.
  ✆ 011 40778131, +91 9786100436
  Email sales@neemranahotels.com
  www.neemranahotels.com

- **WelcomHeritage**
  Chain of 40 heritage hotels across 13 states, WelcomHeritage has properties in Jaipur, Jhunjhunu (Shekhawati), Bijaynagar (Ajmer) and Sawai Madhopur.
  ✆ 011 46035500
  E-mail holidays@ welcomheritagehotels.in
  www.welcomheritagehotels.in

NATURE LODGES

There are several privately owned nature lodges in popular wildlife destinations like Ranthambore (Ranthambore Bagh, Nahargarh, Dev Vilas) and Bharatpur (Birder's Inn, The Bagh), while the emerging parks like Chambal and Sariska have fewer options like Chambal Safari Lodge and Sariska Palace.

TOP-END HOTELS

Most luxury hotels come equipped with a choice of specialty restaurants, all modern amenities, spa and fitness centre, swimming pool, boutiques, travel desk, money exchange and other facilities. Some even offer free pick up and drop to/from the airport or railway station. Besides The Park, Hyatt, Marriott and the Lalit with hotels in Delhi and new entrants like Lebua, these top-end chains have multiple hotels across the Golden Triangle.

♦ **Lebua**
Bangkok's luxury chain comes to India with its Lebua Resort in Jaipur, Lebua Lodge at Amer and Devigarh in Udaipur.
℘ 0141 3050211
www.lebua.com

♦ **Taj Hotels**
With 93 hotels in 55 locations across India and 16 international hotels across the globe, the group targets multiple segments – luxury hotels, resorts and palaces under the brand Taj (Delhi, Gwalior, Jaipur), resort and spa brand Taj Exotica, the upscale mid-market Gateway Hotel (Agra, Jaipur), wildlife lodges Taj Safaris and contemporary luxury hotels Vivanta by Taj (Sawai Madhopur).
℘ 1 800 111 825
www.tajhotels.com

♦ **ITC Hotels**
Part of Starwood's Luxury Collection, ITC has ten hotels across India including ITC Maurya Delhi, ITC Mughal Agra and ITC Rajputana Jaipur.
ITC also runs sub-brands like WelcomHotel Dwarka & Sheraton New Delhi, besides the Fortune and WelcomHeritage chains.
℘ 1 800 102 2333
www.itchotels.in

♦ **Oberoi Hotels & Resorts**
The Oberoi group runs operates 30 luxury business and leisure hotels and three cruisers in five countries with properties at Delhi, Agra (Amar Vilas), Jaipur (Raj Vilas) and Ranthambore (Vanya Vilas).
℘ 011-2389 0606
www.oberoihotels.com

♦ **Trident**
Luxury chain has hotels in Agra, Gurgaon and Jaipur.
℘ 011 23890555, 1800 11 2122
www.tridenthotels.com

WHERE TO EAT
RESTAURANTS

With a large diplomatic community in Delhi, one is spoilt for choice with dining options ranging from North Indian, Punjabi and Mughlai to authentic specialty restaurants *(see a selection of restaurants at the end of Delhi, Agra and Jaipur chapters)* like Bukhara (North-West Frontier cuisine), Yeti (Himalayan cuisine), Megu and Ai (Japanese), Gung the Palace (Korean), Mashrabiya (Lebanese), San Gimignano and Baci (Italian), Smokehouse Grill and All American Diner (American) and China Kitchen (with five private dining rooms dedicated to Sichuan, Hubei, Guangzhou, Anhui and Hunan). Luxury hotels *(see a hotel selection at the end of Delhi, Agra and Jaipur chapters)* have excellent Pan-Asian and Continental cuisine.

Delhi also has fine South Indian restaurants: from pure vegetarian ones like Naivedyam and Sagar Ratna to Dakshin and Swagat. For Choley Bhature, local sweets and snacks, head to Nathus Sweets. For Muslim and Mughlai cuisine, try Karim's in Old Delhi and Nizamuddin. There's a fondness for Dhaba food (highway eatery) and strong street food culture, best experienced at Paranthewali Gali in Old Delhi.

Backpacking havens like Paharganj and Pushkar have rooftop restaurants and cafes serving faux Israeli, Italian and Continental cuisine.

In Jaipur, sweet shops like Laxmi Mishthan Bhandar (LMB) and Rawat Sweets serve great snacks and Rajasthani thalis. For a larger ethnic spread with cultural performances, try Chokhi Dhani. In Gwalior, SS Kachoriwalla and Bahadura are local legends.

Basic Information

BARTERING

Notice boards at popular lodges, restaurants, eateries and cafes at Pushkar, Paharganj and other tourist spots have interesting deals for sale/exchange from motorbikes, bicycles, phones, cameras, books, travel equipment to accessories. With the rise of social networking and Internet exchange, one can even barter things online on travel communities like India Mike or Thorn Tree and dedicated sites like eBay, Booksvilla or Locanto.

BUSINESS HOURS

Most businesses operate from Monday to Saturday 9am–6pm, though government shops and monuments open and close half an hour later/earlier in winters. Malls remain open until 10–11pm, while privately owned shops usually stay open until 8 or 9pm. Various shops, restaurants and eateries have different weekly holidays *(indicated in the Addresses of the Discovering section)*, so it's best to enquire in advance.

COMMUNICATIONS

Postal services, video conferencing, **Internet** facilities and cyber cafes, courier services, phone calls and all forms of telecommunications are available in all major cities and towns across India. Convenient post offices are located near the circle southwest of Connaught Place and the Eastern Court in Janpath. Patience at the post office pays if you opt for speed post rather than courier services to ship anything long distance as the cost can shoot up considerably. **Mobile** connectivity has eased the hassle of communication and spurred business opportunities even in remote rural corners of Rajasthan. **Wi-Fi** hotspots have also cropped up for laptop carriers. Many resorts and hotels in Delhi, Agra and Jaipur have mailing facilities and even offer free Wi-Fi or Internet at a nominal fee. Some shops have privately run phone services and booths that are open late at night in the busier corners of town where one can make local, national or international calls.

NATIONAL CALLS

Travellers can safely make national or international calls from phone booths and shops that proclaim STD/ISD facilities outside. They are located in every nook and corner of the country. Standard Trunk Dialling, or STD, is the easiest way to make calls to any place within India. Enter the area code followed by the landline number that you wish to dial. To dial a mobile number in India from a landline, you must dial (0) followed by the mobile number. An automated bill is generated at the end of the call. The STD code for Delhi is (0)11, Jaipur (0)141, Agra (0)562. Bharatpur (0)5644, Gwalior (0)751.

INTERNATIONAL CALLS

A phone booth with an ISD, or International Subscriber Dialing board, allows you to make calls to other countries. Dial the country code followed by the number and the call usually goes through with a digital indication of the duration of your call. The procedure is the same

as an STD call and a consolidated bill is generated once you disconnect. Charges in most phone booths are based on Government rates, which is approximately Rs.10 per minute to most Western countries. Call-back options are also available at about Rs.3-5 per minute. Calling from hotel rooms is best avoided as charges will always be very high. Internet parlours offer Net2Phone facilities for as little as Rs.2-3/min or download the Reliance Net Call that lets one make telephonic calls online to over 230 countries (www.rnetcall.com). (00) is the International Access (dial) Code used to call overseas from India. (91) is the International Country (Calling) Code for India.

MOBILE PHONES

India has seen an explosion in the use of mobiles thanks to the availability of many service providers across India. The GSM (Global System for Mobile Communications) frequency band for India is the same as Europe and most parts of the world at GSM 900 and GSM 1800. However, the US and Americas GSM is different so US mobile cell phones won't work in India. It is best to get a local SIM card and an unlocked phone that accepts new SIM cards. The power in India is 230-240 volt and 50 Hz, so make sure your mobile phone charger is compatible. It's cheaper and easier to buy a mobile in India for as low as Rs.1500. Tourists can pick up a phone and local SIM card (Rs.300) at the airport itself. However, address proof must be provided along with a letter from a local Indian organisation stating why you need a SIM card. Some cell phone retailers even rent mobile phones to foreign nationals for a limited period. For security reasons, SIM cards become defunct after three months of inactivity. Find out the rates for outgoing, incoming, texting and roaming facilities and get a good service provider as you automatically pay roaming charges outside local coverage area. Service

providers like Vodafone, Airtel, Idea, Tata Indicom, BSNL and Reliance offer varied pre-paid and postpaid deals and operate within different circles. To call a landline number in India, dial the STD code followed by the number. Local calls in India are approx Rs.1 per minute or lower, while international calls cost Rs.5-8 depending on the prepaid plan and the country you are calling.

INTERNET

All large cities and tourist spots have cyber cafes or Internet parlours that usually charge Rs.20-30 for half an hour of browsing. It's safer not to transmit personal or sensitive details on unsecured networks. Most luxury hotels have Wi-Fi connectivity that is free in the lobby, lounge and common areas, but chargeable in the room. Some business hotels offer free Wi-Fi, but it's best to check the hotel policy.

DISCOUNTS

Many hotels offer good discounts on rack rates for booking online in advance or for group travel. Some establishments offer lesser rates for booking on weekdays, longer stays and discounts of up to 20-25% in the off-season.

ELECTRICITY

Most luxury hotels have complete power back up, while smaller entities use inverters. Electricity is generally 50 Hz and 230-240 volts, which alternates at 50 cycles per second. If carrying a device not compatible to these, it's better to carry a voltage converter or a surge protector.

LAUNDRY

New Delhi has **Quick Clean** (www.quickcleanidia.com), a convenient laundromat or walk-in self-service laundry facility that is immensely popular with the public. With several outlets located across the length and breadth of the capital that remain open all-week, people can wash and dry a maximum of 6kg clothes for

1hr (approx Rs.150) in a smart-card operated washing machine in a clean, hygienic, free Wi-Fi and music-filled environment. You also have to the option of getting it washed, dried and neatly folded by their staff. There are plenty of other laundry/dry-cleaning services besides local *dhobis* (washermen) who can do your laundry at a very reasonable rate, but it is advisable that travellers avail these services at their hotel itself. Though hotels and resorts have a higher cost for these services, they are more reliable. Depending on your hotel, your clothes can be washed/dry-cleaned, ironed and delivered the same evening or the following day. Check on the delivery schedule as laundry services take at least a day or two but the staff may give it sooner on prior request, if it's urgent. Avoid giving designer wear or expensive clothes or those that require gentle cleaning to a local *dhobi*. The traditional method used to wash garments usually involves soaping, scrubbing and pounding on a granite slab followed by fierce wringing after rinsing! Many a time, they mix clothes together, so fabrics that don't use fast colours often ruin other clothes. Specify your instructions, if your garments require special care while ironing or need to be washed separately.

LIQUOR LAW

The laws that regulate the sale and consumption of alcohol and the legal drinking age in India vary from state to state. In some states the legal drinking age varies, depending on the different types of alcoholic beverages consumed. Usually the permissible age to consume alcohol is between 18-25 years of age. In Delhi and Haryana, it is 25 years, in Rajasthan it is 21 years, while in Uttar Pradesh it is 18 years. Home delivery of alcoholic beverages is illegal in Delhi except beer and wine by private vendors and departmental stores. The sale of beer at departmental stores, banquet halls and farm houses is legal in Delhi.

Some calendar days are declared Dry Days when the sale of alcohol or liquor is banned or suspended. National holidays such as Republic Day (January 26), Independence Day (August 15) and Gandhi Jayanti (October 2) are dry days that are observed throughout India. Dry days are also announced when elections are held in the state. In addition, a few festivals may also be declared as dry days. On such days, wholesalers will not supply liquor and retail vendors will remain closed. Except on three declared national holidays, service of liquor in licensed bars, hotels, clubs and restaurants is sometimes permissible on dry days.

MAIL/POST

Letter-post items and parcel post can be sent by Surface mail, Surface Air Lifted (SAL) or Airmail, which vary in rate and transit speed. EMS Speed Post is a premium service that reaches faster and there's also an efficient Railway Mail Service (RMS). For details on services, postal rates, pin codes, etc., visit www.indiapost.gov.in.

MONEY

Any foreign traveller arriving on Indian soil can bring in any amount of currency he wishes to, including traveller's cheques but this must be officially declared at the time of arrival in India. If entering the country with more than $10,000, a currency declaration form has to be filled out. While leaving, no more than the amount already declared while entering the country, can be taken out. There is a good network of banks, ATMs and foreign exchange facilities at almost all cities, airports and tourist spots. US dollars are the easiest currency to convert, besides euros and British pounds sterling.

CURRENCY

Regulated by the Reserve Bank of India, the Indian Rupee is the currency across India. In this guide, it is shown as Rs. A hundred paise make one rupee. Notes of 5, 10, 20, 50, 100, 500 and 1,000 rupees and coins of 1, 2, 5 and 10 rupees are in common circulation. While traveling, be careful of people trying to palm off patched up banknotes, which often get worn out after changing many hands. Do not accept torn or damaged notes, as no one is prepared to take them. They can, however, be changed at the Reserve Bank of India or large branches of other big banks.

BANKS

There are hundreds of cooperative and commercial banks in India. Money exchange counters at the airport ensure that you have local currency as soon as you arrive in India. You can also change money at a fair rate through authorised banks, foreign exchange dealers and hotels. Local banks will be able to order currency for you. Retain the encashment certificate for changing foreign exchange at your hotel or bank as you will need to present it while making any payments in Indian Rupees, or while re-converting unused Rupees into foreign exchange at the airport before your international departure. Only a third of the value of the encashment certificate will be re-converted into foreign exchange. Banks are open usually Mon–Fri 10am–2pm, and Sat 10am–12.30pm. The Reserve Bank of India closes annually June 30 and December 31, while others opt for March 31 and September 30.

TRAVELLER'S CHEQUES

Besides carrying cash and plastic money, it's good to have some back-up in the form of traveller's cheques. The advantage over cash is that if lost or stolen, they can be replaced. You pay a small commission (usually 1%) to buy these with cash in the same currency and a little more to convert from a different currency. Thomas Cook and American Express are widely accepted by most leading banks. Encash your traveller's cheques

at least 30 minutes before the official bank closing time.

CREDIT AND DEBIT CARDS

All national and international credit and debit cards displaying Maestro, MasterCard, Cirrus, VISA and VISA Electron logos are accepted in most shops, hotels, top restaurants and airline offices. Such cards can also be used in ATMs of nationalised banks and banks like HDFC, Axis, ICICI, Citibank, Standard Chartered, etc. for cash withdrawals. Be aware of hidden bank charges, both from the bank providing the ATM and the card-issuing bank as they could charge a transaction fee and load the exchange rate to their benefit. For ATM cash withdrawals, the card issuer adds a foreign transaction fee and the Indian bank charges a fee of about Rs.25.

ATMS

Most banks have ATM kiosks attached and as separate kiosks in airports, railway stations, business districts and markets in major towns and tourist spots. An international ATM card will work in any of the nationalised banks' ATMs as well as banks like HDFC, Axis, ICICI, Citibank, Standard Chartered, etc. The limit on ATM cash withdrawals is usually Rs.15,000 with a daily cap that can vary. India's largest bank, The State Bank of India, and its associated banks offer access to more than 26,000 ATMs across India and 40,000 ATMs of other banks under multi-lateral sharing.

NEWSPAPERS AND MAGAZINES

As the centre for all political activity, New Delhi enjoys a great deal of media attention. Several media groups and organisations are headquartered here. The most widely read English dailies here are *Hindustan Times, The Times of India, The Indian Express, The Hindu, The Pioneer, Business Standard* and *Deccan Herald*. *Navbharat Times* is the largest Hindi daily in Delhi while others like *Dainik Bhaskar* and *Dainik*

Jagran and weeklies like *New Delhi Times* and Sunday *Guardian* are also published here. *Outlook,* the weekly news mag, *India Today*, *Time Out*, the fortnightly *Business Standard*, and specials like *Down to Earth* (science and environment) and *Manushi* (women's rights and democratic reforms) are well-known magazines. *Deccan Chronicle, The Statesman* and Hindi dailies *Rajathan Patrika* and *Hindustan* are also available. Many newspapers have an online version that can be read on laptops and mobile phones.

PUBLIC HOLIDAYS

Government Holidays **Republic Day** (Jan 26), **Independence Day** (Aug 15) and birthdays of notable personalities and deities – **Ambedkar Jayanti** (Apr 14), **Mahaveer Jayanti** (Apr 16), **Krishna Jayanti** (Aug) and **Gandhi Jayanti** (Oct 2). Religious festivals like **Milad Nabi** (mid-Feb), **Good Friday** (Apr), **Ramzan** (Aug), **Ganesh Chaturthi** (Aug-Sept), Sarasvati/Ayutha Pooja, Vijaya Dashmi and **Deepavali** (Oct), Bakrid (Nov), Moharram and **Christmas** (Dec) are public holidays, when government shops and offices are closed.

SAFETY

For Women – The Indian Police has a special **helpline** to aid women in distress within minutes of reporting an incident. Never travel alone by auto after 9pm. Take down the license number of a vehicle before you board it. Call for a radio cab *(see p34)* if travelling past 9pm; cab drivers are regularly monitored. Always travel in the **metro** women's compartment (the first compartment of every train is dedicated to women only). Do not accept lifts, drinks or food from strangers. In emergency, call 100 (Police) or 1091 (Women's helpline). **Medicines** – While there are trustworthy chemists in India, some chemists stock counterfeit medicines, and pills that have crossed their expiry dates. Carry enough medications to last you through your visit. Buy medicines only from the bigger chemists in any city. Stock up on basic medications before road trips and visits to smaller towns. In case of an emergency, go to only trusted pharmacies *(see those listed under Health p29)*.

SMOKING

Smoking is banned in all public places, including railway premises, hotels, bars and restaurants. Some hotels and airports have designated smoking zones. Train Ticket Examiners (TTEs) and Railway Protection Force (RPF) officers are authorised to take action against offenders, usually a fine of Rs.200. It's always better to use your discretion before lighting up.

TIME

India is 5½ hrs behind GMT (London) and 10½ hrs behind the US, while 2½ hrs ahead of Singapore/Hong Kong and 5½ hrs ahead of Sydney.

TIPPING AND BAKSHEESH

Tipping is a common practice across North India and depends on the quality of service rendered. Tip the driver of a car hired for a long road trip, and tour guides, porters, and room service personnel at the time of departure. Parking attendants and ushers also expect a small tip. At hotels and restaurants, 10% of the bill is standard practice, but for an average eatery, Rs.10 and/or any loose change is acceptable. It's always good to tip low-paid forest department guides and boatmen. Often, temple attendants or priests double up as guides, help you jump a queue or show you special facets of a temple for a small fee. At homestays and estate bungalows, tip domestic help or caretakers before saying goodbye. Consult the host if there's a common tip box for distribution among all.

TRAVELLERS' TIPS

♦ **Clothing:** Always offer to remove your **footwear** when entering the home of an Indian. Footwear is not allowed in temples, mosques, gurdwaras and other places of worship (it is permitted in churches). Women should avoid bare shoulders and low necklines; legs should be covered. Shorts are considered too revealing and are best avoided by all.

♦ **Hospitality:** Indians are hospitable and always offer a visitor food or drink. They will be offended if the visitor refuses to even try a little bit. Praise what is offered: they will be delighted.

♦ **Greeting:** Place both hands together at chest level, only if you are so greeted. Don't shake hands if not invited to do so. The Hindi greeting for hello is "Namaste".

♦ **Meals:** If there is no cutlery, eat only with your right hand.

♦ **Gifts:** If invited to dinner, sweets are always a safe item to take. Don't expect to be thanked on the spot or your gift to be opened in your presence.

♦ **Toilets:** Carry a roll of toilet paper: many Indian toilets do not have them.

VAT
Value Added Tax is a multi-point tax on value addition, which is collected at different stages of sale. For the buyer, it is a tax on the purchase price. India has a uniform VAT rate that is fixed at 4% or 12.5%, depending on the product, goods, material or service.

Hindi Words and Phrases

On The Road

	Translation
Direction	Disha
Drive faster	Aur tez chalao
Drive slowly	Thoda dheere chalo
East	Purab
In	Andar
In front	Aagey
At the back	Peechey
Left	Baayein
North	Uttar
Opposite	Aamne-saamne
Out	Bahar
Right	Daayein/Dahine
South	Dakshin
Straight	Seedha
West	Pashchim

Time

	Translation
Afternoon	Dopahar
Century	Sadi
Daily	Roz/Pratidin
Dawn	Bhor
Day After/Before	Parso
Decade	Dashak
Evening	Shaam
Month	Maah/Maas/Mahina
Morning	Subah
Night	Raat
Season	Ritu
Winter	Sardi
Spring	Vasant
Summer	Garmi
Autumn	Sharad ritu
Monsoon	Varsha ritu
Time	Samay
Tomorrow	Kal
Week	Hafta
Monday	Somvaar
Tuesday	Mangalvaar
Wednesday	Buddhvaar
Thursday	Brihaspativaar/Guruvaar
Friday	Shukravaar
Saturday	Shanivaar
Sunday	Ravivaar
Year	Saal
Yesterday	Kal
What's the time?	Kya time hua/Kitna samay hua

MENU READER

Aloo Puri	Spiced potato curry with fried flatbread
Bhuna gosht	Pan fried lamb curry
Butter Chicken	Iconic Delhi staple of chicken in rich orange gravy
Choley Bhature	Chickpea curry served with a large, fluffy deep-fried leavened bread
Dal-bati-churma	Rajasthani dish of spicy lentil, wheat balls & sweet topping
Dal Makhani	Rich black lentil gravy finished with butter and cream
Gulab jamun	Cheese dumplings in rose and cardamom sugar syrup
Hariyali Kebab	Green coloured veg/chicken kebab with mint and coriander
Kadhai Paneer	Cottage cheese in gravy with onion capsicum
Ker Sangri	Rajasthani dish of wild berries and dried beans
Lachcha paratha	Crispy, layered whole wheat flatbread
Lal Maas	Red meat in spicy gravy
Mughlai Paratha	Paratha stuffed with eggs and meat
Nalli Nahari	Soupy bone marrow broth
Naan	Flour bread baked in a tandoor either plain, buttered, with garlic or stuffed with cheese
Palak Paneer	Cottage cheese in blended spinach curry
Paratha	Popular pan-fried flatbread with different stuffings – potato, onion, radish, *paneer* or cauliflower
Raita	Finely chopped onion-tomato-cucumber in curd as a side order with biryani or a meal (sometimes with Boondi)
Rajma masala	Red kidney beans in thick gravy
Rogan Josh	Rich aromatic mutton curry cooked with Kashmiri chillis, fennel, ginger, yoghurt and clarified butter
Shahi Tukda	Rich dessert of toast fried in ghee in thickened reduced milk flavoured with cardamom and dry fruits
Shami Kebab	Mutton mince and Bengal gram patties
Tandoori Chicken	Chicken marinated in yogurt, lemon juice and spices, grilled in a clay oven
Thali	A fixed meal with assorted dishes available in regional variants like Rajasthani, Gujarati or Non-veg thali
Veg Jalfrezi	Colourful dish of vegetables and paneer in a tangy gravy

Numbers

1 Ek	16 Solah	14 Chaudah	1000 Hazaar
2 Do	17 Satrah	15 Pandrah	
3 Teen	18 Atharah		
4 Char	19 Unnees		
5 Panch	20 Bees		
6 Chhai	30 Tees		
7 Saat	40 Chalees		
8 Aath	50 Pachaas		
9 Nau	60 Saath		
10 Dus	70 Sattar		
11 Gyarah	80 Assi		
12 Barah	90 Nabbe		
13 Terah	100 Sau		

Shopping

	Translation
Give me a better piece	Achcha wala do
How much is this?	Ye kitne ka hai?
How much will two cost?	Do kitna mein doge

Food and Drink

	Translation
Aam Panna	Raw mango summer cooler
Chai	Tea

Hindu Calendar Months

There are 12 months in the Hindu lunar calendar. Each lunar month is divided into a Shukl paksh or Light half (15 day waxing period of the moon) and Krishna paksh or Dark half (15 day waning period). Most Hindu fairs and festivals are calculated as per the lunar calendar.

Chaitra	Begins March 22	**Ashvin**	Begins September 23
Vaisakha	Begins April 21	**Karthik**	Begins October 23
Jyestha	Begins May 22	**Margarisa**	Begins November 22
Ashaadh	Begins June 22	**Paush**	Begins December 22
Shravana	Begins July 23	**Magha**	Begins January 21
Bhadrapad	Begins August 23	**Phalguna**	Begins February 20

Cheeni	Sugar
Chhaas	Buttermilk
Doodh	Milk
Dahi	Curd
Dhaba	Highway eatery
Garam	Hot
Kachori	fried savoury with spiced lentils
Lassi	Yoghurt drink (sweet or spicy)
Laddu	Sweet of chickpea flour,coconut
Makkhan	Butter
Malai	Cream
Namak	Salt
Nimbu pani	Lemonade
Pani	Water
Pakoda	Deep fried gram flour savoury of onion, vegetables or bread
Sada	Plain
Shorba	Soup
Thanda	Cold

Personal Documents and Travel

	Translation
Airport	Hawai Adda/Viman Sthal
Bus Station	Bus adda
Bill/Receipt	Parchi/Raseed
Ticket	Tikat
Wallet	Batua

Commonly Used Words

	Translation
Hello/Goodbye	Namaste
Excuse me	Maaf keejiye
Thank You	Dhanyavaad/Shukriya

Yes/No	Haan/Nahi
Good morning	Suprabhaat
Good night	Shubh ratri
Stop	Ruko
Go	Chalo
Why	Kyon
When	Kab
Where	Kahan
Who	Kaun/Kisne
Please	Kripya
Less	Kam
More	Zyada

Useful Phrases

My name is _____
 Mera naam _____ hai

What is your name?
 Aap ka naam kya hai?

How are you? Aap kaise hain?

Where are you? Aap kahan hain?

How far is it? Kitna door hai?

What are you doing? Kya kar rahe ho?

Whom should I contact?
 Kisse sampark karein

When does it open? Kab khulega?

What time is it?
 Kitna baja hai?/ Kya samay hua hai?

Which place is this? Ye kaun si jagah hai?

I'm leaving Main ja raha hoon/
 Main chalta hoon

Less sugar Cheeni kam

Watch out! Zara dekh ke

See you later Baad mein milte hain

I don't understand
 Samajh mein nahi aya

Talk slowly Dheere dheere baat keejiye

I want to go to xxx Mujhe xxx jana hai

INTRODUCTION TO
DELHI, AGRA & JAIPUR

Diwan-i-Khas, Lal Qila, Delhi
© Arturo Cano Miño/age fotostock

Delhi, Agra & Jaipur Today

The cities of Agra, Delhi and Jaipur are rich with layers of history that influence and enrich them in myriad ways. In every street, in countless homes, in places of worship, in rituals and ceremonies, the ghosts of bygone eras mingle with the forces of modern times to create a vibrant tapestry of the old and the new, the traditional and the contemporary, the spiritual and the material that is uniquely Indian. It is little wonder that these places are among India's most popular tourist destinations, captivating travellers the world over.

POPULATION
DELHI

With a population of nearly 18 million people, India's second most populous city is also its most densely populated in parts. While a core of the population considers itself native to Delhi, this city has seen heavy immigration from across India and neighboring countries as well. A turning point in the demographic history of Delhi took place in the years surrounding Indian Independence and Partition, with large numbers of Hindus and **Sikhs** leaving the newly created country of Pakistan to build new lives

Chandni Chowk, Old Delhi

© Taka/age fotostock

and careers in India's capital. These years saw the highest rate of growth in Delhi's population. In the earlier decades of the 20C when the capital was moved from Calcutta (now Kolkata) to Delhi, a large number of **Bengalis** followed their jobs to Delhi. Certain ethnic groups tend to cluster in particular enclaves of Delhi: Chittaranjan Park is home to Bengalis; a sizable **Tamil** population lives in Karol Bagh, for example. As more immigrants stream into the city and as fortunes rise and fall, many of these once-rigid boundaries are blurring to mirror the demographic diversity of Delhi.

Hindus, with 82% of the population, are the majority religious group; Muslims make up 10% and Sikhs 5%; Christians, Jains, Buddhists and others compose the remainder (&see Religion below).

AGRA

This teeming city is one of the most densely populated in the state of Uttar Pradesh. Agra is also one of the top 20 most populous cities in India. An estimated 1.7 million people live there now, of which 82% are **Hindu**, 15% are **Muslim**, 1.4% are Jain, with Buddhists, Sikhs and Christians among the remainder. The city and its population are growing in a westward direction, following the Delhi-Agra corridor. Agra has an 81% **literacy rate**, which is higher than the national average, but is skewed in favour of males.

JAIPUR

Jaipur's estimated population is 3 million. By 2025, the metropolis is projected to become one of the top 10 most populous cities in India, with more than 4 million residents. Rapid industrialization, proximity to the nation's capital and inclusion in a national investment zone underpin Jaipur's expected population growth. As the capital of Rajasthan, Jaipur attracts people from nearby villages and small towns who hope to make a better living in the big city. In addition, several well-regarded institutions of **higher education** here attract large numbers of students, many of whom settle here after graduation.

Some 74% of Jaipur's population is Hindu, 20% is Muslim, and 4.5% is Jain. The rest are Christians and Sikhs.

RELIGION

A profusion of religions exist together in northern India, sometimes peacefully, sometimes not, as they have done for centuries. The customs and celebrations of Hindus, Muslims, Sikhs, Christians, Jains and Buddhists all form part of northern India's daily life.

HINDUISM

More than 80% of the population in northern India follows the Hindu religion and its conception of the world. Hinduism is a socio-cultural-religious system that encompasses all aspects of human life. Hinduism concerns daily life and rituals as well as metaphysical reflection on the **Absolute**. One characteristic is the division of society into hereditary and hierarchical communities—called **castes** (*see sidebar below*). One cannot be converted to Hinduism: one is a Hindu if born of Hindu parents. There is no single dogma or centralised clergy, as in "orthodox" religion. Hinduism is a religion that accepts an array of ideas and tenets that can include the belief in a thousand gods or no God at all. This spirit of **tolerance** and syncretism, from which nothing is excluded and everything assimilated, is characteristic of India.

Hinduism was born on the sub-continent some 3,500 years ago, when the early Indo-Aryan inhabitants set about formalising the hymns and liturgies that were initially passed down orally and comprise the four **Vedas** (knowledge). The Vedic pantheon comprises gods (*devas*) who embody natural forces. It is dominated by Indra (god of lightning and war), Varuna (the all-seeing god of the celestial ocean), Agni (fire) and Surya (sun). Some centuries later, the **Upanishads**, (*see Literature*) a group of some 200 texts, were composed, in which the idea of **Brahman**, or the universal spirit, and Atman, or the individual soul, made their first appearance. The **Purana** texts (6-2C BC) describe the lives and deeds of many of the present pantheon of Hindu gods. The most popular gods are endowed with fantastic legends, which gave rise to two epic tales, the *Mahabharata* and *Ramayana* (*see Literature*). The ancient Vedic gods faded away with the ascendancy of new gods, and **Brahma, Shiva** and **Vishnu** moved to the forefront. Brahma, the emanation of metaphysical Absolute, is little known. Shiva and Vishnu, however, are objects of intense devotion. These three gods form the **Trimurti**, or Hindu trinity; they are manifestations of an eternal, all-pervading God who can be neither named nor represented. Hindus have a great many names for God (Vishnu, Krishna, etc.) in his multiplicity of forms and incarnations. One of the most popular hymns in Hinduism is the Vishnu Sahasranamam, which lists the 1,000 names of Vishnu.

The landscape of northern India is mythologically charged, with hundreds

Hinduism's Caste System

The caste system is the organisation of Hindu society into rigidly structured hierarchical groups based on occupation. It originated more than 3,000 years ago. A hymn in the Rig Veda endows a religious foundation to castes in the "Poem of the Primeval Man or Purusha": from the mouth of Purusha came the priest, or Brahmin; from his arms, the warrior-king, or Kshatriya; from his thighs, the commoner-trader and worker or Vaishya; and from the feet, the Shudra, the lowliest of the castes. Outside this system were the most abject, the Untouchables.

In this stratified hierarchy, the castes, determined at birth, were immutable and exclusive. Over the course of history, the lower castes suffered great injustice. The Constitution of India makes caste-based discrimination illegal. However, it still persists. Caste is a major consideration in arranging marriages.

of places associated with the tales and exploits of divine beings, and the line dividing the sacred and legendary from history and reality often does not exist. The myths and legends of Hinduism are full of names of places where this god was born, or that god battled a demon, or a particular goddess married her divine consort. Mathura, which is just 50km from Agra and 90km from Delhi, is believed to be the birthplace of Lord Krishna; Indraprastha, the capital city of the Pandavas of the epic *Mahabharata,* is within present-day Delhi; examples like these are rife. Rivers, trees, and mountains are endowed with a mystical essence. A tributary of the Ganges, the Yamuna River, which touches both Delhi and Agra, is worshipped as one of the holiest rivers in India. Bathing in the waters of the Ganges is believed to wash away the sins of a lifetime.

The **temples** of north India are generally less ornamented and imposing than those of the south (see Architecture). Many of the temples that are used for worship today are relatively recent, particularly in Delhi. The massive Akshardham temple complex on the banks of the Yamuna River was completed in 2005, and is already a favorite with tourists and locals alike.

ISLAM

Islam came to northern India in the 12C with invaders from Afghanistan who eventually settled in India and established a succession of kingdoms. Now, approximately 14% of Indians are Muslims, and India has the third-largest Muslim population in the world.

The majority are **Sunni** (faithful to the orthodox teachings passed down by the first four Khalifs). Far fewer are **Shia** (who follow descendants of Ali, Muhammad's son-in-law), who live in northern India, mainly in Uttar Pradesh.

Muslims worship one God, known in Arabic as *Allah*. The **Quran** is their sacred text, a book that contains God's revelation to the **Prophet Muhammed** in the 7C. Muslims' life purpose is to serve God by observing the **Five Pillars** of Islam: Belief, Worship, Fasting, Giving

of Alms and Pilgrimage. Their places of assembly and prayer are called mosques (*masjid, see Architecture*), which dot all of northern India. Delhi's Jama Masjid is India's largest mosque.

After centuries of assimilation in India, the Islam that is practised here has imbibed many elements of local culture. The pluralistic nature of Indian civilisation has ensured that Islam has been assimilated into the society through a process of integration and synthesis. It is a syncretic blend that has deep roots that developed even amidst times of political and social upheaval. There are Muslim saints and holy leaders who are revered and worshipped across religions.

Islamic mystics called Sufis played a vital role in the spreading of Islam in India. **Sufism** is a dimension or aspect of Islam that emphasises the instillation of knowledge of the religion by teachers, not just from books. Islamic thought and history have been shaped and influenced by these teachers and mystics; among the best-known and most beloved of these are Rumi and **Omar Khayyam**, whose words are admired beyond the Sufi community. In India, the Sufis succeeded in creating a link between Islam and Hinduism, with Sufism's mesmerising music and dance, holy shrines, mystic saints and emphasis on the individual's search for oneness with God.

Dozens of Sufi shrines all over north India are visited by thousands of pilgrims of all faiths. Perhaps the greatest is that of the 13C Delhi saint **Sheikh Hazrat Nizamuddin Aulia Chishti**, who told his followers that what mattered was not ritual or attending a mosque or temple, but understanding that divinity lived within every human being, that to find paradise, one had only to look within. The most eminent of the India Sufi brotherhoods, the Chishti Order, was founded by the Afghan **Khwaja Main ud-Din Chishti** (1142-1236), who lived in Ajmer. His dargah (tomb) is India's most venerated Muslim shrine.

Gurdwara Bangla Sahib, Delhi

© Anurag Mallick, Priya Ganapathy/MICHELIN

SIKHISM

The Sikh religion is young, as far as world religions go. It was founded in Punjab in the 15C by **Guru Nanak** (1469-1539), who was born into a Punjabi Hindu family. Sikhism is forged from Indian thought and history, yet it has a distinct philosophy that sets it apart from Hinduism and Islam, which were the dominant religions in North India at the time of its inception. Sikhism preaches that there is one God who is all-pervasive, and that all human beings are equal. It emphasises the importance of **service** and charity.

As Sikhism spread, northern India reeled under political instability and chaos; attempts were made to curb the growing influence of Sikhs in Punjab. When their ninth guru was beheaded by Emperor Aurangzeb for refusing to convert to Islam in 1699, his successor, **Guru Gobind Singh**, founded the **Khalsa panth** (sect of the pure), a martial brotherhood intended to defend the community. The tumultuous history of Punjab forced the exodus of many Sikhs from their homeland. The Partition of India in 1947 resulted in large numbers of Sikhs fleeing to save their lives. Many of them settled in Delhi, and today they form about 5% of the population there. Sikhs wear **five articles** of faith as prescribed by Gobind Singh: *Kesh* (uncut hair), *Kangha* (a small wooden comb) *Kara* (an iron or steel bracelet), *Kacchera*

(a loose undergarment) and *Kirpan* (a short dagger). Sikh men are instantly recognisable by their turbans and long beards (often neatly combed and tucked under a net).

Gurdwara is the name of the Sikh place of worship. Any person, regardless of religion, age or sex, is welcome. In the main sanctuary, there are no idols, statues or pictures, no candles, incense or bells. The object of veneration and worship here is the holy book of the Sikhs, the **Guru Granth Sahib**, which is revered for its spiritual content, not its material form. Every Gurdwara has a food kitchen called a *Langar,* where free communal meals are prepared.

Gurdwara Bangla Sahib is the most prominent Sikh house of worship in Delhi. It is situated near Connaught Place.

LANGUAGE

Hindi is the most commonly spoken language all over north India. In addition, there are countless dialects that are offshoots of Hindi; in Rajasthan, there are many distinct dialects in addition to the main language of Rajasthani (see below).

Along with **English**, **Hindi** is the official language of India. It and other languages and dialects of north India have their origins in the spoken tongues of Middle Indo-Aryan (of which **Sanskrit** was the literary form). These languages did not develop separate identities until after the 11C; their earliest extant literary works date from around the 12C.

Of the many modern Indo-Aryan languages, Hindi boasts the earliest literary records and a rich heritage. It also has one of the earliest established traditions of secular writing in the form of the 12C Rajasthani classic *Prithviraj Raso*, a chronicle of the life of the great Rajput king Prithviraj, written by his court minstrel Chand Bardai. The renowned Sufi poet, musician and scholar Amir Khusro, of the 13C and 14C, wrote soul-stirring poetry in Hindi and **Persian** that is recited and revered to this day; his works did much to advance Hindi as a language.

Many dialects evolved over the centuries from medieval Hindi and have their own literary works. **Braj Bhasha** was and is the language of a large part of Hindustani music repertoire and of the fine poet-musician Surdas. The *bhajans* of the 15C Krishna devotee Mirabai are written in Braj Basha as well as in Marwari. Braj Basha is spoken today primarily around Agra and Mathura in Uttar Pradesh, and Bharatpur and Dholpur in Rajasthan.

What is spoken and written as Hindi today is of relatively recent origin, dating from the early 19C. It is based on an Indo-Aryan dialect that was popular in Delhi and its environs called Khari Boli. **Modern Hindi**, which is written in the Devanagari script, has absorbed the heritage of its predecessors as it has tapped deep into the grammar and vocabulary of Sanskrit. Modern Hindi is now the medium of communication and education across a vast swath of northern India.

A branch of Hindi called **Rajasthani**, which has its own subset of dialects (like Mewari, Marwari and Shekhawati), is spoken in Rajasthan. Classified as a Western Indo-Aryan language, and sometimes as a Central Indo-Aryan language like Hindi, it shares some aspects with old Gujarati and uses the Devanagari script. It is taught as a language in the universities of Rajasthan, and is recognised as a distinct language by the Sahitya Akademi, the University Grants Commission and the National Academy of Letters. However, the Constitution of India does not recognise Rajasthani as a scheduled language.

Taking into consideration the broadest definition of Hindi (as one that includes many Hindi-like languages and dialects like Rajasthani, Haryanvi, Braj Basha and Awadhi, to name a few), it is spoken by around 40% of the population of India. **Urdu**, which is close to Hindi, but written with an Arabic-Persian alphabet, is spoken in areas with large Muslim populations. The liturgical language, that of the revelation, remains Arabic, which is taught in the *madrasas* (Quranic schools).

GOVERNMENT
DELHI

Delhi is the seat of the Central Government of India, as well as of its own local government.

Delhi Local Government

Delhi is part of several administrative and planning levels. At the macro level, it is part of the **National Capital Region** (NCR), an area created in 1971 by the Town and Country Planning Organisation to direct the future growth of the region. The NCR includes the city of Delhi as well as the bordering *tehsils* (administrative divisions) in the states of Haryana, Uttar Pradesh and Rajasthan. At the micro level, the city of Delhi is a union territory that is called the National Capital Territory or NCT. As a largely ceremonial post, a lieutenant governor, appointed by the President of India, is the head of state of Delhi. The **Chief Minister,** who is the leader of the majority party of the unicameral **Legislative Assembly** of Delhi, is the person vested with the **executive** authority to run the government. The Delhi High Court has **judicial** jurisdiction over the city.

The NCT has three local municipal bodies that handle its civic administration: the Municipal Corporation of Delhi (MCD), the New Delhi Municipal Council (NDMC) and the Cantonment Board, each of which is distinct in terms of function and the geographic area it covers. The MCD is an elected body; the NDMC, an appointed body is largely responsible for New Delhi; and the Cantonment Board, which consists of both appointed and elected members, is responsible for functions like water and public utilities management, sanitation, elementary education and birth and death registration.

CENTRAL GOVERNMENT OF INDIA

The Central Government was established by the Constitution of India and is responsible for the government of the Republic of India. It is based in New Delhi.

The Government of India consists of three branches, the executive, legislative and judiciary. Under the Indian Constitution, **executive authority** is conferred on the President, who is the Head of the Republic of India, the head of the executive, legislative and judiciary of the country and the commander-in-chief of the Indian Armed Forces. The real executive power is exercised in the hands of the Council of Ministers, of which the Prime Minister is the head.

The **President**, who is elected by the representatives of the country's citizens in the parliament of India as well as the state legislatures, serves a term of 5 years, which can be renewed. The President lives in the Rashtrapati Bhawan in New Delhi. A Vice President, elected for a 5 year term by both houses of parliament, serves as the chairman of the Rajya Sabha or Upper House of parliament, and as President when needed.

The primary decision-making body of the executive branch is the Cabinet of India, which consists of the **Prime Minister** and senior ministers called Union Cabinet Ministers, who handle important portfolios like Home Affairs, Defense, Finance and External Affairs. According to the Constitution, all Cabinet members have to be members of either house of parliament. The next rank of ministers are Ministers of State. The **legislature** of India is in the hands of the **Parliament**, which consists of two houses, the Rajya Sabha, or Upper House, and the Lok Sabha, or Lower House. The members of the Rajya Sabha are appointed by the President and elected by state and territorial legislatures; the members of the Lok Sabha are elected directly by the people of India in nationwide elections that are truly a marvel in a country as diverse and populous as India. Together, with 545 members in the Lok Sabha and 245 members in the Rajya Sabha, the 790 Members of Parliament (MPs) serve the world's largest democratic electorate. They meet in separate chambers in Sansad Bhavan or Parliament House in New Delhi, a place that is sometimes the scene of raucous debate, shouting matches and walk-outs as the MPs vie with each other to provide the best for their constituents.

The **judiciary** of India consists of the Supreme Court, High Courts (of the various states) and District and Sessions Courts. It has incorporated many elements of British common law, a legacy of Britain's colonial rule over India. The Supreme Court is the highest court in the land and the final court of appeal; it is headed by the Chief Justice of India who, along with 31 associate judges, is appointed by the President of India. The **Supreme Court** is the interpreter and guardian of the Constitution of India, the supreme law of the land.

AGRA

The city of Agra is governed by the Agra **Municipal Corporation**, known also as Agra Nagar Nigam. The area covered by the corporation has 90 electoral wards and 8 sections for revenue collection that are further sub-divided into several zones. Founded in 1959, it is one of the largest municipalities in all of Uttar Pradesh and is responsible for the civic needs of the people including education, electricity, health, infrastructure, records, water supply and sanitation.

The headquarters of the Agra District, which is one of 75 districts in the state of Uttar Pradesh, are in the city of Agra. Agra District covers an area of more than 4,000 square kilometers, with 6 *tehsils* (administrative divisions) and over 900 villages. The district is overseen by a District Collector or Magistrate, who is an officer of the Indian Administrative Service and is responsible for the smooth running and maintenance of law and order of the district. The District Collector/Magistrate is assisted by several Assistant District Magistrates as well as a City Magistrate and Sub Divisional Magistrates for each of the 6 *tehsils*.

JAIPUR

Jaipur is the seat of the Government of Rajasthan, the governing authority of this state with its 33 districts. It consists of an executive division, a legislature and judiciary.

The **executive branch** is headed by the governor, who is appointed by the President of India. The Governor's post is largely ceremonial; the real reins of executive power are in the hands of the Chief Minister along with the cabinet of ministers of the state. The state **legislature** consists of the unicameral Legislative Assembly or Vidhan Sabha, which has 200 elected members or MLAs. The main seat of the **judicial branch** is in Jodhpur, the location of the Rajasthan High Court; a bench in Jaipur has jurisdiction over neighbouring districts.

In 2005 the Government of Rajasthan launched E-Mitra, an ambitious e-governance portal that offers services like payment of bills and premiums to its citizens through the convenience of a computer, alleviating the need to wait in long lines.

ECONOMY
DELHI

India's capital is a booming, vibrant city with an economy that thrives in multiple areas. Delhi enjoys the country's largest average per capita income. The major part of Delhi's economy lies in the **service sector**, which contributes over three-quarters of the city's Gross Domestic Product, and includes trade, real estate, hotels, restaurants, banking and insurance, among other industries. From the 1990s on, New Delhi has emerged as an important hub in **international banking** and corporate finance. Since Delhi is the seat of the country's government, many of its residents work in the public sector. For centuries Old Delhi has been, and continues to be, a trading and commercial centre in north India.

Delhi's economy has profited from the **information technology** (IT) sector as well. Many of the world's major technology companies like Google, Sony, Microsoft and IBM have offices in the National Capital Region; Gurgaon and Noida, part of the greater metropolitan Delhi area, boast state-of-the-art facilities that satisfy the demands of international companies.

Delhi has invested in its **infrastructure**; its road, railway and aviation networks, public transportation (including the enormously successful Delhi Metro) and water supply are among the best in the country. Combined with a competent and well-educated workforce (Delhi has some of India's best institutions of education), investor-friendly government policies and a booming consumer market, Delhi continues to witness steady economic growth.

Manufacturing plays a significant role, with a surge occurring in the 1980s. Delhi is an important center in the garment export business. Hundreds of garment manufacturing facilities of all sizes here produce clothing for international companies. Footwear, automobile parts, fertilisers, leather goods and medicines are also manufactured in the city.

AGRA

Most people associate Agra with the Taj Mahal and not much else. In reality, Agra and its environs are quite a bustling centre of agriculture, commerce and industry. Agra is a major road and rail junction. The city that was once the capital and commercial nerve centre of the mighty Mughal Empire thrives on **tourism**, thanks to its many architectural and historic sights. The city is a major centre for the leather and footwear business and is India's largest **footwear manufacturing** hub. In addition, Agra is an important centre for the automobile industry: multiple manufacturers of vehicle parts have set up plants here. Many artisans and craftspeople live and work in Agra, often employing skills that have run in their families for many generations. **Pietra dura**, the technique of inlaying colourful stones into marble, is popular here: many skilled practitioners create products that are sold the world over. Hand-woven carpets, jewellery and brassware are also made in Agra.

Approximately 40% of the population in and around Agra earns its livelihood from **agriculture**, with millet, barley, wheat and cotton as the primary crops grown here.

At one time there was talk of developing a commercial hub and amusement parks in an area called the Taj Heritage Corridor, on land between the Taj Mahal and Agra Fort. Protests arose as people feared that resulting pollution would damage the Taj Mahal's marble. In 2003 the Archaeological Survey of India denied clearance for the project, and the Supreme Court of India ordered its suspension. The Uttar Pradesh Forest Department has been asked to draw up a plan to refurbish the entire area, now an eyesore, to ensure clean air and a 'green lung' for the city.

JAIPUR

The economy of Jaipur combines traditional and modern, artisanal and industrial livelihoods. Long-established industries like handloomed textiles, gemstone and jewellery manufacture, pottery, painting and block printing share space with industries like metal and mineral mining and processing and the manufacture of automobile parts, acetylene gas, cables and ball bearings. Revenue from **tourism** has been growing steadily, with the rate of number of foreign visitors growing faster than that of domestic tourists.

From royal times, Jaipur has been a centre of decorative **arts and crafts** production. Development of the arts soared under the reign of Maharaja Rana Singh II, who established the Jaipur School of Art in 1866 to develop local skills and crafts. Boys from hereditary artisan families were given an education

in carpentry, ornamental wood carving and stone carving. New skills like making blue pottery and terra-cotta pottery were taught. Students learned embroidery, clock-making, and a 'western' skill, drawing, as well. Today Jaipur is reputed for the beauty and quality of its crafts.

For centuries, Jaipur has been the place where the world's best gems were sent for cutting, polishing and setting. Maharaja Sawai Jai Singh, the city's founder, employed the best jewellers to make his jewelled sword hilts and other bejewelled adornments. In time, the gem craftsmen of Jaipur became renowned for their artistry, a source of healthy revenues for the city.

The area around Jaipur is rich in **mineral resources**. Feldspar, quartz, limestone, dolomite, silica and soapstone are found in abundance and are a major source of revenue for the state.

However, the **state of Rajasthan** has not remained content to limit itself to traditional sources of trade. In the last decade, it has invested tremendous resources in education and training, infrastructure development, tourism management and the IT sector to ensure that it is a part of modern India's economic boom. It has instituted investment-friendly policies for many industries. Jaipur has an excellent road system and is well-connected by the rail to many of India's key cities. The international airport links Jaipur to cities around the country as well as Dubai, Singapore and other global cities. The Resurgent Rajasthan Partnership Summit of 2007 was an ambitious effort to rebrand Rajasthan as a modern, cutting-edge state, with nearly 300 Memoranda of Understanding (MoU) being signed by leading Indian and international companies across a variety of sectors.

Jaipur is home to state-of-the-art **business facilities** like the 3000 acre Mahindra World City that has attracted companies such as Infosys, ICICI and Deutsche Bank. A popular venue for trade fairs and other events, the Export Promotion Industrial Park is attracting growing numbers of customers.

Priest at Krishna temple, Jaipur

© Anurag Mallick, Priya Ganapathy/MICHELIN

LIFESTYLE

Religion (and for Hindus, caste) are an integral part of the social fabric that influences multiple aspects of life, from birth to death rituals, religious celebrations and more. Social considerations, as well as religion, continue to play a major role in the fundamental aspects of most Indians' daily life, like choice of one's profession, suitor for one's child, what restaurant to visit, or even what food to prepare.

DAILY RITES

The first thing in the morning, after washing and purifying rituals, many Hindus carry out *puja* (worship) of their personal gods on the family or temple altar: the nature of the *puja* varies, but often incense sticks are lit, *ghee* (clarified butter), rice and flowers offered, and mantras (sacred verses) recited. The most pious go to the temple every day to have a *darshan* (vision) of God, participate in the fire ceremony *(arti)* and receive *Prasad* (grace, food offered to the gods and eaten by devotees). At times they will undertake pilgrimages to sacred cities like Mathura and Pushkar.

FAMILY LIFE

In times of need or disaster, Indians look first to their family for help. No major decisions (choice of profession, moving, marriage, etc.) are taken without consulting one's parents and other family elders. Urban youth, although well versed in cell phones and the Internet, are surprisingly conservative with regards to family; the majority remain respectful of their parents' authority.

MARRIAGE

Marriage for love is still an exception to the general rule that marriages are organised by parents, uncles and aunts, who set out to find a suitable son- or daughter-in-law. Backgrounds must be similar, taking into consideration the religious, social and economic circumstance of the prospective candidate as well as reputation. **Dowries** are officially banned today, but many families still observe the practice. Few traditional Hindu marriages are planned without the approval of an **astrologer**: incompatibility of birth charts would lead to the marriage being called off, though this trend is changing now.

The **weddings** of northern India are lavish, boisterous celebrations that sometimes span several days. Hosted by the bride's family, the **Mehendi** ceremony is a popular pre-wedding ritual, wherein the bride's hands, arms, feet and legs are adorned with intricate patterns made of a paste of *mehendi*, or henna leaves, to enhance her beauty. In the **Sangeet** ceremony, the women gather to sing songs. In larger cities and in less traditional families, men attend these ceremonies as well. The bridegroom and his friends and family go to the wedding venue or the home of the bride in a raucous procession called the **baraat**, in which the bridegroom is usually seated on a horse or an elephant. He is elaborately dressed, with a turban adorned with feathers and jewels, a long coat called an *achkan* and tight leggings. Tradition calls for his wearing a necklace of **currency notes** to demonstrate his prosperity. At the wedding site the bride waits, attired in bright red, orange or pink clothes, often embellished with embroidery, and adorned with bangles, sparkling chokers, glittering necklaces, forehead jewels, nose rings, earrings and toe rings. The Rajasthani bride wears an embroidered cloth called an **odhni,** that covers her head, a cherished heirloom passed down through generations.

After the wedding ceremony, the couple moves in with the husband's parents, and the young wife becomes part of her in-laws' household. Little privacy is available in this **joint family**, and the practice is dying out among families in uban settings.

MEDIA

The people of India have a voracious appetite for news. Many local, regional and national **newspapers** in local languages, Hindi and English are read in the smallest villages to the largest cities. All over northern India, the *Dainik Jagram*, a Hindi-language daily, is enormously popular, with its mix of articles on politics, business, Bollywood, cricket, entertainment and lifestyle. According to the Indian Readership Survey, it has the largest readership of all newspapers in India.

Not surprisingly, Delhi is a major centre for the newspaper industry. Many Hindi-language dailies are published here, including the *Navbharat Times*, *Hindustan Dainik* and *Dainik Jagram*. Of the English language newspapers published here, the *Hindustan Times* is the most widely read. Since Delhi is home to people from around the country, many vernacular language newspapers are published here, including the *Malayama Manorama* and *Eenadu*, in Malayalam and Telugu, respectively. Delhi is the centre of several national media agencies, including the Press Trust of India and the Media Trust of India. Doordarshan, India's national television network, and All India Radio, the national **radio** network, both have their headquarters here.

In Rajasthan, the state's most widely read newpaper, *Rajasthan Patrika*, is a Hindi-language daily. It is published in multiple cities in the state, including Jaipur, Jodhpur, Udaipur and Bikaner. Other news publications in Jaipur include *Adhikar Patrika*, *Rashtradoot Saptahik* and *Dhainik Bhaskar*.

Discussing the news in Delhi

© Taka/age fotostock

Television in India is growing in popularity. Just a little more than two decades ago, viewers could watch only one television channel, the nationally broadcast Doordarshan. Today, hundreds of networks broadcast an array of programming, including around-the-clock news in a range of languages, sports, soap operas and movies. Many programs have drawn their inspiration and ideas from within India; others have adapted and Indianised foreign programs like *American Idol* and *Who Wants to be a Millionaire?* into crowd-pleasers *Indian Idol* and *Kaun Banega Crorepathi*. Television has successfully tapped into Indians' love of story-telling, high drama and show-biz —no small achievement in a country of such diversity.

SPORT

Agra, Delhi and Jaipur all have well-developed sports facilities. Delhi, as the nation's capital, has played host to prestigious national and international sporting events. The **Asian Games**, or Asiad, a multi-sport event held every four years with participants from all over Asia, had its debut in 1951 in Delhi. In 1982, these games were again held in Delhi, for which state-of-the art facilities were built, including the imposing **Nehru Stadium**. The city was spruced up with new roads and flyovers, and underwent a remarkable transformation. The games were televised in colour, a first for the country. Delhi has also hosted the 2010 Commonwealth Games and the 2010 Hockey World Cup.

Football is enormously popular here and the **Ambedkar Stadium**, which can hold up to 50,000 spectators, is Delhi's main football stadium; the Nehru Cup tournament is played here.

The Delhi Half Marathon, launched in 2005, takes place every November, attracting **runners** from around the world.

India is a **cricket**-crazed country; the Indian Premier League (IPL) has expanded the game's popularity. Delhi's IPL team is called the Delhi Daredevils. The city also has a first-class cricket team that plays in the domestic Ranji Trophy matches. The **Feroz Shah Kotla Stadium**, India's second-oldest functioning international cricket stadium, is home to Delhi's cricket teams.

Jaipur also has an IPL team, the Rajasthan Royals. **Sawai Mansingh Stadium**, the city's main cricket venue, has a seating capacity of 30,000. Both national and international cricket matches are held here.

Agra's **Eklavya Sports Stadium** hosts cricket, football and other matches. The Sadar Bazar Stadium is another venue for cricket matches. Renovated multiple times, it now offers top of the line facilities.

Cricket on the bank of the Yamuna

© DINODIA/age fotostock

Street food in Agra

© Anurag Mallick, Priya Ganapathy/MICHELIN

CUISINE

Delhi and Agra were the seats of power for the Mughal Empire, and in the royal kitchens of its rulers, the cuisine of these cities was born. Beloved by the Mughals, meat and foods rich in butter, cream and nuts are combined with vegetables and spices from northern India. Delhi-Mughal specialties include **biryani**, a layered dish of rice and spiced meat or vegetables, scented with saffron and **ghee** (clarified butter); **haleem** is made of minced meat, lentils, vegetables and spices and cooked for hours. **Kababs**, marinated and spiced meats, are another legacy of the Mughal era. The Rajputs of Rajasthan also love their meat—lamb, goat and chicken are all prepared here. **Laal maas** (red meat) is a delicious ruddy meat gravy that is enjoyed by non-vegetarians.

The average northern Indian obviously does not eat this kind of food on a daily basis. Everyday meals are far less rich but just as delicious, such as whole-wheat rotis, dals, and a variety of **vegetables**, served with spicy pickles and cool yogurt. Cauliflower, potatoes, carrots, radish and many greens are cooked with lots of ginger, garlic, onions and spices like cumin, coriander, *garam masala* and turmeric.

The profusion of vegetables in the winter makes a colourful spectacle in the vegetable **markets**. The end of winter is the season all over northern India for deep red and purple carrots. The sweet carrot *halwa* and a spicy, digestive drink called *kanji* are examples of how these carrots are prepared in Delhi and the rest of North India. Also in every market, it is common to see long skewers of marinated meat waiting to be seared to perfection in a **tandoor** or clay oven. Delhi's **restaurants** cater to every taste. Cuisines of practically every country in the world are spiced up and adapted to the Indian palate. **Thalis,** an assortment of iconic dishes, is a way to try several ingredients at one sitting. Family-owned Karim's is one of Delhi's oldest restaurants, renowned for superb kebabs, tandoor-cooked meats, and breads; today it has branches all over the city that serve some 40 entrées.

No description of Delhi's food scene is complete without mention of its **street food**. The narrow, crowded streets of Old Delhi are perhaps the best place to sample another side of Delhi's cuisine, a far cry from the rich and heavy Mughlai food. The streets of Chandni Chowk, one of Delhi's oldest and busiest marketplaces, teem with vendors of **chaats**. These cool, crispy crunchy snacks are made from fried lentils and breads, boiled potatoes and raw onions, and smothered with sauces that are fiery hot, tangy, sweet and sour. Some adventurous *chaat* makers have experimented with variations like Chinese *chaat*. The famous Paranthewale Gali in Chandni

59

Chowk is a street filled with small road-side restaurants that serve **parantha**—breads fried in ghee and stuffed with potato, cauliflower, *paneer*, or meat. Every prime minister of India has visited the street at least once and eaten there. In Agra, food is similar to Delhi's. Since this region is the wheat belt of India, many varieties of *rotis* and **parathas** (unleavened and stuffed breads) are common. Two specialties of Agra cuisine are *dalmoth* and *petha*. **Dalmoth** is a salty, spicy, crunchy snack (that goes by the generic name namkeen, or savory snack) made of fried lentils, nuts and spices. **Petha** is a translucent sweet made from white pumpkin. Variations today are made with coconut, saffron and nuts.

The cuisine of **Rajasthan** springs from its distinct history and geography, and varies by region as well as the caste and community of the people preparing the food. A large part of Rajasthan is desert, a factor in shaping the cuisine, particularly of western Rajasthan. In the harsh, dry climate, it is difficult to grow fruits and vegetables, and water is always scarce. In spite of these limitations, the grains, legumes and milk products available here are used creatively. Unique fruits and vegetables grown in the desert include *keir*, a small berry; *methi* or mustard; and *mogri*, a desert bean. These are often dried and

Rajasthani thali

© Anurag Mallick, Priya Ganapathy/MICHELIN

preserved for long-term use. Millet is a staple crop here, used in dishes, both sweet and savory. *Bajre ki khichdi* is a millet porridge eaten with pure ghee, and **Raabri** is a millet soup that is flavourful and hearty. Millet bread is commonly paired with a spicy garlic **chutney**.

Dals (legumes) are common in Rajasthani cuisine, and **urad** is especially popular. An iconic Rajasthani dish is **dal-bati-churma**, in which a variety of *dals* are cooked together and served with flaky, buttery balls of whole wheat flour (*bhattis*). Any leftover dough is deep-fried, crumbled and mixed with sugar and nuts to form *churma*, the dessert component of the meal. Other substantial dishes are made with *dal* flours and pastes to provide nutrition and energy for the harsh desert winters. **Papad ki sui**, made with *papads* prepared from a dried paste of lentils, serves as a satisfying substitute for vegetables. Other dishes using lentils are **aloo mangori** (ground lentil paste with potatoes) and **gatte ki subzi** (made with strips of steamed *besan* or gram flour, cooked in a spicy sauce).

Because of water's extreme scarcity, milk, cream, yogurt and ghee are used. The richness of the food is balanced with the judicious use of asafoetida, ginger, carom seed and black salt, all of which are believed to aid digestion.

It goes without saying that Rajasthanis love their sweets. **Ghewar**, a flat, round wheat cake drenched in sugar syrup, is a famous sweet from the Jaipur region. Jodhpur is well known for its *mewa kachori*, a type of turnover filled with sweetened concentrated milk. Delhi is also full of **halwais**, or traditional sweet makers.

In eastern Rajasthan, including Jaipur, where the land is fertile and rainfall is abundant, the food more closely resembles that of the rest of northern India. And today, with modern infrastructure and roads and railway lines to the farthest reaches of the state, many fresh fruits and vegetables are available all over the country, and have been incorporated into local and regional cuisine.

History

The three great cities of Delhi, Jaipur and Agra, linked together today as glittering points on a geographical 'Golden Triangle', have each had a long and glorious past that stretches far back to the time when legend and fact bubbled together in the same cauldron. Their stories, closely intertwined in some parts while discrete in others, include some of the most intriguing and colourful characters and events in the history of India. Delhi, modern India's capital, has served as the principal city for a succession of dynasties, each of which built a city within Delhi's present boundaries, making this multilayered metropolis one of the most historically fascinating places on earth. Agra, which served for a brief period as the capital of the Mughal Empire, is graced with some of the world's most exquisite monuments. Jaipur, a relatively new city, brilliantly planned, belongs to a region rich with stirring tales of chivalry, treachery and romance.

PREHISTORY

Archaeologists have unearthed evidence of human settlement from the **Paleolithic Era** in the areas around present-day Delhi and Rajasthan. In 1956 Surajit Sinha, an anthropologist, found a small trove of paleolithic tools near the main gate of Delhi University; in the years since, many more discoveries have been made, indicating that the area was a fertile one for Stone Age settlers. Scientists estimate that human habitation in and around this region dates back about 100,000 years. Anangpur, which is in present-day Faridabad, some 30 kilometers east of Delhi, has been extensively excavated and studied, and a rich lode of Stone Age tools has been found here.

In Rajasthan, including the Jaipur area, Paleolithic tools of **Acheulian** hunter-gatherers have been discovered. These early humans, whose variety of stone tools displayed a high level of sophistication, were believed to have lived around the shallow lakes and ponds and the sand dunes of the arid Rajasthan region.

EARLY HISTORY
FIRST CIVILISATIONS: 3300 BC TO 1300 BC

The Indus Valley Civilisation, also referred to as **Harappan Civilisation**, was one of mankind's earliest civilisations, dating from approximately 3300 BC until 1300 BC. It occupied a large swath of territory that lies in parts of today's Afghanistan, Pakistan and north and north-west India. This civilisation was remarkably advanced for its time. Excavations of Indus Valley settlements revealed planned cities with streets, houses made of mud bricks, drainage and sanitation systems, as well as a high level of skill in metallurgy, pottery and jewellery making.

There are significant remains from the later period of this far-sighted civilisation in and around Delhi. Among the most interesting are a large burial site that researchers hope will provide answers to many unanswered questions about this culture and period.

In 2013 Harappan artefacts from both the earlier and later periods were found in parts of Rajasthan. These include fragments of baked bricks, pottery, terracotta bangles and figurines and copper artefacts.

AGE OF THE VEDAS AND EPICS: 1700 BC TO 150 BC

Several theories exist about how and why the Harappan Civilisation came to an end, but not surprisingly, there is no consensus among their various proponents. Drought, a decline in trade with Egypt and Mesopotamia, and invasions by tribes from Central Asia (Aryans) are possible reasons. In the declining centuries of the Harappan Civilisation, starting around 1700 BC and ending more than 1,500 years later, the first scriptures of the Hindu religion, the Vedas (meaning "knowledge"), came into being. They were collections of oral hymns and prayers, but also include mentions of geographic features like rivers and mountains, details of the lives of the people and historical events. Studies of the Vedas suggest that they were written in north and north-western India (including the regions where Delhi, Agra and Jaipur lie today) by Indo-Aryan tribes who were establishing themselves in these parts. Many aspects of Hindu life and culture had their origins in this period. Initially believed to have had a nomadic existence in Eurasia, the Aryans introduced the use of horses and war chariots. Their language evolved into Sanskrit and Prakrit, and their religion, based on rites and sacrifices offered to gods who personified natural elements, developed into Vedic Hinduism.

The most famous of the Indian epics, the **Mahabharata** and the **Ramayana**, were created much later in this period. These stories evolved over a long span of time; in them are myths and legends that are inextricably linked with the history and annals of northern and north-western India.

Some scholars believe that Agra is mentioned in the *Mahabharata* as Agravena, the border of the forest. Myth links it with Raja Kamsa, the maternal uncle of Lord Krishna, whose kingdom is said to have encompassed Agra and its environs. The name Delhi is thought to originate from the King Dilipa of the Solar Dynasty, ancestor of none less than the god-king Rama, the hero of the epic *Ramayana*. It was common practice to anchor places and events in legends and myths to give them an importance and credibility that they might not have otherwise had. Delhi has a significant role in the *Mahabharata* as well: the magnificent capital of the Pandava heroes of this epic, **Indraprastha**, is believed by some to have existed at the site of the present Purana Qila, or Old Fort, in Delhi. Whether or not this is true (archaeological evidence neither proves nor disproves this belief), what is indisputable is that these tales and legends have been woven into the tapestry of this great city.

EARLY REPUBLICS AND KINGDOMS: 600 BC TO 300 BC

Over the centuries, the numerous settlements in northern India coalesced into republics and kingdoms. The history of northern India stepped out of the mists of fantasy and lore into an era when events and personalities were buttressed with the heft of historical proof. The Aryan tribes and other groups developed more defined identities. For example, in the Rajasthan area, the **Meena Clan** established the Matysa Kingdom. The Meenas claim descent from the *matsya,* or fish avatar, of Vishnu; their name derived from *meen*, Sanskrit for fish. In the 6C BC their kingdom was named one of the 16 great kingdoms mentioned in the Buddhist text *Anguttara Nikaya*.

The area in and around Delhi gained strategic commercial importance due to its location on the Uttarapatha, one of the major trade and travel routes that criss-crossed northern India. The **Kuru tribe** established itself in this area, with Indraprastha as its capital.

The early kings made heavy use of rituals, sacrifices and other procedures mentioned in the Vedas. The loosely organised political structures of the early period gave way to organised administrations that collected revenues, maintained armies and built cities. There were frequent struggles between the kingdoms over land. Many tribes developed legends about their rulers, ascribing divine powers and origins to them.

AGE OF EMPIRES
MAURYA EMPIRE: 322 BC TO 185 BC

Founded by **Chandragupta Maurya** in the 4C BC, the Maurya Empire became one of the world's most extensive empires of the time, unifying a vast expanse of India. Chandragupta's military successes—from his conquest of Alexander the Great's eastern provinces to his defeat of the Nanda Dynasty and the countless tiny kingdoms that dotted the land—helped him solidify his power. After consolidation, with the aid of his brilliant minister Chanakya, he set about establishing a strong and efficient administrative structure that ensured the smooth running of his empire. The economy thrived as trade, both within the empire and with external sources, flourished. Art, architecture and culture attained great heights.

The other great emperor of the Maurya Dynasty was Chandragupta's grandson, **Ashoka**, who ruled from 269-232 BC. He expanded the empire, attaining one military victory after another. Tales abound of his exceptional cruelty and ruthless tyranny, which he employed to dispose of his siblings in order to ascend to the throne, and which continued unfettered in the early years of his reign. The culmination of this reign of terror was one of bloodiest battles of all time, in the eastern region of Kalinga. There, the legend continues, he was so appalled by the wanton destruction of life that he renounced his bloodthirsty ways on the spot, embraced the non-violent and life-affirming Buddhist faith, despite having been born a Hindu. He spent the remainder of his reign spreading the doctrine of **Buddhism** through his kingdom, and is credited for single-handedly expanding the message of Buddha far beyond its original boundaries.

Little knowledge was available to separate fact from fiction. Then, in the 19C and early 20C, a series of **inscriptions** carved on rocks and pillars were validated by experts as authentic inscriptions created by King Ashoka. They are a remarkable record not only of the values he held and wanted to spread throughout his kingdom, but also of the administrative procedures and structures he put in place to spread his message, the judicial principles and systems he believed in, and the watershed event of his reign, the battle of Kalinga. In Srinivasapuri, close to Nehru Place in modern Delhi, a rock bears one such inscription from Ashoka's reign. This rock suggests strongly that the Delhi region was part of the Maurya Empire.

Ashoka was succeeded by a series of weak emperors under whose reigns the empire shrank, setting the scene for instability and a splintering into multiple small states.

4C BC   Maurya Empire founded by **Chandragupta Maurya**.

GOLDEN AGE OF THE GUPTAS: 320 AD TO 550 AD

Many kingdoms rose and fell in the centuries following the decline of the Maurya Empire. Then, starting about 320 AD and continuing for more than two centuries, a succession of **Gupta kings** consolidated power in most of northern India, reigning during what has come to be called the **Golden Age** because of the cultural achievements, prevalence of law and order and relative peace of the era. The most prominent of the early Gupta rulers was **Chandragupta I** who, through a combination of marriage alliances and military conquests, expanded his empire to encompass most of northern India. His son and successor, Samudragupta, continued the expansion of the empire while also gaining a name as a patron of the arts. Perhaps the most renowned emperor of this dynasty was **Chandragupta II**, the grandson of the first Chandragupta. His rule, from 380-415 AD saw glorious achievements in art, architecture, sculpture and literature. Kalidasa, surely the most famous poet of classical India, lived and worked during this period. Fa Hsien, a Chinese Buddhist, visited India in 399; his descriptions are a major source of information about the life and times of Gupta India.

HARSHA AND HIS EMPIRE: 7TH CENTURY AD

A major threat to the Guptas' kingdom came in the form of raids (end of 5C) by the fierce **Huns** of Central Asia. Local tribes fled the approaching Huns and gathered in Rajasthan. In the growing chaos, as states formed and dissolved, these tribes established themselves by dominating the local **Meenas** and other clans. They came to be accepted as Kshatriyas, members of the warrior caste, for their bravery and success in fending off invaders; they called themselves **Rajputs**, or sons of kings.

For a period after the decline of the Guptas the political scene was murky; few records remain to clarify matters. Petty kingdoms engaged in constant struggles against each other in their bid to acquire land and glory. For a short period, from 606 to 647, an able and accomplished emperor, **Harshavardhana**, ruled over a large stretch of northern India, including Delhi and Agra. He gained much acclaim for political astuteness, the fairness of his laws, care of his people and patronage of the arts and sciences. Even those states that did not become part of his empire sought his friendship and acknowledged his power. Two excellent sources paint a vivid picture of life under Harsha. One is his court poet, Bana, who penned the Harsha-Charitra, an account of the life and times of the emperor; the other is the Chinese traveler Hiuen Tsang, who wrote a detailed account of the court and actions of Harsha, as well as the living conditions in his empire.

After Harsha's death in 647, his empire fractured into numerous small kingdoms. At the same time, the Arabs arrived at the frontiers of India and started to conquer their way into the country.

RISE OF THE RAJPUTS AND PRATIHARAS: 8C TO 13C

Once again the political picture in North India was one of numerous small states and kingdoms each struggling to gain the upper hand.

This fractured state set the stage for the domination of the Rajputs in Rajputana. With tales of mythological ancestry, the Rajputs created a divine aura around their already strong reputation as valiant warriors. Some clans declared that they were *Suryavamshis*, progeny of the solar race, while others said that they were *Chandravamshis* of the lunar race, and yet others, *Agnivamshis*, children of the fire god. The **Kachwa clan** of Rajputs, from the Suryavamshi line, who have ruled over the Jaipur area for many centuries, is said to descend from Kush, one of the twin sons of the god-king Rama.

As these Rajputs consolidated their hold over Rajasthan, they developed a reputation for chivalry, bravery, an unshakeable honor code and pride: to this day they are admired as heroic men of action. In the centuries to come, they consolidated their strength and position and ruled over multiple kingdoms in the land that came to be named for them, **Rajputana**.

Under the Rajputs, monarchy was hereditary, but their great respect for chivalry and the written law tempered the misuse of power. **Caste** (👉 *see sidebar p49*) formed the basis for the organisation of society, which was unabashedly patrilineal. Religious art flourished, and sculpture and architecture reached glorious heights (👉 *see Art and Architecture*). One of the Rajput clans, the **Tomaras**, ruled the area around Delhi and reputedly founded the city of Dillika (Delhi) in 736 AD.

As rival tribes tried to establish themselves, one of them, the Gurjara Pratiharas, succeeded to a far greater degree than the others. The **Gurjara Pratiharas** (after whom the state of Gujarat is named) were a Rajput tribe whose origins are shrouded in mystery, and have spawned multiple theories. One is that they were initially nomads who traveled with the Huns; another makes the claim that they were once lowly door-keepers to their rivals, the Rashtrakutas; yet another states that they might have been palace officials who rose to power. Whatever the truth might be, they succeeded in seizing power and ruled over much of present-day Rajasthan and large stretches of other territories. At their peak in the 9C and 10C, the Gurjara Pratiharas held lands that may have exceeded those of the Gupta empire in size.

During this period the **Arabs** made repeated attempts to penetrate the country. The Pratihara ruler Nagabhata, who formed an alliance with other Hindu emperors, managed to repel the Arab advance in a series of battles in Rajasthan and Sindh in 738 AD. The Arabs were forced to retreat westwards,

Iron Pillar of Delhi , Qutb Minar

© YellowCrest/Fotolia

Delhi's Name

One well-known legend of how Delhi got its name involves the famous Iron Pillar of Delhi (which dates from the Gupta period) and the Rajput king Anangapala of the Tomara clan. A version of this legend is present in the Rajasthani epic the *Prithviraja Raso*, as part of an episode called Killi-dhilli-katha. The story goes that a learned Brahmin told King Anangapala that the base of the iron pillar had been driven so far into the ground that it rested on the hood of Vasuki, the great serpent who supported the world from the nether regions below. The Brahmin promised Anangapala that his reign would last as long as the pillar stood. Anangapala, whose curiosity was aroused, ordered the pillar to be dug up to see if the head of Vasuki really did lie below it. When the bottom of the pillar emerged, it was covered with the blood of Vasuki, whose head it had pierced. Anangapala realized he had made a horrible mistake, and quickly tried to put the pillar back in place. Every effort to do so failed, and the pillar remained *dhili*, or loose. The story of the *dhili* pillar offers one explanation of Delhi's name. In modern times, the iron pillar is the source of another belief. Anyone who stands with his back to the pillar and makes the fingers of his hands meet around the pillar will have his wish come true. It was a common sight to see people trying to make their fingers join around the pillar, now cordoned off.

and local chieftains solidified their hold over Rajasthan and nearby lands. Constant fighting with their rivals weakened the Pratiharas. Their large kingdom shrank in size, and once again Rajputana became a land of many small states ruled by an assortment of kings.

736	City of Dillika (Delhi) founded.
738	Arab advance repelled in Rajasthan and Sindh.

Prithviraj Chauhan and Muhammed Ghori

Rajputana was divided into several kingdoms, some large, some small. Many of them were strictly local and did not or could not expand their domains beyond their limited borders. One exception was the **Chauhan Dynasty**, descendants of the fire-god Agni. After breaking free of the Gurjara Pratiharas, they settled in the Ajmer area in the 8C; from there they expanded their empire as far as Delhi, where an earlier Rajput clan, the Tomaras, had established themselves in an area called Lal Kot. The most illustrious of the Chauhan kings was Prithviraj Chauhan III, who ruled in the 12C from his twin capitals of Delhi and Ajmer. One of the earliest historically verifiable areas of Delhi, Lal Kot, the fort of the Rajputs, was enlarged during his reign; today it is named Qila Rai Pithora (Prithviraj was also known as Rai Pithora). The history of the city of Delhi is told in the multiple layers of its past; Qila Rai Pithora is often called the **First City of Delhi.** The remains of the walls of this fort are all that is left as evidence of Prithviraj's reign. Much of what is known about him comes from an epic, the *Prithviraj Raso*, written by a Rajasthani bard called Chand Bardai. In this epic, Prithviraj Chauhan is described as a gallant hero who eloped with Samyukta, the daughter of a neighbouring tribe's chieftain. The story of their romance is hugely popular in India and has made them household names all over the country.

In 1191 the Muslim warlord Muhammed Ghori swept into India from Afghanistan; Prithviraj defeated his army, and the chivalrous hero released Muhammed from captivity. That act proved fatal, as the following year, the warlord returned with an even stronger force and defeated the valiant Prithviraj at the battle of Taraori (Thaneswar). Muhammed showed none of the clemency that had saved him; he had Prithviraj beheaded and the fort of Lal Kot burned to the ground.

The **Islamic presence** was thus established in the sub-continent and ended Hindu supremacy in the region.

DELHI SULTANATE: 1206 TO 1526

After the death of Muhammed Ghori in 1206, his general, Qutb-ud-din Aibak, a former Turkish slave *(mamluk)* who had been left behind in India to manage and expand Ghori's territories, made himself ruler of a new dynasty, referred to as the **Slave** or **Mamluk Dynasty**. It was the first of a series of Muslim-ruled dynasties that, together, are known as the Delhi Sultanate.

While the Sultanate dynasties did not rule over a united North India, they were the dominant political force. The sultans were constantly attempting to expand their domain. Although they governed independently in India, they thought of themselves as part of the larger Islamic world, with its centre at the Caliphate of Baghdad. Delhi, strategically placed to allow access to the Gangetic plains as well as central and western India, was their capital city. Under the Sultanate, Delhi became increasingly urbanized.

During the reign of Qutb-ud-din Aibak, the first ruler of the Slave Dynasty, construction of the Qutub Minar in Mehrauli, the second of Delhi's cities, began. Made of red sandstone and marble, it is one of Delhi's prominent attractions to this day, rising to a height of 73m/240ft. He also initiated the building of Delhi's first mosque, the Quwwat-ul-Islam Masjid.

Aibak's rule lasted a short four years: he died while playing polo in Lahore. He was succeeded by his son-in-law, Iltutmish, who completed the Qutub Minar and the mosque and expanded the kingdom. Under his rule an efficient monetary system was put into place.

During the reign of Iltutmish, the Mongols, led by **Genghis Khan**, appeared on the banks of the Indus River in 1221. For the time being, their entry deeper into India was stalled by the might of Iltutmish.

The Slave Dynasty came to an end in 1290 when the last ruler of this dynasty was murdered by a Khilji chief, thereby setting the stage for a new dynasty, the **Khilji Dynasty**, of **Turkish** origins, which held sway from 1290 to 1320.

The best known of the Khilji rulers was Alaudin, feared for his cold-hearted ruthlessness and repressive rule. He was frequently attacked by the Mongols, but Alaudin's army managed to beat them back every time. The cruelty with which the Mongol army was treated caused them to eventually suspend their attacks for the duration of his reign. He then launched attacks all over India, and was successful in bringing much of southern India under his control. His plundering and looting earned him an enormous booty of elephants, horses, gold and precious stones. He is believed to have captured the famous Koh-i-noor diamond, which is now part of the British crown jewels.

Alaudin Khilji also attacked the Rajput kingdoms of Rajasthan, vanquishing Ranthambore in Rajasthan, then Chittor, Malwa, Ujjain and numerous other places. His attack on Chittor in 1303 and his capture of its beautiful queen, Padmini, is the stuff of legend—the story is told in the epic poem *Padmavat*.

For all his cruelty, Khilji was also a far-sighted administrator and controlled his lands with an iron hand. He organised the revenue system of his kingdom and kept prices down with his market policies. He built his fort at Siri, another of the ancient capitals in the modern city. After the Khiljis came the **Tughlaqs**, whose best-known ruler, **Muhammed-bin-Tughlaq** (ruled 1325-51), was one of the most eccentric in history. He took charge when the Delhi Sultanate was at its peak, and succeeded in setting in motion the events that would lead to its weakening and eventual downfall. While his reputation was that of a brilliant man and effective strategist, Tughlaq also gained notoriety for his cruelty and lunacy, as hapless citizens fell victim to his spells of paranoia and mad experiments. He levied high taxes on his people at a time when they were reeling from famine; he moved his capital from Delhi to Daulatabad and then back to Delhi, each time forcing his miserable subjects to make the move. The new coins he minted were easily forged, thus negating their value. The Tughlaqabad Fort in Delhi was built by the first of the Tughlaqs ((i) *see Architecture*).

The Tughlaq Dynasty was followed by the **Sayyids**, who ruled from 1414 to 1451. The Sayyids inherited a weakened empire, as the Sultanate had been decimated by repeated attacks by the ferocious Mongol leader **Timur**, also known as Tamerlane. Timur sowed carnage along the paths he traveled, and in 1398 he entered Delhi, where his men wrought terrible destruction and death. They captured a number of slaves, who were sent to Samarkand to build its famous Jama Masjid. Timur, who had no intention of staying on in India, returned to Samarkhand, leaving thousands massacred and villages destroyed.

The Sayyids managed to consolidate their power, and in 1451, the last Sayyid ruler abdicated power to Bahlul Khan of the Afghan Lodhi tribe, thus bringing the **Lodhi Dynasty** to power, which lasted until the accession of the great Mughal Dynasty in 1526.

One Lodhi ruler, Sikander Lodhi, is credited with founding the city of **Agra** (in 1504) which, until this point, lay in history's shadows. In order to invade Rajasthan effectively, he made Agra his capital.

Sikander Lodhi's son, Ibrahim, was the last Lodhi ruler, and with the end of his reign came the end of the Delhi Sultanate. His rule was riddled with intrigue, turncoat politics and instability, and in this milieu, two Afghan noblemen who felt slighted by Ibrahim tried to extract their revenge by inviting **Babur**, a prince of Kabul, to invade Delhi. Utilizing his highly organised army and weapons that included gunpowder-fueled firearms, artillery and cavalry, Babur was victorious at the **Battle of Panipat** in 1526. He took control of Delhi and established what would become the great Mughal Dynasty.

1206	Death of Muhammed Ghori and beginning of the rule of Qutb-ud-din Aibak, the Slave or Mamluk Dynasty.
1221	Mongols, led by Genghis Khan, appeared on the banks of the Indus River.
1290	The end of the Slave Dynasty, and the beginning of the Khilji Dynasty.
1303	Legendary attack on Chittor and capture of Queen Padmini by Alaudin Khilji.
1526	Battle of Panipet

MUGHAL DYNASTY: 1526 TO 1857

Having captured Delhi, Babur turned his attention to Rajasthan, where a group of princely states had formed an alliance under the leadership of the formidable Rana Sanga of Mewar. Once again, Babur's disciplined army and its superior firepower proved too much for the heroic Rajputs; at a brutal battle at Khanwa, Rana Sanga's troops were defeated. Babur next defeated a coalition of Afghan leaders; with this victory, became the uncontested ruler of most of northern India. He retained Agra as the capital of his empire, and built a Persian-style garden, the Aram Bagh. Babur died in Agra in 1530, and was succeeded by his eldest son, Humayun.

An iron hand was needed to control and consolidate Babur's wins, and **Humayun**, a gentle 23-year-old, was ill-equipped to handle the staggering responsibilities and hostile elements both in and outside his family, who were waiting for an opportunity to seize the throne. The Afghan leader **Sher Shah Suri**, with clever mobilising of his forces, wrested control of Humayun's territories. Humayun himself managed to escape, and lived the life of a vagabond for 15 years, waiting for the right opportunity to strike back.

Eventually, after the death of Sher Shah, Humayun was able to regain the throne in 1555. Older and wiser, he succeeded in recapturing much of what he lost earlier. He was unable to enjoy the fruits of his efforts, however: in the following year he died after an accidental fall on his library's staircase. His tomb in Delhi is an early example of a garden-tomb, and one that set a high standard for Mughal mausoleum architecture.

Humayun's son, **Akbar**, was the third, and most renowned, Mughal emperor. Succeeding his father at the age of 13, he inherited a difficult throne, surrounded as he was by adversaries eager to dispossess him of his sovereignty. The Rajput kingdoms asserted their independence and power in Rajputana and other places. Unfazed, Akbar embarked on a campaign of conquest and annexation and succeeded in adding state after state to his kingdom. He was a farsighted and wise ruler who realised that there were many more Hindus than Muslims in the country, and that it would not do to antagonise them entirely. He also recognised that the Rajputs, with

their power and bravery, would make good allies. He therefore sought to build relations with them, and even though he conquered several of their states, he made efforts to accommodate their religion and beliefs and did not attempt to impose his values on them. He married the daughter of the Rajput king of Amer (also spelled Amber) near present-day Jaipur, and later married the princesses of Bikaner and Jaisalmer.

However, one Rajput leader, Maharana Pratap, whose family's kingdom of Chittor had been usurped by Akbar, was eager to reclaim his territory. Pratap spurned all of Akbar's attempts to settle the situation peacefully. His army met the Mughal army in combat at Haldighati, where Pratap was forced to flee. This battle, and tales of Pratap's bravery, are an important part of Rajasthani folklore.

Akbar made it a point to ensure that key administrative positions in his empire went to both Hindus and Muslims. Rajputs were given important positions.

One of the most remarkable features of Akbar's rule was his religious tolerance. A truly broad-minded and intellectually curious thinker, he invited people of all faiths to his court so that he could learn more about their belief systems.

Akbar died in 1605, and soon thereafter his son, **Jehangir**, was crowned emperor. His reign got off to a rocky start as his eldest son, Khusrau, attempted to usurp the throne. Khusrau was captured and imprisoned, and his followers, killed. This act of sons rebelling against their fathers was to be repeated by future members of the Mughal royal family. During Jehangir's reign, representatives from the English **East India Company** visited his court and won themselves valuable privileges, including the right to trade.

Jehangir was addicted to women, alcohol and opium and had a cruel streak as well, in spite of his interest in literature and the arts. The real reins of power were in the hands of his wife, **Noor Jahan**. Highly ambitious, she secured important positions for her father and brother in Jehangir's court, and married her daughter to Jehangir's youngest son, Shahryar.

When Jehangir died, in 1627, it was Noor Jahan's wish that Shahryar be crowned the new emperor. However, another son, Shah Jahan, murdered his younger brother and other contenders to the throne, and proclaimed himself emperor at Agra in 1628. Later, he moved his capital to Delhi, where he built the walled city, **Shahjahanabad**, which lies in today's historic Old Delhi.

Shah Jahan successfully crushed several revolts during his reign. The most serious was an uprising by the Afghan prince Khan Jahan Lodhi, who was supported by many Maratha and Rajput chiefs. Shah Jahan defeated him and purportedly had him and his sons cut up in pieces.

Under Shah Jahan's rule, Mughal architecture achieved its pinnacle. The most stunning monument built by him was the **Taj Mahal** in Agra, a mausoleum for his beloved wife Mumtaz Mahal, who died during childbirth. The Jama Masjid and Red Fort in Delhi were other architectural marvels erected during his rule. Shah Jahan's reign came to an unhappy end. He had named his eldest son, Dara Shukoh, as his successor. However, even while he was emperor, a brutal struggle for succession broke out among his sons. **Aurangzeb**, Shah Jahan's third son, succeeded the throne in 1658 by murdering his brothers and imprisoning his father in the Agra Fort, where he died, a miserable, broken man in 1666.

Aurangzeb was a cruel and fanatical ruler, and with his reign began the decline of the once mighty Mughal Empire. He could not have been more unlike his tolerant and inclusive great-grandfather, Akbar: he imposed harsh taxes on his Hindu subjects, banned the building of new temples and enforced a strict reign devoid of joy. In 1678 he claimed Jodhpur in Rajasthan for himself, an act that led to an all-out war with the Rajputs. These once-faithful allies of the Mughals now became their bitter enemies. Aurangzeb's own son, aghast at his father's divisive actions, joined the Rajputs.

Aurangzeb enjoyed a number of military successes, but his empire—vast, unwieldy and filled with unhappy and resentful subjects—became difficult to control as revolts occurred all over the country. After his death in 1707, the empire was ruled by a succession of weak emperors who dealt the death blow to the Mughal Empire. In the chaos that prevailed, the Marathas and the Persians swooped in and made gains in territory and control. The **Marathas** resided in the coast ranges of the western Ghats near Maharashtra. Both these groups, with the Persians led by Nadir Shah, and the Marathas under their leader Shivaji, bled Delhi dry, and soon the Marathas turned their attention to Rajasthan, where they conquered large stretches of territory.

1530	Death of Babur, a prince of Kabul, in Agra.
1555	Humayun takes the throne after the death of Sher Shah.
1605	Jehangir crowned emperor, during whose reign representatives of the English East India Company visit and are granted the right to trade.
1678	War with the Rajputs erupts after Emperor Aurangzeb claims Jodhpur in Rajasthan for himself.

THE FOUNDING OF JAIPUR: 1727

During the disintegration of the Mughal Empire, armies in and around Jaipur State were constantly at war with each other and the Marathas. In 1699 **Jai Singh II**, a Kachwaha Rajput, became king of Jaipur State. His capital was at Amer, but with the growing population and scarcity of water in that area, he decided to build a new capital. Jai Singh was a brilliant, creative man who had a diverse court with advisers from a variety of religious and intellectual backgrounds. Under his rule, no religion or group had the bigger voice. He maintained good relations with the Mughal court.

He designed his new walled city, **Jaipur,** with a grid of broad boulevards that

The Spark of the Revolt

In the spring of 1857, a rumour began to circulate among the East India Company's sepoy (Indian conscript) troops stationed in northern India that the new cartridges supplied by the army had been greased in cow or pork fat. (Cows are held sacred by Hindus, and pigs are considered impure by Muslims.) The cartridges had to be bitten off before being loaded. When the conscripts refused to use the cartridges, the English officers threatened them with imprisonment. The clash of wills ignited the already highly tense atmosphere. On May 10, 1857, mutiny broke out in Meerut (now in Uttar Pradesh). Three battalions massacred the Europeans living there, before heading to Delhi. That city soon became the centre of the sepoy uprising; but with its ineffective administrative infrastructure, Delhi lacked the capability and competence to maintain the mutiny. The British, taking advantage of the disarray and limited means of the rebels, crushed the rebellion; Delhi crumbled. After witnessing unimaginable horrors and bloodshed, this once-great city lay in ruins.

were lined with shops and temples. Construction began in 1727, and the city was one of the best-planned in India. Later emperors erected fine buildings like the Hawa Mahal, the Diwan-i-Khas and the Diwan-i-Am, adding to the charm of an already beautiful city. In 1828, in honor of the visiting Prince of Wales, the buildings were painted a rosy pink: Jaipur has been called the Pink City ever since.

1727   Construction of the walled city of Jaipur begins.

COLONIAL PERIOD: 1600 TO 1947

The 1600s saw a number of European powers, including the Portuguese, the French and the English, attempt to set up shop in India to profit from its spices, silks and other riches. Of these powers, the British had by far the greatest impact and influence on the course of Indian history. Their presence in India began with the **East India Company**, an English joint-stock company whose initial goal was to establish trading relations with India. The Mughal emperor Jehangir granted them trading rights and their first trading outpost was established in Surat in Gujarat. In time, their trading pursuits took a back seat to their ambition to acquire land and power. They played dynasty against dynasty, Hindu against Muslim, and succeeded in establishing a strong foothold dur-

ing the chaos that prevailed. Many of the Rajput states signed treaties with the British that placed them under their protection and yet granted them local autonomy. Calcutta became the capital of colonial India.

The British domination extended over large parts of India. They ceased to be merely traders and became heavily involved in the administration of territory. They began to impose high taxes on Indian goods and flood the markets with their cheap goods, an act that destroyed local livelihoods. As Indians from all strata of society felt sidelined and imposed upon in their own country, resentment mounted toward the British. Matters came to a head in 1857 with the First War of Independence, or the legendary **Indian Mutiny** (🕮 *see sidebar opposite*).

Practically the whole of northern India was up in arms. Only the Punjab Sikhs remained loyal to the British. In Rajasthan, although the population turned against the Western colonists, most of the Rajputs, aware of what they owed the British, remained loyal to them and stood up to the rebels. Thanks to the support of the Sikh battalions, the British managed to maintain control. A month after it began, the uprising was quashed. The last of the Mughal emperors, Bahadur Shah Zafar II, who had sided with the mutineers, surrendered. His sons were executed, many in plain sight of their father, now a broken old man. After spending time in a Delhi prison, where, in silence, he wrote poetry on the walls with a burned stick, he was exiled to Rangoon on a bullock cart. Thus ended the once-mighty Mughal Empire.

The 1857 uprising revealed how vulnerable the East India Company was and how incapable it was of administering such a vast territory. In 1858 control of India passed from the company to the British Crown. A large part of India was now under British rule.

1857   First War of Independence, also known as the legendary Indian Mutiny.

INDEPENDENCE

Feeling oppressed by British rule, many Indians agitated for freedom and independence. Remarkable Indians like Gandhi, Nehru and Rajaji made great sacrifices to achieve this goal.

In 1911, the British decided that the capital should be moved back to Delhi and with this transfer, the last of Delhi's cities, New Delhi, was built.

After a long and eventful struggle, India won its independence in 1947. **New Delhi** was its capital. At the time of Independence, Rajasthan consisted of 19 princely states, two chieftains and the British-administered Ajmer-Merwara Province. Over the next several years, it acquired its present shape as princes signed the Instrument of Accession. They were granted generous allowances in the form of a **privy purse**, which was abolished in 1971.

The city of Agra lost its importance after the death of the Mughal Empire. However, it is one of the best-known cities in India because of its stunning architectural monuments.

1911   India's capital moved back to Delhi.
1947   Independence is won.

Father of the Nation

Mohandas Karamchand Gandhi was born on October 2, 1869, in Porbandar (Gujrat), into an upper middle-class Hindu family. After law studies in England, he practiced law in South Africa for 20 years. On returning to India in 1914, he devoted himself to the struggle for Independence, and was regularly imprisoned as a result. His greatness lay in the fact that he was tolerant of all religions; he fervently believed that the underlying truth in all religions was the same. He campaigned for the development of villages and defended the lot of the 'untouchables'. His desire to serve and help India's different religious communities earned him the hostility of extremists.

© DINODIA/age fotostock

Jawaharlal Nehru (left) and Mohandas Karamchand Gandhi (right)

On January 30, 1948, he was assassinated in Delhi by a member of a Hindu nationalist organisation that hated Gandhi's conciliation towards Muslims. Gandhi was heart-broken at the breaking up of the country into India and Pakistan; he was not present at the Independence ceremony.

Architecture

Northern India's architecture is the product of wave after wave of dynasties that dominated the region for more than 2,000 years. Hindu, Islamic, Rajput and British Colonial are the major architectural styles that emerged from this period. Delhi, Agra and Jaipur preserve temples, tombs, mosques, forts and palaces constructed by the region's successive rulers. Yet as early as the 11C, Muslim invaders set about razing Hindu and Jain shrines. In the 16C religious and other buildings came to be erected once again in this part of the country. Delhi's sultans and the Mughal emperors who succeeded them commissioned magnificent monuments, including the Taj Mahal, that rank among the wonders of world architecture. *Italicised words are listed in the Glossary of Terms at the end of the chapter.*

EARLY TEMPLES

Nothing survives of India's earliest wooden, bamboo and thatch shrines. The first structural temples built of brick and stone date only from the 5C-6C. **Hindu temples** (*mandirs*) replicated mountains, the abodes of gods and goddesses, and were thus provided with lofty towers. In northern India these towers take the form of curved super-structures known as *shikharas*, or peaks. Laid in corbelled masonry courses with hollow interiors, **shikhara towers** rose over temple sanctuaries, their summits coinciding with the emblem of the image of the deity housed in the sanctuary beneath.

A particular feature of religious architecture in Rajasthan is the region's 11C- 15C temples dedicated to the Jain *tirthankaras*, or saviours. Examples at Mount Abu and Ranakpur are fashioned entirely of local white marble. These spectacular, glistening complexes have towered sanctuaries approached through multi-storeyed columned halls roofed with intricate corbelled domes.

UNDER THE DELHI SULTANS

Delhi's first Islamic monuments introduced to India new architectural forms, such as the **courtyard mosque** and **domed tomb**, while preserving long-standing Indian (indigenous) building techniques and decorative motifs. The Quwwat-ul-Islam Masjid, begun in 1192 by Qutb-ud-din Aibak, the first of Delhi's Mamluk ('Slave') sultans, was intended as a place of prayer for the conquering troops. It consists of a spacious courtyard surrounded by colonnades on three sides, with a **prayer hall** on the west, facing towards Mecca. The hall's multi-arched façade imitates the prayer halls of Central Asia and Iran; but its pointed-arched openings are cut out of sandstone slabs laid horizontally, without any binding mortar, in the traditional Indian building method. Excerpts from the Quran are etched in high relief around the arches, yet the Arabic letters are interwoven with naturalistic blossoms and stalks, like temple sculpture. The same decoration adorns the nearby Qutb Minar, the lofty cylindrical tower raised by Qutb-ud-din Aibak as a victory monument in 1202; it was extended upwards in later times until it reached an astounding height of more than 73m. Its tapering sides are relieved by circular and angled flanges, divided into stages by circular balconies, recalling earlier **minarets** in Afghanistan and Iran.

Under the Tughlaqs in the 14C, Delhi's Islamic architecture incorporated elements that were more characteristically Indian, as in the immense fortifications of Tughlaqabad, capital of Sultan Ghiyathuddin. This mammoth citadel employs colossal **ramparts** strengthened with massive **circular bastions** to define an irregular quadrangular zone almost 3km across. To the south, a large artificial lake has an island on which Ghiyathuddin erected his own tomb before his death in 1324. The tomb features sloping **red sandstone** walls topped with a smooth, white marble dome. Its location in the middle of the lake recalls Hindu monuments that overlook sacred rivers and pools.

The final phase of Sultanate architecture in Delhi is represented by the tombs of the 15C Lodhis, who raised elegant royal mausoleums within lush settings, as in Delhi's Lodhi Garden. Crowned with domes, these tombs have small rooftop **pavilions** with slender columns bearing small domes known as *chhatris*. Deriving from look-out towers of Indian forts, *chhatris* became a distinctive feature in later Mughal and Rajput architecture.

PALACE CITIES OF THE MUGHALS

As the supreme rulers of northern India for 200 years, the Mughals proved to be ambitious builders. In 1533 Humayun laid out the **Purana Qila**, a huge citadel next to the Yamuna River in Delhi. Like Tughluqabad, its massive walls define a huge quadrangular fortified zone, but with imposing arched gates embellished with polychrome decoration. The style of the small mosque within its walls, erected in 1540 by Sultan Sher Shah Suri, who expelled Humayun from India, recalls earlier sultanate traditions.

Soon after assuming the Mughal throne in 1556, Akbar moved the Mughal capital to Agra. His grandly scaled residence there, built up to the bank of the Yamuna for protection, is surrounded by massive red sandstone walls, hence the name Lal Qila, or **Red Fort**. It is entered through gateways set between huge bastions relieved by polychrome decoration and in one example, sculpted elephants. Of Akbar's palaces inside the Red Fort, only the (mis-named) **Jehangir Mahal** survives. Its red-sandstone façade has arched recesses edged with white marble strips; *chhatris* punctuate the corner towers. Chambers opening off its central court employ Islamic-styled domes as well as flat ceilings supported on angled struts, in imitation of local wooden construction.

Under construction from 1571 to 1573, but occupied by Akbar for only 14 years, **Fatehpur Sikri** is the most complete example of an early **Mughal palace city** that has survived. This red sandstone complex is approached along a bazaar street entered through a ceremonial triple-arched portal. The palace structures within are amazingly diverse. The **Diwan-i-Am** is a pavilion with a two-storey exterior bearing corner rooftop *chhatris*; its interior, in contrast, is a single, double-height chamber with a central column supporting a circular dais, perhaps intended for Akbar to sit on when privately meditating. The pavilion is overlooked by a pyramidal open structure crowned with a small *chhatri*. Jodha Bai's palace nearby takes the form of a Rajput *haveli*, or courtyard mansion. Its residential apartments look inwards on four sides of a square court; Raja Birbal's House has a pair of exquisitely decorated domed chambers joined in an unusual diagonal formation.

All these palaces were serviced by wells, kitchens, workshops, and *hammams* (steam rooms, Turkish bath).

A short distance from Akbar's palace rises Fatehpur Sikri's **Jama Masjid**. The central arched portal of its prayer hall recalls Central Asian mosque designs, but its interior is roofed partly with flat ceilings carried on slender columns, as in Indian wooden architecture. The graceful, white marble tomb of Shaykh Salim Chishti, Akbar's spiritual preceptor, stands in the spacious courtyard in front. The Sufi saint's grave is housed in a domed chamber surrounded by a broad corridor lined with *jalis* with delicate geometric designs.

Mughal palace architecture was much expanded under Shah Jahan, whose projects were built mostly with white marble facing and **pietra dura** decoration. This emperor's additions to Agra's Red Fort include the Diwan-i-Am of 1637, the interior of which is divided into aisles by lines of broad lobed arches. Shah Jahan's building program reached a climax in Shahjahanabad, his namesake capital laid out in 1639-48 beside the Yamuna in Delhi. Its palace, also known as the Red Fort, begins with a bazaar street inside the main gate that leads to a Diwan-i-Am, which imitates the **audience hall** at Agra, with a throne recess set into its rear wall embellished with the finest pietra dura panels. Overlooking the river beyond is a line of flat-roofed white marble pavilions intended for the emperor's private use, through which runs a continuous, refreshing water channel. The complex also contained several *char-bagh* (gardens), with planted plots and central fountains. Shajahanabad's Jami Masjid of 1656 outside the palace is raised high above the city streets, its huge courtyard accessed by steep flights of steps on three sides. The prayer hall on the west side of the courtyard has a red sandstone façade framed by a pair of slender **minarets** topped by *chhatris*. Three white marble domes with slightly bulbous profiles rise above.

MUGHAL GARDEN TOMBS

Funerary architecture under the Mughals begins with one of the most majestic constructions of the era: the **mausoleum** of Humayun in Delhi, completed in 1571 during the reign of the youthful Akbar. The tomb stands in the middle of a vast *char-bagh*, divided by water channels and fountains into 36 plots; the platform on which the tomb is raised occupies the central four plots. Its red sandstone exterior features central higher arched portals and angled shorter side portals on all four faces, as well as angled side faces. The whole composition is topped by a magnificent dome, with an empty space between its outer white-marble cladding and the interior plasterwork, the first instance in India of Central Asian **double-dome construction**.

Subsequent Mughal funerary monuments are more typically Indian, even though tombs continued to be located at the midpoint of symmetrically laid out *char-baghs*. Akbar's mausoleum at

Sikandra outside Agra, completed by Jehangir in 1614, rises in a pyramid of terraces lined with arcades and *chhatris*. It is crowned not with a dome, but with a marble enclosure containing the emperor's **cenotaph**. The same flat-topped scheme is found in the tomb of I'timad-ud-Daulah in Agra, built in 1628-30 by Noor Jahan, Jehangir's queen, for her parents. This small but exquisitely finished building is adorned externally with dense, geometric patterns fashioned from rare stones set in marble slabs. Its interior chamber is roofed with a low dome divided into interlocking, painted geometric facets.

With the Taj Mahal at Agra, erected by Shah Jahan in 1632-53 in memory of his beloved queen Mumtaz, the garden tomb of Iranian-Central Asian origin reaches its zenith, unsurpassed in all Islamic architecture. Unlike its predecessors, the mausoleum does not stand in the middle of a garden, but on a terrace overlooking a vast *char-bagh*, with the Yamuna River providing an uninterrupted backdrop. Framed by a quartet of slender cylindrical minarets, the building is topped by a **bulbous dome** soaring above a cubical chamber. The chamber features central **arched portals** flanked by double tiers of lesser arched recesses on all four sides, repeated on the shorter, angled corners. White marble is employed throughout, relieved by black stone Quranic inscriptions running around the portals, and carved floral panels on the lower walls. Exquisite pietra dura workmanship embellishes the octagon of marble jali screens that surrounds the graves of Mumtaz and Shah Jahan within.

RAJPUT PALACES AND HAVELIS

The buildings of the Rajputs represent a different tradition from that of the Mughals, as evidenced by the fortified citadel at Amer, overlooking a pass in the rugged terrain of north-eastern Rajasthan. Built by Man Singh, the Kachhwaha raja, at the end of the 16C, the complex consists of a sequence of courtyards, audience halls and private

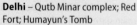

UNESCO World Heritage Sites

Delhi – Qutb Minar complex; Red Fort; Humayun's Tomb

Agra – Taj Mahal; Red Fort

Fatehpur Sikri – Palace

Jaipur – Janta Mantar observatory

apartments. These elements are laid out not in geometric regularity, as in a Mughal palace, but on successive levels, beginning with **Jaleb Chowk,** where troops and animals were assembled, and ending with Man Singh's private residence, later converted to a *zenana* (abode for women of the harem, who lived a segregated life, or *purdah*). The Diwan-i-Am and residential Sukh, Jai and Jas Mandirs of the intermediate courts were added by Mirza Raja Singh I in the early 17C. These pavilions are built in Mughal style, with **lobed arches** and pietra dura decoration and gardens in front. They include a gleaming *sheesh mahal*, its interior covered with tiny mirrored pieces.

Founded in 1727 by Maharaja Sawai Jai Singh II as the new Kachwaha capital, the city of Jaipur is laid out on a nine-square plan, with the City Palace occupying the central plot. This configuration conforms to a typical Indian *mandala*. A sequence of courtyards lead to a main wing arranged on seven levels, with an audience hall at the bottom and private apartments with terraces above. The painted lobed arches and vaults of the interiors are typically late Mughal in style. However, the remarkable astronomical instruments of the Janta Mantar in the outermost courtyard, fashioned of masonry for Jai Singh's personal use in 1734, were modelled on the 15C observatory in Samarkand.

Rajput nobles in the service of the Kacchwahas built grand *havelis* at their country estates on the outskirts of Jaipur, as well in the capital itself. These private residences are entered from the street through imposing arched gateways that give access to walled gardens within. **Havelis** in the Shekhawati region north of Jaipur are conceived more as fortified residences, with massive outer walls to guarantee protection. Like the Jaipur havelis, they feature double-height **reception rooms** with brightly painted ornament, often hung with family portraits and crystal chandeliers, as in European interiors, which became fashionable in Rajasthan.

THE BRITISH IMPACT

From the 19C on, the British presence is seen in European-style churches and bungalows, as in Agra's cantonment area. Yet **Samuel Swinton Jacob**, chief engineer for the State of Jaipur, promoted the revival of Rajput building arts. His Albert Memorial and Rambagh Palace skilfully incorporate finely crafted Rajput *chhatris* and jalis.

The design of New Delhi may justly be considered the most enduring British architectural contribution to India. Dating from 1911, the plan for the new capital is truly imperial in scale, with broad avenues providing dramatic approaches to major public monuments. The pinnacle of the capital's buildings was the Viceroy's House (now Rashtrapati Bhavan), with its assemblage of Buddhist stupa, Mughal domes and Rajput *chhatris*. That such typically Indian elements could be incorporated into a British Colonial monument is testament to the imagination of New Delhi's principal architect, Sir **Edwin Lutyens**.

GLOSSARY OF ARCHITECTURAL TERMS

cantonment – British quarter of an Indian city, originally for the military
char-bagh – garden divided into four equal squares
chhatri – rooftop open pavilion with a small dome
chowk – courtyard
Diwan-i-Am – hall of public audience
Diwan-i-Khas – hall of private audience
hammam – steam room, Turkish bath.
haveli – courtyard mansion
jali – perforated screen, often of stone
kotla – fort
mandala – cosmic diagram composed of multiple squares
mandir – temple or hall
masjid – mosque
minar – minaret
pietra dura – technique of inlaying pieces of semiprecious stones into marble
sheesh mahal – mirror palace
shikharas – (peak) curved tower
zenana – harem women's apartments in a palace or house

RAJPUT ARCHITECTURE

FAÇADES

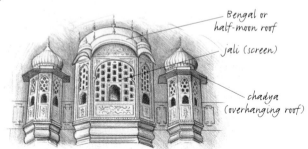

Bengal or
half-moon roof

jali (screen)

chadya
(overhanging roof)

JHAROKHA (COVERED BALCONY)

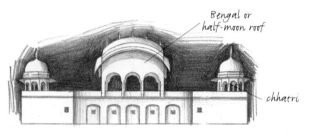

Bengal or
half-moon roof

chhatri

PAVILIONS

THE CENOTAPH

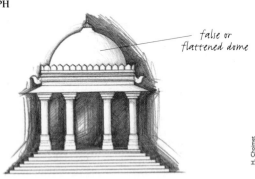

false or
flattened dome

H. Choimet

CHHATRI (PAVILION WITH BALDACHIN OR KIOSK WITH DOME)

INDO-ISLAMIC ARCHITECTURE

THE TOMBS (RAUZA)

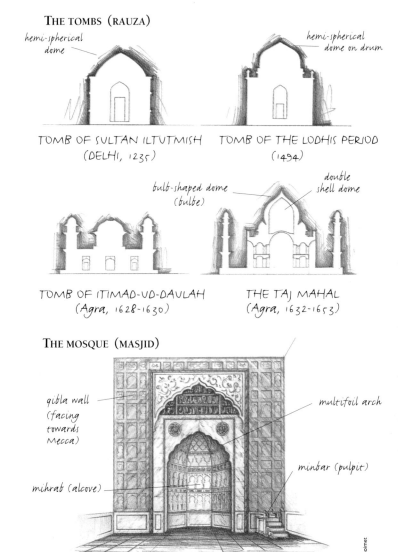

hemi-spherical dome

TOMB OF SULTAN ILTUTMISH
(DELHI, 1235)

hemi-spherical dome on drum

TOMB OF THE LODHIS PERIOD
(1494)

bulb-shaped dome (bulbe)

TOMB OF ITIMAD-UD-DAULAH
(Agra, 1628-1630)

double shell dome

THE TAJ MAHAL
(Agra, 1632-1653)

THE MOSQUE (MASJID)

qibla wall (facing towards Mecca)

multifoil arch

minbar (pulpit)

mihrab (alcove)

MIHRAB

H. Cholmet

77

Art

Indian artistic traditions date back more than 2,000 years, though it is mainly sculptures of Buddhist and Hindu divinities that have survived the country's severe monsoonal climate. Such vestiges are represented by stone and metal images displayed in Delhi's National Museum. Of the paintings and decorative arts that must also have flourished in early time, there are almost no traces, apart from the splendid murals of the 5C at Ajanta in Maharashtra, which still endure in situ. Paintings on paper, decorative arts in metal and cotton cloth remain only from the Mughal period. Most of these works of art are closely identified with the imperial courts at Agra, Delhi and Fatehpur Sikri, as well as the courts of their Rajput contemporaries, as at Amer and Jaipur. The finest examples of such arts in India are those displayed in Delhi's National Museum and in the palace museums of Jaipur, Udaipur, Kota, Bikaner and Jodhpur.

PAINTING

Painted **watercolour** illustrations are known mainly from paper pages bound in books or albums. Though orthodox Islam strictly forbade depictions of living creatures, miniatures produced for the Muslim Mughal emperors and their courtiers represent historical events and legendary stories crowded with lifelike people, animals and birds. This exuberant figural art was accompanied by intricate geometric patterns and sinuous foliate motifs, the latter betraying accurate observation of the natural world. Painted **calligraphy** is also known from the period, especially pages recording *suras* (chapters) of the Quran or verses of popular Persian poetry.

MUGHAL MINIATURES

The Mughals were avid collectors of paintings, and set up specialised workshops near their palaces. Renowned artists from Persia, Afghanistan and Central Asia found employment here, benefiting from the personal interest of the emperors themselves. In Akbar's ateliers in Agra and Fatehpur Sikri, these foreign masters trained talented Indian artists, and so was born the **Indo-Persian school** of miniature painting. Mughal pictures fused long-standing Persian traditions with the brilliant tones and naturalistic details of those works of previous **Indian schools** of painting sponsored by Hindu patrons. Examples are illustrated versions of the *Bhagavata Purana*, the popular story of the God Krishna, produced in the Delhi-Agra region in the early

Mughal miniature painting, City Palace Museum, Alwar

© Anurag Mallick, Priya Ganapathy/MICHELIN

Murals in Mandawa

© Anurag Mallick, Priya Ganapathy/MICHELIN

16C. These compositions have bright, flat areas of red and yellow, serving as backgrounds for vigorous figures of the youthful hero, whether he appears battling with his enemies or engaging in amorous adventures with the *gopis*, the girls who tended the cows. Foreign visitors to the Mughal court from the end of the 16C, especially Portuguese missionaries, introduced Mughal artists to **engravings** in Bibles and other Christian texts, many of which were imitated by Indian artists. Thus is explained the appearance of **European perspective** and shading in Mughal painting.

The impact of indigenous schools of painting on early Mughal art is best seen in the more than 1,000 illustrations for the *Hamzanama*, a famous Persian epic popular at the Mughal court. Executed in watercolour on **cotton panels**, with identifying labels on the reverse, these paintings provided Mughal artists with ample opportunities to portray lively battles with heroes and demons in naturalistic settings, not unlike the Krishna paintings just mentioned. Later in his reign, Akbar commissioned **miniatures on paper** for the Persian language biography of his grandfather, the *Baburnama*, and also for his own chronicle, the *Akbarnama*. The latter was crammed with scenes from Akbar's childhood and hunting exploits of his youth, as well as his later military conquests and courtly receptions at Agra and Fatehpur Sikri.

Under Jehangir in the early 17C, Mughal painting attained a greater **realism**, with naturalistic portraits of the emperor and his prominent nobles, and delicate studies of flowers, birds and animals. Painting for Shah Jahan, like architecture, was harnessed to the task of creating a majestic, imperial presence. Miniatures served as official **documents**, recording official gatherings in the Diwan-i-Ams of Agra and Delhi, as well as receptions of foreign guests, reconciliations with rebellious sons, performances of musical concerts, and other ceremonies. Aurangzeb took less interest in the arts than his predecessors, with the result that Mughal painting declined markedly by the end of the 17C.

RAJPUT MURALS AND MINIATURES

Inspired by the Mughals, many of the Rajput prices also became energetic patrons of painting. Their audience halls and private apartments were cloaked in **murals** depicting typical scenes within the palace, as well as pleasurable and military excursions outside the walls of their cities. Among the finest examples of such murals are those at Bundi and Kota. Murals also covered the walls of the fortified residences of the nobles who served under the Rajputs. Havelis in Shekhawati preserve lively paintings that offer a pictorial 'window' into everyday life. Mythological topics were also popular in the murals in Rajasthan: notably episodes from the Krishna and Rama stories, as well as depictions of pilgrimages to local Hindu shrines.

In emulation of Mughal workshops, artists at Rajput courts also produced watercolour **miniatures on paper**. In time they developed distinctive visual idioms to portray rulers in the company of their retinues within the palace, riding in procession through the streets of their capitals, or enjoying hunting expeditions in the surrounding landscapes. Rajput rulers are also shown savouring more private pleasures: sitting on the upper terraces of their palaces in the cool of the evening smoking hookahs; in the company of their consorts; observing musical or dance performances.

Hindu devotional topics are particularly popular in Rajput painting, especially illustrations of the *Ramayana*, such as the episodes showing the rescue of Sita, or the climactic battle between heroic Rama and demonic Ravana. The Krishna story was also a favourite, and numerous Rajput paintings depict the youthful hero dallying with adoring *gopis*, especially with Radha, the god's favourite.

Another genre of Rajput painting is represented by the *Ragamala* series. Here, graceful maidens accompanied by peacocks, sitting in swings or waiting for lovers are identified with musical ragas, as well as quasi-poetical moods. Such subjects continued to be produced at painting ateliers in Rajasthan until the 19C.

DECORATIVE ARTS

Today there is a vigorous revival of inlaid stonework, metal crafts, printed cotton textiles and woven carpets, as may be seen from the wares on sale in innumerable shops in Delhi, Agra and Jaipur. Many of these arts date back to Mughal times, the finest examples being those displayed in the National Museum and Jaipur's City Palace Museum.

METALWORK, JEWELLERY AND JADES

From its peak (2600 BC to 1800 BC), the sophisticated Indus Valley civilisation has left a few rare **metallic statuettes**, including the famous 'dancer' from Mohenjo-Daro (now in Pakistan), that can be seen in the National Museum. Later metalwork is represented by Buddhist and Hindu **sacred icons** dating from the 5C to the 13C, like those in the National Museum.

Engraved copper and brass vessels were also produced in northern India during these early centuries, but almost none predate the Mughal period. From this era date elegant **metallic vases** and bowls, some inscribed with Persian verses bestowing good wishes on the user. The finest metallic trays and *huqqa* bowls are embellished with gleaming floral designs in silver and brass strips, a technique known as *bidri*. Circular trays and **pandan boxes** for storing betel leaves, fashioned out of pure gold inlaid with emeralds, rubies and bright enamels, were usually reserved for the emperor.

Ceremonial **weapons** are also showcases of the metalworkers' art, as in the blades of swords with dedicatory inscriptions in gold, and the daggers, arm-guards and bows enhanced with inlaid arabesques.

Gems were always appreciated by the Mughals, who had a preference for blood-red spinels from Afghanistan and emeralds from Colombia, as well

© Francis Leroy/hemis.fr

Making bidri work

© Anurag Mallick, Priya Ganapathy/MICHELIN

Making block-printed cotton at Dastkar Kendra, Ranthambore

as Indian rubies and diamonds, all set into gorgeous necklaces and turban ornaments. The most spectacular jewelled object of the period, however, was the legendary **Peacock Throne,** commissioned for Shah Jahan and set up in the Diwan-i-Am in Delhi. Though the throne was dismantled in the 18C, representations of it are seen in contemporary miniatures.

Precious jade imported from China was much valued by the Mughals, especially **wine-cups** of milky white nephrite fashioned for the emperors' personal use. White jade *huqqa* bowls were adorned with lattice designs of gold strips framing minute pieces of lapis lazuli and green jade. Jade hilts of ceremonial **daggers** carried by the emperor and his nobles are inlaid with designs of gold and rubies, or carved into the semblance of naturalistic animal heads.

CARPETS, TEXTILES AND COSTUMES

Interiors of Mughal audience halls and private apartments were devoid of furniture, but laid with sumptuous carpets, cloths and bolsters. The great **carpets** manufactured in the imperial workshops under the supervision of skilled weavers generally followed Persian conventions, with repeated floral motifs on bright red backgrounds, or blossoms contained in

geometric lattice frames. Some carpets featured flowering bushes, inhabited by realistic and fantastic animals and birds. Floor spreads, **wall hangings** and awnings were made of cotton, enlivened with stencilled and printed designs. The bright sprays of regularly arranged flowers on these textiles contributed to the splendour of palace interiors and tented encampments. The same designs were embroidered in silk threads onto gorgeous jackets worn by the nobles on important ceremonial occasions, as were sashes with brightly printed floral borers. Under the encouragement of the emperors, **woollen shawls** began to be produced in Kashmir, and were exported to Europe, where they became extremely fashionable.

Though some Mughal carpets, cloths and costumes found their way to Rajput courts, Rajasthan developed its own textile traditions, like the decorative, **block-printed cottons** produced in the towns around Jaipur. Characteristic of Rajasthan textiles are the painted cotton cloths hung as backdrops in the Krishna shrine at Nathdwara in Rajasthan. Such cloths, known as *picchwais*, were produced for pilgrims visiting Nathdwara. They show, for the most part, the stone Krishna image being venerated by pious patrons, or attended by enraptured *gopis,* and at times even docile cows.

Literature

The earliest literary works of northern India were the body of Hindu religious works that first emerged more than 3,000 years ago. They were composed in Sanskrit, which has sometimes been called the language of the gods, as some of these works were believed to have been divinely transmitted. Sanskrit, still in use today, was the language of ancient Hindu scriptures, utilised by the Hindu priesthood as well as by scholars as a literary language.

MAJOR HINDU TEXTS

The earliest known Sanskrit works are the **Vedas**, which came about when the early Indo-Aryan settlers established themselves in northern India more than 3,000 years ago. They are believed to have been divinely transmitted, and for many centuries, the Vedas remained an **oral literature** that was passed on with meticulous accuracy from generation to generation. These sacred texts consist of hymns and chants for rituals and religious occasions such as wedding and funeral ceremonies.

ANCIENT COLLECTIONS

Later, over a span of time that might have stretched from 3,000 to 2,000 years ago, came the **Upanishads**, a collection of some 200 texts. In these, the early concepts and tenets of Hinduism make their appearance, presented as conversations between people and animals.

Another important series of Hindu texts arose around 2,000 years ago, collectively called the Dharmasastras, of which Manu's *Manusmriti* is the best known. These works pertain to Hindu religious and legal duties and laws, and lay out the guidelines for the ideal Hindu way of life.

The **Puranas**, a collection of stories and allegories about Hindu gods, appeared initially in oral form. Written versions came later and were modified through the 16C.

GREAT EPICS

During the Maurya and Gupta empires, more than 2000 to 1500 years ago, new forms of religious devotion emerged, largely focused on the gods Vishnu and Shiva. The two great Hindu epics, the **Mahabharata** and the **Ramayana**, were composed in the ancient classical language of Sanskrit and form the core of Hindu literature today. Part of *Mahabharata*, the **Bhagavad Gita** is the most influential text of Hinduism; millions of Hindus turn to this text today for guidance and inspiration. Countless versions of the *Ramayana* and *Mahabharata* have since been, and continue to be, written in a variety of languages, with the stories being retold from multiple points of view. Some well-known contemporary versions in English have been written by C. Rajagopalachari, Ramesh Menon and Devdutt Patnaik.

Much of dramatic literature and poetry have been written in Sanskrit. Bhasa was one of the earliest of the ancient

Ramayana and Mahabharata

Composed between the 4C BC and the 4C AD, the **Ramayana** relates the exploits of **Rama**, the seventh incarnation of Vishnu. Driven from his kingdom by palace intrigue, Rama, crown prince of Ayodhya (now in Uttar Pradesh), lived in exile in the forest in the company of his brother and his wife, **Sita**. The latter was kidnapped by the demon-king Ravana, who held her prisoner on his island, Lanka. With the help of the loyal **Hanuman** and his army of monkeys, Rama managed to free Sita, and returned to Ayodhya once his period of exile ended. Dating from roughly the same period, the **Mahabharata** recounts the rivalry and war between two clans of the region of **Indraprashta** (Delhi): the five Pandava brothers and their cousins the Kauravas. The *Mahabharata* includes the **Bhagavad Gita**, a masterpiece of philosophy.

Sanskrit playwrights. He is believed to have lived over 2,000 years ago. His plays were based on the *Ramayana* and *Mahabharata*. Kalidasa is the most celebrated of the Sanskrit poets; his works are taught and performed even today. The rich lode of Indian Mythology forms the basis for his poems, which include *Raghuvamsa* and *Kumarasambhava*. Among his best known plays are *Malavikagnimtram* and *Shakuntalam*.

EARLY YEARS: 10C TO 14C

During the tumultuous period of wars and conquests in the 11C and 12C, the modern vernacular languages of northern India were taking shape. They were born of the older forms called Middle Indo-Aryan, of which Prakrit, the language of the masses, was one of the best known. They also shared roots with **Sanskrit**, the language of the sacred and classical texts of Vedic times and beyond. The newly evolving languages developed a grammar and syntax that linked them to the Hindi and Urdu languages of modern times.

From the 11C on, while the Rajputs were establishing their kingdoms and struggling against the invading Muslims, their courts employed bards who celebrated the heroic exploits of their leaders in songs and poetry. The **chronicles** of these bards form some of the earliest examples of Hindi literature as well as of secular writing. They adopted a type of **lyrical poetry** called *raso* for their martial-themed works. The best-known of the bardic works from this period is the *Prithviraj Raso* by Chand Bardai. It is a stirring account of the desperate battles between the 12C Rajput leader Prithviraj and those who sought to defeat him and destroy his kingdom. Though unwieldy and verbose, it is a moving and imaginative blend of legend and fact.

Bards were numerous in the early centuries of the newly growing and maturing Hindi language and its dialects, but many of their works were lost, or survive in bits and pieces. Among them are Jagnayak, a contemporary of Chand Bardai, and Sarang Dhar, of the 14C, who narrated the events of the kingdom of

Mythological depiction at Sone ki Dukan, Mahansar

© Christophe Boisvieux/age fotostock

Ranthambore. Such works of literature are valuable as records of earlier times. A major figure in **Hindi literature** from the 13C and 14C was the Sufi poet Amir Khusro. This accomplished poet, musician and scholar was truly a multicultural person who blended his Persian roots with the culture of his homeland, India. The versatile poet wrote about a variety of topics in a range of styles; his writings are rich in **metaphors** and descriptive language. As court poet to several rulers of the Delhi Sultanate, he wrote riddles, jokes and songs that delighted the common man and are quoted even today. Amir Khusro's contribution to the development of the language and literature of Hindi is lauded by modern scholars. During this period the *doha*, or **couplet,** emerged as a popular form of poetry. In time, the *doha* achieved high standards of excellence in the hands of skilled poets. Today Hindi poetry, with its well-developed prosody, is full of *dohas* of enchanting rhythms.

BHAKTI MOVEMENT: 14C TO 16C

The 15C saw a burgeoning Bhakti, or **devotional**, movement all over northern India. The Muslim invasions created tremendous havoc in society, and perhaps as a response to the chaos, Hindu religious movements flourished in this period. The **Vaishnavite form** of Hinduism composed a large part of this movement. From this outpouring of devotional fervor came vast literary output. Much of it was in the Hindi language of the time, as the objective was to appeal to the common masses, for whom Sanskrit, the language of the classics and the priests, was impenetrable and inaccessible.

One of the most influential people of the Vaishnavite group was Ramananda, an ascetic who lived and preached around Varanasi in the 15C. An ardent devotee of Ram, he eschewed the strictures of caste and welcomed all into his fold. His audience was the common man, whom he addressed in Hindi, thus doing much to advance the language. From the point of view of Hindi literature, Ramananda's significance lay in the fact that the literary works generated by his movement were almost entirely in Hindi.

Ramananda's best known disciple was Kabir (1398-1518), a poet and saint who is revered by Hindus and Muslims alike. He is remembered for his **dohas**, which school children in India are taught to this day. These couplets, written for the average person, are rustic and simple, yet full of profound symbolism, rich imagery and lyrical beauty. Through these *dohas*, Kabir shared his thoughts and philosophy. He opposed dogma, ritual and the caste system and emphasised simple living and devotion to achieve the union of the self with the soul. The followers of Ramananda and Kabir generally praised Vishnu in the name of Lord Ram.

Another branch of the Vaishnavite form celebrated another incarnation, Lord Krishna. In the mid-15C, one of the most famous poets of the Hindi language, Mirabai, lived in western India, in present-day Rajasthan. A Rajput princess, she was a devotee of Krishna; her intense adoration for the blue-skinned god is expressed in her melodious poetry. Her words, many of which have been set to music, are alive and beloved throughout India today. One of Mahatma Gandhi's favorite songs was a *bhajan* by Mirabai, "Hari, Tuma Haro". After his assassination, radio stations all over India played this song repeatedly.

One of the venerated names in Hindi literature from the Bhakti movement is that of Tulsidas (c1532-1624), a poet-saint whose fervor and reverence for Lord Rama was expressed in exquisite songs and poetry. His best known work is the *Ramacharitramanas*, the "Lake of the Deeds of Rama", a retelling in Hindi of the great epic *Ramayana*. Written in expressive Hindi, this masterpiece has captivated readers from all over the Hindi-speaking world.

Another well-known poet of the Bhakti era was Surdas. This blind poet and musician lived in the 15C, and composed thousands of devotional songs dedicated to Lord Krishna.

The literature and religious works of this period are a vital part of the foundation for many of the beliefs and values of modern northern India.

MUGHAL AND RAJPUT COURTS: 15C TO 19C

Many of the Mughal emperors were admirers of literature. Hindi and Urdu literature experienced a significant flowering in their time. Under their patronage and that of the later Lucknow and other courts, **Urdu** grew into a language of polish and sophistication.

Todar Mal, Emperor Akbar's finance minister, was influential in encouraging Hindus to learn the Persian language. He translated the Sanskrit *Bhagavata Purana* into Persian and wrote verses in Hindi, many on morals and good behaviour. The Urdu language stemmed from this interaction. Today, Hindi and Urdu are complementary versions of the same language, almost identical at the spoken level, but each layered with a distinct cultural orientation that serves to set them apart from one another. Urdu literature is written in the Perso-Arabic script and is permeated with the influence of Persian language and culture.

Birbal, who was first a poet in the Jaipur court, later joined the court of Akbar, where he became the emperor's most trusted advisor. A highly skilled poet, he was awarded the title of Kavi Rai, or poet laureate, by Akbar. Witty and humorous, his poetry is enjoyed to this day.

Akbar's successors continued to promote Hindi literature, which entered a golden period when a great many works of a high literary quality were written. However, by Emperor Aurangzeb's reign, as the Mughal Empire began to decline, Hindi literature suffered a dearth of excellence. Yet the great Urdu poets Ghalib and Zauq were renowned for the beauty of their works (and their rivalry) in the reign of the last Mughal emperor, Bahadur Shah Zafar II. Ghalib is known for his **ghazals**, a poetic form consisting of couplets and a refrain, usually on the themes of love and separation. His ghazals are a popular part of the Hindustani music canon.

The Rajput kings were also great patrons of the arts and literature. The **bardic tradition** continued to flourish, and many works that chronicle the life and times of the kings of the region are extant today. During the reign of Maharaja Jai Singh (1621-67), *riti* or **scholarly literature** reached great heights. Jai Singh encouraged literature in both Braj Bhasha (literary Hindi) and Sanskrit. Under his patronage, the poet Biharilal wrote one of the masterpieces of *riti* poetry, *Biharisatsai*, a collection of 700 poems.

COLONIAL INFLUENCE: 19C TO 20C

The colonial presence had an influence on Hindi literature as the Indian people came into contact with Western literature and technology. The **printing press** played a significant role in spreading European literary traditions. Early presses set in the **Devanagari** (an Indian alphabet used to write Hindi; since the 1800s it has been used to write Sanskrit) script were not a success, but a lithographic press set up in Delhi in 1837 opened the floodgates for the printing of books, magazines and pamphlets.

Hindi literature enjoyed a renaissance, and **prose**, as well as a new literary dialect, flourished. Lallu Ji Lai worked with Dr. John Gilchrist, head of Fort William College in Calcutta (now Kolkata), and wrote works of a high literary standard in prose, helping to establish the popularity of this hitherto little-used form in Hindi. By expelling words of Persian and Arabic origin from Urdu and substituting words from Sanskrit or Hindi, he helped create what is sometimes called 'High Hindi', which became the new literary Hindi. He wrote the *Prem Sagar*, his version of the 10th chapter of the *Bhagavata Purana*, an ancient work in Sanskrit. One of the highly regarded writers of the modern era is Bharatendu Harischandra (1850-1885). Often called the father of **modern Hindi literature**, he wrote prose, poetry and drama under the pen name Rasa. His works reflect the trials and difficulties of the middle class.

Another star in modern Hindi's literary firmament is Munshi Premchand (1880-1936). A pioneer in literary realism in Hindi, this one-time government servant resigned from his job and settled down in a village where he observed the mundane ordinariness of daily life, which became his theme. His novels and short stories had a major influence on modern Hindi literature.

Mahaprasad Dwivedi wrote in the early years of the 20C about nationalism and social reform, reflecting the concerns and issues of his time.

HINDI LITERATURE TODAY

Throughout the 20C and beyond, Hindi literature has continued to flourish. Poets and novelists have experimented with different styles and genres. Essays and dramas have been embraced by Hindi writers as well as by their readers. Harivanshrai Bachchan (the father of the Bollywood superstar Amitabh Bachchan), Nagarjun, Mahadevi Verma, Shivani, Bhisham Sahni and Ramdhari Singh Dinkar are among those who have distinguished themselves in pre- and post- Independence India.

Today, Hrishikesh Sulabh, Geet Chaturvedi, Vyomesh Shukla, Mrinal Pandey and Krishna Sobti are among the many writers who ensure that the literature of the Hindi language continues to thrive.

Cinema

There is nothing quite like India's Bollywood (Hindi film) industry anywhere in the world. It is the country's primary source of mass entertainment, providing a fantasy-filled escape from life's mundane realities for millions of people in both urban and rural areas. Yet, its popularity is not limited to India alone; Bollywood movies are enjoyed in countries as far-flung and diverse as Japan, Germany, Russia, the United Kingdom and Pakistan, to name just a few. Based in Mumbai, Bollywood is one the India's three major film producers: Telugu cinema (aka 'Tollywood') operates out of Hyderabad, and Tamil films (dubbed 'Kollywood') issue forth from Chennai, but Bollywood is reputedly the world's largest film industry.

FILM'S DEBUT

This multi-billion dollar industry had its beginnings in the colonial era, in the waning years of the 19C. Cinema first came to India in the 1890s, during the British colonial years. It took root in the three most 'British' cities of the time: Bombay (now Mumbai), Madras (now Chennai), and Calcutta (Kolkata). **Film halls** began to appear to enable audiences to view the new medium, and soon Indians were making their own films.

Early movies were **silent,** without sound. The first film of note, *Raja Harischandra*, released in 1913, was India's first full-length feature film shot entirely with an Indian crew. This movie, like many subsequent ones, got its inspiration from the rich lode of stories found in **Indian mythology** and legends.

SOUND AND MUSIC

As technology improved, a new element, **sound**, was added to Indian movies beginning in 1931. India's first public limited film company, Bombay Talkies, was established in 1934. Its studios used the latest in technology and set a high standard of professionalism for the movie business. Several of Indian cinema's most beloved stars like Raj Kapoor, Madhubala and Dilip Kumar, had their careers launched by Bombay Talkies.

The advancement of sound opened the floodgates for one of the most popular features of Bollywood movies: **music.** In the first 'musical' movies, the actors actually sang. With the advent of **playback technology** in the 1930s, a new branch of film-making, the playback singing industry, was created. A host of playback singers began recording songs for movie soundtracks, for which lead-

A cinema in New Delhi

© DINODIA/age fotostock

ing actors and actresses lip-synced the words on camera. Playback singer Lata Mangeshkar's sweet, high-pitched voice and undulating delivery have come to epitomise Bollywood's signature **female vocal style**. In this era, it was common for movies to have as many as 40 songs in them. Today's movies commonly have only 8 or 9 songs, but the enduring popularity of the song-and-dance sequence in movies ensures that they are here to stay. Without songs, a Bollywood movie is just not an authentic Bollywood movie.

The music for the movies generated its own galaxy of stars: music directors, lyricists and of course, the singers themselves. Among the most revered names associated with Bollywood music are music directors R.D. Burman, S.D. Burman and A.R. Rahman; lyricists Gulzar, Anand Bakshi and Javed Akhtar; and singers Lata Mangeshkar, Kishore Kumar and Muhammed Rafi. Their names are given equal billing with those of the actors and actresses, as often, it is the music that can make or break a movie. **Cinematic songs** are one way that movies unite the entire country: a hit song is listened to and sung in the tiniest villages to the most densely populated cities across the length and breadth of the country. It is a common bond that people from widely divergent backgrounds share: the unifying power of the Bollywood movie is a remarkable phenomenon.

CINEMA'S GOLDEN AGE

The 1940s, 50s and 60s, sometimes hailed as the Golden Age of Hindi cinema, saw the birth of the big-budget period-costume **epic movies**. One movie from this era that made a splash in India as well as abroad was *Awaara*, starring Raj Kapoor. Dev Anand, Vijayantimala Bali and Dilip Kumar were some of the other stars of the earlier part of this period. Later came Rajesh Khanna, who was surely every Indian woman's heart throb. Sharmila Tagore and Mumtaz were two of his most popular heroines. The majority of movies in these decades centred on romance, personal relation-ships between a man and woman, told with an abundance of songs and dance. This period was a time of great turmoil and anxiety in India stemming from the struggle for freedom and independence. There was a need for light, frothy, **escapist entertainment**, and Bollywood supplied it in droves. Audiences lapped up the fantasyland of beautiful lovers, dashing heroes, scheming villains, gorgeous scenery and to cap it all, melodious songs and **riveting dances.**

The Bollywood movie was an unambiguous world of good and bad, hero and villain, joy and sorrow, with a happily ever after ending. It was the ideal getaway from the ambiguities and problems of daily life.

TOWARDS VIOLENCE

The 1970s brought political instability and economic uncertainty in India. Bollywood movies continued to deliver escapist fantasies, but now with the added dimension of violence. A whole slew of *dishoom-dishoom* films, with **angry anti-heroes** who defied and beat the system (all for a good cause), cropped up. A new star was born as a result of these movies: Amitabh Bachchan, Bollywood's beloved Angry Young Man (who is neither young nor angry these days); the movie that skyrocketed him to fame was *Sholay*, directed by Ramesh Sippy, in 1975. One of Bollywood's highest-earners, this movie has won countless accolades and awards. Amitabh's most popular heroines were his wife, Jaya Bhaduri, as well as Rekha. The film is credited with introducing the genre of **action films**, nicknamed 'curry westerns' and reflective of Italy's 'spaghetti westerns' that launched American actor Clint Eastwood's career.

STARS ARE BORN

Indian cinemagoers had much to choose from. Bollywood was churning out hundreds of movies every year and the galaxy of stars acting in them was expanding and bright. Some of the other well-known names of actresses and actors from the 1970s and 1980s

Aamir Khan in Lagaan: Once Upon A Time In India (2001)

include Shashi Kapoor, Rishi Kapoor, Neetu, Zeenat Aman, Hema Malini and Sridevi.

In the 1980s and 1990s, Bollywood continued to produce lavish fantasies. New names came into the picture as the next generation of actors and actresses made their debut on the silver screen, including Shah Rukh Khan. He acted in **blockbusters** like *Kabhi Kushi Kabhi Gham* and *Kuch Kuch Hota Hai*. His films straddle multiple genres, from romantic comedies to action thrillers. Other top names from this period and beyond are Salman Khan, Juhi Chawla, Madhuri Dixit, Om Puri and Irfan Khan.

BRIGHT FUTURE

Today Bollywood continues to turn out flamboyant blockbusters. More than a thousand movies are made each year, generating **revenues** of some 3 billion dollars. In the last 5 years mega-hits have earned hitherto unheard of earnings of over Rs. 100 crores (around $20 million) each. These top-grossing films include *Ghajini*, full of blood and gore; the much tamer *Three Idiots*, and *Krrish 3*. A recent movie that has been making waves is *Dhoom 3*, a Hindi language action thriller that has earned the multiple distinctions of being the most expensive Bollywood movie to date as well as the first to be released in the **IMAX movie** format.

None of the technological developments like television or the Internet have dented Bollywood's popularity. To the contrary, India's version of TV quiz show *Who Wants to be Millionaire?*, hosted by Bollywood superstar Amitabh Bachchan, led the way for the international mega-hit *Slumdog Millionaire* (2008); though not a Bollywood production, the blockbuster brought venerated Bollywood music director A.R. Rahman two Academy Awards and raised global awareness of the talents, resilience and pluck of India's people. It was a film in which East and West came together to make a movie of universal appeal.

Today's **superstars** like Katrina Kaif, Deepika Padukone, Priyanka Chopra, Kareena Kapoor, Salman Khan, Hrithik Roshan, Ranbir Kapoor and Aamir Khan have immense drawing power. They endow the industry with tremendous glamour and allure. Their efforts are acknowledged by a wide range of civic and professional **awards** bestowed annually at industry award ceremonies. Aamir Khan, for example, won Best Actor in 2002 for his role in *Lagaan: Once upon a Time in India*, which was selected as the Best Movie of 2002, and in 2009, Movie of the Decade.

Bollywood movies are gaining in popularity abroad as well as within India. The future looks bright indeed for the country's Bollywood film industry.

Music

Music forms a vital part of the devotional and entertainment landscape of the country. Northern India has its own form of classical music called Hindustani music, and the folk music culture is vibrant throughout this region as well. While there are marked differences in the history, repertoire and other aspects of these musical genres, they share lilting melodies and infectious rhythms that are sourced from the same wellspring.

HINDUSTANI MUSIC

The classical music of northern India has ancient roots and a rich, fascinating genealogy. The complex history of the region has contributed many elements to the music to further enhance and refine it.

It is believed that all **classical music** in India has its roots in the *Sama Veda*, an ancient religious text that is more than 3,000 years old. The chants described in this text eventually evolved, using 3, then 5, then 7 notes. The notes were organised into groups that later came to be known as **ragas**, which are akin to melodic modes; they form the backbone of all Indian Classical Music. Every *raga* is made up of a unique combination of the notes and microtones within an octave. The word *raga* means colour, and its notes can be thought of as a palette of colours with which beautiful musical pictures are painted, often using lightning-fast oscillations and ornamentations called *gamaks*.

Another major element is the **rhythmic cycle** of the music, called the *taal*. There are a wide variety of *taal* cycles, many of which are fiendishly complex.

In the early centuries of its existence, Hindustani music served primarily as a means to praise divinity. Organised music of songs in praise of God was performed in temples, where the audience consisted of devotees.

As the political landscape of northern India changed and as princely states and royal courts established themselves, kings became major patrons of music and vied with each other to have the best musicians and performances at their **courts**. As Hindustani music moved from temples to the courts, a new elegant style of singing, the *dhrupad*, evolved. New themes emerged as well. In addition to the religious songs already prevalent, **romantic songs** and songs praising the king became popular. A major influence on Hindustani music arose during the 13C and 14C, a period of Islamic invasions in northern India. A series of dynasties, starting with those of the Delhi Sultanate in the 13C-15C, and culminating with the great Mughal

Miniature painting showing musical instruments

Dynasty of the 16C-19C, ruled the region. The invaders introduced their culture into multiple aspects of life in the parts of the country they controlled: food, dress, architecture and of course, music. The music of northern India was altered forever as Arabic, Turkish and Persian melodies, themes, motifs and instruments fused with existing local music. Amir Khusro, a 13C poet, musician and scholar of Turkish origin who worked in the courts of several Delhi Sultanate rulers, played a significant role in melding **Islamic** musical aspects into Indian music. To this day he is revered as a musical saint in the world of Hindustani music. At this time and largely due to such influences, classical music in India separated into two distinct streams. The music of northern India, now augmented with the musical elements of the Islamic rulers, became Hindustani music; the music of southern India, with its own and different set of influences, became **Carnatic music**.

In the royal courts, under the patronage of many kings who had a deep appreciation of culture, Hindustani music blossomed and enjoyed a period of great growth and popularity. The courts, populated by families of musicians, became well-known for their own special *gharana*, or musical style and ideology, that was the hallmark of each family. For example, the Jaipur *gharana*

Sitars in Jaipur

stood out for its use of rare and intricate *ragas*, rhythmic complexity and high-speed vocal ornamentations; the Agra *gharana*, on the other hand, emphasised slower vocal ornamentations, voice culture and particular rhythmic patterns.

Emperor Akbar, the most enlightened of the Mughal rulers, was renowned for the high standard of the music of his court. One of the brightest stars in Hindustani music's firmament, **Mian Tansen**, lived and worked in Akbar's court, and composed and performed sublime music that is a vital part of the Hindustani repertoire today.

As **royal patronage** became entrenched, a subtle change occurred in how music was perceived—from a purely religious form to a means of entertainment and pleasure. Music transcended religious boundaries and was performed and enjoyed by Hindus and Muslims alike.

Hindustani music continued to evolve as new forms of songs were composed, many in regional languages. Until the 19C, Hindustani music was transmitted **orally** from teacher to student, most often within the palace environment. It was a highly fragmented system, nonstandardised, and only a few people had access to training. During the British presence in India, the power and influence of many of the kings waned, and there was a real danger that the music that had blossomed in the nourishing environment of the courts would wither away. At this critical juncture, two acclaimed musical scholars, Vishnu Digambar Paluskar and Vishnu Narayan Bhatkhande, stepped into the breach and ensured that the music continued to thrive and grow in the tumult of the changing political and social milieu. They organised music conferences, founded schools that were open to anyone interested, and standardised the notation used to write the songs. Thanks to their efforts, the music survived and has emerged strong and vibrant.

Today the music of northern India is taught, performed and enjoyed around the world. It has imbibed outside elements and evolved into an art

© Anurag Mallick, Priya Ganapathy/MICHELIN

Gwalior's Tansen Samaroh festival of classical musicians

form that is highly elaborate, requiring years of dedicated training to master it. Its variety ranges from devotional and serious to light-hearted and romantic compositions in hundreds of *raags* and a mind-boggling array of *taals*.

The music is performed vocally, or on several instruments, among the most well-known of which is the **sitar,** a stringed instrument that is plucked; it evolved from the long-necked lutes of Central Asia. Rhythmic accompaniment is usually provided by the *tabla*, a pair of **drums** made of goatskin membranes that are played with the hands. The **harmonium** is a portable keyboard instrument with hand-pressed bellows.

RAJASTHANI FOLK MUSIC

Folk music can be found all over India, but the traditional genre has a particularly dynamic presence in Rajasthan. It is an integral part of the life and identity of the state, and the songs and rhythms add to the region's vivid character.

The folk music of Rajasthan is built on the same structural foundation of *raags* and *taals* as classical music, but it is not bound by the rigourous rules that govern the latter. Many communities of people who are musicians by birth and custom keep the traditional songs and performances alive.

Rajasthani folk music is characterised by melodious tunes and toe-tapping rhythms. A vast variety of songs are sung at different occasions and times

of the year. Devotional songs called *bhajans* and *banis* sing the praises of various gods and goddesses. Particularly popular are the songs of Mirabai, a 15C Rajput princess who devoted much of her life writing poems and songs in honour of her beloved Lord Krishna. Her soulful songs are popular throughout India today.

There are folk songs about the life and adventures of folk and epic heroes. Rajasthan abounds with tales of chivalry and heroism, many of which have found their way into the folk music canon. They are sometimes performed against the backdrop of a painting depicting the incidents described in the song, making for a truly multi-media performance.

Rousing, spirit-lifting songs are sung to accompany **chores** and duties like harvesting, camel-saddling, and water-gathering as well as joyous events like festivals, births and marriages. A wide variety of string, wind and percussion instruments accompany the songs. They are rarely performed the same way each time; **improvisation** and audience participation ensure that the songs remain fresh and engaging every time.

One of the most well-known and sophisticated of the Rajasthani folk music forms is the **Maand**, which originated in the Rajput courts as songs in praise of the kings, and is now regarded as a quasi-classical form, sung by both folk and classical musicians and appreciated by all.

91

Dance

Northern India has a rich tradition of classical dance that dates to the remote past. Over the centuries, this dance has absorbed Islamic and other influences and emerged as one of the most exhilarating and graceful dance forms in the world today.

TRADITIONAL KATHAK

The classical dance form of northern and central India is called Kathak. The name is derived from the term *katha*, which means **story**, and *kathakar*, which denotes storyteller. Kathak traces its origins to ancient times when *kathakars* roamed the land performing tales from the epics and from other mythological sources. Some of these *kathakars* told their stories through dance, movement and acting: these performances were the forerunners of the Kathak dance tradition that developed in the centuries that followed.

As empires and dynasties came and went in northern India, kings began to patronise dance and dancers. Accounts from travelers like Fa Hien (5C) and Hieun Tsang (7C) reveal the important role that dance played in the **royal courts**. It became customary for kings to support large numbers of musicians and dancers as part of the regal entourage. In return for providing top-notch entertainment, these artists were provided accommodation, financial security and the freedom to pursue their art form.

The Bhakti (Devotional) Movement, which swept over North India in the 15C, had a major impact on Kathak. Many songs and lyrics, including the Raas-Leela with its stories of Lord Krishna became an important part of the Kathak repertoire. A distinct style of dancing developed, using **mnemonic syllables** to echo the rhythmic patterns danced by the feet.

During the peak years of the Mughal Dynasty, Kathak became even more popular as courts lavished attention on its dancers. Emperor Akbar's wife, Jodha, a Rajput princess from Rajasthan, was passionate about dance and ensured that it thrived at her husband's court. Perhaps the most ardent royal supporter of Kathak was Wajid Ali Shah, the 19C Nawab of Oudh (a kingdom near Lucknow in Uttar Pradesh). So enamoured was he by Kathak that he himself took lessons from his court's dance guru. The best dancers graced his presence, and the region became renowned for the superb quality of its cultural life. The **gharana,** or style of dance born here called the Lucknow Gharana, to this day is acclaimed as one of Kathak's premier *gharanas*, praised for the elegance and grace of its movements, the evocativeness of its *abhinaya* (facial expressions) and the variety of compositions that form part of its repertoire. Another outstanding *gharana* developed in the Jaipur courts; this Jaipur *gharana* is known for its powerful and difficult footwork, lightning-fast spins and complex rhythms. The different styles of Kathak that evolved and flourished in the courts have immeasurably enriched the dance form.

As with Hindustani music, Islamic elements were incorporated into the dance, making it distinct from other Indian classical dances. Kathak acquired its specific characteristics and form during and after the Mughal period. Some of these elements include the **straight-leg stance** as opposed to the *demi-plie* that is seen in other Indian dances; the profusion of **bells** tied around the ankles to provide a tinkling counterpoint to the rhythmic complexities of the footwork; and the **spins**, or *chakkars*, that flash by and that are believed to be inspired by the whirling dervishes of Sufism.

Kathak endured a shaky period during the British rule of India; they deemed the dance, and the whole system of royal patronage, as base and unwholesome. However, passionately dedicated dancers and patrons ensured that the dance remained alive, and today, it enjoys a wide popularity.

Bhavai dance

© DINODIA/age fotostock

RAJASTHANI FOLK DANCES

The desert landscape of Rajasthan might be brown and bleak, but its folk dances are vibrant and exuberant. A large variety of folk dances are performed in the state by different groups on various occasions. Many of the rituals and festivals of Indian life are enlivened by these dances. Some of the most popular and colourful are described below.

Ghoomar Dance: Performed by women dressed in vividly coloured and embellished clothes, the Ghoomar dance is performed on happy occasions like marriages. The women spin and whirl, and the sight of their twirling skirts and the sounds of the tinkling bells on their feet add to the festive air.

Kacchi Ghori: This dance is performed by men wearing brightly coloured turbans as well as *dhotis* and *kurtas*. Richly decorated horses constructed of bamboo paper and cloth are used in **mock fights** accompanied by the brandishing of swords and quick footwork. The dances tell of confrontations between desert bandits and traveling merchants in times of yore.

Bhavai: Another hugely popular, exciting and extremely difficult folk dance, the Bhavai is performed by women who balance a number of **pots** (as many as nine) on their heads and then perform intricate foot movements on top of a brass plate or even the edge of a sword. The Bhavai is believed to have evolved among tribes who criss-crossed the Rajasthan desert carrying pots of food and water on their heads to sustain them during their long journeys.

Fire Dance: This is another difficult dance, performed by men who dance **barefoot** on live burning wood and charcoal. They enter a trance-like state dance with **fire rods** in their hands and kerosene in their mouths to the accompaniment of drums that beat a tempo of growing speed and intensity. This dance is performed on festive occasions like Holi and the birth celebrations of Lord Krishna.

Tera Taali: In this highly specialised folk dance, small brass **castanets** called *manjeeras* are tied to parts of the body; these are struck with a different set of hand-held *manjeeras*. A variety of rhythmic actions are performed to the sound of these castanets, often while a sword is balanced in the dancer's mouth.

Nature

Rajasthan is India's largest state, covering an area of 342,239 sq km in the north-western part of the country. The Tropic of Cancer grazes its southernmost tip, situating it in the subtropical and tropical zones of the Northern Hemisphere. Delhi and the National Capital Region lie to the north-east. Contrary to the common notion that its terrain is largely desert, Rajasthan possesses great geographical diversity, from forests and dry scrubland to desert and marshes. Blessed with an abundance of minerals, metals and other natural resources, it also supports a wide assortment of flora and fauna.

Colonel James Tod, a cadet in the East India Company's army in the early years of the 19C, was dazzled by Rajasthan and its people. He conducted detailed, and among the earliest, studies of the land. He penned the first **written geography** of Rajasthan which, while incomplete and considerably rosy-eyed, contains many useful facts that provide insight into the region of his time, and serve as a basis for assessing its environmental health today.

The Government of Rajasthan has made great strides in its efforts to protect the state's natural environment. As one of India's top travel destinations, Rajasthan is an ideal location for the development of **sustainable tourism**. Framed in 2010, the Government's Eco Tourism Policy outlines specific guidelines for the implementation of impactful ecotourism initiatives for its parks and sanctuaries.

PHYSIOGRAPHIC AREAS

Rajasthan is shaped like an irregular diamond. Running diagonally across the state from the south-west to the north-east, like an inclined spine, the **Aravalli mountains** are among the oldest in the world, at about 1.5 billion years in age. This range extends 800km in length north to Delhi where, as the **Delhi Ridge**, it traverses south Delhi and tapers to an end as Raisina Hill. These mountains divide Rajasthan into two distinct sections: the western arid Thar desert and the fertile eastern plains with higher rainfall.

Rajasthan's major physiographic areas are the Western Desert, the Aravalli Range and Hilly Region, the Eastern Plain, and the South-Eastern Hadoti Plateau.

Dunes of Thar Desert, Rajasthan

© 19photos/Fotolia.com

WESTERN DESERT

Desert occupies nearly 60 percent of the state and includes the districts of Jaisalmer, Barmer, Jodhpur and Jhunjhunu, to name a few. The great **Thar Desert** encompasses vast expanses of sand interspersed with ridges, dunes, **thorny scrub**, salt marshes and hillocks. The river Luni, which originates in the Aravalli range, flows in a south-westerly direction across part of the desert before draining into the Rann of Kutch in neighbouring Gujarat state.

The **climate** here can be brutal, with searing hot summers, sparse rainfall and cold winters. Fierce **dust storms** sometimes rage in the summer months. Phenomena of terrible beauty, these storms form and re-form sand dunes, resulting in an ever-changing landscape. Despite its unforgiving climate and terrain, the Thar Desert nurtures a bountiful **biodiversity** of habitats and ecosystems. Several national parks and sanctuaries in this area harbour a wide variety of wildlife. Here rare and endangered animals and **birds** can be seen, including several varieties of vulture, grouse, quail, falcon and eagle, as well as chinkaras, desert foxes, desert cats and black buck. The parks are also home to the highly endangered **state bird** of Rajasthan, the Great Indian Bustard. One of the world's heaviest flying birds, the bustard lost out in popularity to the peacock, partly due to the combined misfortune of its infelicitous name and its less than spectacular looks. Destruction of its habitat has resulted in an alarming decline in number.

Among the most popular parks is Desert National Park in Jaisalmer, which offers the eco-friendly and popular option of a camel safari.

Due to perennial water shortages in this region, the Rajasthan Canal System was developed to irrigate parts of the desert and assure a supply of drinking water. Now, vast swathes of formerly bone-dry land support lush fields of mustard, cotton and wheat.

ARAVALLI RANGE AND HILLY REGION

The Aravalli Mountains stretch across the western part of the country. They bifurcate the state of Rajasthan, forming the watershed that divides the rivers of the western and eastern parts of the state. The highest peak, near Mount Abu in southern Rajasthan, is **Guru Shikhar**, which rises to a height of 1,722 meters. These pre-Cambric mountains are rich in **metal and mineral deposits,** a fact that is both a boon and a curse for the state. They abound in zinc, lead, quartzite, marble, clay, silver, copper, garnet and jasper: Rajasthan is one of India's leading suppliers of these metals and minerals. The marble that was used to build the Taj Mahal, for example, came from Makrana, in this range. Such bounty, however, has resulted in rampant and unregulated **over-mining**: large expanses of once-green hills are now bald and bare. The Supreme Court of India has attempted to stanch the damage by banning mining activities across the Aravalli Range, but illegal mining continues. A mere three decades ago, a handful of mines operated in southern Rajasthan; today there are more than 1,500 of them, all contributing to the devastation of the ecosystem. Also located in southern Rajasthan, the **Kumbalgarh Sanctuary**, named for the historic fort in the area, sits within the Aravallis. A showcase for the wildlife and biodiversity of these mountains, it is inhabited by wolves, leopards, sloth bears, hyenas, jackals, chinkara, nilgai and chaisingh. Many bird species can be found here as well, like jungle fowl, peacocks, parakeets, red spur owls, golden orioles and the white-breasted kingfisher.

EASTERN PLAIN

The eastern plain accounts for 24 percent of the total area of the state, and 40 percent of the population. This is Rajasthan's most **fertile area**, crisscrossed by several rivers, the major among which are the **Chambal**, the Banas and the Gambhiri, which drain into the Ganga-Yamuna river system.

Tigress, Ranthambore National Park

The state's capital, Jaipur, lies in this area, as do Bharatpur, Bhilwara, Tonk and Alwar. In stark contrast to the barren sands of western Rajasthan, this area is flat with rich **alluvial soil** prone to flooding. Wheat, rice, cotton and tobacco are grown here. In the southern extremity of the eastern plain, **teak forests** thrive in the humid climate.

The most popular nature reserves here are the **Keoladeo Ghana National Park** in Bharatpur, and the Sariska Tiger Reserve. Located 55km west of Agra, Keoladeo National Park is one of the best birding havens in India and indeed, the world, attracting birding aficionados from experts to amateurs. Formerly known as the Bharatpur Bird Sanctuary, the land was originally the duck hunting preserve of one of the Bharatpur Maharajas who created shallow wetlands there. A staggering variety of birds, fish, amphibians and flowers thrive here among the marshes, dry deciduous forests and grasslands of the sanctuary. The **sarus crane**, the world's tallest flying bird, is found here. Thousands of migratory birds spend the winter and breeding seasons here. The park was declared a World Heritage Site by UNESCO in 1985 to protect its environment and wildlife.

Just north-west of the park, the **Sariska Tiger Reserve** (*see Sariska*), thick with dry deciduous forest, lies at the foothills of the Aravalli mountains. This former

preserve of the Maharajas of Alwar retains only the ruins of their temples and pavilions, today occupied by langurs. Other animals here include leopards, jungle cats, hyenas, jackals and of course, tigers. Bird species include the peafowl, grey partridge, bush quail, crested serpent eagle and the great Indian horned owl.

SOUTH-EASTERN HADOTI PLATEAU

Kota, Jhalawar, Balawar and Bundi districts fall into this region characterised by a diverse topography of low hills, plateaus and higher hills that are part of the Vindhya mountain range. Crops like wheat, barley, sugarcane and cotton grow in the region's thick black soil, which retains moisture well. The Chambal River traverses the **Hadoti Plateau**, adding to its rich floral diversity. Other waterbodies and dense forests attract migratory birds who fly here from as far away as China and Russia.

One of India's premier tiger sanctuaries, **Ranthambore National Park**, once the hunting grounds of the erstwhile Maharajas of Jaipur, straddles the eastern plain and the Hadoti Plateau. Bounded by the Chambal River in the south and the Banas River in the north, Ranthambore comprises steep rocky hills, dry deciduous forest, grassy meadows, lakes and rivers. In addition to its popular tigers, the park hosts langurs,

leopards, hyenas, jackals, marsh crocodiles, wild boar, bears, deer and many
bird species. The dramatic landscape
of Ranthambore includes ruins of a 10C
fort, which add another dimension to
the wildlife preserve.

NATURAL DELHI

India's capital city and the area
surrounding it, collectively referred to
as the **National Capital Region**, spread
out over 1,483sq km, making it the country's largest metropolis physically. For
a city that is situated on the edge of a
desert (the Thar desert of Rajasthan), it is
a remarkably green place that is home to
more than 200 varieties of trees, in addition to being rich in bird and animal life.
Delhi has three primary **geographical
features**: the Delhi Ridge, the Yamuna
River, and the Plain that is part of the
great Indo-Gangetic plain system. The
older areas of Delhi fall into a rough
triangle marked by these features.
The tail end of the Aravalli mountains,
known here as the Delhi Ridge, lies in
the western and southern sections of
the city; the Yamuna River enters Delhi
at its north-eastern end and flows in a
south-easterly direction to feed the Agra
Canal just south of Delhi; in-between
lies a broad, fertile alluvial plain. Each of
these areas is marked by flora and fauna
that are distinct to that particular ecosystem and habitat.

DELHI RIDGE

The northern extreme of the Aravalli
mountains tapers to an end at Delhi,
terminating in what is known as the
Delhi Ridge. Stretching 35km in a south-
east to north-west direction, the Ridge
protects parts of the city from the hot
desert winds that blow like sand-laden
gusts of fire in the scorching summer
months. The dry deciduous forests of
the Ridge, often called **Delhi's green
lung**, teem with a profusion of birdlife
that has earned Delhi the distinction
of being the capital city with one of
the largest bird populations, second
only to Nairobi in Kenya. Thorny trees
like **acacias** and seasonal herbaceous
plants grow in the furrows and hillsides

of this area. Much of the greenery of the
Ridge was planted during the period of
the Delhi Sultanate, when these rulers
enjoyed hunting in and around their
capital. Colonial planners who helped
to develop New Delhi as the nation's
new capital also contributed to the
reforestation of the Aravalli ridges,
planting large numbers of American
Mesquite and other trees.
The Ridge's ecosystem plays a vital
role in reducing pollution, recharging
groundwater and cooling the city. Lack
of adequate protection from construction and **pollution** has resulted in
rampant destruction of habitat. Many
animal species, like leopards, hyenas,
foxes, wolves and jackals that roamed
the ravines and hills of the Ridge in large
numbers have vanished. Measures have
been taken to protect and conserve this
habitat, but it is an ongoing endeavour.
The city of Delhi has recognised that
education is a vital element in preserving natural habitats. To this end, it has
set up **biodiversity parks**, with more
in the planning. One of these, Aravalli
Biodiversity Park, about 5km north-
east of the city's airport, showcases
the micro and macro ecosystems of the
Aravalli mountains. In the southern edge
of the Ridge, near its merger with the
Indo-Gangetic plain, the Asola Bhatti
Wildlife Sanctuary shelters a wide array
of birds and an impressive assortment
of reptiles, amphibians and mammals.
Monkeys, which have become a men-
ace in many parts of Delhi, have been
successfully relocated here, where they
are welcome.

YAMUNA RIVER

Born in the Himalaya mountains,
the Yamuna, a major tributary of the
Ganges, is one of India's holiest rivers.
Accounting for more than 70 percent
of Delhi's water supply, it enters the city
in the north-east and snakes its way
southward. Delhi sits astride the river,
primarily on its west bank. However,
large-scale industrial activity and dump-
ing of sewage have severely polluted
the Yamuna. An interceptor **sewage
system**, due to be completed in mid-

2014, should reduce pollution levels dramatically, once it is fully functional. The Yamuna is extensively **dammed,** and for much of the year, water levels in the Delhi area are low, resulting in mudflats and shallow pools that invite flocks of **wading birds** like Greater Flamingoes. Wild boar, several species of fish, and the occasional crocodile can be seen in and around the Yamuna. On its banks, riverine vegetation like weeds and grasses thrive. As part of its effort to conserve this habitat and make people aware of its distinct features, the Delhi Development Authority has set up the Yamuna Biodiversity Park, covering some 400 acres near Wazirabad in north Delhi. Miniature versions of the **ecosystems** of the Yamuna River have been developed here, from subtropical mixed evergreen forests and tropical dry deciduous forests to tropical thorn forests. With its abundance of birds and butterflies, the park is becoming a popular nature destination in Delhi.

THE PLAIN

In Delhi's broad alluvial plain, the most abundant of the city's many trees and flowering plants are the **sheesham** trees (with their dark and durable timber), neem, jamun, gulmohur, mango and peepal. When the new city was in

Jantar Mantar in New Delhi, surrounded by trees

© Kamini Dandapani/MICHELIN

the planning stages in the early 20C, expert horticulturists debated the types of trees to plant along the newly constructed, broad roads. Initially, a list of 13 trees was drawn up, including neem, jamun and imli, which still dominate New Delhi today, even though other varieties were planted in later years. These trees, many with brilliantly coloured flowers, along with seasonal flowering plants like chrysanthemum, phlox and verbena, make the city one of the greenest capitals in the world.

The Delhi government's efforts to add forest and **tree cover** to the National Capital Region are succeeding: more than 229 sq km, or 20 percent of the area, were under forest and tree cover in 2009, a dramatic jump from 1993, when a mere 1.48 percent was canopied. Recognising that strong measures had to be taken to tackle the alarmingly high pollution levels in the city, the Delhi government decreed in the early years of the new millennium that its entire fleet of **public buses** had to be converted to use compressed natural gas. This conversion earned Delhi the Clean City International Award in 2003.

AGRA'S GREENWAYS

The city of Agra lies on the banks of the Yamuna River, some 200km southeast of Delhi. It sits on the great Indo-Gangetic plain, whose terrain is largely flat, with the ravines and badlands of the Chambal River valley pock-marking the extreme south-west. In an area known more for agriculture, industry and tourism than natural beauty, places of keen interest to nature lovers lie practically at the Taj Mahal's doorstep.

TAJ NATURE WALK

Starting half a kilometer from the Taj Mahal's east gate, Agra's **green belt** stretches to the banks of the Yamuna. An area of high grasslands dotted with thorny and broad-leafed trees, the greensward is part of a ravine ecosystem. It is a place of scenic beauty, enhanced by views of the Taj Mahal from several perspectives.

Crocodile, National Chambal Sanctuary

© Anurag Mallick, Priya Ganapathy/MICHELIN

Created in 1998, this **nature preserve** has a healthy population of pheasants, bulbuls, pigeons, parakeets, kingfishers, hoepoes and peacocks, as well as mammals such as hyenas, jackals, blue bulls and hares. The **bird population** soars during the months of migration. Reptiles and butterflies are also found here.

SUR SAROVAR SANCTUARY

This little-known 400-hectare sanctuary lies just 20km west of Agra. A haven from that city's bustle, this **wetland** preserve has been described by eminent ornithologists as one of the best places in the world to observe migratory birds. Birdlife International has designated it as an Important Bird Area.

The main feature of Sur Sarovar is the man-made **Keetham lake**, which occupies more than half of the sanctuary's acreage and is dotted with small islands. Vast numbers of pelicans, flamingos, storks, sarus cranes and other birds flock to its hospitable shores.

Sur Sarovar is also home to the **Agra Bear Rescue Center,** the world's largest sloth bear holding facility. More than 200 former dancing bears, forced to perform from a young age, have been brought here for care. Injured and orphaned Asian elephants are also taken here for care and shelter.

PATNA BIRD SANCTUARY

This bird sanctuary, which is approximately 60km north of Agra, might be small in size at 108 hectares, but its bird population is large and varied. Gerbs, cormorants, herons, egrets and ducks are just some of the birds that can be found here, in addition to animals like jackals, mongooses, hares, nilgai, monkeys and foxes. Many **migratory birds** spend the winter here (◔November through February are the best months to visit). Within the sanctuary, the ancient Shiva temple adds the sound of its pealing bells to the songs of thousands of birds.

NATIONAL CHAMBAL SANCTUARY

Straddling the three states of Rajasthan, Madhya Pradesh and Uttar Pradesh, this sanctuary (◔*see Chambal*) showcases the ecosystem of the ravines and gullies of the Chambal River basin. Situated approximately 70km south-east of Agra, it is best known as the preserve of the critically endangered crocodilian species the **gharial**, as well as the Gangetic dolphin. Chinkaras, sambhar deer, nilgai, leopards and foxes, varieties of turtles, and local and migratory birds can be found in this large preserve.

Amer Fort in Amer, near Jaipur
© Christian Heeb/John Warburton-Lee Photononstop

Delhi★★★
and around

Highlights

Traffic outside Jama Masjid
© Jon Arnold/hemis.fr

Delhi★★★

The National Capital Region of India (made up of Delhi, Noida and Gurgaon; the national capital itself is properly New Delhi) is the country's second city in size (after Mumbai, formerly Bombay, and before Kolkata, formerly Calcutta). It combines a wealth of history and art with a vitality that makes it one of the most interesting cities in the whole of South Asia, while embodying all the contrasts that characterise modern India.

It takes barely a quarter of an hour to travel several stations on the ultra-modern metro, from New Delhi's grid of magnificent, airy avenues to the labyrinth of alleyways criss-crossing the market at Chandni Chowk in Old Delhi. Here, you will find yourself in the middle of indescribable traffic jams where pedestrians, cycle rickshaws, motorbikes and scooters vie for right of way. The untutored eye will find it hard to take in all the physical types and styles of clothing in this incredible human maelstrom. Everyone goes about their business with great energy, spawning a thousand small additional tasks and jobs as a result of this great and sincere sense of enterprise.

In addition to this, modernisation has been undertaken at a breakneck pace with the metro extension, a perpetual building project expected to last until 2021; this colossal enterprise has cut a swathe of construction across the city from one side to the other. All this commotion may be trying for visitors used to slightly more regulated environments: the first reaction of all new arrivals is to try to find a bit of peace and quiet. So it is a good idea to take refuge in one of the parks surrounding the majestic Indo-Islamic monuments in the southern districts. A walk in Lodhi Garden or the grounds of Humayun's Tomb should be enough to persuade you of Delhi's real charms.

OLD DELHI★★★

(Shahjahanabad) Map II

▶ *Tour* 1 *marked in green on map departing from the Lahore Gate at Red Fort. Allow a day for walking and taxi.*

Delhi locals call this district, which corresponds to the city founded in the 17C by Muhal emperor **Shah Jahan** (1627–58), 'Old Delhi' (Purani Dilli). Surrounded by defensive walls of which there are still considerable traces (in the east), it retains a sufficient sense of unity to give an impression of being a city within a city. Until the partition of India in 1947, it was a mainly a Muslim city, teeming with a mix of Turks, Afghans and Persians. It witnessed the flourishing of the most sophisticated Indo-Islamic culture, notably in the Urdu poetry kept alive in the *ghazal* (*see Literature*).

THE RED FORT★★ (LAL QILA)

M° Chandni Chowk. Access via Lahore Gate. ⏰ *Open Tue–Sun sunrise–sunset.* 🎟 *Rs.250; video Rs.25. Allow 1hr.*

👥 **Sound and Light Show:** *Nov–Jan 7.30pm; Feb–Apr and Sept–Oct 8.30pm; May–Aug 9.00pm.* 🎟 *Rs.80, 1hr.*

Shah Jahan moved his capital city from Agra to Delhi in 1638 and set about building a formidable 'forbidden city' that included the imperial residence, and government offices. The construction program entailed tearing down an 11C fortress built by the Tomara Rajputs. This palace was the heart of the empire and the official imperial residence until Bahadur Shah Zafar, the last Mughal, was exiled after the Indian Rebellion of 1857. The palace suffered considerable damage from ongoing pillaging in the 18C as well as from demolition by the British in the wake of this rebellion: to facilitate the defence of the fort, the British razed the district surrounding it to the ground, creating a vast walkway (along which the monument is now accessed), and destroyed a section of the palace within, replacing it with monumental barracks now occupied by the army.

▶ **Population:** 17.8 million.

ℹ **Info:** A number of travel agencies, especially around Connaught Place and in Paharganj) style themselves the 'Government Tourist Information Centre' to attract clients, sometimes with dishonest intentions. Be cautious and trust only the addresses listed in the tourism info box:

▶ **Location:** 203km north of Agra, 232km north-east of Jaipur. For a detailed map of Delhi, buy an **Eicher City Map** from a bookshop.

👥 **Kids:** Sound and Light show at Red Fort; astronomy instruments at Jantar Mantar; paddle boat ride in the lake at the Purana Qila.

⏰ **Timing:** Use the metro (the quickest way to get around) whenever possible. Avoid Old Delhi on weekends (shops at Chandni Chowk are closed Sundays) and on Mondays (when the Red Fort is closed). Gain valuable time by walking or travelling by cycle rickshaw; by contrast, having to travel miles in the dusty environment of **New Delhi** will teach you the value of the auto rickshaw; when visiting the southern districts, hire a taxi for the day. Most of the monuments are open sunrise to sunset (approx. 7.30am–5pm in winter, 7am–6.30pm in summer); the price of admission often includes permission to take photographs, but expect to pay a surcharge for video camera use. Visit the Mughal Gardens of Rashtrapati Bhawan mid-Feb–mid-March if you can.

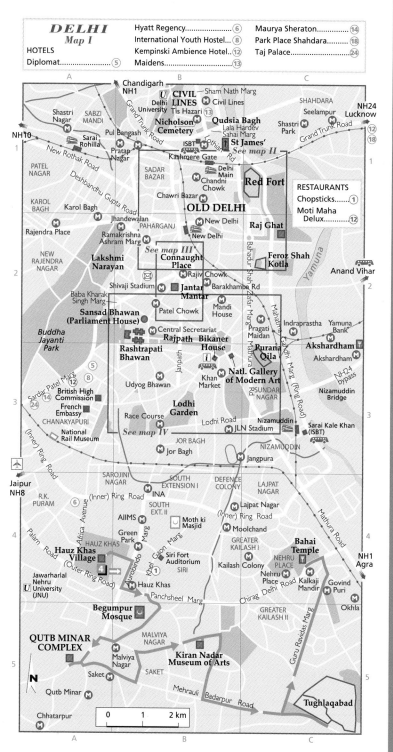

DELHI
Map 1

HOTELS

Diplomat......................⑤
Hyatt Regency....................⑥
International Youth Hostel...⑧
Kempinski Ambience Hotel...⑫
Maidens............................⑬
Maurya Sheraton...............⑭
Park Place Shahdara.........⑱
Taj Palace........................㉔

RESTAURANTS

Chopsticks........①
Moti Maha
  Delux............⑫

GETTING THERE/LEAVING

BY PLANE– Indira Gandhi International Airport (IGIA) – *off map, Map I A4.* 20km south-west of Connaught Place. ☎ 0124-3376000 and 0124-4797300 (toll-free numbers). www.newdelhiairport.in. Also known as **Terminal 3** (Terminal 1 is wholly domestic and Terminal 2 is out of commission), it is served by international flights and somef domestic flights. Only ticket-holding passengers may enter the airport. The main airport hall has bureaux de change (open 24 hours), ATMs and booking centres for train and flight tickets (🕐 open8am–8pm).

🕸 **Worth knowing** – Book domestic flight tickets well in advance. Check departure time and terminal from which the flight is to take off before you leave for the airport (it takes about 20min to get from T1 to T3). A free Airport Authority of India (AAI) **shuttle** provides a connection between the various airport terminals. **Airport tax** – This tax is included in the price of your flight ticket.

Getting to city centre from airport
TAXI – The **pre-paid taxis** desk, run by the Delhi Traffic Police, is located outside. You pay the fare before entering the cab, and you will receive a receipt indicating the amount paid and the taxi number. Don't give the receipt to the driver until you arrive at the hotel. **Easy Cabs** (☎ 011-43434343. www.easycabs.com), **Meru Cabs** (☎ 011-44224422. www.merucabs. com) and **Mega Cab** (☎ 011-41414141. www.megacabs.com) have desks at the airport. **Ashok Travels & Tours** (☎ 011- 25654501. www. attindia tourism.com) is a reliable car hire agency that provides tourist taxis at the airport.

🕸 **Worth knowing** – International flights often arrive in the middle of the night and some taxi drivers might try to convince tired tourists to book into a hotel that will pay the driver a commission. Make sure you book your taxi only at the counters of the service providers recommended above.

METRO – The Orange Line connects the airport with New Delhi Railway Station (M° New Delhi); one-way 40–50 minutes. Every 15mins from 5.15am until 11.35pm. Rs.150.
BUS – Number 780 bus departs for Connaught Place (9am–7pm; journey approx. 1hr) from bus stop outside the airport. Air-conditioned DTC (Delhi Transport Corporation) buses leave for the city centre every 20mins departing opposite the Centaur Hotel, which you can reach via the shuttle from the airport (every 15mins, 24hrs).

🕸 **Worth knowing** – Departing from Delhi – If you have to leave your hotel early in the morning to get to the airport, ask the hotel to book a taxi the previous evening.

Airlines

Air India – At the airport, Terminal 3. ☎ 011-24622220. www.airindia.com.
Air France – ☎ 1 800 1800 077 (toll-free number). ☎ 0124-2723000 (from abroad). www.airfrance.in.
Air Canada – *Map III C3.* Next to the Hindustan Times Building, 2nd floor, 16 Kasturba Gandhi Marg. ☎ 011-41528181. www.aircanada.com.
British Airways – ☎ 1 860 180 3592 (toll-free number). ☎ 0124-4120715 (from abroad). www.britishairways.com.
Jet Airways – *Map III C3.* G-11/12 Outer Circle, Connaught Circus. ☎ 011-39893333. www.jetairways.com. 🕐 Open Mon–Sat 9am–6pm. Also at: Jetair House, 13 Community Centre, Yusuf Sarai. ☎ 011-26523357.

BY TRAIN– Four stations serve Agra and Rajasthan: Delhi's largest station, **New Delhi Railway Station (NDLS** *Map II B3, 700m* north of

Connaught Place. M° New Delhi), is on the same line as Delhi Main, but has connections to Mathura, Agra, Bharatpur, Sawai Madhopur, Kota, Jaisalmer, Udaipur and Jaipur. New Delhi is also the departure point for Shatabdi trains, which are slightly more expensive but fast, comfortable and air-conditioned One serves Alwar, Jaipur and Ajmer; another serves Agra, arriving 8am, making a day trip to Agra from Delhi possible – take the train back to Delhi at around 8.30pm.

Delhi Main Railway Station (DLI) – *Map II C1.* North of Old Delhi. M° Kashmere Gate. Note that to get here from Connaught Place you will have to cross Old Delhi, which is often congested. Departures are principally for Alwar, Jaipur, Ajmer and Jodhpur.

Nizamuddin Railway Station (NLZ) – *Map I C3.* East of New Delhi. Trains for Mathura, Agra, Bharatpur, Sawai Madhopur and Kota; some depart from New Delhi before stopping at Nizamuddin, others leave directly from Nizamuddin.

Sarai Rohilla Railway Station (DEE) – *Map I A1.* Approx. 5km north-west of Connaught Place. This station serves Bikaner and Udaipur via Jaipur, Ajmer and Chittaurgarh.

⊛ **Worth knowing** – Check your ticket to see what station your train will leave from. You can find timetables and fares online at www.erail.in and www.indianrail.gov.in. For more details check www.irctc.co.in.

Tickets – Best to book train tickets via a travel agency, paying a small commission but saving on time and effort. Otherwise, computerised booking centres are in every station (8am–8pm). An office reserved for foreigners is the **International Tourist Bureau** – *Map II B3*, on the 1st floor of New Delhi Station, ✆ 011-42625156 (also information for all stations), ⏰ Mon–Sat 8am–8pm, Sun 8am–2pm. Take advantage of seat quotas reserved for foreigners; pay in dollars, Euros, sterling or rupees upon

production of your passport. Buy your Indrail Pass (⦿ *see GETTING AROUND below*) here or from the computerised booking centres.

⊛ **Worth knowing** – Watch out for pickpockets and touts around the stations, especially in New Delhi. They often target the most popular tourist routes between Delhi, Agra and Jaipur. ⦿ *See also Safety below.*

Maharaja Trains – Details and reservations for the Palace on Wheels and Heritage on Wheels from the **Rajasthan Tourist Office**, www.rtdc.in. **Gujarat Tourism** handles the Royal Orient, www.royalorienttrain.com – *Map III A3*, A-6 Baba Kharak Singh Marg, ✆ 011-23734015.

BY BUS– Main bus stations: **Bikaner House** – *Map IV D2.* Pandara Rd. ✆ 011-23383837. www.rtdc.in. Reservations 6am–7pm. Rajasthan State Transport Roadways Corporation (RSTRC) Super Deluxe bus: Silver Line (no air-conditioning) and Deluxe (air-conditioned) buses depart for Jaipur daily 6am and midnight (6hr journey). This is the best way to get to Jaipur if you don't take the Shatabdi. Fares and timetables at http://rsrtconline.rajasthan.gov.in/.

Inter-State Bus Terminal (ISBT) – *Map I B1.* Old Delhi, north of Delhi Main station. M° Kashmere Gate. Reservations at Bikaner House or ✆ 011-23868836, 7am–7pm. Pre-paid taxi and rickshaw service. The departure point for private buses (avoid those with on-board video) and some scheduled RSTRC buses.

Sarai Kale Khan Bus Terminal (New ISBT) – *Map I C3.* Mahatma Gandhi Rd, east of Nizamuddin station. Buses for Ajmer, Alwar and Jaipur leave from here, as well as for Agra via Mathura.

Anand Vihar Bus Terminal – *off map, Map I C2.* Trans-Yamuna. A rather out-of-the-way bus station located east of the city and run by Uttar Pradesh State Transport Roadways

Corporation (UPSTRC). Buses leave for Mathura and Agra, but it is better to take the train to these destinations.

GETTING AROUND

METRO – Delhi Metro system (www. delhimetrorail.com) is the fastest way to get around the city. The metro runs 6am until 11pm. A single-journey token costs between Rs.8 and Rs.30. Metro cards are also available, but are not suitable for sightseeing. 1-day or 3-day tourist cards can be purchased for unlimited travel. Network maps are available from every station. No large bags allowed on the metro. North–south **Yellow Line** connects the Civil Lines district to the Qutb Minar, calling at Chandni Chowk, New Delhi station, Connaught Place, Rajpath, Lodhi Garden and Hauz Khas Village. East–west **Blue Line** for for Connaught Place and Paharganj (Mº R.K. Ashram Marg). **Red Line** stops at Kashmere Gate but is little used by tourists, much like the **Green Line** which extends the route to the west. **Orange Line** serves the airport; change for Yellow Line at New Delhi station. **Violet Line** serves Janpath and Khan Market.

RICKSHAW – Delhi's **auto-rickshaws** have meters but drivers often refuse to turn them on, in which case, discuss/haggle the fare before you get in. Rickshawallahs have a chart in which you can look up **fares** but they will often present the unwary tourist with the taxi fare chart instead, with the heading cut off. Agree on a fixed price, based on a rate of Rs.15/km; add 25% to the usual price for journeys made between 11pm and 5am. A pre-paid rickshaw kiosk is on Janpath (opposite Janpath Market) and in front of train stations. **Cycle rickshaws** are not allowed in Connaught Place and in most of South Delhi.

TAXI – Delhi taxis are black and yellow cars of Indian make with no air-conditioning and often dilapidated. As the Delhi government regularly hikes the hire charge and rate per kilometre, make sure the meter is up-to-date before setting off; if it isn't, the fare will be higher than that indicated on the meter. **Tourist taxis** are in much better shape than black-and-yellow cabs and can be hired from taxi stands. But it's best to ask your hotel to arrange one.

Day hire – Negotiate directly at the taxi stand or with the driver. Most taxi stands have fixed rates based on the number of hours and the kilometres plied (for 4hr and 40km expect to pay Rs.500; double for 8hr and 80km).

Pre-paid taxis – Easy Cabs (☏ 011-43434343. www.easycabs.com), **Meru Cabs** (☏ 011-44224422. www.merucabs.com) and **Mega Cab** (☏ 011-41414141. www.megacabs. com) are reliable companies.

Fares – Rates are routinely changed according to fuel costs. Expect to pay a surcharge of 25% between 11pm and 5am; also to pay a fixed rate of Rs.10 per piece of luggage.

BUSES – Delhi Transport Corporation (DTC)'s red buses are air-conditioned (fares start from Rs.20); green buses are not air-conditioned (fares start from Rs.15). ☹ *Beware of pickpockets.* Travelling by bus is the cheapest, and for the adventurous, gives insight into the city's people.

Tourist buses – Hop-on/Hop-off sightseeing buses follow 2 circuits (green line and red line), stopping at Delhi's main monuments Tue–Sun, every 30 to 60 minutes 8.30am–5pm. There is also a night bus timetable. Fares Rs.300 to Rs.500. Further information at www.hohodelhi.com.

CAR HIRE – Hire from travel agencies. Cars come with a driver, minimum mileage and a rate per kilometre. Expect to pay between Rs.1,200 and Rs.1,800, and more for an air-conditioned larger vehicle.

HEALTH

🔊 **Advice** – If an emergency, head to the nearest big hospital or pharmacy.
Max Multi Speciality Clinic - N 110, Panchsheel Park, ☎ (0) 8860444888. For branches www.maxhealthcare.in.
Pharmacies:
On Connaught Place: **Nath Brothers** (*Map III B2*), G-2 Radial Rd 3 and **Chaturbhuj & Bros** (*Map III B2*), G-45 Outer Circle. Khan Market: **Crown Drug Store** (*Map IV C3*), 28-B.

EMERGENCY SERVICES

Ambulance – ☎ 102.
Fire service – ☎ 101.
Police – ☎ 100.

SAFETY

🔊 **Worth knowing** – Once your plane has landed, someone may approach you offering to take you to the 'tourist office'. It is a **scam**; refuse point blank. Fake offices may bear the slogan 'approved by Government') and the cost of going there directly from the airport will be far more expensive than if you wait until you are already in the city. Real tourist offices are closed at night.
Don't take any advice from passers-by who purport to want to help you, especially around New Delhi railway station or Connaught Place. Gullible tourists are prey to rip-offs and confidence tricks.

Lahore Gate★★

The red sandstone **ramparts** run around a perimetre of more than 2km; entrance is gained first through a former military outpost and then via the **Lahore Gate**. This imposing portal, designed as a pointed arch topped with small white domes, also has symbolic value: it was from here that the flag of an independent India flew for the first time on 15 August 1947. Every 15 August since, the prime minister has addressed the nation from this vantage point.
The gate leads to **Chhatta Chowk**, a covered gallery filled with souvenir stalls that is immediately reminiscent of a bazaar from the time of Shah Jahan. At its far end, you will find the **Naubat Khana** or Naqqar Khana ('House of Drums'), a space dedicated to musicians during ceremonies. A small **military museum** (India War Memorial on the 1st floor of the central building, 10am–5pm, no charge) displays weapons from the Mughal period to World War I.

Diwan-i-Am★

At the end of the court garden.
The emperor would assemble his court in this Hall of Public Audiences to receive subjects or foreign envoys. Despite the depredations of attacks on Delhi in the 18C, the Diwan-i-Am still boasts a frontage of elegant, engrailed arches. It houses a marble **throne★★★** beneath a canopy and a 'Bengal' roof.
Note the superb **pietra dura** work that continues round to the back of the throne: floral swirls, birds and even an Orpheus that is said to be the work of a Florentine or French artist.

Palaces on the Yamuna

Past the Diwan-i-Am.
You now enter the gardens of the **private apartments**. These included a succession of six palaces (five have survived) lined up on the east side, looking out over the Yamuna River. Try to imagine them swathed in precious tapestries and draped in red silk suspended between the walls to form intimate courtyards or awnings to guarantee some shade.
Opposite, in line with the Diwan-i-Am, the **Rang Mahal★★**, is divided into six apartments that were occupied by the first wife of the emperor. A basement provided respite from the heat that preceded the monsoon, and the perfumed water of the Nahar-i-Behisht ('Stream of Paradise'), a small watercourse flowing beside all the palaces in the fort, provided coolness. A security barrier prevents access, and it is not possible to walk under the arcades (this restriction is also true of

the Khas Mahal and the Diwan-i-Khas). The next palace as you head north is the **Khas Mahal★★**, where the emperor lived. Some spectacular **jali** stonework has been preserved, decorated with the scales of justice, one of Shah Jahan's favourite symbols. From the balcony of the octagonal tower, the emperor would appear each morning, offering his *darshan* (literally, view) to his people. Continuing north, you arrive at the jewel in the crown of the fort, the **Diwan-i-Khas★★★** ('Hall of Private Audiences'). Its white marble walls housed the famous **Peacock Throne**, a priceless treasure encrusted with precious stones. In 1739, the king of Persia, Nadir Shah, took possession of this prize during the sack of the city and removed it to Tehran, where it remains to this day. Fifty years later, Shah Alam II was blinded in this very place by an Afghan chief, enraged at his failure to find the Mughal treasure. The **hammam★** *(closed to the public)*, has three marble bathing chambers encrusted with fine jewels. Opposite, the **Moti Masjid★★** (Pearl Mosque) *(closed for renovation)* was built by emperor Aurangzeb in 1659 for his exclusive use. Notice the grills on the windows with their extremely ornate shapes.

The Gardens
Continue north.
Pass the **Hayat Bakhsh Bagha**, the 'Life-Bestowing Garden' (*on the left*). The Persian taste for geometrically arranged gardens enclosed by walls, conceived as images of paradise, was introduced to India by Mughal emperor Babur and gave rise to a host of gardens designed in the Mughal style (divided into four quarters by two bodies of water that meet in the middle). Past a small pavilion rises the **Musamman Burj** tower; the sovereign worked in one part of it. At the base, a mechanism drew water from the Yamuna to feed the Nahar-i-Behisht.

Archaeological Museum
Far southern end of the palaces, beyond the Rang Mahal. Open 9am–5pm.
Return south across the gardens with their late Baroque-style pavilions, the middle one of which, surrounded by water, was built for Shah Zafar, the last emperor. End the tour in the small **archaeological museum**, whose miniatures, small objects in ivory and mother of pearl evoking life at court, are housed in the **Mumtaz Mahal**, once the apartment of the harem.

Sri Digambara Lal Jain Mandir
Opposite the Red Fort, on the corner of Chandni Chowk. Open 5am–noon and 6pm–9pm. Remove your shoes before entering.
This Jain sanctuary for the *digambara* ('sky-clad') sect, looking like a colonial mansion, was founded in the 17C. It is famed for its **bird hospital**, to which the Jains, keen protectors of all life, bring injured birds. The **tower** (*shikhara*) rising behind it is typical of Hindu sanctuaries in northern India and belongs to the **Gauri Shankar Mandir** ('temple'), dedicated to Shiva and his consort Gauri.

CHANDNI CHOWK BAZAARS★
M° Chandni Chowk. A majority of the stores are closed on Sundays; the restaurants and barbershops stay open, and local grocers ply their trade along the main roads.
Chandni Chowk ('Moonlit Square') owes its name to the reflection of the moon in the waters of the canal that once surrounded it (but is now completely filled in). This canal, the **Nahar-i-Behisht**, flowed through the Red Fort. In the late 19C, Chandni Chowk was a sleepy avenue, shaded by large trees; nowadays, it is a bazaar engulfed in a confusion of cycle rickshaws, ox-carts and porters, who struggle under sacks and boxes as pick their way through the crowd, while scooters and backfiring auto rickshaws weave in and out, with much honking of horns, along a roadway colonised by a motley collection of stalls – paste jewellery, shoes, crockery and gadgets for a few rupees.

☺ **Worth knowing** – The best way to explore the bazaars is to stroll the alleys and *katra* ('covered lanes'), where *baniya* ('Hindu merchants') lay out metres of

Districts of Delhi

Located on a gravel plain, Delhi extends for nearly 30km from north to south along the banks of the Yamuna, a tributary of the Ganges that is sacred to Hindus; yet the city seems to turn its back on the river. The history of the city and its different districts has resulted in the main points of interest being spread out across a number of sites, some of which are rather far from the city centre and are not handily distributed between Old and New Delhi.

Old Delhi (*Map I BC1–2 and Map II*) – The 17C city includes the **Red Fort, Jama Masjid** and, around **Chandni Chowk**, bazaars that are teeming with life. Visit this district on foot to discover the picturesque streets of traditional India.

Connaught Place and Rajpath (*Map I B2 and Maps III and IV*) – Located further south, the commercial and administrative heart of the city, designed by Lutyens in the 1910s and 1920s, extends around **Connaught Place** (airlines, banks, luxury shops, restaurants) and **Rajpath** (central government buildings, National Museum, National Gallery of Modern Art).

The Residential Area – The most spacious and peaceful part of the capital is located just south of Rajpath. To the west, **Chanakyapuri** (*Map I A3*), the 'Diplomatic Enclave', is occupied by embassies and a few luxury hotels, while at its southern end **Lodhi Road** (*Map IV*) snakes between the converted grounds surrounding Muslim mausoleums. .

Southern Districts – These are a disparate succession of less charming new areas that nonetheless include a few quiet havens such as the **Qutb Minar complex** (*Map I A5*) and **Hauz Khas Village** (*Map I A4*). Visit by rickshaw or car.

Civil Lines (*Map I B1*) – Built by the British in the 19C, this spacious, green district to the north is mainly of note for those interested in the colonial era.

Bara Gumbad, Lodhi Garden off Lodhi Road

© Anurag Mallick, Priya Ganapathy/MICHELIN

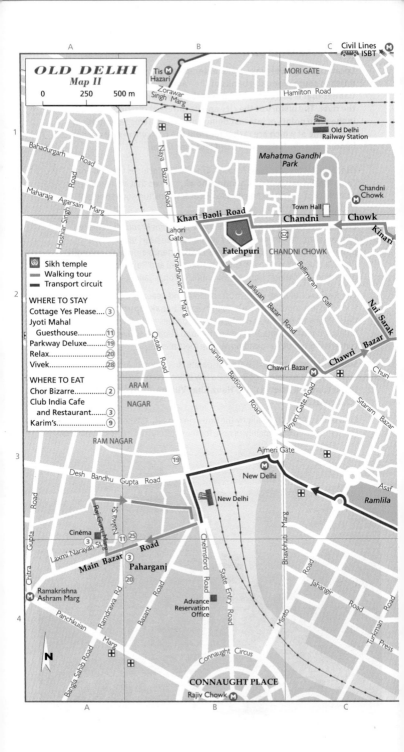

OLD DELHI
Map II

0   250   500 m

Civil Lines
ISBT

MORI GATE

Tis Hazari
Zorawar Singh Marg
Hamilton Road

Bahadurgarh Road

Maharaja Agarsain Marg

Hoshiar Singh Marg

Naya Bazar Road

Old Delhi Railway Station

Mahatma Gandhi Park

Chandni Chowk

Town Hall

Khari Baoli Road

Lahori Gate

Fatehpuri

Chandni   Chowk

Kinari

CHANDNI CHOWK

Shradhanand Marg

Lalkuan Bazar Road

Ballimaran Gali

Nai Sarak

Sikh temple
Walking tour
Transport circuit

WHERE TO STAY
Cottage Yes Please.... ③
Jyoti Mahal
   Guesthouse.............. ⑪
Parkway Deluxe......... ⑲
Relax........................... ⑳
Vivek........................... ㉘

WHERE TO EAT
Chor Bizarre.............. ②
Club India Cafe
   and Restaurant...... ③
Karim's....................... ⑨

Qutab Road

Garstin Bastion Road

ARAM NAGAR

RAM NAGAR

Chawri   Bazar

Chawri Bazar

Churi

Sitaram Bazar

Ajmeri Gate Road

⑲

Desh Bandhu Gupta Road

Ajmeri Gate

New Delhi

New Delhi

Asaf

Ramlila

Gupta Road

Chitra

Cinéma
③
Raj Guru Marg
JS Marg
⑪ ㉕
Main Bazar Road
③
Paharganj
⑳

Laxmi Narayan St.

Ramdrawa Rd

Basant Road

Chelmsford Road

State Entry Road

Bhavbhuti Marg

Jahangir Road

Road

Turkman

Press

Ramkrishna Ashram Marg

Panchkuian

Bangla Sahib Road

Advance Reservation Office

Minto

Connaught Circus

N

CONNAUGHT PLACE

Rajiv Chowk

112

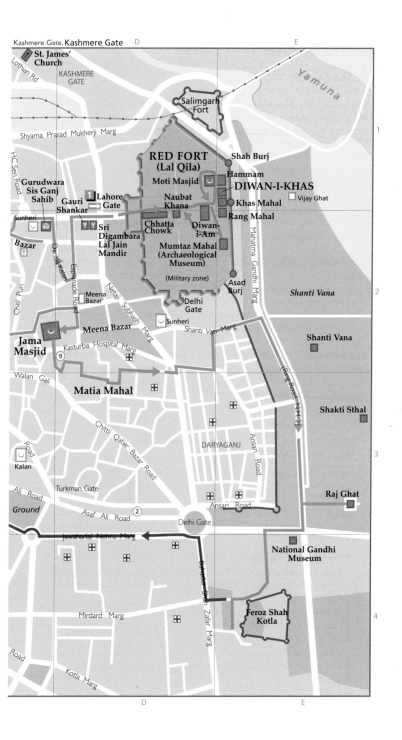

Kashmere Gate, **Kashmere Gate**

St. James'
Church

Lothian Rd

KASHMERE
GATE

Shyama Prasad Mukherji Marg

Salimgarh
Fort

Yamuna

HC Sen Road

RED FORT
(Lal Qila)

Shah Burj

Hammam

DIWAN-I-KHAS

Gurudwara
Sis Ganj
Sahib

Moti Masjid

Gauri
Shankar

Lahore
Gate

Naubat
Khana

Khas Mahal

Vijay Ghat

Sunheri

Sri
Digambara
Lal Jain
Mandir

Chhatta
Chowk

Rang Mahal

Bazar

Diwan-
i-Am

Chel Puri

Danda Kalan

Esplanade Road

Netaji Subhash Marg

Meena
Bazar

Mumtaz Mahal
(Archaeological
Museum)

(Military zone)

Mahatma Gandhi Marg

Shanti Vana

Asad
Burj

Meena Bazar

Kasturba Hospital Marg

Delhi
Gate

Sunheri

Shanti Van Marg

Shanti Vana

Jama
Masjid

Walan Gali

Matia Mahal

Chittli Qabar Bazar Road

(Ring Road NH 2)

Shakti Sthal

Road

Kalan

DARYAGANJ

Ansari Road

Ali Road

Ground

Turkman Gate

Asaf Ali Road

Ansari Road

Raj Ghat

Delhi Gate

Jawaharlal Nehru Marg

National Gandhi
Museum

Bahadur Shah Zafar Marg

Mirdard Marg

Feroz Shah
Kotla

Road

Kotla Marg

cloth. Within this labyrinth, small courtyards hold unexpected calm, reminiscent of the medieval East.

Dariba Kalan★

East of Chandni Chowk.
This is the street of jewellers; while the real jewellery-makers seem to be disappearing, this street, true to its traditions, is now a concentration of shops selling gold and silver encrusted with cameos or semi-precious stones. Make a brief stop at the far end, right on the corner of Chandni Chowk, at the Old Famous Jalebiwala, which is said to make the best *jalebi* (deep-fried wheat flour batter soaked in sugar syrup) in the capital.

Gurdwara Sis Ganj Sahib★

Go down the avenue to the left.
Cover your head and remove shoes.
The presence of bearded, turbaned men betrays the proximity of one of the largest **Sikh temple** in Delhi. It was constructed where the ninth Sikh guru, **Teg Bahadur**, was beheaded for his faith in 1675 on the orders of Emperor Aurangzeb. The faithful come to pray in the main hall, where the refrain of *kirtan*

('religious songs'), accompanied by the *tabla* and harmonium, is constant.

▶ Head west along Chandni Chowk.

Pass a small square with a fountain (*on the right*) and turn left into **Paranthe wali Gali**, a small street overseen by three families who have specialised in *paratha* (fried stuffed whole wheat bread) for generations. Cauliflower or apple *parathas* turn a golden brown in a *karahi* (bowl-shaped frying pan).

Kinari Bazaar★

Further along beyond Paranthe wali Gali, on the left.
Red and gold colours dominate the street, which is devoted to accessories for Hindu weddings and to lace-making. Costumes are also sold here: monkey or bird masks, the bow and quiver of the Lord Ram, and cardboard figures of his faithful ally (monkey god Hanuman).

Fatehpuri Masjid and Market

Far eastern end of Chandni Chowk.
This elegant mosque was built in 1650 by Fatehpuri Begum, one of Shah Jahan's

---

Your Itinerary in Delhi

If you only have 2 days

1st day – Morning and lunch around Connaught Place. Afternoon, whistle-stop tour of the main sights of Delhi (Red Fort, Jama Masjid, Humayun's Tomb) with the DTTDC. An evening at the cinema or at a dance show.

2nd day – Visit the Qutb Minar and shop at Hauz Khas Village; lunch around Khan Market. Afternoon at the Crafts Museum and Purana Qila (stay for the Sound and Light show).

If you are spending 4 days in the capital

1st day – Bazaars at Chandni Chowk and Jama Masjid; lunch at Karim's; for the afternoon, the National Gandhi Museum and the Red Fort (stay for the Sound and Light show).

2nd day – Jantar Mantar, Gurdwara Bangla Sahib and Hanuman Mandir. Lunch at Connaught Place. See crafts at the State Emporia and a stroll at Paharganj. Dance spectacle in evening.

3rd day – Lodhi Garden and National Museum in the morning. Lunch around Khan Market. Crafts Museum, Purana Qila and Humayun's Tomb in the afternoon.

4th day – Akshardham and the Bahai Temple in the morning. Shop at Hauz Khas Village and visit the Qutb Minar in the afternoon.

wives. Directly behind it, **Khari Baoli Road★** and the adjoining streets make up the largest **spice market** in Asia; sacks with red chillis, black pepper, turmeric, dried raisins and cardamoms. This is the place to buy loose Assam tea.

Chawri Bazaar
South of Chandni Chowk.
Students come to **Nai Sarak**, which connects Chandni Chowk to Chawri Bazaar, to buy books and writing pads. **Chawri Bazaar**, where many of the stalls are run by Jains, specialises in anything to do with paper: wedding invitations and greetings cards decorated with symbols of good fortune, such as the *swastika*.

JAMA MASJID★★★
M° Chawri Bazaar. Approx. 800m from the Red Fort, main access is via the east gate, but you can also enter from the north and south. ⏱ *Open 7am–noon, 1.30pm–6.30pm (30mins before sunset; hours vary by about 1hr, depending on season). No charge, photo and video ✆ Rs.200. Closed to non-Muslims at noon and evening prayers. Remove shoes; cover your head.*
Begun in 1644 and completed in 1658, the 'Friday (*jama*) mosque (*masjid*)', referring to the day of the week with the greatest congregation, stands on high ground opposite the Red Fort. Access is via the main entrance (the eastern gate), reached past the open-air stalls of the **Meena Bazaar**, which is full of shops

that start right on the pavement and sell all sorts of kitsch objects intended for pilgrims and Indian tourists.

A vast set of steps leads up to the gate, which features a deep *iwan* ('a vaulted entrance space').

As you enter the **courtyard**, you begin to get an idea of the scale of the construction. The layout of the Jama Masjid in Delhi, the last great mosque built by the Mughals and the largest in India, represents the apotheosis of the Indo-Islamic style of mosque with a courtyard (♨ *see Architecture*): a large space enclosed on three sides (north, east and south) by identical arcades that feature at their centres a monumental gate known as a *pishtaq*. The porticos house a sort of collection of booths in which the doctors of the faith can meditate and children can learn the Quran. A basin for ritual washing before prayers (*namaz*) stands in the middle of the courtyard.

At the far western end (the direction of Mecca), the actual **sanctuary** itself is found, flanked by two minarets and topped with three towering, onion-shaped white domes. The engrailed arch of the great central gate (*pishtaq*) leads to the **prayer hall★** whose walls are decorated with calligraphy representing quotations from the Quran. The back wall, known as the *qibla*, indicates the direction of Mecca. Its centre is marked with a *mihrab (representation of the house of God)*, an empty niche, a symbolic aperture allowing access to God.

Domes and minaret of Jama Masjid
© Brad Pict/Fotolia.com

End of a Tyranny

After the death of Aurangzeb (1707), the Mughal Empire went into sharp decline but northern India slowly regained its religious freedom. The Hindus made use of this period to reconstruct their temples and the Sikhs did the same for their *gurdwaras* , but not without conflict in many cases. In 1783, Baba Baghel Singh, the chief of a Sikh group, took control of the Red Fort and forced the emperor Shah Alam to negotiate: to recover his property, he was obliged to allow the Sikh community to build temples in Delhi.

Climb the **south minaret** (*to the right as you leave the prayer hall, Rs.100, no admission for unaccompanied women*) for a superb **panorama**★★ of Old Delhi.

Matia Mahal District

Leave the mosque by the southern gate.
From the top of the enormous flight of steps you see a part of the district that surrounds the mosque on its southern and eastern sides: its narrow lanes, mostly frequented by men, are dominated by signs in Urdu, the Perso-Arabic script used by the Muslims.

The fish and meat market (*to the left*) is next door to the low-budget restaurants of **Matia Mahal**, a crowded district where authentic Mughlai food is prepared. Cauldrons containing lamb *korma* sit next to piles of *naan* (leavened white bread) taken straight from clay ovens in the ground, with kebab skewers and roasted chickens in the window displays of the restaurants.

▶ After exploring Matia Mahal, take a rickshaw to Shanti Vana Park.

SOUTH OF THE RED FORT

A ring road runs along the eastern side of the Red Fort, serving **Shanti Vana**, which extends along the Yamuna and contains monuments marking sites where notable people were cremated.

Shanti Vana Cenotaphs

The most visited cenotaphs are **Shanti Vana** (literally the 'forest of peace'), commemorating Jawaharlal Nehru, India's first Prime Minister, who died in 1964, followed, to the south, by **Shakti Sthal** (dedicated to Indira Gandhi) and especially **Raj Ghat**★ (*Map II E3*)

(*from sunrise to sunset*), the monument to **Mahatma Gandhi** (◖ *see sidebar at end of History*). The *samadhi* (memorial) to the 'father of the nation' is composed of a black marble plaque, decorated with flowers, and engraved with the words '*He Ram*' ('Oh God'), Gandhi's last words at his assassination on 30 January 1948. The small **National Gandhi Museum** (*Map II E4*) (◷ *open Tue–Sun 9.30am– 5.30pm, closed public holidays; no charge; small bookshop; film at 4pm weekends*) on the other side of the boulevard has a display of several objects from the Gandhi period and some of his photos and personal effects, including his spinning wheel, as well as the pistol used in the assassination.

Feroz Shah Kotla

South of the museum.
The fortress of Ferozabad was a former city founded in 1354 by Sultan Feroz Shah Tughlaq. Visit to experience the tranquility of its park. Rising above the palaces and ruined mosques is an **Ashoka pillar**, a monolith on which the Maurya emperor had one of his famed edicts engraved in the 3C BC. Feroz Shah brought it back as a trophy after a campaign against the ruling Hindus.

▶ Take a rickshaw to the area around New Delhi station.

PAHARGANJ

M° Rama Krishna Ashram Marg or M° New Delhi.The end of Main Bazar Rd. is located opposite the station, to the left.
For decades, Paharganj has been one of the places favoured by visitors who come to India intent on re-creating scenes from the hippie years. **Main**

Bazar Road, the principal thoroughfare through the district, has a collection of low-rent hotels, second-hand clothes shops, mass-produced craftwork stalls, cybercafes and travel agencies.

As soon as you move away from this touristy street, local life picks up. In the neighbouring lanes customers at tiny *chai (tea)* shops (a camping stove and two wooden benches) sip milky tea beside a mason's workshop or a street vendor's barrow. Pass the street of potters *(parallel to Qutab Rd.)* and the street of quilt-makers to find craftworkers and small traders. Cows roam the streets all the time. Tandoors (earthen ovens) and piles of *lady's fingers* (okra) announce the entrance to a vegetable market.

CONNAUGHT PLACE★ AND AROUND *Map III*

❯ *Tour* 2 *marked in green on map departing from M° Rajiv Chowk. Allow 3hr on foot, not counting Lakshmi Narayan Temple.*

Connaught Place actually refers to the traffic island in the middle of the square, but by common consent the name includes the three concentric roads surrounding it, Inner Circle, Middle Circle and Outer Circle (or **Connaught Circus**), as well as the rest of the district. Generally considered the nerve centre and shop window of the capital, the place attracts dealers, touts, tellers of tall tales and scoundrels who will take their chances at relieving well-off passers-by (both Indian and foreign) of a few rupees. *The colonnades of Connaught Place and neighbouring streets, especially those near the station, are a magnet for tricksters trying their luck on tourists who have just arrived in Delhi.*

CONNAUGHT PLACE★

M° Rajiv Chowk. ◷ *Square comes alive when shops open at 10am or 11am.*

An immense square enlivened by the constant traffic, **Connaught Place** symbolises the business-focused nature of the Indian middle classes. Surrounded by Colonial-style buildings, it was opened in 1931 and named in honour of the Duke of Connaught, King George V's uncle. The square was in fact re-named 'Indira Chowk' in 1995, with Connaught Circus becoming 'Rajiv Chowk', but the inhabitants of Delhi stuck to using the original name or the familiar nickname 'CP'. The traffic jams at CP, unlike those of Old Delhi, bear the mark of the modern world: there are no cycle rickshaws or ox-carts here (ox-carts are banned), only auto rickshaws and poorly regulated motor vehicles, among which zigzag countless two-wheelers.

JANTAR MANTAR★

M° Rajiv Chowk. Entrance on Parliament St. ◷ *Open from sunrise–sunset.* ◉ *Rs.100, video Rs.25.*

👥 This **astronomical observatory** from the early 18C was designed on the orders of emperor by **Jai Singh II**, the maharajah who founded Jaipur. As a devotee of astronomy, he had established that measuring instruments made of brass were not very reliable due to their small size and the amount of play in their axes. He decided to construct instruments that were immovable and a hundred times the size, giving rise

The 'New Hippies'

Some hotels and restaurants in Paharganj are overflowing with young Westerners, sometimes scruffy looking or sporting extravagant piercings, who are off to Goa, Pushkar or Nepal. However, many of these 'new hippies' would rather eat spaghetti bolognaise, chips and veggie burgers than Indian food. Having usually just spent the winter in pampered idleness, they generally soon realise the distance that separates them from Indian society, or its conservative elements at least; this lack of understanding most often elicits arrogance on both sides.

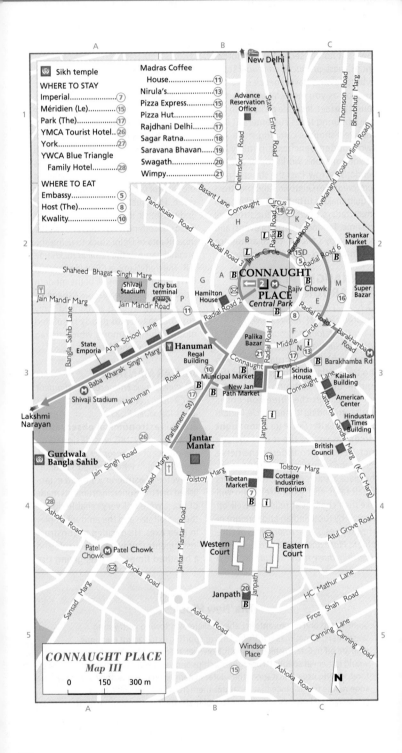

Sikh temple

WHERE TO STAY
Imperial.....................⑦
Méridien (Le)............⑮
Park (The)..................⑰
YMCA Tourist Hotel..㉖
York...........................㉗
YWCA Blue Triangle
    Family Hotel............㉘

WHERE TO EAT
Embassy......................⑤
Host (The)..................⑧
Kwality.......................⑩

Madras Coffee
    House....................⑪
Nirula's....................⑬
Pizza Express............⑮
Pizza Hut..................⑯
Rajdhani Delhi..........⑰
Sagar Ratna..............⑱
Saravana Bhavan......⑲
Swagath....................⑳
Wimpy.....................㉑

CONNAUGHT PLACE
Map III

0   150   300 m

to the Jantar Mantars in Delhi and in Jaipur, as well as modest ones in Varanasi (Benares), Ujjain and Mathura (this last has now been lost).

These astonishing structures worked well and were so reliable that they made it possible to correct errors in the astronomical tables of the era's greatest thinkers. Nowadays, the large buildings surrounding them in a somewhat surreal manner render them impossible to use. The **Samrat Yantra★** is an enormous sundial (or gnomon) with a central staircase. Next to it is the **Jai Prakash Yantra**, invented by Jai Singh II to check other instruments' calculations.

HANUMAN MANDIR

M° Rajiv Chowk. From Jantar Mantar, walk back to the Outer Circle, Connaught Place. Take Baba Kharak Singh Marg, the first road to the left, and continue for 150m. Remove your shoes before entering.

Built by Jai Singh II, creator of Jantar Mantar, and altered several times, the temple is dedicated to the monkey God. While of minimal architectural interest, this shrine, dear to Delhi's citizens, provide insight into the religious fervour of Hindu devotees. Crowds are particularly large on **Tuesday**, the day dedicated to Hanuman. At the stalls selling carnations or rice cakes, buy an offering for the God, before climbing the steps. People visit the temple when the mood takes them to experience **darshan** (literally, view). The devout leave an offering in front of their chosen God, never forgetting to bow to the other divinities.

GURDWARA BANGLA SAHIB★

M° Patel Chowk. End of Baba Kharak Singh Marg (approx. 500m from the Hanuman Mandir), just before Ashok Circle. Cover your head and leave your shoes and any cigarettes outside.

You can see the golden dome of the Gurdwara Bangla Sahib, the largest **Sikh temple** in Delhi, from some distance away. Built at the end of the 18C, it is located on the site of the house where Harkrishan Dev, the eighth guru, lived during his stay in Delhi (1664). The entrance to the temple is surrounded by stalls selling copies of the **Guru Granth Sahib**—the holy book of the Sikhs—as well as turbans, daggers and metal bangles—traditional Sikh accoutrements. Follow the pilgrims and enter the prayer hall, which resounds with *kirtan* (hymns) composed to the glory of God and the 10 founding gurus of the community. One grill protects the Guru Granth Sahib, the principal object of veneration; the faithful prostrate themselves, make their offering of money and then rejoin the congregation, taking care never to turn their backs on the holy book.

Before leaving the temple, worshippers may wash in the immense **basin** in the courtyard; having been blessed by Harkrishan Dev, the basin's water is said to cure cholera and smallpox. Beside the entrance, a flight of stairs leads to a basement converted into the Baba **Baghel Singh Museum** (*no charge*). Colourful tableaux recount the dramatic history of the community's 10 gurus.

You may be invited to take a meal in the communal **dining hall** (*langar*); you sit on the floor with other pilgrims and the faithful wait on you (the notion of service for the benefit of the community is essential to Sikhs). The menu will include dal (lentils) and *roti* (wholemeal bread) for all.

LAKSHMI NARAYAN TEMPLE

1km from the gurdwara. Head left on Baba Kharak Singh Marg to the roundabout and turn right onto Kali Bari Rd; at the end, turn right (in front of the small Buddhist temple) onto Mandir Marg. ⏰ Open daily 7am–noon and 2pm–9pm. Remove shoes. Cameras not permitted (locker at the entrance).

Also known as the **Birla Mandir**, this **Hindu shrine** made entirely of white marble was built by the wealthy Birla family, originally from Shekhawati. The temple is dedicated to Vishnu-Narayan and his consort Lakshmi, the Goddess of abundance, who is much cherished by the Marwari merchants. Mahatma Gandhi agreed to inaugurate the temple in 1938 on the condition that it would be open to the 'untouchables', which was not always the case with Hindu temples.

Nonetheless a notice announces that the building is closed to 'people suffering infectious diseases' (lepers).

NEW DELHI★★

Map IV, see inside front cover.

▶ *Tour* ③ *marked in green on map departing from Vijay Chowk. Allow 5hr for a visit by rickshaw, 6hr including Akshardham.*

M° Central Secretariat ('Sansad Bhawan' exit). **Vijay Chowk** *(Map IV B2), 'Victory square' is 400m away. Distances between monuments (1–2km) and long avenues of deafening traffic may dissuade you from completing the journey on foot.*

This tour through green and spacious districts, and museum halls, starts at **Rajpath** (king's way), the old route followed by the monarch, an immense avenue 2.5km long that culminates to the west in a series of symbolic monuments to Indian democracy: Rashtrapati Bhawan, the official residence of the president; North Block and south Block, the main ministries; and Sansad Bhawan (formerly called Parliament House), the parliament building. Built by the British in the early 20C to plans by the architect **Lutyens**, these buildings were initially intended for the administration of the British Empire in India, known as the **Raj**. The furthest building in the row to the east is the Purana Qila. To the south white colonnaded bungalows from the 1920s nestle among the greenery in rows along **a grid of avenues** planted with large trees. Today these bungalows are residences of minsters, generals, etc.

GOVERNMENT BUILDINGS★

Not open to visitors. Only the Mughal Gardens behind Rashtrapati Bhawan are accessible mid-Feb–mid-Mar. Changing of the guard Sat 8am–8.30am (summer), 10am–10.30am (winter).

Rashtrapati Bhawan★

On the high ground of Raisina Hill.

This 1929 edifice was once the residence of the British Viceroy. Since 1947, it has been occupied by the President of the Republic of India . The buildings of the

Secretariat – North Block and South Block, which house the ministries of the Indian Republic – lead up to it on both sides of the hill. The climb to the summit of **Raisina Hill** reveals the large dome of the residence, which was inspired by the Buddhist stupa (reliquary) at Sanchi (in Madhya Pradesh state).

Sansad Bhawan (Parliament House)

To the north of Rajpath.

This vast, circular structure, surrounded by a colonnade, was built in 1927 and once housed sessions of the Chamber of Princes and the Assembly, the two symbolic legislative bodies imposed by Britain in 1935. It is now used as the seat of the republic's two chambers, the **Rajya Sabha** (Council of States) and the **Lok Sabha** (House of the People).

NATIONAL MUSEUM★★

M° Central Secretariat or Udyog Bhawan, 1km from metro. www.nationalmuseumindia.gov.in.
🕐 *Open Tue–Sun 10am–5pm.*
🎫 *Rs.300; photo permit Rs.300; no video permitted. Audioguide included in admission price (very useful as only a few information panels). Allow 2hr for your visit.*

The most striking feature of the Delhi's National Museum, located at the junction of Rajpath and Janpath (once known as Queen's Way), is its remarkable **collection of statues★★★**, on display on the ground floor.

Ground floor

The visit begins with a hall devoted to the Mohenjo-daro and Harappan civilisations, which ruled north-west India until the arrival of the Aryans around 1600 BC. The display cases house a variety of statuettes, including the famous Mohenjo-daro 'dancing girl' in bronze, and objects unearthed during excavations in Sindh (now in Pakistan) in 1921. Don't miss the terra-cotta objects and the statues from the Maurya and Sunga periods (3C and 2C BC) in the next rooms. Graeco-Buddhist busts evoke the art of the Gandhara period (1C to 3C AD), which influenced the Mathura School of

Rashtrapati Bhawan

© Rohan Dandapani/MICHELIN

Art. Buddhist art is to be found in the collections from the Nagarjunakonda site in Andhra Pradesh (friezes, plaques and columns sculpted in the 3C) and the Gupta era (5C terra-cotta and 6C sculpture).

The next rooms are devoted to southern statuary from the Chalukya (8C), Pallava (9C), Chola (11C) and Hoysala (12C) periods, with a series of bronzes representing Hindu divinities.

The **miniatures**★★ room has examples from a range of local Indian schools *(kalam)*, arranged in larger regional movement: Mughal, Rajput, Rajasthani, Pahari ('from the mountains'; don't miss the superb Kangra school) or from the Deccan Plateau. Among the **manuscripts** in the collections that follow is an 8C Quran.

The **decorative arts**★★ rooms house jewellery boxes, jade vases encrusted with semi-precious stones, objects in ivory and silver filigree, and doors made of silver and wood; celadons (stoneware with a green glaze) and ceramics enhance the collection.

The **jewellery**★★ collection includes necklaces, bracelets, diadems and a host of other treasures from the Harappan to the Mughal period.

Further along are panels following the evolution of **Indian script** in India and Southeast Asia (the Thai, Khmer and Burmese alphabets were largely inspired by south Indian writing).

First floor

Once past two rooms exhibiting antiquities from Central Asia, you reach the **Maritime Room**, whose tableaux bring to life the Hindu imperialism of the 7C to the 11C, when the ruling Chola and Pallava dynasties sent boats as far away as the coasts of Java and Sumatra. One room presents the cultures of Central Asia in the form of a collection of objects from the early 20C. The room devoted to numismatics will be of interest principally to coin enthusiasts.

Second floor

Taking a slightly more ethnographical slant, this floor exhibits a display of **tribal costumes**★ from Nagaland, weapons (including eye-catching armour for war elephants), magnificent **fretwork** from south India and a collection of traditional **musical instruments**★ such as a sitar, sarod, tabla and many more.

INDIA GATE

At the far eastern end of Rajpath.

The **triumphal arch** was built in the middle of the octagonal square in memory of the 100,000 Indian soldiers killed fighting for the United Kingdom during World War I.

As evening falls, locals assemble here with their families to take in the air among the ice cream and balloon sellers. On the right-hand side of the roundabout (standing with your back to Rashtrapati Bhawan), you will see the city homes of the Maharajahs of Bikaner and Jaipur: **Bikaner House** (now the Rajasthan tourist office; and **Jaipur House**, occupied by the **National Gallery of Modern Art**.

NATIONAL GALLERY OF MODERN ART★★

At the end of Rajpath. www.ngmaindia. gov.in. ◷ *Open Tue–Sun 10am–5pm, closed major holidays;* ⊙ *Rs.150; no photography.*

Established in 1954 by the Government of India, the Delhi branch of the National Gallery of Modern Art, or NGMA, is housed in the former residence of the Maharaja of Jaipur. The gallery maintains more than 14,000 works of art and sculptures by Indian as well as international artists, with the oldest exhibits dating back to 1857. Collections include works by Amrita Sher-Gill, Jaya Appasamy and Raja Ravi Verma, among many others. Throughout the year the gallery hosts several exhibitions; check the website for information about ongoing and upcoming exhibitions.

▷ Walk down Shershah Rd and then turn right onto Mathura Rd.

PURANA QILA★★

M° Pragati Maidan. East of Rajpath, on the other side of Mathura Road. ◷ *Open sunrise–sunset.* ⊙ *Rs.100; video permit Rs.25.*

Sound and Light Show: *(1hr) In English starting between 8.30pm and 10pm depending on the season. Ticket bookings (*◷ *open daily 9am–9pm) at the Central Reservation Office, Coffee Home, Baba Kharak Singh Marg, opposite the Hanuman Mandir (Map III B3),* ✆ *011-23365358,* ⊙ *Rs.80.*

Perched on a small hill that has been converted to a park, the **'Old Fort'** is a favourite place for Delhiites to take a Sunday outing: for a picnic or peddle-boat ride on the lake at the base of the walls.

This hill was the site of the legendary city of **Indraprastha** of the *Mahabharata*, in other words the first Delhi. Objects unearthed in archaeological excavations seem to confirm the myth *(small museum,* ⊙ *Rs.2).* These objects date back to the era of Humayun, the second Mughal emperor, who founded the fort at the beginning of his reign, earning it the name of Dinpanah, 'refuge of the faith'. Yet, in 1540, the usurper Sher Shah took over the site, as well as much of the rest of the empire. Humayun succeeded in reclaiming what was rightfully his in 1555, before dying the next year in a fall from his library steps. A village known as Indrapat also existed within the ruins of the fort until the 1910s.

The walls have **four monumental gates**. The fort contains only three buildings, including the **Sher Shah Mosque**, which marks an architectural transition from the time of the Lodhis dominated by Hindu building techniques, to the Mughal era with its Persian influences. Note the importance given the central arch of the façade: the one here is higher than the others and features a large border with epigraphic bands, creating a *pishtaq* (monumental gateway). The decorative mosaics and multi-hued earthenware are remarkable in their subtlety. The neighbouring tower, **Sher Mandal**, with its many iwan niches and topped with a *chhatri* (pavilion), houses Humayun's library (⊙ *closed).* Between the two monuments is a *baori* (stepwell).

CRAFTS MUSEUM★★

M° Pragati Maidan. Bhairon Marg. ◷ *Open Tue–Sun 10am–5pm. No charge; photography permitted only outside. No information panels but guides offer their services at entrance for* ⊙ *Rs.150/h. Allow 45min.*

This museum provides a fascinating insight into Indian craftwork and rural arts and traditions. It is laid out like a village, with a series of houses arranged around courtyards. Admire decorative murals (including reproductions of the frescos at Shekhawati), woodwork and a wealth of finely sculpted doors.

One room houses temporary collections of popular artists, while in the rooms nearby, **bronze statues** and **sacred** carvings from south India are indicative of Dravidian temples. In the room dedicated to **court craftwork** an 18C *jharokha*, an ornately carved wooden balcony, is decorated with jali from the palace of a Gujarati nawab. The same room also contains a replica of a **historic Gujarati house** with superb carvings. A **collection of textiles** displays weaving styles and saris, Kashmiri shawls and printed cotton fabrics from Bagru and Sanganer (Rajasthan).

In winter, the **park** holds exhibitions where you can buy items by craft workers from various Indian states. There are also reconstructions of **traditional homes** as used by various tribes and regions in the country.

▶ Take a taxi or rickshaw to temple at Akshardham, 8km to the east.

Façade of Sher Shah Mosque, Purana Qila

© donyanedomam/Fotolia.com

AKSHARDHAM★★

M° Akshardam. www.akshardham.com. ⏱ *Open Tue–Sun 9.30am–6.30pm. No charge. Correct dress required (arms and legs covered). Make sure your pockets and bags are secure, as this temple holds the city record for crime. Bags, mobile phones, cameras and any other item, apart from money and passports, must be left in a locker (at your own risk). Allow 1hr to look round.*

This colossal temple on the left bank of the Yamuna, a hymn to the grandeur of Hinduism and to kitsch in equal measure, was inaugurated at the end of 2005. Gold, marble, a riot of sculptures, musical fountains (there is nothing here that is not done to excess). Once through security checks that are more rigorous than at the airport, you will pass through **Bhakti Dwar** (the 'Gate of Devotion'), then **Mayur Dwar** (the 'Gate of the Peacock') to reach a pool where water pours from conches onto footprints marked with the 16 sacred signs: the footprints belong to **Bhagwan Swaminarayan** (1781–1830), a holy man considered an avatar of the divine by the Swaminarayan Sampraday sect.

▶ Enter the main path leading to the shrine.

👤👤 Long colonnades of red sandstone on either side of the temple separate it from two great gardens. One garden features a gigantic **baori** where a musical fountain show is held every evening *(just after sundown, Rs.30)*. An exhibition room shows educational films in a loop (🔁 *Rs.170*) introducing the life of the guru and celebrating the cultural past of India and its moral values. The second garden contains a giant lotus flower designed in stone, an image of purity emerging from the muddy soil of the world, with inscriptions of the words of some of the world's inspiring people.

The actual **shrine**, at the end of the main thoroughfare, is laid out in a cruciform arrangement topped with cupolas. Extended colonnades support a proliferation of sculpted figures (more than 20,000) with elephants featuring heavily. In a nod to traditional Indian architecture, the temple was built using no steel at all, just pink sandstone for the exterior and white marble for the interior. It houses a gilded statue of Bhagwan Swaminarayan surrounded by statues of four divine couples: Radha-Krishna, Sita and Rama, Lakshmi and Narayan, and Shiva and Parvati. Every last inch of the impressive cupolas, the walls and the pillars has been carved.

A City Created Ten Times Over

The foundation of Delhi goes back to the time of legend: it is said to have been created at the behest of the Pandavas, the heroes of the Mahabharata and was known as Indraprastha ('city of Indra', one of the main gods in the Vedic pantheon). However, this first Delhi may not be as mythical as you might think: between 1955 and 1973, the Archaeological Survey of India unearthed pottery dating from around 1000 BC at Purana Qila, evidence of a city of great antiquity. Seven centuries later, the city had become sufficiently important for the Emperor Ashoka to have an edict engraved in stone there. Another millennium later, the Rajputs of the Tomar clan founded the fortress of Dilli several kilometres south of Indraprastha, around the 8C.

MUSLIM INVASIONS AND THE SULTANATE

The Rajputs of the **Chauhan** clan, based in Ajmer (Rajasthan), took control of Dilli in the 12C and the Muslims arrived on the scene soon after that: Sultan **Muhammed of Ghori** arrived at the gates of Delhi from Afghanistan in 1192 and defeated the army of Prithviraj III, the last Hindu king of Delhi at the Battle of Tarain. Before returning to the Afghan hills, he entrusted the city to his general, **Qutbuddin Aibak**, once a Turkish slave, who proclaimed himself 'sultan' on Muhammed of Ghori's death, establishing the dynasty known as the Mamluks. He built his capital near the present Qutb Minar and the **first 'Muslim Delhi'** was born.

Two new Turkish dynasties, the **Khiljis** and the **Tughlaqs**, ruled in succession from 1290 to the end of the 14C, witnessed the creation of four new cities at Delhi. The power of the sultans was greatly depleted when the Turko-Mongol **Timur** (or Tamburlaine) sacked the capital in 1398, leaving a devastated city behind him that took more than a century to recover its splendour. One of Timur's Afghan lieutenants settled in Delhi to found the **Sayyid** Dynasty (1414–50), which was succeeded by the **Lodhis** (1450–1526), who went on to found the city of Agra around 240 kilometres south of Delhi, and began to govern his kingdom from there. Worn down by internecine clan strife, the sultans were unable to resist a new invader from Afghanistan: **Babur**, a descendant of Gengis Khan on his father's side and Timur on his mother's, who founded the **Mughal** Dynasty.

Portrait of Shah Jahan from 17C manuscript

© De Agostini G Dagli/age fotostock

FROM THE MUGHAL EMPIRE TO THE BRITISH RAJ

Having defeated Sultan Ibrahim Lodhi in 1526 and the Rajput confederation in 1527, Babur settled at Agra; his son **Humayun** (1530–40 and 1555–56) returned the capital to Delhi and fortified the site at Indraprastha. He struggled to defend his throne for 15 years before finally ceding it to Sher Shah, an Afghan lieutenant. While the Grand Mughals Akbar and Jahangir governed from Agra and Lahore (in present-day Pakistan) their successor **Shah Jahan** (1627–58) chose Delhi as his capital, building the ninth city on the site, **Shahjahanabad**, and creating what is now Old Delhi, where he built his most renowned monuments: the Red Fort and the Jama Masjid.

The power of the Mughals barely survived the demise of the Emperor **Aurangzeb** in 1707 and Delhi, the capital of a weakened and war-torn empire, was pillaged three times, first by the king of Persia, Nadir Shah (1739), then by an Afghan chief, Ahmed Shah (1756), before a final sack by the Jat rajah of Bharatpur (1764). The Mughal throne was no more than symbolic.

As they gradually took control of the peninsula, the **British** left the emperor on his throne as a puppet king but installed a Viceroy who actually governed the capital. When the **Indian Rebellion** (1857) broke out, the poet emperor **Bahadur Shah II**, aged 80, took the part of the insurgents. In a series of bloody battles, the British crushed the insurrection and captured Bahadur Shah Zafar (Zafar, the 'sword', was his nom de plume) who had fled behind the walls of Humayun's Tomb. He was exiled to Rangoon and his two sons were hanged in public.

Since the 18C, the new rulers had governed from Calcutta, in Bengal; however, distrusting the political agitation that dominated in the Bengali territory, the British chose to transfer the capital to Delhi – after all, wasn't it the legitimate capital of the empire? The decision was announced in 1911 by King George V. Construction of the tenth Delhi, **New Delhi**, was entrusted to the architect **Sir Edwin Lutyens**. A whole city worthy of the might of the Indian Empire, the **Raj**, began to spring up from 1918 onwards, and was officially inaugurated in 1931.

CAPITAL OF THE WORLD'S LARGEST DEMOCRACY

With the arrival of independence in 1947, the creation of a Muslim majority in Pakistan provoked great population movements in the capital of the new republic. Thousands of Muslims abandoned their houses in Delhi to move to their new homeland in **Pakistan**, while the Hindus and Sikhs who had left everything behind in **Pakistan's Punjab**, arrived with only their spirit of enterprise.

Administratively, Delhi has had the status of **National Capital Territory** since 1956, distinguishing it from its neighbouring states of Uttar Pradesh and Haryana. Politically, it vacillates between the BJP ('Bharatiya Janata Party', the Hindu nationalist party) and the Indian National Congress, but in the recent elections, Delhi voted in the new grassroots Aam Aadmi Party (AAP). However, AAP's chief minister resigned 48 days later; reelections will be held.

Connaught Place, New Delhi

© Olaf Krüger/imagebroker/age fotostock

▶ After leaving the temple, take the metro to Jor Bagh and then a rickshaw to Safdarjung's Tomb, at the far end of Lodhi Road.

ALONG LODHI ROAD★★

Allow 3hr to tour by rickshaw, not including a visit to the Tibet house.
This tour includes a series of well-kept parks *(the flower beds are best Feb–Mar)* marking the southern end of the residential area built by Lutyens. The tombs and mausoleums give an insight into the evolution of Indo-Islamic architecture from the 15C-18C. The end of the tour is heralded by a picturesque district that is a popular centre of Islamic pilgrimage.

Safdarjung's Tomb★★

M° Jor Bagh. ◷ Open sunrise–sunset. ✆ Rs.100.
Often cited as the last masterpiece of Mughal art, this building is the tomb of **Safdarjung**, a wazir to emperors. Built in 1754, it has the typical features of all the Indo-Islamic tombs dating back to 1560: it is positioned at the centre of a Mughal garden *(char-bagh)*, divided into four sections by watercourses and enclosed by walls and is placed on an elevated base to create a pyramid effect. The quality of the decoration (marble mosaics on the corner towers and platforms of stucco stalactites) is notable.

Lodhi Garden★★

Follow Lodhi Rd for 300m. Left-hand side. ◷ Open sunrise–sunset.
A haven of peace and greenery, this large park features **tombs** *(rauza)* dating from the Sayyid and Lodhi eras. The southern entrance leads to **Sultan Muhammed Shah's Tomb** (1450), once surrounded by walls and now guarded by royal palm trees. It was the first example in Delhi of an **octagonal tomb**: a central chamber with eight sides topped with a spherical dome *(gumbad)* and surrounded by a gallery supporting eight *chhatris*, a throwback to Hindu architecture. While the sharply projecting awning *(chhajja)* is a typical feature of the Hindu tradition, the pointed arches are evidence of Persian influence.

At the centre of the park, two **rauza** with an almost identical cruciform floor plans house the tombs of two unidentified but undoubtedly important people of the sultanate. The **Bara Gumbad** ('Big Dome',1494) has doorways typical of pre-Mughal architecture: a lintel supported by two opposing corbels. A mosque beside the tomb is little more than a prayer hall. Opposite, on the other side of a fountain, is a hostel for pilgrims, and beside it the **Shish Gumbad** ('Glass Dome'), which has retained a few blue earthenware tiles. Inside, there is a pretty mihrab on the eastern wall.
At the far north of the garden, a **Sikandar Lodhi's tomb** (1517) rises in the lee of a crenellated wall. It echoes the octagonal shape of the rauza of Muhammed Shah, but does not have its pavilions.

▶ Follow Lodhi Rd to far east end.

Stop at the **Tibet House** (◷ *open Mon–Fri 9.30am–5.30pm; ✆ Rs.10*), whose library boasts more than 4,000 books. A small museum exhibits *tangka* (religious painting on fabric), ritual objects, jewellery, musical instruments and more.

HUMAYUN'S TOMB★★★

◷ *Open sunrise–sunset. ✆ Rs.250; video permit Rs.25.*
Listed in 1993 by UNESCO as a perfect example of a Mughal garden tomb, this complex is situated in a green space that also contains the tombs of several other important people.
Just beyond the entrance, a door in a crenellated wall *(to the right)* accesses **Isa Khan's Tomb★** (1548), the last resting place of a dignitary from the era of the usurping Sher Shah. An octagonal building with a veranda, the tomb is in the style that had been adopted a century earlier (as seen in Lodhi Garden).

▶ Return to the main thoroughfare leading to Humayun's Tomb.

Enter the walled **Mughal gardens**, at the centre of which the **tomb★★★** was built in 1565. On entering, note the con-

Humayun's Tomb

© Anurag Mallick, Priya Ganapathy/MICHELIN

trast between the red sandstone and the white marble. The inconsolable widow of Emperor Humayun entrusted the design of the monument to a Persian architect. He created a work that was virtually perfect and served as a prototype for all the Indo-Islamic mausoleums that followed, finding its apotheosis in the construction of the Taj Mahal at Agra. The tomb stands on an elevated base; a large central *iwan* (vaulted space) breaks up the solid wall on each of the four sides, creating a sense of lightness. Four chhatris surrounding the dome at the top of the pyramidal structure, provide a convergence point for all the architectural lines of the tomb. The flattened **interior dome** is not the same size as the exterior dome (which is slightly wider and taller), leaving a gigantic empty space between the two domes; this was the first example of a **double-dome** in India. Before approaching, notice the Iranian features: the depressed arches that replaced the lintels and consoles of Hindu inspiration, as well as the succession of bays and iwan niches running along the monument, alternating light and shade.

▶ Stairs at the centre of the platform lead to the terrace.

The octagonal **burial chamber** within is a masterpiece of sobriety and balance. The surrounding rooms are closed off with jali stonework that plays with the contrast of darkness and light. From the terrace you will see two domes rising from the eastern wall: the one covered in blue earthenware conceals a 17C tomb; the one in white marble adorns a gurdwara, a Sikh temple commemorating the visit of the guru Gobind Singh in 1707.

NIZAMUDDIN DARGAH★★

Leave the Humayun's Tomb complex and return to the roundabout with the 17C Sabza Burj tower (the 'green tower'), turn left into Mathura Rd and take the 1st turning on the right.

This tour takes you to Nizamuddin, a mainly Muslim residential district, named after Hazrat Nizamuddin Auliya, a mystic Sufi saint of the Chishti order who died in 1325. The saint's **dargah** (tomb) is reached along a winding street that becomes increasingly narrow, snaking between small restaurants that, as you progress, slowly give way to stalls selling religious books and music shops flooding the bazaar with the latest *qawwali* that are in fashion in Pakistan. In all this austerity, populated by bearded men and beggars, it is left to the shops selling rose petals and jasmine (with which the pilgrims decorate the tomb) to add cheerfulness that is amplified by the brilliant green of the chaddars (elaborately decorated lengths of cloth) hanging in the window displays, ready to be bought by devotees and be laid out on the tomb of the saint.

Nizamuddin Dargah

© Tibor Bognár/age fotostock

The lane opens out into the **dargah courtyard** *(please cover your head and take off your shoes)*. Notable people have contrived to be buried near the saint, to whom many miracles are attributed. So you will see the tomb of the famed poet Amir Khusrau (1253–1324) *(opposite the entrance)*, a disciple of the saint; the tomb of Jahanara, the favourite daughter of Shah Jahan, with its jali surrounds; and the tomb of the emperor Muhammed Shah (18C) *(opposite the last-mentioned, on the right)*.

The **tomb of the saint** (1562) stands in the centre of a courtyard in a mosque, next to the prayer hall. It is visited by pilgrims who seek a blessing or make a vow (represented by a piece of cotton thread tied to the jali of the tomb). It is brought to life every day by the sacred chants of the *qawwal* accompanied on the harmonium. Don't be intimidated by the somewhat official-looking beggars who will present you with books bearing the names of supposed celebrity donors in the hope of earning some money from your visit.

SOUTHERN DISTRICTS★★

Map I

▶ *Tour 4 marked in green on Map I. Allow 6hr for tour by taxi, or 3hr30min if you omit Tughlaqabad or Bahai Temple.*

Pockets of lower-middle and middle class residences alternate here with upmarket districts and old villages, with no overall urban plan providing any order in this rather anarchic development.

HAUZ KHAS VILLAGE★

M° Green Park or Hauz Khas.
9km south of Connaught Place.
Until the end of the 1980s, this village was a semi-rural settlement with buffaloes and *charpoys* (woven beds), just like others that exist today, slotted in among the city's residential districts. But then the fashionable elite arrived, and the village became a centre for fashionable ethnic chic with its rows of designer boutiques, eateries and clubs. In the early 14C, Sultan Alauddin Khilji dug a reservoir *(hauz)* here to supply water to his new city of Siri (Map I B4), and several **tombs** were built on its banks at the end of the 14C, notably that of the sultan **Feroz Shah Tughlaq**, with its domes on top of pillars in a Persian style. A madrasa (educational institution) was added to the well-preserved ruins. Timur (also known as Tamberlaine) is said to have camped among the monuments before attacking Delhi in 1398.

BEGAMPUR MOSQUE★

M° Hauz Khas.
Follow Aurobindo Marg south;
after the Outer Ring Rd roundabout,
take the first road on the left, which
crosses a residential district and then
doubles back suddenly, just before
you reach the mosque.
The building marks the centre of this oasis of calm which has lost none of its village feel. On Sundays, the charpoys are pulled up to the front of the mosque, where men play card games or smoke hookahs (Oriental pipes).

The fortified mosque on the hill, the best-preserved monument of what was once **Jahanpanah** (14C), one of the three cities founded by the Tughlaq Dynasty, is now used as a playground. The central arch of the prayer hall was once flanked by two minarets. Climb the stairs and tour the curtain walls to discover the ruins of the old Jahanpanah fort, a few hundred metres to the north.

QUTB MINAR COMPLEX★★★

M° Qutb Minar. 3km south of Hauz Khas Village. ◷ *Open sunrise–sunset.* ☞ *Rs.250; video permit Rs.25. Allow at least 1hr for your visit.*

This beautiful park features a mosque, tombs and buildings generally dating from the 13C and 14C, of which the most celebrated is the Qutb Minar, the monument that symbolises Delhi.

This minaret tower, now a UNESCO Heritage Site, commemorates the victory of Muhammed Ghori (and Islam) over the Hindu king Prithviraj III at the Battle of Tarain (1192). Its name honours general **Qutbuddin Aibak**, who commanded Muhammed's troops and became first governor and then sultan of Delhi (1206–10).

Qutbuddin built a city beside Prithviraj's, which was expanded and enriched for more than a century. Two earthquakes, in the 14C and 19C , damaged the Qutb Minar and the surrounding buildings seriously.

Qutb Minar

The main path leads to an esplanade, dominated on the left by the Qutb Minar. The slightly conical outline of the **minaret** is well known. At 73m in height, it comprises five successive sections composed of stone corbels *(muqarna)* supporting a gallery; it is decorated with bands of Kufic script that resemble armbands.

Just behind the minaret is a cube-shaped building with an arch, the **Alai Darwaza**. Pass through and view its other side, the one facing the faithful as they enter the mosque. This gate was added in 1310 by Sultan Alauddin. The Hindu artists hired locally carved interlacing, swooping Quranic inscriptions that cover every square inch of the monument, with a *horror vacui* (literally, 'fear of empty space') that is characteristic of Indian art. On the right is the **Imam Zamin's Tomb** from the early 16C.

▷ Retrace your steps to the Qutb Minar.

Quwwat-ul-Islam

A small flight of stairs to the left leads down to the courtyard of the oldest mosque in India, **Quwwat-ul-Islam** ('the power of Islam'), which was begun in 1193 and extended twice in the course of 100 years. It was built with materials recovered from about 20 Hindu and Jain temples that had been destroyed in the name of the Muslim faith. The pillars of the gallery are therefore constructed of two superimposed, square columns that are typical of 8C–10C Hindu art. All that remains of the mosque's prayer hall are the majestic **pointed arcades** of the entrance, covered in vine branches and Quranic inscriptions. The profusion and subtlety of the ornamentation

Columns in Qutb Minar Complex

© Olivier Brossollet/MICHELIN

bear witness to the extreme mastery of the Indian sculptors. Standing almost in the centre of the courtyard is an iron pillar – with not a single spot of rust! – the last intact evidence of the Hindu period: dedicated to Vishnu in the 4C, it was used as a flagpole, according to its Sanskrit inscription.

▶ Pass through the arcades and head left.

Tombs

The ruins of **Alauddin Khilji's Tomb** (sultan at the turn of the 14C) are located in a madrasa. This combination of a tomb and a school is typical of Seljuq tradition and recalls the Turkish origins of the first Muslim rulers of India.

▶ Return to the arcades, but continue straight on without passing back through them.

The **tomb of Iltutmish**, Qutbuddin's successor, was built during his lifetime in 1235. This square building was originally topped with a cupola that rested on corbels at the corners. It was the first monumental tomb built in India and served as a prototype for Indo-Persian mausoleums until the Mughal era. The intricacy of the carved decoration is testament to the skill of the local artists. In the centre of a lawn, a pile of stones *(to the left as you head towards the exit)* is evidence of an abortive attempt by Alauddin to build a minaret, the **Alai Minar**, which was to have been twice the height of the Qutb. The sovereign died in 1316.

KIRAN NADAR MUSEUM OF ARTS★

M° Malviya Nagar. 4km east of the Qutb Minar – 145, DLF South Court Mall. 𝒫 *011-49160000. www.knma.in.* 🕐 *Open Tue–Sun 10.30am–6.30pm.*
An impassioned collector of art, Kiran Nadar assembled a hoard of some 500 works from the 1980s onwards, ranging from Mughal miniatures through colonial-era oil paintings to modern

plastic works by Indian artists. In 2010, she decided to open her collection to the public and began the project that became this dynamic museum. Temporary exhibits of paintings, sculptures and installations provide a privileged insight into the modern and contemporary art of the Indian sub-continent.

TUGHLAQABAD FORT★

At the south-eastern end of Delhi – 8km from the Qutb Minar on the Merhauli Badarpur Rd. 🕐 *Open sunrise–sunset.* 💰 *Rs.100.*
Perched on a promontory, this gigantic citadel was begun in 1320 by the sultan **Ghiyasuddin Tughlaq** and abandoned a few years later, supposedly because of a curse pronounced by the Sufi saint Nizamuddin Auliya. It is recognisable from a distance *(to the left of the road)* by the shape of its perimeter wall, where visitors are met by troops of monkeys. The interior, which is largely wasteland, is composed of shapeless ruins that delight romantics. On the opposite side, to the right of the road, the **tomb of Ghiyasuddin** was built by his son after the former's assassination in 1325. Constructed of red sandstone set off with white marble, it is hidden behind a crenellated wall and surrounded by a lake (now dried up), a sort of mini-fort. Its angled walls reinforce the impression of a fortification.

BAHA'I TEMPLE★ (LOTUS TEMPLE)

From Tughlaqabad, continue heading north and turn left into Chiragh Delhi Rd, which you follow to Nehru Place. www.bahaihouseofworship.in. 🕐 *Open Tue–Sun Oct–Mar 9.30am–5.30pm, Apr–Sept 9am–7pm.*
Set in a superbly well-tended garden, this temple was completed in 1986 to symbolise the unity and peace advocated by the adherents of **Bahaism**. In the basement is a bookshop and a museum providing information about the religion, which first appeared in Iran in the 19C, founded on tolerance, personal mystic experience, and religious unity.

CIVIL LINES

Map I

▶ *Allow 1hr30min. M° Kashmere Gate or Civil Lines.*

Right across the Indian sub-continent, the British, wishing to locate themselves apart from the masses, settled beyond the city centres in districts that were specially constructed for them, the **'Civil Lines'**: containing administrative buildings, a church and residential bungalows. A stroll through Delhi's Civil Lines, an area somewhat out of the way in the north of the city, is a reminder of the British families who were resident here in the 19C, and of the Indian Mutiny of 1857, which almost sounded the death-knell of European domination in northern India. The round-trip, in fact, stops at the southern approach to the Civil Lines, the least agreeable section but with the most interesting relics from the time.

St. James' Church (Skinner's Church)

South of M° Kashmere Gate, on Lothian Rd.

One of Delhi's oldest churches, St. James' Church was built in 1836 by Colonel James Skinner. Lying wounded on a battlefield, the colonel, an adventurer with a Scottish father and a Rajput mother, vowed to build a church if he survived. He did and duly built the church. His cavalry unit, Skinner's Horse, went on to carve itself a reputation as an elite regiment on in many battles right up to World War II. Skinner's house, with its vast hemispherical dome, is located behind his church (closed to the public).

Kashmere Gate

Approx. 100m to the north, on Lothian Rd.

Kashmere Gate, a remnant of the ramparts of Shahjahanabad, marks the beginning of the road to Kashmir and now marks the southern end of the Civil Lines. There were bloody battles here during the Indian Rebellion and parts were blown up in an explosion.

St. James' Church

© DINODIA/age fotostock

▶ Continue north to the large junction of Lothian Rd and Lala Hardev Sahai Marg.

Qudsia Bagh

On the other side of Lala Hardev Sahai Marg, on the right. It is better to take the metro from Civil Lines as it is impossible to cross Lala Hardev Sahai Marg on foot.
Qudsia Bagh is an old Mughal-style garden containing ruins and a mosque, but the charm of the overall effect is much diminished by the noise of the traffic.

Nicholson Cemetery

From Qudsia: on the other side of Sham Nath Marg.

One of the oldest British cemeteries on the sub-continent, it is now over-run with brambles, wild grasses and monkeys. General John Nicholson, who lost his life defending the Kashmere Gate, is buried here and lends his name to a place made more touching still by the ramshackle condition of some parts of it.

You can extend your walk by exploring the old secretariat which is now the town hall, the Mutiny Memorial or the Ashoka pillar.

ADDRESSES

🛏 STAY

Coins indicate the price range for a double room in high season (Nov–Feb). *See the inside front cover.* In **low season** (mid-Apr–Sept) in Delhi, as in the region, many hotels offer discounts of around 30%. They also all provide a laundry service.

PAHARGANJ

M° *Rama Krishna Ashram Marg*
Main Bazar Rd, the main thoroughfare in Paharganj district, has a good number of cheap hotels (Rs.800–1,000), but hygiene and comfort may be questionable.

⊖ **Cottage Yes Please** – *Map II A4. 1843 Laxmi Narayan St.* ☏ *011-23562100. www. cottageyesplease.com.* 📧 🖃. *Wi-Fi, lift, travel agency. 45 rm. Rs950/2,000.* This hotel set back from Main Bazar Rd offers large, well-maintained rooms and is conveniently located close to the metro.

⊖ **Vivek** – *Map II B3. 1534–50 Main Bazar Rd.* ☏ *011-46470555. www.vivekhotel.com.* 📧 ✗. *Left luggage, Internet and pool table, lift. 14 rm. Rs.960/1,900.* ⊠ *Rs.100.* Some rooms have refrigerators. This is one of Paharganj's institutions, so it is best to book in advance. Have breakfast among flowers on the well-maintained roof terrace. Wi-Fi available for a fee.

⊖ **Relax** – *Map II B4. 4970 Ram Dawra Rd.* ☏ *011-23562811. vidur109@hotmail.com.* 📧 ✗🖃. *23 rm. Rs.1,000/1,700.* Relax is located away from Main Bazar Rd, opposite the vegetable market. Has rooms looking out onto attractive public areas decorated with plants.

⊖ **Parkway Deluxe** – *Map II B3. 8591 Main Qutab Rd.* ☏ *011-23531125. www.hotelparkway.in.* 📧. *Lift. 25 rm. Rs.1,500/2,200.* Located north of Paharganj and about 100m from the railway station, this is usually the hotel of choice for Indian businessmen. Handily located but lacking charm, it has large, dark rooms, apart from those looking out onto the street; rather noisy. Although decorated in a 1970s style, the rooms still look quite fresh and are well maintained.

⊖ **Jyoti Mahal Guesthouse** – *Map II A3. 2488 Nalwa St.* ☏ *011-23580523. www.jyotimahal.net.* 📧 🖃. *Wi-Fi. 34 rm. Rs.2,200/2,500* ⊠. The architecture of this hotel situated in a small, pedestrian-only street harks back to the Indo-Mughal style with its archways and tiny patio. The prices are justified more for the building than the rooms themselves, which are clean but gloomy.

CONNAUGHT PLACE

M° *Rajiv Chowk*
The centrally located district of Connaught Place has hotels of every category with the added advantage of being close to the restaurants and shops. The location explains the rather high prices for the services on offer.

⊖ **YWCA Blue Triangle Family Hotel** – *Map III A4. Ashoka Rd.* ☏ *011-23360133. www.ywcaofdelhi.org.* 📧 ✗. *39 rm. Rs.2,250/2,850.* A 10min walk from Connaught Place, this austere-looking red-brick building (which, despite belonging to the YWCA, does not cater solely to women) has no-frills rooms that are spotlessly clean.

⊖ **YMCA Tourist Hotel** – *Map III A3. Jai Singh Rd.* ☏ *011-43640000. www. newdelhiymca.in.* 📧 ✗ ⊼. *101 rm. Rs.3,325/4,335* ⊠. Nothing out of the ordinary in terms of comfort, but the atmosphere is agreeable. The cheapest rooms have shared bathrooms. You are not allowed to stay longer than 15 days. Travel agency, exchange, fitness room.

⊖ **York** – *Map III C2. K-10 Connaught Circus.* ☏ *011-23415769.* 📧 ✗. *28 rm. Rs.4,500.* A well-maintained hotel with understated and immaculate rooms that are a little expensive for their size. Ask for one with a bathtub: these are larger than the rooms with showers – or a view of the large communal terrace. Travel agency.

⊖⊖⊖ **The Park** – *Map III B3. 15 Parliament St.* ☏ *1 800 102 7275. www.theparkhotels.com.* 📧 ✗ 🍷 ⊼. *Internet, spa, fitness room. 220 rm. Rs.10,000/12,500* ⊠. *Rest. Rs.1,500.* The nearest fancy hotel to Connaught Place, but it lacks the style of most of the other hotels in this category. Restaurants offering Indian and Mediterranean cuisine, plus a 24hr coffee shop.

⊖⊖⊖⊖ **Le Méridien** – *Map III B5. Windsor Place.* ☏ *011-23710101. www. starwoodhotels.com.* 📧 ✗ 🍷 ⊼. *355 rm. Rs.13,000/17,000* ⊠. *24hr coffee shop, spa, beauty salon.* Built of glass and steel at the end of the 1980s, with a central tower. The decoration is understated, but the rooms, which are equipped with a safe, are a little on the small side.

⊖⊖⊖⊖ **Imperial** – *Map III B4. 1 Janpath.* ☏ *011-23341234. www.the imperialindia.com.* 📧 ✗ 🍷 ⊼. *Wi-Fi, shops, beauty salons. 231 rm, starting from Rs.18,000* ⊠. The approach road is lined with king palm trees. Opened in the 1930s, the hotel has been restored in a Victorian style with a touch of Art Deco, combining luxury with good taste. Dine in one of several restaurants, or linger for a drink on the terraces and in the gardens.

CIVIL LINES DISTRICT

M° Civil Lines

This residential district situated 10km north of Connaught Place lies away from the urban bustle of the old city.

Maidens – *Map I B1. 7 Sham Nath Marg.* 011-23975464. *www. maidenshotel.com.* *Internet, wi-Fi. 56 rm. Rs.8,500/9,500.* Situated in a beautiful colonial-style building which has retained much of its old-world allure (it dates from 1903), this is a lovely, charming hotel without being overly luxurious. Horse riding is available and there is a tennis court.

SOUTH OF CONNAUGHT PLACE

M° Jor Bagh (near Lodi Garden) and Khan Market. All the reputable hotels offer suites.

Jorbagh 27 – *Map IV C4. 27 Jorbagh.* 011-24694430. *www. jorbagh27.com.* *18 rm. Rs.5,700/7,000. Rs.100.* Situated 5km from Connaught Place, but only a minute's walk from Lodhi Garden and the market at Jorbagh. This hotel in an upmarket residential area has a small garden and attractive rooms, but the service is a little disorganised.

Hyatt Regency – *Map I A4. Bhikaji Cama Place, Inner Ring Rd.* 011-26791234. *www.delhi.regency. hyatt.com.* *Large shopping arcade. 507 rm, starting from Rs.13,000.* An excellent hotel, always buzzing, which has become a focal point of life in the capital. The 'luxury' rooms have complimentary access to the gym, sauna, spa and tennis court.

The Ambassador (Taj Group) – *Map IV D3. Sujan Singh Park, Khan Market.* 011-66261000. *www. vivantabytaj.com.* *Internet, Wi-Fi, spa, shops. 88 rm. Rs.13,000/18,000.* Corridors lined with imitation wood panelling might be a little lacking in 'class', but the rooms are enormous, light and well maintained. Pleasant location on the eastern margins of New Delhi.

The Claridges – *Map IV C3. 12 Aurangzeb Rd.* 011-39555000. *www. claridges.com.* *Internet, Wi-Fi, safe. 137 rm. Rs.15,000/20,000.* Situated in an area of avenues lined with

The Taj Mahal

© Graham Crouch/Taj Hotels Resorts and Palaces

buildings by Lutyens and large white bungalows, this hotel has retained some of its Old World charm and intimacy. Sunday brunch is a buffet (noon–3.30pm, Rs.2,600).

The Oberoi (The Oberoi Group) – *Map IV E3. Dr. Zakir Hussain Marg.* 011-23890606. *www.oberoihotels. com.* *Shops. 279 rm, starting from Rs.21,000.* Looking over the golf course and Humayun's Tomb, this hotel caters for businesspeople. The restaurants are stylish and include Taipan (Szechuan and Cantonese cuisine) and Threesixty°, with its fine wine cellar.

The Taj Mahal (Taj Group) – *Map IV C3. 1 Man Singh Rd.* 011-23016162. *www.tajhotels.com.* *Tennis court. 294 rm. Rs.25,000/30,000.* Located 400m from Khan Market and popularly known as the Taj Mansingh, this is one of the most pleasant and lively hotels in Delhi. A large, glass atrium looks out over a garden with trees and shrubs.

SUNDAR NAGAR

The Sundar Nagar district should be served by the metro by 2015. Several old houses in this verdant residential area 4km south-east of Connaught Place are now small hotels with manicured lawns perfect for strolling.

Shervani New Delhi – *Map IV E3. 11 Sundar Nagar, opposite the zoo.* 011-24351000. *www.shervanihotels.com.* *Internet, Wi-Fi, safe. 19 rm. Rs.3,500/5,000.* Non-smoking. Well maintained, the rooms are decorated with taste in understated, warm tones. The least expensive rooms have tiny bathrooms.

Devna & Atul – *Map IV E3. 10 Sundar Nagar.* 011-24351798. *www. tensundernagar.com.* *Internet, Wi-Fi.*

5 rm. Rs.5,500 ⬚. A charming hotel with large rooms and balconies decorated with flowers. The owner, an art collector and antiques dealer, has furnished the whole place with carefully selected pieces.

⬚⬚ **Jukaso Inn** – *Map IV E3. 50 Sundar Nagar.* 📞 *011-24350308.* 🖥 ✕. *Internet, Wi-Fi. 24 rm. Rs.5,000/6,500* ⬚. The reception hall and corridors of this well-maintained hotel near the market are all in marble, which, combined with the high glass roof, makes things a little noisy. The rooms are slightly on the small side for the price.

⬚⬚⬚ **La Sagrita Tourist Home** – *Map IV E3. 14 Sundar Nagar.* 📞 *011-41507013. www.lasagrita.com.* 🖥. *Wi-Fi. 19 rm. Rs.5,500/7,800* ⬚. Deluxe rooms have large windows and imitation parquet. Standard rooms, with carpeted floors and bare walls, are a little drab. Choose a room looking out over the garden, which are a little more expensive. The hotel was renovated in 2013.

CHANAKYAPURI
5km south-east of Connaught Place. The embassy district, often called the Diplomatic Enclave, is close to shops and restaurants in Malcha Marg Market, to the north-west.

⬚ **International Youth Hostel** – *Map I A3. 5 Nyaya Marg.* 📞 *011-26116285. www. yhaindia.org/hostels/index/5.* ✕ 🍷 ⬚. *7 rm, 15 dorms with 4 to 10 beds; some with air-conditioning (expect to pay Rs.500/bed). Rs.800/1,400* ⬚. This clean hostel nestles among greenery. Non-members of the Youth Hostels Association of India must buy a membership card (Rs.165) when they arrive. You are not allowed to stay for more than 7 days. Booking advised.

⬚⬚⬚ **Diplomat** – *Map I A3. 9 Sardar Patel Rd.* 📞 *011-23010204. www. thehoteldiplomat.com.* 🖥 ✕. *25 rm. Rs.7,000/9,500* ⬚. This well-maintained hotel in an attractive modern building surrounded by greenery is quiet. Each of the 8 suites is decorated differently.

⬚⬚⬚⬚ **Maurya Sheraton (ITC Group)** – *Map I A3. Sardar Patel Marg.* 📞 *011-26112233. www.starwoodhotels.com.* 🖥 ✕ 🍷 ⬚. *Shops, safe, Wi-Fi, tennis court. 515 rm. Rs.15,000/19,000* ⬚. The hotel is always lively and is considered one of the best in the capital.

⬚⬚⬚⬚ **A Taj Palace (Taj Group)** – *Map I A3. 2 Sardar Patel Marg.* 📞 *011-26110202. www.tajhotels.com.* 🖥 ✕ 🍷 ⬚. *422 rm. Rs.20,000/28,000* ⬚. A less lively atmosphere than at the Sheraton, but the service is excellent and the rooms are comfortable, with bathrooms in black marble. Three restaurants, including a French one and a Vietnamese one.

EAST DELHI
Park Plaza Shahdara – *32 Central Business District, Shahdara, New Delhi 110095,* 📞 *011 45630000, www.parkplaza. com, 91 rooms,* ♿, *free Wi-Fi, all-inclusive meal plan, cards accepted.* Decent offering from a popular hospitality chain set in the IT, Industrial and Business hub of East Delhi. Makes up for lack of great view with European style décor, value for money, good service and fresh food at The Promenade (multi-cuisine), Chingari (traditional Indian) and Shish - open-air Mediterranean theme dining area (grills, roasts and wood-fired pizzas). Relax at Rouge-Lounge bar or mineral bath at spa and salon. Nearest metro is Karkarduma (1.8km). Tariff: Rs Rs 4,500-Rs 9,500.

Kempinski Ambience Hotel – *1 Central Business District, Maharaja Surajmal Road, Near Yamuna Sports Complex, Delhi 110032* 📞 *011 4908 8888 www.kempinski.com, 480 rooms,* ♿, ⬚, *cards accepted.* With water bodies, landscaped gardens and a marble façade, this city resort comes with a Greek temple-inspired spa with Asian and European therapies and four bars and restaurants serving Italian, Oriental and Indian cuisine. East Delhi's premiere address has fitness centre, great swimming pool and one of the largest hotel ballrooms in India. Rs 12,000-14,500.

🍽 EAT
The food served in Delhi is usually a mix of Punjabi and Mughlai (Mughal) flavours. The more expensive hotels have a coffee shop open 24 hours, where a meal (buffet or extensive menu of Indian and international dishes) costs approx. Rs.1,500. They also normally have at least three good-quality restaurants, specialising in different cuisines: Mughlai, from the former Northwest Frontier Province, Chinese, Thai, French or grill classics. 🪙*For coin ranges, inside front cover flap.*

PAHARGANJ
⬚ **Club India Cafe and Restaurant** – *Map II B4. 4797 Main Bazar Rd, on the square, upstairs.* 📞 *011-23589392.* 🍷 ⬚. *8am–11pm. Rs.250/400.* Enjoy tandoori chicken, biryani and chicken burgers

in the dining room on the 2nd floor or on the roof terrace; the menu has been adjusted to suit the tastes of a generally Western clientele. Wi-Fi.

CONNAUGHT PLACE
M° Rajiv Chowk

🍽 **Madras Coffee House** – *Map III B2. P-5/90 Connaught Circus.* 🕿 *011-23363074.* 🍴. *9am–10pm. Rs.200/350.* Spicy Indian cuisine and imitation leather banquettes in quaint but reasonably clean surroundings; opt for the coconut rice if you tend to have a sensitive stomach. Entirely vegetarian menu with snacks from southern India.

🍽 **Rajdhani Delhi** – *Map III C3. 9A Atmaram Mansion, near Scindia House, Outer Circle.* 🕿 *011-43501200. www.rajdhani.co.in.* 🍴. *Noon–3.30pm, 6.30pm–11pm. Rs.300/400.* The counterpart to Rajdhani in Mumbai, the outlet in the capital is a credit to the reputation of this chain specialising in all-you-can-eat thali.

🍽 **Sagar Ratna** – *Map III B2. K-15 Connaught Circus.* 🕿 *011-23412470. www.sagarratna.in.* 🍷. *8am–11pm. Rs.300/500.* Serving vegetarian South Indian delicacies, this unpretentious restaurant is very popular with Delhiites. Spread over two floors, it also serves ice-creams, shakes and fresh juices. If you are hankering after some **Western-style fast food**, try the noisy and packed 🍽 **Wimpy** (*N-6 Radial Rd 1; 10.30am–11pm*) or a fairly pleasant 🍽**Pizza Hut** (*M-20 Outer Circle*). 🍽**Pizza Express** (*D-10 Inner Circle*) is expensive but it is the best and serves alcohol.

🍽 **Nirula's** – *Map III C3. N-64 Connaught Circus, 1st floor.* 🕿 *011-41230404. www.nirulas.com.* 🍷. *11am–midnight. Rs.400/750.* Decorated with artificial plants, this popular eatery is sometimes a bit noisy with a young crowd. Pizzas, burgers, Indian dishes, ice cream and a decent salad buffet. It is often full.

🍽 **Kwality** – *Map III B3. 7 Regal Building, Parliament St.* 🕿 *011-23742310. www.kwalitygroup.com.* 🍷. *Noon–11pm. Rs.500/650.* Dine in pretty rooms decorated in shades of pink and apricot. There is a general lack of space and the service is hurried, but the tandoori dishes are good; specialities incude the chicken dishes and Mughlai lamb.

🍽 **York's** – *Map III C2. At the York Hotel.* 🕿 *011-23415819.* 🍷. *11.30am–11.30pm. Rs.500/700.* The comfortable dining room

houses one of the best restaurants on Connaught Place. The house speciality is lamb or chicken kebabs. Try the murgh malai or reshmi kebab.

🍽 **Embassy** – *Map III C2. D-11 Inner Circle, Radial Rd 6.* 🕿 *011-23416434. www. embassyrestaurant.in.* 🍷. *10am–11pm. Rs.600/900.* Founded in 1948, the Embassy is still catering to Delhi's political and middle classes amid a hubbub of conversation. The tables are too close together for any real privacy. Avoid the dishes with sauces, which are a bit fatty, and stick to the tandoori specialities or the chicken chaat.

🍽 **The Host** – *Map III C3. F-8 Inner Circle.* 🕿 *011-23316381.* 🍷. *10am–11pm. Rs.800/1,200.* A comfortable dining room decorated with mirrors and bare stone walls for a clientele of regulars. Similar to the United Coffee House (☕ *see TAKING A BREAK*), but the food here is better.

NORTH OF CONNAUGHT PLACE
🍽 **Karim's** – *Map II D2. 16 Jama Masjid, Gali Kababiyan, Old Delhi. M° Chawri Bazar.* 🕿 *011-23269880. www.karimhoteldelhi.com.* 🍴. *11am–3.30pm, 6.30pm–11pm. Rs.400/750.* A restaurant that has been flourishing in a working-class Muslim part of town since the 1930s. Enjoy authentic Mughlai cooking – delicious, but very rich. Try the burra kabab, biryani or mutton pasanda. Sheer delight!

🍽 **Chor Bizarre** – *Map II D3. Rest. at the Broadway Hotel, Asaf Ali Rd.* 🕿 *011-43663600. www.chorbizarrerestaurant.com.* 🍷. *Noon–3pm, 7.30pm–11.15pm. Rs.700/ 1,100.* The décor is rather eclectic but original (the starters buffet is in a convertible classic car), and the atmosphere is chic. The menu offers a range of excellent Kashmiri and Mughlai dishes.

SOUTH OF CONNAUGHT PLACE
🍽 **Saravana Bhavan** – *Map III B4. 46 Janpath.* 🕿 *01123317755. www. saravanabhavan.com. 8am–11pm. Rs.200/350.* This exclusively vegetarian restaurant has brought the culinary traditions of southern India from Madras: finely prepared thalis and dosas served near a tempting display of sweets. Their second restaurant is on Connaught Place, Block P, Outer Circle.

🍽 **Dastar Khwan-e Karim** – *Map IV E4. 168/2 Jha House, Nizamuddin West, next to the mosque.* 🕿 *011-41827871. www. karimhoteldelhi.com. Noon–3.30pm, 6.30pm–9.30pm. Rs.300/500.* A branch of the famous Karim's in Old Delhi, with even more stylish décor but the Mughlai food is not quite as tasty.

🍲🍽 **Gulati and Veg Gulati** – *Map IV D2. 8 Pandara Rd Market. ☏ 011-23388839. www.gulatirestaurant.in. Noon–midnight. Rs.550/800.* A similar place to Pindi (*see below*). Tuck into a buffet lunch (Rs.589).

🍲🍽 **Ginger Moon** – *Map IV C3. 73 Middle Lane, Khan Market. ☏ 011-43593000. 🍷. Noon–midnight. Rs.600/ 1,000.* Good Chinese cooking with dishes such as coconut soup and noodles with prawns, celery tofu and chicken with black mushrooms in this popular restaurant. It helps if you don't mind eating in front of a large flat-screen TV!

🍲🍽 **Pindi** – *Map IV D2. 16/17 Pandara Rd Market, behind Bikaner House. ☏ 011-23387932. Noon–midnight. Rs.600/900.* The market in the residential area of Pandara Park contains a huddle of restaurants renowned for their very rich Punjabi-Mughlai cooking. The butter chicken is the local speciality served at any hour.

🍲🍽 **Chopsticks** – *Map I B4. Siri Fort, Khel Gaon Marg. ☏ 011-26493628. 🍷. 12.30pm–3.30pm, 7.30pm–11.30pm. Rs.750/900.* A popular Chinese restaurant. After a concert at the nearby Siri Fort Auditorium, try the fish in ginger or the garlic prawns.

🍲🍽🍽 **Swagath** – *Map III B5. Rest. at the Janpath Hotel. ☏ 01123340070. 11am–11pm. Rs.800/1,200.* North and south Indian specialities in intimate surroundings. The curries are delicious but spicy for Western palates. Try the saag gosht (lamb cooked in spinach) with some appam (soft pancakes made with fermented rice). The restaurant has branch in Defence Colony Market.

🍲🍽🍽 **Machan** – *Map IV C3. Rest. at the Taj Mahal Hotel. 🍷. 24hrs. Rs.1,500/2,500.* One of the nicest coffee shops in Delhi, light and lively with safari-style décor (the restaurant is named after a *machan* or elevated platform among the trees for observing animals). Sunday brunch 12.30pm until 3.30pm.

CHANAKYAPURI

🍲🍽 **Moti Mahal Delux** – *Map I A3. 20/48 Malcha Marg Market. ☏ 011-26118698. 🍷. Wed–Mon 12.15pm–4pm, 7pm–midnight. Rs.500/800.* Dine on tasty tandoori and Punjabi cooking in comfortable surroundings, amid décor that is a little on the heavy side. Try the 'family' naan or the dal makhani, which is creamy and full of flavour.

🍲🍽🍽 **Dum Pukht** – *Map I A3. Rest. at the Maurya Sheraton Hotel. ☏ 011-26112233. 🍷. No children under 12. Mon–Sat 7pm–11.45pm, Sun 12.30pm–2.45pm, 7pm–midnight. Rs.1,500/2,000.* A sophisticated basement dining room serving *awadhi* cuisine (Lucknow region), especially *dumpukht* (stew simmered and steamed in stone pots sealed with a layer of dough). House specialities include koh-i awadh (chicken with cardamom and saffron), dal with yoghurt and garlic.

🍲🍽🍽 **Bukhara** – *Map I A3. Rest. at the Maurya Sheraton Hotel. ☏ 011-26112233. 🍷. No children under 12. 12.30pm–2.45pm, 7pm–11.45pm. Rs.4,500/6,000.* Offering Mughlai cuisine and renowned kebabs, Bukhara is decorated in traditional Peshwari style. Through a window you can watch your meal being cooked in the clay ovens. Limited choice, but the food is superb. Booking is essential.

TAKING A BREAK

Wengers – *Map III B2. A-16 Inner Circle. ☏ 011-23324594. www.wengers.in. 🍽. 11am–8pm.* This excellent bakery serves cakes and pastries, vegetarian and other sandwiches and mini-pizzas, if you want a small snack or are eating on the hoof.

United Coffee House – *Map III C2. E-15 Inner Circle, Connaught Place. ☏ 011-23416075. www.unitedcoffeehouse.com. 🍷. 11am–11.30pm.* The Indian equivalent of a French brasserie, with regulars who read the paper or talk politics for hours, although foreign tourists are now discovering it. The coffee is good; pair it with cinnamon apple pie served

United Coffee House

© René Mattes/hemis.fr

with fresh cream. Meals are a little disappointing.

Gaylord – *Map III B3. 16 Regal Building, Connaught Circus. 011-23360717.* 10.30am–11pm. Opened in 1952, the this restaurant serves different cuisines in an upmarket tearoom atmosphere. Teatime snacks are good. Visit for the ambience, than for the food.

Bengali Market – *1.5km east of Connaught Place.* Visit Nathu's Sweet and Bengali Sweet House, two spacious, well-known sweet shops for a sugary snack or a taste of Indian fast food before going to an exhibition or a concert at the several auditoriums near Mandi House.

BARS

The Gem Bar – *Map III B3. 1050 Main Bazar Rd, Paharganj. 011-23588165.* 11am–midnight. As evening falls, you'll find all the weekend revellers gathering here, in unpretentious surroundings.

@Live – *Map III D2. K-12 Connaught Circus, next to the York Hotel. www.qba.co.in.* Noon–1am. Brick, wood and leather combine to warm up the atmosphere for the live band every evening at 8.30pm.

1911 Bar – *Map III B4. Bar/brasserie at the Imperial Hotel. 011-23341234. www. theimperialindia.com.* 11.30am–12.45am. Highly regarded by the regulars for its chic and relaxed atmosphere, 1911 has its terrace and lawns. Louis XVI armchairs make an inviting place for a good chat. The hotel's other bar, Patiala Peg (12.30pm–11.45pm) serves draught beer in teak-panelled surroundings with prints of the famous Maharajah Bhupindra de Patiala and his cavalry.

Insomnia Bar – *Map IV D3. Bar at the Ambassador Hotel.* 1pm–1am. A themed bar with jazz, blues and country evenings and food and drinks served in colonial-style surroundings. Good selection of rare whiskies.

SHOPPING

MALLS

The shopping area in **Old Delhi** (*Map II*) has traditional stalls (*open Mon–Sat*), while the shops in **Connaught Place** (*Map III*) are modern (*open Mon–Sat*), but the rich middle classes like to splash the cash at **Khan Market** (*Map IV CD3*) (*open Mon–Sat*) and **South Extension** (*Map I B4*) (*open Tue–Sun*). Popular for 'ethnic' fashion and interior décor are **Santushti Shopping Complex** on Kamal Ataturk Rd

(*Map IV A4*) (*open Mon–Sat*) and **Hauz Khas Village** (*Map I A4*), which was started in the 1980s by young designers, but has since seen prices skyrocket (*open Mon–Sat*). The **Qutb** district (*Map I A5*) is gradually going the same way, with two centres close to one another: **The Qutb Colonnade**, H-5/6 Mehrauli Rd, at the north-western corner of the wall round the Qutb Minar and the **Ambawatta Complex** at the entrance to the village of Mehrauli, 15km to the south-west (*partially closed Sun and Mon*).

CRAFTS

Delhi specialises in glazed blue pottery, small lacquered objects decorated with fragments of mirror, and stuffed animals made of black cloth and gold braid that are produced by members of the Bhat community from Rajasthan who have settled in Delhi. But you can buy craftwork from all over India.

Cottage Industries Emporium – *Map III B4. On the corner of Janpath and Tolstoy Marg. www.cottageemporium.in.* 10am–7pm. Textiles, turned wood, leather goods and papier mâché are sold at slightly elevated prices, but the quality is good and the prices are fixed and clearly indicated.

State Emporia – *Map III A3. Baba Kharak Singh Marg.* 10am–7pm. Four imposing buildings house shops and outlets from 18 states, including **Rajasthali**, which represents Rajasthan. In the 3rd building there is a small exhibition space containing a superb collection of minerals.

The gift shop at the **Crafts Museum** is normally well stocked and regularly invites a dozen or so top-quality artists to work in the courtyard.

February sees two craft fairs: the open-air **Surajkund Crafts Mela**, held in the village of Surajkund, just outside Tughlaqabad (*off map, Map I C5*), and the **Indian Handicrafts & Gift Fair** celebrating India's artisans, at Pragati Maidan, on Mathura Rd (*Map IV E1*).

Chatta Chowk Bazaar – *Map II D2. In the Red Fort.* You can buy Indian and Tibetan 'antiques' here.

Hanuman Mandir Mela – *Map III B3. Baba Kharak Singh Marg, on the esplanade in front of the Hanuman Mandir.* This is a small open-air market that is particularly busy and full of life on Tuesdays and Saturdays, the days sacred to the Hindu deity Hanuman. Along with some modest examples of local craftwork, you can buy pretty glass bangles.

Tibetan market – *Map III B4*. Janpath, north of the Imperial Hotel. A dozen or so shops sell clothes, turquoise necklaces, masks and other items in bronze, all imported from Tibet.

FABRICS AND CLOTHES

Janpath Lane – *Map III B3-4*. Embroidered Rajasthani and Gujarati fabrics encrusted with fragments of mirror are sold in the shops along Janpath, as well as at the roadside by women from Rajasthan.

Khadi Gramodyog Bhawan – *Map III B3. 24 Regal Building, Connaught Place. Open Mon–Sat 10am–7pm*. This is a large shop noted for its Gandhi-style cottons and hand-woven silks.

Joyce International Handloom – *Map III C2. 49 Shankar Market, 3rd lane*. This shop sells a cotton fabric which, once washed, looks like hand-woven silk.

Two good places to go on Connaught Place for silk are **Kalpana**, F-5, and **Handloom House**, Block A, Radial Rd 3. Don't miss **Tex-Styles India**, the fabric fair held at Pragati Maidan in February/March (*Map IV E1–2*).

For good-quality table and bed linen, scarves, bags and Indian clothes in traditional fabrics: **Anokhi**, Santushti Shopping Complex and 32 Khan Market (also in Greater Kailash 1 N Block Market); **The Shop**, 10 Regal Building, Parliament St; **Tulsi**, Santushti Shopping Complex and 30 Hauz Khas Village; **Fabindia**, Greater Kailash I, N Block Market (also in Greater Kailash 1 M Block Market, Khan Market, Select City Walk mall in Saket, and several other locations) (*Map I BC4*) (*Wed–Mon*); **Good Earth**, Santushti Shopping Complex and Khan Market (*Map IV CD3*) (fabrics, ornaments and pottery); **Shyam Ahuja**, Santushti Shopping Complex and Greater Kailash II (*Map I C5*) (dhurri and silk).

For saris and embroidery with gold or silver thread and pearls, look around in in **Hauz Khas Village: Theme for a dream**, **Neelam Jolly's** and **The Marwari's**. For clothes (silk or linen blouses), try **Ensemble**, Santushti Shopping Complex and Ambawatta Complex; **Christina**, Santushti Shopping Complex.

WESTERN BRANDS

These are sold in the shopping complexes, malls and on **Connaught Circus and Connaught Place** (*Map III BC2–3*).

LEATHER AND SHOES

Traditional chappals (sandals) from Kolhapuri in Maharashtra and juttis (camel leather slippers), with their curved tips, can be bought on **Janpath**, in shops number 61 and 62. European brands are available on **Connaught Place**, at **Woodland** (F-18) for shoes and **Da Milano** (E-12) for clothes, bags and accessories.

JEWELLERY

DaribaKalan – *Map II CD2*. In Old Delhi. This road is a centre for jewellers specialising in gold, silver and fine or semi-precious stones.

Hanuman Mandir Mela – *Map III B3*. Near Connaught Place. This shop sells glass bracelets.

Sundar Nagar Market – *Map IV E3*. A number of jewellers and goldsmiths selling tribal ornaments, vintage pieces and copies.

Antique and modern jewellery Kanjimull & Sons – *Map III C3*. Scindia House, on the corner of Janpath.

Sumtidass & Bros – *Map III B3*. 18 Regal Building, on Connaught Circus.

Bharany's – *Map IV E3*. 14 Sundar Nagar Market. Since 1906: an institution among the jewellers that have been reinterpreting Mughal jewellery traditions.

Nirmal Vijay & Co – *Map III B2*. B-7 Connaught Place, Radial Rd 3. Nirmal Vijay's modern pieces are designed by Nirmal himself, who has worked for Cartier.

CARPETS

Dhurris from **Shyam Ahuja** in the Santushti Shopping Complex and Greater Kailash II malls.

Indian and Persian carpets, antique or modern Carpet Cellar – *Map I B4*. 1 Anand Lok, Khel Gaon Marg, north of Siri Fort.

Cottage Industries Exposition (CIE) – *Map III B4*. DCM Building, 16 Barakhamba Rd, on the corner of Tolstoy Marg.

ANTIQUES

☺ **Worth knowing** – The export of antiques more than 100 years old is subject to prior authorization; further information from the Archaeological Survey of India.

Indian Arts Palace – *Map III C2. 19-E Connaught Place, Radial Rd 7. ☎ 011-65809885. www.indianartspalace.in. Open Mon–Sat 11.30am–7pm*. Jewellery, miniatures, vintage wood and fabrics: some good items at high prices.

COSMETICS AND BEAUTY CARE

Most of the large hotels have a beauty salon.

Biotique – *Map IV CD3*. Khan Market. A classic outlet for Ayurvedic products made with plants.

Shahnaz Husain Herbal – *Map III B2.* B-13 Connaught Place. Presided over by Shahnaz Husain, the high priestess of pampering. Numerous other shops, including one in the Santushti Shopping Complex.

Hanuman Mandir Mela – *Map III B3.* Open-air market opposite the Hanuman Temple. On Tuesdays and Saturdays, the *menhdiwali* (henna artist) will cover the palms of your hands or the soles of your feet with arabesques in henna (menhdi).

PERFUME

Gulab Singh Johri Mal – *Map II CD2. 320 Dariba Kalan, Old Delhi.* Joss sticks, ittar (perfumed essential oils), soaps and scented candles.

Natural Perfume & Essential Oils – *Map II B3. 1115 Main Bazar Rd, Paharganj. 11.30am–8pm.* Good ideas for small gifts, stylishly presented.

CULINARY SPECIALITIES

Khari Baoli Rd and the two adjacent roads – *Map II C2.* In the western part of Old Delhi. A gigantic **spice market** also selling dried fruit and condiments, supposedly the largest in Asia.

In the **Connaught Place** area – *Map III B3.* **Bharat Dry Fruit Mart**, 3 Municipal Market, at the beginning of Janpath; **Cheap Dry Fruit Mart,** 5 New Janpath Market.

At **Bengali Market** – *off map, Map III C2.* 1.5 km east of Connaught Place. **Nathu's Sweet** and **Bengali Sweet House** sell *mithaiyan* (confectionery) and *namkin* (spicy or sweet and sour appetisers), as well as the finest Bengali sweets.

On **Chandni Chowk** – *Map II C2.* **Annapurna Bhandar, Haldiram Bhujjiawala**, near Annapurna, for Delhi-style confectionery, and **Ghantewala**, on the opposite side of the road (a shop established in 1790) for Bengali sweet treats.

MUSICAL INSTRUMENTS

Rikhi Ram – *Map III B2. G-8 Marina Arcade, Connaught Circus.* ✆ *011-23327685.*
Marques and Co – *Map III B2. G-14 Connaught Circus.* ✆ *011-23324234.*
A. Godin & Co – *Map III B3. 1 Regal Building, Parliament St.* ✆ *011-66303435.* Godin sells sitars and tablas.

RECORDED MUSIC

The Music Shop – *Map IV CD3. 18-AB Khan Market.* ✆ *011-24618464.* Classic Indian music available on CD and DVD.

ART GALLERIES

The galleries are generally open Mon–Sat 11am–6pm.

Dhoomi Mal Art Gallery – *Map III B2.* A-8 Connaught Place, 1st floor. The oldest contemporary art gallery in India.
Kumar Gallery – *Map IV E3.* 11 Sundar Nagar Market.
Triveni Kala Sangam – *Map IV D1.* Mandi House Circle.
Lalit Kala Akademi – *Map IV D1.* Rabindra Bhawan, Mandi House Circle.
Galerie Romain Rolland – *Map IV C4.* Alliance française, 72 Lodhi Estate. Nature Morte

BOOKSHOPS

There are some good bookshops on **Connaught Place** (*Map III*) selling beautiful books on India, and novels and magazines, many in English:
E. D. Galgotia & Sons – *Map III B2. B-17.* ✆ *011-23713227.*
The Bookworm – *Map III B2. B-29 Radial Rd 4.* ✆ *011-23322260.*
Oxford Bookstore – *Map III C3. N-81 Connaught Place.* ✆ *011-33503291.* There are a number of good book stalls in **Khan Market** (*Map IV CD3*): **Bahri Sons** – ✆ *011-24694610;* **Faqir Chand** – 15-A, ✆ *011-24618810.*
Jacksons Books – *Map II A4. 5106 Main Bazar Rd, Paharganj. 11am–10pm.* Jacksons sells photography books and a large selection of second-hand books.

STATIONERY

New Delhi Stationery Mart – *Map III B2. C-8 Connaught Place, Radial Rd 4.*

ENTERTAINMENT

Listings for cinemas, concerts and shows in the weekly publications sold at the kiosks and at www.timescity.com/delhi.

CINEMA

The capital has some 70 screens showing Bollywood masala movies, which are commercial Hindi films, as well as several Hollywood films; centrally located cinemas include the **Odeon** – *Map III B2,* **Connaught Place**, and **Regal** – *Map III B2,* in the Regal Building.
Priya – *Map I A4.* Community Centre, Vasant Vihar. Foreign films are also shown in cultural centres.

Siri Fort Auditorium – *Map I B4.*
Khel Gaon Marg. Festivals show
contemporary releases.

CONCERTS AND DANCE

Several performances of Indian music
and dance are organised every evening,
generally during the high season (Oct–
Apr). They start around 6.30pm and
tickets are often free; see the press for
details of where they can be obtained.
Most of the auditoriums are situated
close to Mandi House Circle (*Map IV D1*):
Kamani, Triveni Kala Sangam (205
Tansen Marg), **Shri Ram Centre** (Mandi
House). The **India International Centre
(IIC)** is 5km to the south, on Max Mueller
Marg, and the **India Habitat Centre**
(www.indiahabitat.org) is on Lodhi Rd
(*Map IV C4*). **Siri Fort Auditorium**, the
largest hall in Delhi, is to be found on
Khel Gaon Marg (*Map I B4*).

SPORTS AND ACTIVITIES

SWIMMING POOLS

👥 Hotels open their pools February–
November. Claridges and the Park Hotel
accept non-residents, as do some others.

GOLF

Delhi Golf Club – *Map IV D3. Dr Zakir
Hussain Marg.* 📞 *(011) 24 36 27 68. www.
delhigolfclub.org.* An excellent 27-hole
course dotted with monuments from
the Lodhi period. Approx. Rs.3,000/day
during the week, Rs.4,550/day at the
weekend.

POLO

Jaipur Polo Ground – *Map IV B4.
Kamal Ataturk Rd.* If you wish to catch a
match, polo has two seasons: October–
November and February–March.

MUSIC AND DANCE COURSES

Sangeet Natak Akademi – *Map IV D1.
Rabindra Bhawan, on Mandi House Circle.*
📞 *011-23387246. www.sangeetnatak.gov.in.*
Kathak Kendra – *Map III B2. Bahawalpur
House.* 📞 *011-23381317. http://kathak
kendra.org.*

YOGA AND MEDITATION

**Morarji Desai National Institute for
Yoga** – *Map III A4. 68 Ashok Rd.* 📞 *011-
23721472. www.yogamdniy.nic.in.*
Sri Aurobindo Ashram – *Map I B4–5.
Aurobindo Marg.* 📞 *011-65684153.
www.sriaurobindoashram.net.*

EXCURSIONS

🌀 **Worth knowing** – Agra's Taj Mahal
is closed Friday; sights are jam-packed

weekends. Avoid tours touted by the
little bus companies on Janpath as
these don't always stick to the
destinations they advertise and like to
stop at shops.
Rajasthan Tourist Office and
**Rajasthan Tourism Development
Corporation (RTDC)** – *Map IV D2. Bikaner
House, Pandara Rd.* 📞 *011-23383837
and 23389525. www.rajasthantourism.
gov.in. Open daily 10am–1.30pm,
2pm–5pm (closed 2nd Sat of the month).*
For information about Rajasthan or
reservations for the Maharaja Train and
Rajasthan's RTDC hotels.
**Delhi Tourism and Transportation
Development Corporation (DTTDC)** –
The DTTDC organises coach trips to
Agra three times/week (7am–10.30pm,
Rs.1,200 in an air-conditioned bus) or
combined trips to Agra-Jaipur (Rs.4,800).
Also all-inclusive trips (transport,
accommodation at an RTDC hotel
and a guide).
Alwar and Sariska – **Indian Railways**
organises a weekly two-day excursion
on the Steam Express, the oldest steam
train still in operation, departing from
Delhi at 9am Saturday and returning at
6.45pm Sunday, with visits to Alwar and
the Sariska National Park and staying
overnight in the Tiger Den Resort.
Rs.2,245 or more. Further information
from the International Tourist Bureau,
New Delhi Railway Station, 1st floor.

EVENTS AND FESTIVALS

Republic Day – 26 Jan. A military parade
and procession of floats along Rajpath.
Beating of the Retreat – 29 Jan. Military
music and fireworks opposite the
Rashtrapati Bhawan.
Urs of Nizamuddin Auliya – Apr–May
and Nov–Dec. Singers and musicians
celebrate the Sufi saint as night falls at
the *dargah* (tomb) of Nizamuddin.
Independence Day – 15 Aug. A speech
is given by the prime minister at the Red
Fort. Parades and pageants.
Phool Walon Ki Sair, Mehrauli district,
near the Qutb Minar – Late Sep–early Oct.
'Procession of the florists' symbolises
traditional links uniting Muslims and
Hindus, held at the dargah (tomb) of
Khawa Qutbuddin Bakhtiar Kaki and the
Hindu Yogmaya Mandir temple.
Gandhi Jayanti – 2 Oct. The birth of
Mahatma Gandhi is commemorated at
Raj Ghat.

Mathura★

Situated on a fertile plain at the heart of the Braj (or Vraj Bhumi) region, Mathura is first and foremost one of the seven cities sacred to Hinduism. Krishna himself, one of the most popular gods in India, was born here, and spent his youth in the surrounding countryside. Every corner of the region is sacred to the God with the blue skin. Mathura was already a large city when the Buddha came to preach here in the 6C BC. The new faith took root and the town became an important religious hub boasting monasteries and stupas. A school of sculpture here reached its apotheosis under the Guptas (4C–6C), but was stopped in its path by the invading Huns at the end of the 6C.

SIGHTS
GOVERNMENT MUSEUM★

🕐 *Open Tue–Sun 10.30am–4.30pm.*
🎟 *Rs.25; photo permit Rs.20.*

The museum's remarkable sculptures recall Mathura's glorious past as an ancient Buddhist centre and politico-cultural capital of the Kushan Empire, where Gandhara art flourished in the 1C. Most sculptures and bronzes discovered in the area date from 1C–6C. This era (ruled by the Kushans and Guptas) witnessed the zenith of the **Mathura school** of art, which was characterised by the use of a red sandstone mottled with cream-coloured flecks.

Highlights include the figure of a **young man standing**; the bust of **Parshvanatha**, the 23rd tirthankara; a 1C (Kushan era) **Buddha** in the *abhaya* position (with the right hand raised in a gesture of peace); Kushan-era **pillars**; and a statue of the **Buddha** from the 5C (Gupta era), and the **four-armed Vishnu** (Hindu Middle Ages, 7C–12C).

▶ **Population:** 380,000.

🡒 **Location:** 145km southeast of Delhi, 58km northwest of Agra.

👥 **Kids:** A boat trip on the Yamuna, departing from the ghats at Mathura.

😊 **Don't Miss:** Chhatta Bazar and the ghats (stepped areas) on the banks of the Yamuna; the sculptures in the museum.

🕐 **Timing:** Allow a half-day for Mathura, staying locally or making an excursion from Agra. Stroll along the ghats, enter a shrine where the faithful intone *bhajans* (religious hymns) to the glory of Krishna, the heavenly herdsman.

Krishna, the Blue-Skinned God

Knowledge of the *Bhagavata Purana*, composed in south India around 10C, had spread throughout the north by the 12C, bringing the legends of Krishna to a wider audience. The Braj region thus became a place of pilgrimage for Vishnuists (Krishna is an avatar of Vishnu), drawing in saints and poets, including the 15C princess Mira Bai and Chaitanya, the Bengali reformer. The accounts of the life of Krishna vary among the *Mahabharata, Bhagavad Gita* and *Bhagavata Purana*. When the Earth was threatened by the demon Kamsa, king of Mathura, Vishnu elected to take on an eighth incarnation to save the world. Krishna was thus born among the Yadav community and brought up by adoptive cowherd parents in Vrindavan, rapidly achieving renown for his mighty deed, mischief and female conquests. Having killed Kamsa, he left to found the town of Dwarka (Gujarat) and act as charioteer for the warrior Arjuna during the final battle described in the *Mahabharata*. He went on to die in Dwarka of an arrow wound to his heel, the only vulnerable part of his body.

GETTING THERE/LEAVING
**BY TRAIN– Mathura Junction
Railway Station** – Located to the
south-west, approx. 4m from the
Yamuna. ☎ 139 (booking centre).
Frequent departures for Agra
Cantonment (approx. 1hr). Superfast
(2hr) and Express (3hr) trains for
Delhi (New Delhi or Nizamuddin
stations); the fastest train, the
Shatabdi (45min), leaves around
7.30am. Frequent departures for
Bharatpur (30min), Sawai Madhopur
(3hr) and Kota (4hr30min); the most
practical connection to these last
two cities is the morning Superfast,
the Golden Temple Mail.
BY BUS – New Bus Stand –Agra Rd.
The timetables are only in Hindi.
Frequent departures for Delhi (but
take the train instead since the bus
journey can be very long; there
are several stops en route to Delhi)
and Agra (1hr30min) via Deeg
(1hr), Jaipur (5hr); a few buses for
Govardhan (1hr).

GETTING AROUND
A walk on the road by the Yamuna is
pleasant; otherwise, take a rickshaw,
tempo (shared taxi) or tonga (horse-
drawn carriage).
BY RICKSHAW – The ride from the
station to town centre costs approx.
Rs.40 in an autorickshaw and Rs.25
by cycle rickshaw.

HEALTH
Maheshwari Hospital –Masani
Bypass, Delhi Rd. ☎ 0565-2530381.
Private clinic.

SAFETY
Police – ☎ 0565-2405979.

SHRI KRISHNA JANMABHOOMI
Take a rickshaw to get here.
The street leading up to this shrine
('Birthplace of Lord Krishna') is lined with
religious stalls. A statue of Krishna above
the entrance gate depicts him driving
Arjuna's chariot, recalling the occasion in
the *Mahabharata* when the God brought
the *Bhagavad Gita* to mankind.
Built in 1975, the **Temple of Krishna**
with its pink façade and red *shikhara*
is the most recent reconstruction. The
most significant rebuild took place in
the 17C: not content with razing the temple to the ground, Aurangzeb replaced it
with a mosque *(on the right)*. The current
temple is thus not located on the exact
'birthplace' of the god.
The **interior** is decorated with kitschy
paintings depicting the life of Krishna
and his games with the *gopi*. The statue
of the flute-playing divine herdsman on
the altar is hidden behind curtains that
are drawn back several times a day for
darshan, when the God is revealed for
the adoration of the faithful.
The red sandstone **mosque,** which now
stands on the same spot where Krishna
was born, has nothing to do with worship of the divinity. Hindus consider
its presence an outrage against Indian
traditions. A gallery leads to the **birthplace of Krishna**, a small basement
underneath the mosque. The God is
said to have been born in this cell while
his parents were imprisoned by Kamsa,
the *asura* (demon) king.

AROUND THE YAMUNA
Follow the road towards the city centre. .
The 17C Jama Masjid has nothing of
interest beyond its green paint and the
white minarets. Linger a while at the
vegetable market in the neighbouring square, then follow the pilgrims to
the **Temple of Dwarkadhish** (🕐 *open
mornings and after 4pm; remove your
shoes; no photography*), from 1814,
sacred to the 'master of Dwarka' (or
Dwarkanatha), otherwise known as
Krishna. The façade and painted gates
conceal a rather garish interior decked
with mirrors and paintings. Darshan
takes place eight times a day: the statue
of Krishna is revealed to his devotees.
Follow Ramdas ki Mandi for 100m.
The road beside the Yamuna features
shops selling religious items, traditional

barber's stalls and tiny grocer's shops that are as likely to sell soap as incense. Take one of the lanes to the left leading to the Yamuna; the banks of the sacred river, known as **Vishram Ghat★**, are lined with ghats *(take off your shoes at the top of the steps)*, where Krishna is said to have bathed to purify himself after killing Kamsa. Pilgrims come to make ablutions in the morning and, once evening has fallen, the area is filled with the sound of bells heralding *aarti (a ritual during puja)* in the shrines nearby.

ADDRESSES

🏨 STAY

🛏 **Agra Hotel** –*Bengali Ghat.* ☎ 0565-2403318. 🖥✗🚿. *14 rm. Rs.500/600.* A traditional inn for pilgrims on the banks of the Yamuna. The rooms are basic but not unbearable if you have one looking out over the river.

🛏 **Brij Bihar** – *Holy Gate St.* ☎ 0565-2501090. 🚿. *40 rm. Rs.600/900.* The rooms are very plain but better value for money than the hostels on the ghats. The rooms on the road have balconies.

🛏 **Sheetal Regency** – *Deeg Gate, Masani Rd.* ☎ 0565-2404401. www.hotelsheetal regency.com. 🖥 ✗. *Internet, travel agency. 28 rm. Rs.2,550/2,950.* 🚅 *Rs.185. Rest. Rs.175/200.* This city-centre hotel has all the comforts expected by its clientele of commercial travellers.

🛏 **Brijwasi Royal** – *State Bank of India Crossing, Station Rd.* ☎ 056- 2401224. www.brijwasihotels.com. 🖥✗🍷. *40 rm. Rs.2,600/3,000* 🚅. This well-maintained hotel is situated between the bus and train stations. The décor is pleasant and the rooms comfortable, even if the over-all effect leans more towards functionality than charm.

🛏🛏 **Hotel Duke Palace** – *Sarswati Kund, Masani Bypass, Delhi Rd, 3km from the city centre.* ☎ 0565-2430354. 🖥 ✗. *25 rm. Rs.2,600/4,000.* The great ceremonial hall of this hotel regularly plays host to couples who have come to get married here from all over India.

🛏🛏🛏 **Radha Ashok (Best Western)** – *Masani Bypass, Delhi Rd.* ☎ 0565-2530395. www.radhaashok.com. 🖥✗🍷🏊. *Wi-Fi. 28 rm. Rs.5,200/9,800* 🚅. *Rest. Rs.450/600.* Located on the edge of fields at the

Shri Krishna Janmabhoomi

© Anurag Mallick, Priya Ganapathy/MICHELIN

northern exit to Mathura, this slightly charmless hotel boasts every comfort far from the bustle of the city.

🍽 EAT

🛏🛏 **Radha Ashok** –*Hotel restaurant.* 🍷. *6.15am–10.30pm. Rs.450/600.* A range of cooking styles including non-vegetarian dishes, which is rare in this town of pilgrims. The surroundings are light and clean.

SHOPPING

Bazaars – The souvenir shops on the road leading to the shrine of Shri Krishna Janmabhoomi, in **Chhatta Bazar** and along the ghats sell images of the blue god Krishna, flutes (the instrument with which he beguiled the female population of Braj) and scarves bearing the mantra 'Hare Rama, Hare Krishna'.

Everyday items –Tilak Bazar and Vikas Bazar.

EVENTS AND FESTIVALS

Krishna Janmashtami – 8th–9th day after the full moon in Aug–Sep (5–6 Sep 2015) commemorates birth of Krishna that is celebrated at the Janmabhoomi temple and in Vrindavan in particular.

Diwali – 11 Nov 2015, 30 Oct 2016, 19 Oct 2017. Park yourself near Vishram Ghat for photographs; once night falls, devotees launch their oil lamps onto the Yamuna.

Kamsa ka Mela – Oct–Nov. A Ramlila (a play on the life of Rama) is enacted to celebrate Krishna's victory over Kamsa.

Vrindavan★

If you are tired of Mathura's bustle, head 15km north to Vrindavan, the 'forest of basil' and scene of the exploits of the young Krishna. Hermits and Vaishnavite thinkers have come to settle here over the centuries and many temples and ghats have been built in their honour. The centre of this large town has retained the charm of a village living to the rhythms of yesteryear; cows and monkeys share space with people in its tranquil bazaars.

▶ **Location:** 15km north of Mathura. Tempo departures opposite the New Bus Stand or south of the temple of Shri Krishna Janmabhoomi in Mathura, (35min, 🚌 Rs.10/person). Allow a half-day.

🕐 **Timing:** Plan your excursion around the temples' opening hours (approx. 5am–11am and 4.30pm–8pm).

Vrindavan's streets are lined with old houses and temples. The Yamuna flows at the foot of the ghats north of the town; near the Chir Ghat boatmen tout for business. From here, a stroll east-wards along the ghat will take you to a little bridge (approx. 500m); the sound of loudspeakers broadcasting non-stop prayers will accompany you everywhere.

TEMPLE OF GOVIND DEV

On the right down the main road from the bridge. North-east of the town.
After its destruction by Sultan Sikandar Lodhi in the 15C, the temple was rebuilt by the maharajah of Amer in an Indo-Islamic style in 1590. This massive red sandstone structure originally had seven storeys, but the top four were destroyed by Aurangzeb a century later. In antici-pation of the emperor's iconoclastic inclinations, Maharajah Jai Singh II had the shrine's main statue of Govind Dev (the 'herdsman god') transferred to his city of Jaipur.

TEMPLE OF RANGAJI

Opposite the Temple of Govind Dev. No photography inside.
Immediately recognisable by its high *gopuram* (pyramidal tower at the entrance to a temple precinct), this astonishing temple was built in 1851 in a highly eclectic style; it too is dedicated to Krishna and is staffed by priests from south India.

TEMPLE OF KRISHNA BALARAM

Approx. 4km from the last two, south-west of the town. Take a rickshaw here.
The Indian headquarters of **ISKCON** (International Society for Krishna Consciousness), a sect known as Hare Krishna, stands in a park alongside local administrative buildings, a hostel for pilgrims and a white marble **tomb** (at the entrance to the complex) com-memorating the founder of ISKCON, who died in 1977. Pilgrims with white skin and shaven heads stream from the complex, dancing and tapping their drums to honour Krishna.

ADDRESSES

🏨 STAY

📧 **Shri Krishna Balaram Guest House (ISKCON)** – *Bhaktivedanta Swami Rd, on the road beside the temple of Krishna Balaram.* 📞 *0565-2540022. www.iskcon vrindavan.com.* ✗ 🚿. *44 rm. Rs.300* 🍽. A sanctuary for Western converts to the cult of Krishna. The interior is light and clean. Hot water but no heating in winter. Book at least a fortnight in advance.

📧 **Dhanuka Ashram** – *Parikrama Rd, 2nd little road on the right after the Temple of Krishna Balaram.* 📞 *0565-2540075.* ✗ 🚿. *35 rm. Rs.300* 🍽. A sunny garden. The rooms are relatively clean and boast hot water. No heating.

Neemrana

Located south-west of Delhi in the Alwar district of Rajasthan, Neemrana is a major industrial city whose key interest to visitors is its sprawling 15C fort-palace. Set against the Aravalli hills, the renovated fort hotel sits unperturbed on its hillside perch amid industrial surroundings. The spiked gates of Surajpol once defended the fort against charging war elephants, often blinded to batter down the gates.
Today, these portals open wide to welcome global guests to an ancient setting overflowing with beauty and wonder.

▶ **Population:** 7,143.

Info: Neemrana Hotels: ✆+91-11-4666 1666. www.neemranahotels.com .

Location: 122 km south-west of Delhi off NH-8 (Delhi-Jaipur highway) between Shahjahanpur and Behror in Alwar district.

Timing: Access is restricted to walk-in visitors on days of marriages and events.

Guided Tours: Neemrana's self-guided audio tour costs Rs.250/player. For local touring arrangements, contact Balwant Soni of Tresors d' Inde (Unique Tours of Rajasthan) ✆+91 9929066854.

After the death of Prithviraj Chauhan in 1192 at the hands of his archenemy Muhammad Ghori, his descendants fled southwest to Rajasthan. Over the next three centuries they fought battles and set up three capitals: Mandhan, Mandawar and Neemrana. Nimola Meo, a defeated local chieftain, begged the Chauhans to lend his name to his lost kingdom. When Raja Rajdeo Singh laid the foundation of the fort in 1464, the Chauhans kept their word and named the village Neemrana after Nimola. The desolate region was called Raath. Sadly, when Raja Rajendra Singh moved out in 1947, local villagers pillaged doors, windows, girders and whatever had not been sold off. Aman Nath and Francis Wacziarg bought the property on a whim in 1986 for Rs.8 lakh. After 15 years of painstaking renovation at the cost of Rs.7 *crore*, the ruins of the fort-palace were transformed into a luxury resort, now one of India's oldest heritage hotels.

The film *Major Saab* was shot at Neemrana Fort Palace, which serves as an ideal filming location besides being a popular venue for weddings and conferences. Stop by the 18C **stepwell** one kilometre away, besides shops like Shri Shyam, Bijoux de Rajasthan, Neemrana Silver Craft and Sadguru's (open since 1857).

NEEMRANA FORT PALACE★★★

For non-guests, Neemrana charges an entry fee of Rs.500/person (Mon–Fri), Rs.750/person (Sat–Sun), valid for a 2hr visit, including a tour of the interior.
Cascading down a hillside of the Aravali hills over 12 tiers of lushly landscaped terrain, the fort's seven formidable palace wings—a blend of Sultanate,

18C stepwell

© Anurag Mallick, Priya Ganapathy/MICHELIN

Neemrana Fort Palace

© Anurag Mallick, Priya Ganapathy/MICHELIN

Rajput, Mughal and Colonial archi-tectural styles—overlook six acres of magnificent gardens, terraced patios and secluded alcoves. Hotel guests are immersed in luxurious indoor and out-door spaces and given attentive service. Self-guided **tours**, open to the public, start at Suraj Pol gate, past a winding entrance, taking in 11 key sights within the palace, including Shatranj Bagh, Chand Pol, Hawa Mahal, Raj Mahal, Tulsi Chowk, Baradari and Sheesh Mahal. Neemrana Fort Palace offers **camel rides** (⊜ Rs.200), camel cart rides to the 18C stepwell (⊜ Rs.500), 5km vin-tage-car ride (⊜ Rs.1,000) and a 5-track zipline, the first in India by Flying Fox (&+91-1494 297100; 10am–4:30pm; Rs.1999, Rs.1699 children).

⊛ **Worth knowing – Stepwells** are carved stone wells, usually massive, built to store water, and often have stairs descending to the body of water.

ADDRESSES

☚ STAY

⊜⊜⊜⊜ **Neemrana Fort Palace** – 122nd Milestone, Off Delhi-Jaipur Highway. &01494 246007, 9310630386. www.neemranahotels.com. 65 rooms, no wheelchair access, ⌣, Wi-Fi. Rs.4,000-18,000. Each room at Neemrana is

unique – Paashan Mahal (Palace of the Rocks) integrates the Aravali rockface into the interiors, Uma Vilas has great hill views, Chandra Mahal was once the Hall of Justice, while Francisi Mahal is a French suite. Enjoy alfresco dinners, Ayurvedic massages (Rs.1,000-5,000) and two swimming pools. Mahaburj restaurant serve Rajasthani and North Indian *thalis* on weekends. Being a hill fort, be prepared to walk and climb steps to reach different levels.

⊜⊜⊜ **Ramada Neemrana Jaipur Highway** – M 2 Riico Industrial Area, Shahjahanpur. & 91 1494 677777, www.ramada.com, 102 rooms, ♿, ⌣, Wi-Fi. Rs.6,000-9,000. This new hotel at Shahjahanpur near NH-8 between Delhi and Jaipur and RIICO Industrial area offers all creature comforts, a 2nd Floor pool, 24x7 room service and a coffee shop, besides free hot breakfast buffet, Japanese restaurant and business centre. Rooms include 33 twin bedded and 63 king-size rooms and many suites. Ideal for families and business groups.

⊜⊜ **Cambay Sapphire** – Neesa Square, Plot No. CC-11, Industrial Area. & +91 1494 246432. www.thecambay.com, 70 rooms (87 planned), ♿, breakfast not included, Wi-Fi. Rs.5500. This modern hotel aimed at business travellers visiting Neemrana's industrial hub has a spa, swimming pool and fitness center besides Indus multi-cuisine restaurant, and Oishii serving Japanese cuisine.

Kurukshetra

Located 155 km north of Delhi, in Haryana, Kurukshetra is a large city of almost a million residents. Its cityscape teems with sacred lakes, groves, temples and nearly 360 sites linked to the *Mahabharata*. The sacred Kurukshetra or Land of Kuru, ancestor of the Kauravas and the Pandavas, is the site of the legendary battlefield where the 18-day Mahabharata War was fought. The city is also a place of annual pilgrimage as well as an academic hub. The Kurukshetra Festival (usually in December) is celebrated here to mark the birth anniversary of the *Bhagwad Gita*, and the Bhagwad Katha (week-long *shloka* recital) is conducted with great reverence.

SAROVARS

Kurukshetra has a number of sacred water bodies where Hindu pilgrims flock on solar eclipses and *amavasya* (no moon night) for a dip to attain salvation. The **Sannihit Sarovar** is reputed to be the confluence of the seven sacred Saraswati rivers. In the middle of **Brahma Sarovar**, the world's largest man-made pond, stands a mammoth bronze chariot on the small island of Purushottam Bagh; it depicts Arjuna and his charioteer Krishna.

Just off NH6, 6.5km west of town, the Lake of Illumination (through knowledge) or **Jyotisar**, marks the spot where

▶ **Population:** 964,655.

ℹ **Info:** Haryana Tourism runs Parakeet Lodge ✆ 01744 230250 at Pipli and Neelkanthi Krishna Dham Yatri Nivas ✆ 01744 291615 in Kurukshetra.

▷ **Location:** 155 km north of Delhi on the Grand Trunk Road (NH-1) between Karnal and Ambala (3hr by road).

👥 **Kids:** Kurukshetra Panorama and Science Centre.

Lord Krishna narrated the *Bhagwad Gita* to Arjun. The immortal banyan tree stands as witness to the celestial song, and the ancient Shiva temple, as the sign proclaims, saw several foreign invasions. **Bhishma Kund**, south of the NIT Kurukshetra campus, signals the site where Arjuna shot an arrow into the earth to quench the thirst of Bhishma Pitamah.

TEMPLES

The Sthaneshwar Mahadev Temple in Kuber Colony gives the industrial town of Thaneswar its name (👣 *see below*). It was the original *taposthali* (place of penance) of King Kuru, and the Pandavas are believed to have prayed here to Lord Shiva before the war.

In addition to the **Sri Saraswati temple** at Jyotisar, there are temples dedicated to **Sri Tarakeshwar Mahadev** and

Brahma Sarovar

© Alamer/age fotostock

Bhishma Pitamah, with kitschy interiors and statues. Bhishma is depicted in *baan-shaiyya* posture—reclining on a bed of arrows. At the **Sri Lakshmi Narayan Swamy Temple** (*near the Panorama Museum*), devotees offer yellow objects for wish fulfillment.

OTHER SIGHTS
SriKrishna Museum★

In Science Park 🖉 *01744-291288. www.kurukshetra.nic.in/tour/Museums/ShriKrishnaMuseum/index.htm* 🕐 *Open Tue–Sun 10am–5pm. Cameras not allowed.*
Established in 1987, the museum houses six galleries of artefacts and art devoted to Krishna. The Mahabharata and Gita Gallery displays archaeological artefacts from the same period as the epic tale, lending substantiation to its validity; paintings on exhibit depict Krishna and his exploits.

Kurukshetra Panorama and Science Centre★★

Pehowa Rd. 🖉 *01744-226100. www.kurukshetra.nic.in/tour/Museums/Panorama/index.htm.* 🕐 *Open Tue–Sun 10am–4pm.*
This unique centre of learning showcases India's scientific and technological advancement across 4,500 years of history and mythology. At the centre of the cylindrical hall, ten 34ft high digital paintings offer scientific explanations to justify key episodes of the Mahabharata war: from Sanjay's war commentary to various *yantras* (devices) and *astras* (weapons). Interactive exhibits engage visitors in aspects of modern science as well as ancient astronomy. Decorative arts, sculpture, tools, weaponry, and dinosaur models are on display.

Sheikh Chilli ka Makbara

In Thanesar, north of the Panorama Museum at Kalyan Nagar.
The nearby industrial town of Thanesar (on the NH-8) is the twin town of Kurukshetra. The Sheikh Chilli ka Makbara here is the tomb of Mughal Prince Dara Shikoh's Sufi master Abd-ur-Rahim

Abdul-Karim Abd-ur-Razak, popularly known in folk tales as Sheikh Chilli. In addition to the marble-domed tomb, the monumental complex includes a mosque built of red sandstone, rooftop pavilions (*chhatris*) with slender columns, tunnels and a large Mughal-style garden (*char-bagh*).

ADDRESSES

🛏 STAY

🛏 **Hotel Pearl Marc** – *Railway Rd.* 🖉 *01744 226614. www.hotelpearlmarc.com. 10 rm. Wi-Fi. breakfast not included. Rs1500-Rs.2500.* A decent stay option near the railway station, this modern hotel has clean rooms, a terrace garden and Shell restaurant serving good food.

🛏🛏 **Hive Panipat** – *Opposite Pillar Number 41, near SBI Bank, BMK Market, GT Rd, Panipat.* 🖉 *0180 4093000, www.hivehotels.co.in/panipat. 45 rm. Wi-Fi.* ♿, 🖥. *Rs.3000-Rs.5000.* Located just 1km from the railway station, this accommodation has well-appointed rooms in 3 categories: club, deluxe and suite with business facilities. Basic comfort, all-day dining and a bar.

🛏🛏🛏 **Noor Mahal** – *40 km from Kurushetra, 4 km from Karnal. Noor Mahal Crossing, NH-1, Sector 32, Karnal* 🖉*0184 3066 666. 125 rm. Wi-Fi,* ♿, 🖥. *Rs.7,500-Rs.9,500.* Blending history and Mughal-Rajputana luxury, the palatial hotel is set on a sprawling 8 acre property. The first courtyard, Diwan-i-Am, on the lobby level is accessible from all sides. A tiny doorway leads to the Diwan-i-Khas or courtyard on the first floor surrounded by rooms and balconies with low lattices and *chhajjas* (ledges). The hotel complex has four stunning 100 ft high *Hiran minars* (golden towers) capped with octagonal canopies. Open-air restaurant, Indian specialty fine dining, 24hr coffee shop, Polo Bar plus a patisserie.

Pataudi

Set at the foot of the Aravalli hills south-west of Delhi, Pataudi is a small village within the district of Gurgaon, a booming suburb of the capital city. Attractions include the Pataudi Palace and Sultanpur National Park, 7km away and known for its bird sanctuary around Sultanpur Lake. At Thakran Farms (👣 see STAY), 6km from Pataudi Palace, guests can experience life on a rustic farm.

▶ **Population:** 16,064.

Info: Haryana Govt. Tourist Bureau ☎ 011-23324910. Haryana Tourism Corporation Limited. ☎ 0172 2702955-57.

◐ **Location:** 26km south-west of Gurgaon and 60km south-west of Delhi.

◔ **Timing:** The Pataudi Palace is being renovated and part of it will open as a museum.

The story of Pataudi is a heady mix of cricket, cinema and royalty. The Nawabs of Pataudi, a 137sq km non-salute princely state near Delhi, trace their lineage to Salamat Khan, who came from Afghanistan more than 500 years ago. About 1480 AD, when Bahlul, an Afghan of the Lodhi tribe was governor of Punjab, a mass migration of Afghans took place to India. As skilled horsemen, Salamat Khan's clan was chosen to quell the Mewati tribe. His successors helped Mughal rulers in many battles against the Rajputs and were bequeathed Kalam Mahal (later Pataudi House) near Delhi Gate as the family residence. After Faiz Talab Khan aided the British in their battle against the Marathas, they established Pataudi (a small principality named after a Rajput ruler called Pata) as a princely state in 1804 and made him the first Nawab.

The small region left its imprint on the world map when Iftikhar Ali Khan, the 8th Nawab of Pataudi, represented both England and India (as captain) in Test cricket. Ibrahim Kothi or Pataudi Palace was built in 1938 for his wife and designed after the Colonial mansions of Imperial Delhi. His son, Mansoor Ali Khan Pataudi, the 9th Nawab, became the world's youngest cricket captain at 21.

PATAUDI PALACE★★

On the outskirts of the village.
☎ *+91-9813440454.*
This two-storey palace is set within 10 acres of gardens with rosebushes, palm trees and fountains. A large swimming pool dominates the grounds. The palace

has served as a filming location for movies like *Veer Zara, Mangal Pandey,* and **Julia Roberts'** Hollywood hit *Eat, Pray, Love* (a cottage is named for Roberts). After being run as a heritage hotel by the Neemrana Group, the palace was handed back to the owners in January 2014. Plans are afoot to convert it into a cricketing memorabilia museum.

ADDRESSES

🍴 STAY

🛏🛏 **Thakran Farms**§ – *6km from Palace on Malpura Rd, Village Lohaka near Village Lokra, Pataudi Tehsil, Haryana.* ☎ *+91 124 427 7771. www.thakranfarms.com. 5 rm. Rs.6,000, includes all meals.* This farm, run by Nakul and Madhulika Thakran, features bungalows within a spacious countryside setting. Besides 20-25 camping tents and upcoming Swiss luxury tents on a 4.5 acre patch, 15 acres have been set aside for activities such as paint ball and ATV riding. Spend time among cows, buffalos, ducks and farm animals, see the herb garden and vermi-compost or take part in farm work such as harvesting wheat in April.

🛏 **Rosy Pelican Guesthouse** – *Sultanpur National Park, Haryana (www. sultanpurbirdsanctuary.com).* ☎ *0124-2015670, 9311533922 (JP Shekhawat). www. haryanatourism.gov.in. 14rm. Rs. 3,500-Rs. 5,000, includes all meals for 1night/2days and entry to the park.* Run by Haryana Tourism, this guest house has cottages as well as rooms, a bar and restaurant in a good location for a night in the wild. .

Agra
and around

Highlights

- Taj Mahal *p151*
- Agra Fort *p156*
- Fatehpur Sikri *p165*
- Tomb of I'timād-ud-Daulah *p160*

Thanks to the fame of the Taj Mahal, the city of Agra is known throughout the world. For some visitors to India, their only aim is to see this mausoleum, built by the emperor Shah Jahan in the 17C as a sublime love song in memory of the wife he adored. Along with Delhi and Lahore (in modern-day Pakistan), Agra was one of the three most beautiful cities of the Mughal Empire, yet its architectural splendour doesn't reside solely in the Taj Mahal. Some of the finest creations of the 17C are here: magnificent palaces, majestic mosques and monumental tombs fuse together in one grand masterpiece of white marble and red sandstone amid a background of gardens inspired by Allah and Paradise. Sadly, the rather grubby centre of the city, disfigured by unattractive structures and assaulted by constant, chaotic traffic, somewhat dulls the lustre of these marvels.

Taj Mahal in morning fog over the Yamuna
© Frank Bienewaldimage/age fotostock

Agra★★★

🐾WALKING TOUR *See Map*

TAJ MAHAL★★★
🕐 *Open Sat–Thu sunrise–sunset.*
☞Rs.750. Night viewing 2 days before and after full moon, except Fri and month of Ramadan Rs.750. Tickets can be purchased up to 24 hours in advance at the Booking Counter of the Archaeological Survey of India (☞ see p164). Visit at sunrise (around 6am) to avoid the crowds. Allow 1hr.
Ideally, visit the monument at different times of the day to truy appreciate its magnificence: from dawn's pink reflections and full glare of the midday sun to the magical glow of twilight and lunar light of night's full moon, every moment of the day and night reveals another view of this enchanting building.

Enter by the western, eastern or southern gate, and cross a large courtyard to the monumental **gateway** of red sandstone inlaid with white marble. As you leave the archway, the Taj seems almost unreal in its all-encompassing whiteness. Sit for a moment on one of the benches on either side of the gateway to admire the building, before get-

▸ **Population:** 1.64 million.
▷ **Location:** 203km southeast of Delhi, 58km southeast of Mathura, 232km east of Jaipur.
🛕 **Don't Miss:** Taj Mahal and Agra Fort in the city centre; the tomb of I'timād-ud-Daulah and the tomb of Akbar the Great at Sikandra.
🕐 **Timing:** Allow one day for a visit to Agra, two days to include an excursion to Fatehpur Sikri or Mathura (hire a car and combine the excursion with a visit en route to Sikandra). To avoid the crowds, visit the most famous sights as soon as they open on a weekday. Take a rickshaw from the Taj Mahal to the fort.

ting closer. A canal lined with cypresses (these once alternated with orange trees) guides the eye towards the Taj. It stands—an object placed for contemplation—on a vast plinth, following a pattern established 70 years earlier for Humayun's Tomb in Delhi. Unlike

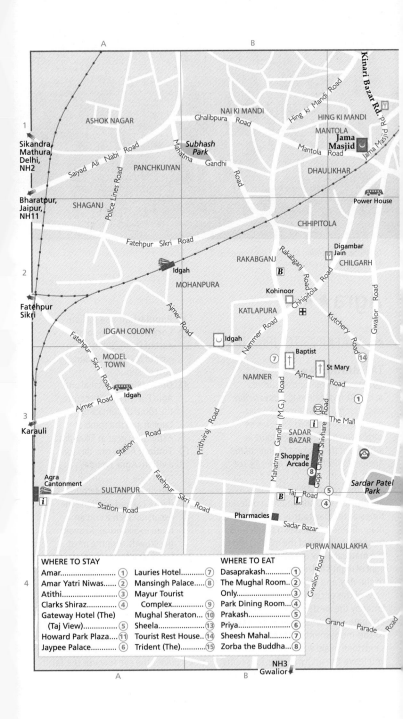

WHERE TO STAY

Amar..........................	①
Amar Yatri Niwas......	②
Atithi........................	③
Clarks Shiraz.............	④
Gateway Hotel (The)	
(Taj View).............	⑤
Howard Park Plaza....	⑪
Jaypee Palace............	⑥
Lauries Hotel............	⑦
Mansingh Palace.....	⑧
Mayur Tourist	
Complex..............	⑨
Mughal Sheraton...	⑩
Sheela..................	⑬
Tourist Rest House...	⑭
Trident (The).........	⑮

WHERE TO EAT

Dasaprakash.............	①
The Mughal Room...	②
Only..........................	③
Park Dining Room...	④
Prakash....................	⑤
Priya......................	⑥
Sheesh Mahal..........	⑦
Zorba the Buddha...	⑧

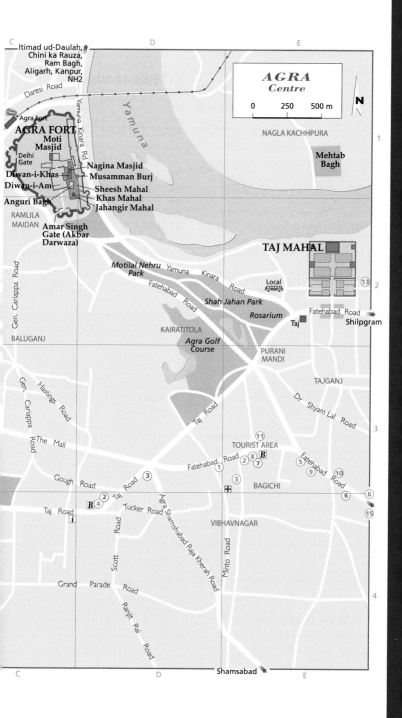

AGRA
Centre

0   250   500 m

N

Itimad ud-Daulah,
Chini ka Rauza,
Ram Bagh,
Aligarh, Kanpur,
NH2

Daresi Road

NAGLA KACHHPURA

Yamuna Kinara Rd

Yamuna

Agra Fort

AGRA FORT
Moti
Masjid

Mehtab
Bagh

Delhi
Gate

Diwan-i-Khas
Diwan-i-Am

Nagina Masjid
Musamman Burj

Sheesh Mahal
Khas Mahal
Jahangir Mahal

Anguri Bagh

RAMLILA
MAIDAN

Amar Singh
Gate (Akbar
Darwaza)

TAJ MAHAL

Motilal Nehru
Park

Yamuna Kinara Road

Local

13

Fatehabad Road

Gen. Cariappa Road

Shah Jahan Park

Rosarium

Fatehabad Road

Taj

Shilpgram

KAIRATITOLA

BALUGANJ

Agra Golf
Course

PURANI
MANDI

TAJGANJ

Gen. Cariappa Road

Hastings Road

The Mall

Dr Shyam Lal Road

Taj Road

11

TOURIST AREA

Fatehabad Road

2 8 B
1   7

5
9   10

Gough Road

3

3

BAGICHI

6

6

B 2
4

Taj Road

Tucker Road

Agra Shamshabad Raja Kheral Road

15

Taj Road

i

VIBHAVNAGAR

Scott Road

Minto Road

Grand   Parade   Road

Ranjit Rai Road

Shamsabad

GETTING THERE/LEAVING

BY TRAIN– Agra Cantonment Railway Station – *Map II A3.* In the Sultanpur district. ☏ 139 (booking centre). The best way to get to Delhi is to take one of the nearly 30 trains that serve the capital daily (2hr–4hr journey time) via Mathura (50min). Almost all of these call at New Delhi station and some continue to Nizamuddin (20min). Go for the Karnataka Express in the morning, the Jhelum Express (which leaves around 5pm) or the Shatabdi (which leaves Agra around 8.30pm) – they are a bit more expensive (Rs.930), but are comfortable, air-conditioned and speedy (2hr10min). Two departures a day for Jaipur (approx. 4hr).

Agra Fort Railway Station – *Map II C1.* Near the Fort. Info ☏ 139. Reservations ☏ 0562-2364163. Provides connections with Rajasthan (Jaipur, Sawai Madhopur); 4 trains a day for Fatehpur Sikri (1hr). Taking trains from Agra Cantonment, when there are any, is a better option.

BY BUS – The state bus company, Uttar Pradesh State Roadways Transport Corporation (**UPSRTC**), www.upsrtc.com, runs two bus stations. The main one is **Idgah Bus Stand** – *Map II A3*, on the corner of Ajmer Rd and Fatehpur Sikri Rd, ☏ 0562-2367543, 24hr, booking centre 8am–8pm. Departures for Delhi (4hr30min) via Mathura every 30mins from 5am until 8pm, and for Fatehpur Sikri (1hr) every 45mins from 6am until 8pm. Buses for Jaipur (6hr) via Bharatpur (1hr30min) every hour from 6am until 11.30pm; 4 buses continue to Ajmer. One express bus in the late afternoon for Udaipur (12hr). Other departures from the **Power House Bus Stand** – *Map II C1*, Gwalior Rd, to the west of the fort, 6am–10pm, no reservations. Buses serving the towns of Uttar Pradesh leave from here in an indescribable chaos of noise and dirt. Local buses for Mathura (1hr30min).

🕙 **Worth knowing** – Some long-distance trains arrive hours late, especially in winter (due to fog).

GETTING AROUND

Use a motor vehicle to travel between the main sights: the distances are quite long. Traffic is free-flowing in the Cantonment, the residential area stretching along the Mall, and between the Taj Mahal and the fort, but very congested in the districts north of the Ajmer Rd, to the west and north of the fort; vehicles are prohibited around the Taj.

BY TAXI – The Agra Cantonment railway station taxi-drivers have formed a union offering a range of fixed-price deals; they are not the cheapest fares, but they are convenient. If you are coming from Delhi for a day trip on the Shatabdi, you can hire a taxi for Rs.800–1,100 that you can keep all day until your return train departs, even if this is at 11pm. Allow 1hr to get to Fatehpur Sikri because of the traffic jams getting out of Agra.

BY RICKSHAW – There is a pre-paid rickshaw booth at Agra Cantonment railway station. Expect to pay Rs.100 for the Taj Mahal. Day hire: approx. Rs.350 for 8hrs in a cycle rickshaw (Rs.500 for an auto-rickshaw).

BY CAR HIRE – Rates (with driver included) range from Rs.1,500-2,000/day. Remember to add on the total cost of tolls and parking, which is about Rs.500, if you have to cross the Rajasthan border.

🕙 **Worth knowing** – Paying commission to rickshaw- and taxi-drivers by merchants, hoteliers and restaurateurs is prevalent; be firm with the drivers and categorically refuse any detour that you have not asked for. Watch out also for scams of every kind, starting with con tricks involving precious stones.

EMERGENCY/HEALTH

Ambulance – ☎ 102.
Amit Jaggi Memorial Nursing Home – *Map E3*. Minto Rd. ☎ 0562-2330600. Private clinic.
Pharmacies – *Map B4*. Sadar Bazar St, on the corner of M.G. Rd.

SAFETY

Police and Control Room – ☎ 100.
Tourist Police – Fatehabad Rd. ☎ (mobile) 9454402764.
Fire service – ☎ 101.

Humayun's Tomb, which is located in the middle of a park, the Taj is at the far end of a superb **Mughal Garden**, known as a *char-bagh*. A further innovation in comparison with Humayun's Tomb is to be found in the four **minarets** framing the tomb and standing in isolation at the corners of the plinth. Echoing a technique used earlier in the tomb of Jahangir (father of Shah Jahan), at Lahore, they serve to anchor the monument centrally on its plinth; without them, the colossal tomb would give the impression of tipping over backwards. As with Humayun's Tomb, the building has a **square floor plan** divided into sections; each side is deeply recessed to enclose a central *iwan* (vaulted space) framed by a *pishtaq* (monumental gateway), with two storeys of niches. The overall impression is more delicate than that of Humayun's Tomb, however, due in part to the over-sized **dome** on top: the dome is the same width as the *pishtaq*, a visual effect that generates a sense of great upward movement. Note the four omnipresent *chhatris* (pavilions) around the dome (👉 *see Architecture*).

The **reflecting pool** is located in the exact centre of the garden; its size was calculated to ensure that the Taj would be mirrored in its entirety. The tomb and its ghostly *doppelgänger* seem freed from earthly weight, lifted up as they are by the blue of the sky and the water. 🙂*Remove your shoes at the foot of the steps leading to the tomb's plinth.*

Set against the whiteness of the marble quarried at Makrana (near Ajmer), the **tomb's plinth** reveals an elegant decoration that combines floral motifs carved in bas-relief with curves and Quranic inscriptions inlaid with semiprecious stones using the **pietra dura** technique (👉 *see Architecture*). Access to the interior is via the central *iwan*, whose vaults are covered with a network of lines depicting geometric motifs. The **octagonal interior** of the tomb contains the imperial couple's **cenotaphs** under a low cupola (the actual tombs are in a crypt); the cenotaphs were originally surrounded by a golden screen inlaid with precious stones. Aurangzeb is said to have replaced it with the current marble balustrade with its subtle openwork and ornamental floral curves.

Two identical structures in red sandstone flank the Taj, separated from it by pools that are large enough to contain their whole reflections in another playful use of mirrors and images. The building on the left, facing west, is the only one that is actually a mosque. Its partner, which lacks a *mihrab* (the niche indicating the direction of Mecca), is used by pilgrims or poets and musicians who have come to pay homage to the dead and proclaim the greatness of Allah at celebrations and parties held in the gardens. You can also view the Taj from the opposite bank of the Yamuna (*access via the railway bridge open to pedestrians*). After passing through several busy villages (🙁*don't linger after nightfall*), you will reach the **Mehtab Bagh,** all that remains of old Mughal gardens (👉 *see Architecture*). The view is just right. You should have no trouble finding a boat to take you back (🚢 *approx. Rs.100*).

🙂 **Worth knowing** –Air pollution remains a serious problem, but Agra has benefited from government efforts to curb it in the last few years by the introduction of battery-operated transport in the area around the Taj Mahal.

AGRA FORT★★★

🕐 Open sunrise–sunset. 🎟 Rs.300 (Rs.250 with a ticket for the Taj dated the same day); video permit Rs.25. Allow 1hr30min for a visit. www.agrafort.gov.in.

There is no mistaking the military purpose of the formidable Agra Fort (also known as the 'Red Fort'), given its **double red-sandstone walls** surrounded by a deep **moat**. Today the site is occupied by the army and only the south-eastern section, which contains the most interesting buildings, is open to the public.

it was originally built by Akbar in 1565 on the site of a Rajput fortress constructed by the Chauhan tribe. His grandson, Shah Jahan, added palaces and mosques in white marble; however, the site has suffered much damage and pillage. The fort endured its last siege in 1857, during the Indian Rebellion; the British held out for four months behind its walls before being relieved by reinforcements arriving from Delhi.

Walk across the bridge leading to **Amar Singh Gate (Akbar Darwaza)★**, the southern gate, ignoring any harassment from rickshaw-drivers, souvenir-sellers and pseudo-guides hunting for their next generous client.

Amar Singh, a prince of Jodhpur, who was not well disposed towards the Mughals, was executed here on the orders of Shah Jahan in 1644.

The gate in the second wall opens onto a ramp leading to a courtyard garden flanked on the left by the red façade of the **Jahangiri Mahal★★**, the palace of Jahangir. Akbar had the palace built around 1585, which was lived in by his son Jahangir. The façade is punctuated by a series of mihrab-shaped blind arches on either side of a deep central *iwan*, through which you can enter the palace. Arranged around two courtyards, the rooms incorporate Hindu architectural forms (canopies, projections, plinths) along with Persian features (pointed arches), a blend of elements that is typical of Mughal architecture.

As you leave the palace and head back towards the ramp, pass through a monumental double door into the second courtyard garden. Admire the understated elegance of the **Diwan-i-Am★** ('Hall of Public Audiences') to the right, a pillared gallery in sandstone covered in stucco in which the emperor would receive guests regally in all his pomp.

A passage to the right leads to the fort's private apartments.

The **Anguri Bagh** ('Grape Garden'), a Mughal terrace surrounded by arcades on three sides, takes its name from some 300 bunches of grapes, made of gold,

Diwan-i-Khas, Agra Fort

© Anurag Mallick, Priya Ganapathy/MICHELIN

City of the Taj Mahal

Although mentioned in the *Mahabharata* **(5C–4C BC) and Ptolemy's** *Geographia* **(125 AD) under the name of Agrabana, the town does not emerge from the fog of history until 1492, when Sikandar Lodhi, the sultan of Delhi, established his court there. His successors preferred Delhi, but Agra regained its position as capital in 1526 under the reign of Babur, the first Mughal ruler. His son Humayun settled in Delhi before being driven out by Sher Shah, but a period of prosperity began for Agra with the rise to power of the emperor Akbar (1556–1605), attracting merchants, artists and scientists from all over the world.**

A CAPITAL SHUNNED

Akbar did not rule from Agra, a capital shunned In fact, for more than the first 15 years of his reign; in 1570 he transferred his capital to the entirely new city of Fatehpur Sikri, 38km east of Agra and then to Lahore, returning to Agra only to live out his last days. **Jahangir** (1605–27), Akbar's son, did not dally on the banks of the Yamuna either, shuttling instead among Lahore, Delhi and Agra. **Shah Jahan** (1627–58) definitively moved the capital to Delhi. His extravagant buildings enriched Agra, however, and none more so than the Taj Mahal.

AN UNGRATEFUL SON

In 1657, Emperor Shah Jahan was almost killed in an attempt on his life. False rumours of his death spread across all of northern India, causing three of his sons, Murad, Shuja and Aurangzeb, to begin a merciless struggle for the throne. When the true state of affairs was revealed, it did not stop Aurangzeb, the youngest, from seizing power; he imprisoned his father in Agra Fort in 1658 and eliminated his brothers. The death of Shah Jahan in 1666 marked the end of the architectural excesses of the Mughal Era: Aurangzeb's main contribution in the field was to destroy Hindu temples and replace them with mosques of no great artistic value.

PILLAGE AND DECLINE

The empire went into decline after the austere reign of Aurangzeb, with the rulers barely able to govern their own capital from their base in the Red Fort at Delhi. Agra was sacked by **Jats** from Bharatpur (1761) and Hindu **Marathis** (1770) before the British took control of the region in 1803. After independence, the old capital became no more than a city of middling size.

Taj Mahal Mosque

© Anurag Mallick, Priya Ganapathy/MICHELIN

rubies and emeralds, that once decorated it—treasures that are likely to have been looted by the Jats in 1761.

Opposite, the **Khas Mahal**★★ ('Private Palace'), a white marble structure used as an apartment by the emperor, is flanked by pavilions with half-moon Bengali roofs that overlook the Yamuna. You can just make out the silhouette of the Taj in the distance.

To the left is the **Shish Mahal** ('Palace of Mirrors') with its two small hammams, one for bathing in hot water and one for cold water.

The **Musamman Burj**★★ (octagonal tower) behind the bathhouses was used first as an apartment for Mumtaz Mahal, then as a prison—a gilded cage—for her husband, Shah Jahan, in the last years of his life; here he is said to have received visits from courtesans, who came to cheer him in his old age. He was able to look out on his beloved Taj Mahal from the window.

The stairs starting opposite the tower lead to a patio overlooked by a terrace where Shah Jahan built his **Diwan-i-Khas**★★ ('Hall of Private Audiences') to receive notable guests.

As you continue round the courtyard on the upper floor, you reach the delightful **Nagina Masjid**★, a miniature mosque reserved for the women of the palace; from the terrace you can see the domes of the **Moti Masjid** (Pearl Mosque, 1646), which is renowned for its elegance. It is located in the part of the fort that is closed to the public.

AROUND THE JAMA MASJID

Leave the fort and take a rickshaw to the Jama Masjid, on the other side of the railway tracks.

The **Jama Masjid** ('Friday mosque') was finished in 1648 but is less spectacular than its namesake in Delhi, which was also built by Shah Jahan. Situated at the end of a courtyard surrounded by arcades of multi-lobed arches and topped with three red and white striped domes, the mosque features a prayer hall covered with blue paintwork.

To the north is **Kinari Bazar Road**, the main thoroughfare through this traditional commercial district; few tourists come to stroll through its immense bazaars, so you won't be pestered as much here as elsewhere, while you explore a more authentic India.

ALSO SEE
LEFT BANK OF THE YAMUNA★

Hire a rickshaw or a taxi to visit these sights, which are spread out over a distance of approx. 4km down the Yamuna (there is nothing to be gained from walking it). Allow 2hr for the trip.

Tomb of I'timād-ud-Daulah★★

Located approx. 3km north-east of the Agra Fort. 🕐 *Open sunrise–sunset.* 📷 *Rs.110; video permit Rs.25.*

While Emperor Jahangir devoted himself to the pleasures of poetry and wine, his wife Noor Jahan governed the state with her father, the Persian **Mirza Ghiyas Beg**, who had been honoured with

A Good Wife

Shah Jahan lost **Mumtaz Mahal**, his favourite wife, the 'Chosen One of the Palace', as she was giving birth to their 14th child in 1631. The emperor decided to build her a mausoleum that matched his grief, a sort of palace of love: the 'Mumtaz Mahal', the 'Palace of the Chosen One'. In time, the name was changed to the 'Taj Mahal' ('Crown of Palaces' or 'Palace of the Crown') as the 'z' and the 'j' were represented by the same letter in Hindi. Work started in 1632 and lasted 12 years. Although the name of the chief architect cannot be established with any certainty (there is a 19C tradition that names the Persian Ustad Ahmad Lahauri), there is no doubt that Shah Jahan had some input in designing the plans. One story brought back by European travellers of the time relates that Shah Jahan intended to build an exact replica of the Taj Mahal—in black marble—on the other side of the Yamuna, which would be his own tomb.

the title I'timad-ud-Daulah ('Pillar of the State'). She built him this tomb upon his death in 1628 (four years before work was started on construction of the Taj Mahal), creating a delicate masterpiece that resembles a precious ivory box covered in carvings and inlay work.

The square floor plan, with four stocky minarets at its extremities, is reminiscent of the design chosen for the tomb of Jahangir in Lahore, but with more modest dimensions (Ghiyas Beg was not of royal blood!). A Hindu-style corbelled canopy juts out from the roof of the ground floor and the pavilion at the summit, blending with the Persian arches. The **façades★★** seem to have been painted by a pointillist or stitched by a lacemaker: the decoration is uninterrupted, alternating fine jali screens, white marble and **multi-coloured stone inlay**. This tomb was the first Mughal building to be made entirely of white marble using the pietra dura technique.

The walls and ceilings of the interior are painted in subtle shades of blue, brown and green that echo this technique in delicate motifs evoking the delights of Paradise: cypresses, pomegranates, irises, and phials containing the elixir of eternal life. The two sarcophagi of Noor Jahan's parents are located in the burial chamber on the ground floor; the first floor (🕐 *closed to the public*) houses cenotaphs set on paving stones whose curves and whorls resemble a carpet.

Chini ka Rauza
Located 1.5km further north. 🕐 *Open sunrise–sunset.* 🎟 *No charge. Worth a visit only if you have the time.*
This 'Tomb of Tiles' looking out over the river has been the resting place since 1639 of **Afzal Khan**, a Persian poet and Shah Jahan's prime minister. Only a few enamelled tile panels have survived on the walls of the abandoned tomb.

Ram Bagh Garden
600m to the north. 🕐 *Open sunrise– sunset.* 🎟 *Rs.100.*
Growing tired of Afghan parks, the emperor Babur had this walled garden

built upon his arrival in Agra. His mortal remains were interred here in 1530 before being transferred to Kabul. This Mughal garden or *char-bagh* ('garden in four sections'), one of the oldest in India, features pleasure pavilions and hammams on the banks of the Yamuna. The whole site echoes the Iranian symbolism wherein a garden resembles Paradise, but instead of being divided into eight sections like its Persian forerunners, it is separated into four by two canals that intersect at right angles in the centre.

Mehtab Bagh Garden
To the south, opposite the Taj Mahal. 🕐 *Open sunrise–sunset.* 🎟 *Rs.100.*
The 'Moonlight Garden' offers a unique view over the Taj Mahal complex, with the Yamuna in the foreground. The site was once a Mughal garden, and ages ago there were fountains surrounding a large octagonal pool. Its advantageous position has long provided support for Shah Jahan's unrealised 'black Taj'.

TOMB OF AKBAR THE GREAT AT SIKANDRA★★
Located 10km from the city centre on the road from Mathura and Delhi (approx. Rs.200 return fare by autorickshaw, with 1hr waiting time at the

Tomb of I'timād-ud-Daulah

Akbar, Enlightened Ruler of the East

Holding dominion over a territory the size of Europe and with a population of a hundred million inhabitants, Akbar has come down through history as the greatest ruler of northern India after the emperor Ashoka (3C BC). An adept politician and a great reformer, he centralised power and unified the currency, the language (imposing Persian as the language of the court) and his subjects: in order to minimise the differences between Muslims and non-Muslims, he abolished the taxes imposed on non-believers, disestablished Islam as the state religion and permitted inter-faith marriage. His curiosity and tolerance led him to surround himself with philosophers and theologians from every religion and to organise long ecumenical debates among them. He provided one of his sons with a Christian tutor, and under the guidance of a Zoroastrian master, even dreamt of creating a syncretist religious system that would subsume every existing tradition.

site). 🕐 *Open sunrise–sunset.* 🎟 *Rs.110. Allow 1hr if you are travelling by car. Complete this trip with a half-day excursion to Fatehpur Sikri or Mathura.* Here, on a site in the capital founded by Sikandar Lodhi, lies one of the major figures of Indian history: **Emperor Akbar the Great**, buried in a tomb appropriate to his stature, and constructed from plans he drew up himself. Work began in 1602 and was completed by his son Jahangir in 1613, eight years after Akbar's death.

The impressive **entrance gate** to the park is entirely covered with a multicoloured mosaic of red sandstone inlaid with white marble and decorated with purely geometric patterns. In a square at about mid-height that is repeated on both sides of the iwan you can see a Hindu swastika among the octagonal motifs, a hooked cross that was a symbol of good fortune. Once through the gate, you will find yourself in a pleasant park through which you can stroll at the end of your visit, accompanied by deer and a troupe of Langurs.

The **tomb**, the last of the Mughal era to be built in red sandstone, is located in the centre. It resembles a four-level pyramid adorned with galleries and chhatris (pavilions), in a style that has little in common with the Persian tradition despite the four pishtaqs surrounding it. The topmost floor, constructed entirely in white marble, is made up of a terrace surrounded by a jali or fretwork screen gallery.

The first chamber (as you enter) in the building is decorated with murals, gilt work and Quranic inscriptions. A dark corridor leads down to the **crypt**, which is entirely empty apart from the tomb; this was originally decorated with frescoes depicting the various religions of the world, but the fundamentalist Aurangzeb painted over them. Akbar's mortal remains were taken and scattered by the Jats in 1761, but the place can still evoke deep emotions (when less respectful visitors are not shouting to test the echo in the vault). True to the double burial tradition practised by the royals of the time, there is a false tomb or cenotaph on the terrace of the last floor. About 400m away on the right, in the direction of Delhi, you will see the **Tomb of Mariam-uz-Zamani** (🕐 *open sunrise–sunset;* 🎟 *Rs.100*), the last resting place of Heer Kunwari (known as Mariam in her Muslim incarnation), Akbar's Rajput first wife and the daughter of the maharajah of Amer.

😊 From Agra, you can add on a visit to Mathura or Bharatpur; the trip to Fatehpur Sikri, which is often advertised as an excursion from Agra, can also be made from Bharatpur if you prefer to stay in a less touristy atmosphere.

Entrance gate, Tomb of Akbar the Great at Sikandra

© Anurag Mallick, Priya Ganapathy/MICHELIN

ADDRESSES

🏨 STAY

Even though you may have pre-booked your accommodation, once in a taxi you may be offered a number of reasons to divert you from your initial choice, especially as the best-known hotels don't pay a commission: your hotel has burnt down/closed/is full (the driver may even phone in front of you and make you talk to 'reception' for proof!). You will find a plethora of low-budget guest houses, especially in the small roads south of the Taj Mahal, but no truly pleasant hotels, and certainly none in the luxury bracket. The area west of Fatehabad Rd, 5km from Agra Cantonment railway station, is an uninterrupted succession of hotels, restaurants and shops for tourists. Agra suffers daily power cuts: pick a hotel with a generator or get hold of a torch and some candles. Most of the hotels offer a 10–20% discount between April and September. The 'luxury' tax is 5%. There also a 7.42% service tax.

AROUND THE TAJ MAHAL

🛏 **Sheela** – *Map E2. East gate of the Taj.* ☎ *0562-2331194. www.hotelsheelaagra.com.* 📺✕🚿. *22 rm. Rs.600/800.* A hotel that stands out from the innumerable guesthouses of variable quality in the area. The rooms are simple and there is a garden full of flowers. Left luggage.

AROUND SADAR BAZAR

🛏 **Tourist Rest House** – *Map C4. 4/62 Kutchery Rd, Baluganj.* ☎ *0562-*

2463961. www.dontworrychickencurry.com. 📺✕🚿. *Internet. 30 rm. Rs.750/1,100.* 🛏 *Rs.150. Rest. Rs.250/350.* The best low-budget accommodation in Agra. The rooms are arranged in a U-shape around a little courtyard. The upstairs rooms get more light and have a veranda. The atmosphere is welcoming and everything is well maintained. The manager organises circular tours of Rajasthan.

🛏 **Lauries Hotel** – *Map B3. M.G. Rd, Pratap Pura.* ☎ *0562-242-14-47.* 📺🚿. *28 rm. Rs.975.* A large and rather decrepit white building that has clearly seen better days, with a vast lawn. There are single-price rooms that are large but poorly maintained. The hotel is nonetheless peaceful and the service is as friendly as it is respectful.

FATEHABAD RD

🛏 **Amar Yatri Niwas** – *Map E3. Fatehabad Rd.* ☎ *0562-2233030. www.amaryatriniwas.com.* 📺✕. *41 rm. Rs.1,300/2,500.* Rather more basic than its parent hotel, the Amar, but they will give you a warm welcome. Ask for a room with plenty of light (the windows are small). It's a pity that the paintwork and finishing leaves much to be desired.

🛏🛏 **Mayur Tourist Complex** – *Map E3. Fatehabad Rd.* ☎ *0562-2332302. www.mayurcomplex.com.* 📺✕🏊. *Internet. 24 rm. Rs.3,500* 🚿. Away from the road, with a family-friendly feel. Arranged around a pleasant flower garden, the bungalows have a bathtub and heating. There's a play area for children, as well as fountains.

Atithi – *Map E3. Set back from Fatehabad Rd, in a little street next to Pizza Hut.* 📞 *0562-2330880. www. hotelatithiagra.com.* 🖃 ✕ 🛏. *Internet. 44 rm. Rs.4,000/5,200.* 🍽 *Rs.250. Rest. Rs.400/450.* Everything is clean and the staff is pleasant, but the décor of the almost-identical rooms is lacking in warmth. Restaurant and coffee shop on the terrace.

Amar – *Map D3. Fatehabad Rd.* 📞 *0562-2331885. www.hotelamar.com.* 🖃 ✕ 🍷 🛏. *Spa, Ayurvedic massage, travel agency. 68 rm. Rs.3,300/5,800* 🍽. Good value for money, especially in the more expensive rooms. Twelve large suites that are truly kitsch. Avoid the rooms with no windows and those with fitted carpets. Smoking and non-smoking rooms. It is often full, so book in advance.

Howard Park Plaza – *Map E3. Fatehabad Rd.* 📞 *0562-4048600. www. howardplazaagra.com.* 🖃 ✕ 🍷 🛏. *79 rm. Rs.6,200/7,300* 🍽. A modern and very comfortable hotel, but with a slightly sad air to it and an atmosphere that is less pleasant than at the Mansingh. A beauty salon, and a good restaurant looking out onto the Taj.

Clarks Shiraz – *Map D4. 54 Taj Rd.* 📞 *0562-2226121. www.hotel clarksshiraz.com.* 🖃 ✕ 🍷 🛏. *Shopping arcade, beauty salon, spa, gym, Internet. 237 rm. Rs.7,000/9,500.* 🍽 *Rs.400. Rest. Rs.700/800.* This old hotel set in a 3-hectare garden is undeniably extremely chic. Coffee shop open 6am–midnight.

Mughal Sheraton – *Map E3. Fatehabad Rd, Taj Ganj.* 📞 *0562-4021700. www.starwoodhotels.com.* 🖃 ✕ 🍷 🛏. *Pool table, beauty salon, shops, fitness room, tennis court. 285 rm. Rs.7,500/10,000* 🍽. Some of the rooms have a distant view of the Taj Mahal. High standards and everything is fine, from the décor and fittings through to the restaurants and service. Often lots of groups stay here, so be sure to book in advance.

Mansingh Palace (Mansinghgroup) – *Map II E3. Fatehabad Rd.* 📞 *0562-2331771. www. mansinghhotels.com.* 🖃 ✕ 🍷 🛏. *97 rm. Rs.9,500/10,500.* 🍽 *Rs.700. Rest. Rs.1,200.* A modern hotel with style and a good reputation. Everything is as it should be, from the halls to the rooms and bathrooms. Good value for money even if the overall effect is lacking in warmth and has seen better days.

Jaypee Palace – *Map E4. Fatehabad Rd.* 📞 *0562-2330800. www. jaypeehotels.com.* 🖃 ✕ 🍷 🛏. *Pool table, spa, nightclub, tennis court. 350 rm, starting from Rs.13,000.* A luxury hotel out in the country. Its contemporary architecture and the materials used (lots of glass) make it a good example of its type.

Gateway Hotel (Taj Group) – *Map II E3. Fatehabad Rd, Taj Ganj.* 📞 *0562-6602000. www.thegatewayhotels.com.* 🖃 ✕ 🍷 🛏. *Shopping arcade. 100 rm. Rs.13,500/17,500* 🍽. Also known as the Taj View. A beautiful garden sheltered from the road with a swimming pool set among palm trees. Very tastefully decorated corridors and rooms. You can see the Taj Mahal from the more expensive rooms.

The Trident – *Map E4. Fatehabad Rd, Tajnagri Scheme (2km from the Tourist Area).* 📞 *0562-2335000. www. tridenthotels.com.* 🖃 ✕ 🛏. *Shops, Internet. 138 rm, starting from Rs.15,000* 🍽. The hotel maintains its own small kitchen garden for the restaurant.

🍴 EAT

AROUND THE TAJ MAHAL

The German bakeries are thriving in the little streets south of the Taj, alongside greasy cafes with often poor standards of hygiene, that have set up in the courtyards or on the roofs and attract young travellers on restricted budgets. On the menu: thalis, macaroni, banana crêpes, Israeli dishes. Sensitive stomachs

Frying jalebis

should pass: the food is not always as fresh as it might be.

AROUND SADAR BAZAR

Prakash – *Map B4. 49 Taj Rd. Open Sat–Thu 11am–10.30pm. Rs.100/150.* There's a choice of four types of thalis and chicken dishes amid décor that has been stripped back to the basics. Ideal for a quick lunch.

Dasaprakash – *Map C3. Meher Theatre Complex, Gwalior Rd. 0562-4016123. Noon–10.45pm. Rs.400/600.* This branch of the Dasaprakash in Delhi is a comfortable and stylish place to try the vegetarian specialities of the south. Some European dishes. The ice creams are renowned throughout Agra. The service is impeccable but the atmosphere noisy: the price of success.

Park Dining Room – *Map B4. 183-A Tal Rd, on the corner of Gopi Chand Shivhare. 0562-2226323. 10am–11pm. Rs.400/600.* Veggie, chicken and lamb dishes served in Mughlai, tandoori or Chinese style in a room with over-the-top décor. The service is efficient and speedy.

Zorba the Buddha – *Map B3. E-19 Shopping Arcade, Sadar Bazar. 0562-2226091. Closed in Jun. Noon–10pm. Rs.550/750.* Disciples of Osho will enjoy this clean small white room where fruit and vegetables are given pride of place on the menu, with soups and salads accompanied by cheese or spinach naan.

AROUND FATEHABAD RD

Devotees will stop off at the Pizza Hut on Fatehabad Rd next to the hotel Amar Yatri Niwas. The large hotels offer buffet meals: try the Clarks Shiraz and the Gateway when in a group (approx. Rs.800), and the Mughal Sheraton.

Only – *Map D3. 45 Taj Rd. 0562-2226834. Noon–10pm. Rs.500/700.* Depending on the weather, you can take a seat on the lawn or in a large, bamboo-panelled room. The service is a bit hectic and the tablecloths could do with a good wash, but you will enjoy the tasty and well-executed Mughal dishes (although it has been adapted to Western tastes). Live music in the evenings.

Priya – *Map E4. Fatehabad Rd. 0562-2231579. Noon–10.30pm. Rs.650/800.* The dining room, which is clean and austere, is decorated with just three kitsch prints. Unimpeachably classic Mughal cuisine, especially the

shahi korma gosht (lamb with cream and dried fruit). There is a pleasant terrace upstairs and the service is attentive. Buffet for Rs.350 at noon and in the evenings.

Sheesh Mahal – *Map E3. The Mansingh Palace Hotel restaurant. Noon–3pm, 7pm–midnight. Rs.700/1,000.* Serves Mughal dishes, accompanied by ghazals from 8pm.

The Mughal Room – *Map D4. Rest. on the 5th floor of the Hotel Clarks Shiraz. 12.30pm–2.45pm, 7pm–11.30pm. Rs.1,200/1,500.* The setting is agreeable and the service stylish. Try the *murgh begum baha*, stuffed chicken with a cashew nut sauce. *Ghazals* from 8.30pm.

TAKING A BREAK

Ripples – *Coffee shop at the Mansingh Palace Hotel. Fatehabad Rd. 24hr.* People come here for the ambience and the airy, light surroundings, as neither the Indian nor the international cooking holds many surprises.

BARS

Maikhana – *Bar at the Mughal Sheraton Hotel. Noon–midnight.* The soft banquettes and hushed atmosphere are very welcome at the end of the afternoon when it's time for a beer or a cup of tea. Music group 6 days a week.

Tapas – *Bar at the Jaypee Palace Hotel. Noon–midnight. Admission fee.* Numerous themed bars. Pool table, table tennis, video games, bowling, disco.

SHOPPING

EVERYDAY ITEMS

Sadar Bazar – *Map B3. Wed–Mon.* The largest commercial district in the **Cantonment**. Come here for products for everyday use.

HANDICRAFTS

The handicrafts and souvenir shops *(open daily)* are concentrated south of the Taj Mahal and in the **Tourist Area**. Take particular care as scams and tricks are par for the course in Agra. Avoid paying by bank card and negotiate firmly on prices.
Cottage Industries Exposition (CIE) – *Map II D3. 39 Fatehabad Rd. 8.30am–8pm.* Located in a pretty bungalow perched on a rise between the Amar Hotel and the Only restaurant, with handicraft items from the Agra and Kashmir regions

(shawls, embroidery, carpets). Rather high prices, but quality products.

Shilpgram§ – *off map, Map E2. 1km east of the Taj Mahal.* This complex of open-air stalls was created by Uttar Pradesh Tourism to showcase different artisans every month. Poorly maintained and most often deserted, it is of little interest apart from during the annual Taj Mahotsav festival (⊙*see EVENTS AND FESTIVALS below*).

INLAID MARBLE
You will find boxes, glass placemats and table tops in the artisans' stalls in the small street south of the Taj Mahal. Don't confuse genuine marble or alabaster inlaid with precious stones using the *pietra dura* technique with the imitations in soapstone and coloured glass, which are sold in the less scrupulous souvenir shops. Remember that fine materials requiring hours of painstaking work are also more likely to command higher prices. There are two reputable manufacturers at Sadar Bazar (⊙ *open daily*): **Subhash Emporium**, *18/1 Gwalior Rd* (⊙ *open daily 10am–7pm*), and the slightly more expensive **Oswal Emporium**, *30 Munro Rd* – both are privately owned.

CARPETS
People have been making woollen and silk carpets in Agra since the time of the Great Mughals, but these days the carpets are more likely to be artificial than natural, despite what some of the sellers may tell you. You will find carpets and dhurris (rugs) in the Main Bazaar and the Tourist Area.

JEWELLERY
Kohinoor – *Map B2. 41 M.G. Rd, on the corner of Chhipitola Rd. ☏ 0562-2460856. www.kohinoorjewellers.com. 10am–7pm.* A jeweller's shop renowned for five generations for the quality of its precious stones. There is also a small embroidery museum.

EMBROIDERY
Muslim craftworkers have developed a type of embroidery known as *zari*, using silver or gold thread on black velvet. Another speciality is surface embroidery, which is much prized in the Middle East, where it is used to make three-dimensional tableaux. One of the most renowned artisans is Sheikh Shasuddin, who shows at Kohinoor.

CULINARY SPECIALITIES
Agra's edible treats, which are sold in namkeen shops and sweet shops, include *dalmoth*, a mixture of fried and savoury yellow lentils, *petha*, crystallised gourd flesh, and *gazak*, with a brown sugar and sesame base.

BOOKSHOPS
Modern Book Depot – *Map B4. Taj Rd, Sadar Bazar. ☏ 0562-2225695. Wed–Mon 10am–9pm.* Several classics about India. Good bookshops at the Clarks Shiraz, Mughal Sheraton and the Gateway (Taj View) hotels.

IN THE EVENING
Archaeological Survey of India – *Map B3. 22 The Mall, opposite the Indian tourist office. ☏ 0562-2227263. www.asi.nic.in. 10am–6pm, book a day ahead.* If you would like to admire the Taj by night under a full moon in a group of 50 people closely surrounded by police, buy your ticket here (*Rs.750, 40min visit*).

SPORTS AND ACTIVITIES
Swimming pool – Several hotels (Amar, Atithi, Agra Ashok, Mansingh) open their swimming pools to non-residents. Expect to pay Rs.150-200/day.

EXCURSIONS
All the travel agencies offer guided tours combining the Taj with Agra Fort as well as trips to Fatehpur Sikri and Sikandra. It will cost from Rs.1,800 for a half-day excursion and Rs.2,500 for the whole day. For Mathura, allow 1hr30min travelling time and Rs.3,000–3,500 for a day trip, including Vrindavan. For Bharatpur, allow 1hr15min travelling time.

⊙ **Worth knowing** – Organised tours often attract criticism for preferring to stop at shops rather than spending time at the sights themselves. Remember that all these trips are easy to make on your own, too, either by bus or car.

EVENTS AND FESTIVALS
Taj Mahotsav – *www.tajmahotsav.org. 10 Jan–Feb.* Fair bringing craftworkers from all over the country to the Shilpgram. 'Mughal' procession with elephants, dromedaries and food-tasting stalls.

Fatehpur Sikri★★★

The road from Agra crosses a well-cultivated, fertile plain. Along it you may see some 'tame' bears with black fur, accompanied by their masters, always willing to enforce some twirls and dance steps for a few rupees (do not encourage them). The red walls of the ghostly city suddenly rise before you, the glorious remnants of the old Mughal capital, perched on a low hill. Fatehpur, the 'City of Victory', has a rather tranquil air, and for good reason: the old city, the former capital of Emperor Akbar, has been virtually uninhabited for four centuries, except for the stone masons whose ancestors built the astonishing palaces in red sandstone that survive to this day.

🐾 WALKING TOUR

JAMA MASJID★★★

🕐 *Open sunrise–sunset.* 💰 *No charge. Take off your shoes and keep them with you during your visit. Allow 3hr. Start the visit from the south.*

Enter the **'Friday mosque'** through the **Buland Darwaza★★★**, the triumphal entrance built by Akbar in 1575 to commemorate his victory over the sultan of Gujarat. 'The world is a gate. Pass over it, but build no houses upon it' is inscribed in Persian on the inside wall. The vast red sandstone courtyard is enclosed on three sides by arcades topped with square *chhatris* (pavilions) arranged at regular intervals.

Upon entering, your eye is drawn to a marvellous construction in white marble: the **Tomb of Sheikh Salim**

▶ **Population:** 31,000.

ℹ **Info:** 38km from Agra, 26km from Bharatpur. ♿ See also Getting There/Leaving.

🕐 **Timing:** Allow 2hr to visit the essentials, 3hr30min to see everything. Take a half-day excursion from Agra (where you can hire a car) and combine the trip with visiting the tomb of Akbar the Great at Sikandra (Agra). It is easy to make the trip on your own from Bharatpur; allow a half-day. Avoid the weekend – the site is crowded.

Buland Darwaza

GETTING THERE/LEAVING

BY TRAIN– The railway station is 1km south-east of Jama Masjid. There are 4 trains a day for Agra Fort (1hr).

BY BUS – The buses stop on the main road opposite Buland Darwaza (southern entrance to the mosque, 5min walk). Frequent departures for Agra (approx. 1hr) from 6am until 8pm. Approx. 6 buses a day for Bharatpur (30min).

BY TEMPO – Shared taxis for Bharatpur and Agra on the main road 1km north-east of the site; they leave when they are full (approx. every 20min).

SIGHTSEEING

A visit to Fatehpur Sikri is included in a range of organised tours leaving from Agra and Delhi. Further information from the travel agencies in these two cities.

Chishti★★ *(cover your head and make a small donation)*. The *pir* (Muslim saint), a descendant of the Sufi saint buried at Ajmer, used to withdraw to this place to pray. Upon his death in 1572, Emperor Akbar had a tomb built here in red sandstone, which was later enclosed in a galleried pavilion with jali screens of incomparable delicacy, under the rule of Jahangir in 1606. It was the first Mughal monument to be built entirely of white marble. Note the prominent cornice supported by elegant curved brackets. To one side of this, the red sandstone **Tomb of Islam Khan** houses the last resting place of one of the saint's nephews, who was governor of Bengal at the turn of the 17C. Gravestones marking the tombs of relatives and disciples of Sheikh Salim Chishti are spread out between the two tombs: there are only men here; the women are buried in the arcades running behind the two tombs; this sacred place is known as **Zanana Rauza**.

The **prayer hall** of the Jama Masjid, located on the west side of the courtyard, is identified by a gigantic *pishtaq* (monumental gateway).

Inside, there are three *mihrabs* (niches) to indicate the direction of Mecca. The central one, lavishly accentuated with enamelled tiles, features a *minbar*, the pulpit from which the imam preaches the Friday sermon.

▶ To reach the palace, leave the mosque via the **Badshahi Darwaza** ('Royal Gate'), the entrance used by the emperor.

THE PALACES★★★

🕐 *Open sunrise–sunset.* 📷 *Rs.260; video Rs.25. Guides offer their services at the entrance (Rs.200 for 2hr). Brochures in English.*

In the 16C, Fatehpur had as many inhabitants as Agra. Nowadays, the private houses made of brick have disappeared from the hillsides on which they once stood and only the red sandstone palaces remain. These palaces perfectly express the syncretism so beloved of Akbar in their blend of Turko-Persian features (clearly defined structures, pointed arches) and elements from the Hindu tradition (entablature with cornices and brackets, an overabundance of ornamentation).

Birbal's House★★★

Take a left turn immediately after the ticket office to reach the **lower Haramsara**; this vast courtyard probably housed the quarters of the harem servants, rather than stables, as was once thought. At the far northern end is **Birbal's** House (the residence of one of the emperor's advisors), which was, in fact, the home of one of Akbar's wives or daughters. The whole building is covered with a network of curves and interlacing patterns of extraordinary delicacy, carved to resemble woodwork.

▶ Turn right.

Detail of the carving work, Birbal's House

© Tibor Bognár/age fotostock

Jodha Bai's Palace★★

This palace was named in honour of one of Akbar's Hindu wives, daughter of the maharajah of Jodhpur.

Take the eastern entrance through a porch overlooked by *jharokhas* (covered balconies) and flanked by niches in which stand armed eunuchs. The rooms are arranged around a single central courtyard. Note the small sanctum installed on the western side, opposite the entrance, for the Hindu wives.

▷ Exit from the palace.

Haramsara★ ('Women's Quarters')

To the south-east.

According to Father Monserrate, a Portuguese Jesuit who stayed at the emperor's court, this harem housed up to 300 wives, who were guarded by Rajput warriors and eunuchs.

Maryam's House

To the left as you leave Jodha Bai's Palace. Also known as the 'golden house', this house was the home of both Akbar's mother and his first wife, the daughter of the maharajah of Amer (both were given the name Maryam in their Muslim titles). The corbels of the façade feature carvings of geese and elephants, typical Hindu motifs, as well as of gods Rama and Hanuman, while inside, the blue paint and gilt is gradually fading. The Lady's Gardens are located at the rear.

A Fleeting Mughal Capital

In 1570, at the height of his power, Emperor Akbar (who reigned 1556–1605), undertook the removal of his capital from Agra to a site at Sikri of no particular strategic or economic interest. His main motivation, aside from the kudos of founding a new city, was to be closer to **Sheikh Salim Chishti**, a Sufi saint he venerated. The saint had prophesied the birth of three sons to the emperor, who at the time was still without issue; when a child (the future Jahangir) glimpsed the light of day the following year, he was named Salim in honour of the saint. Akbar then had an entire town built on the promontory at Sikri, surrounded by ramparts on three sides and flanked on the fourth by a lake that is now partially filled in. It proved difficult to supply the city with water, however, and the location was also too far from the empire's main roads and vulnerable borders. Akbar decided to abandon it from 1585 and transferred his court to Lahore (now in Pakistan). An outbreak of plague at the turn of the 17C finally emptied the city of its inhabitants.

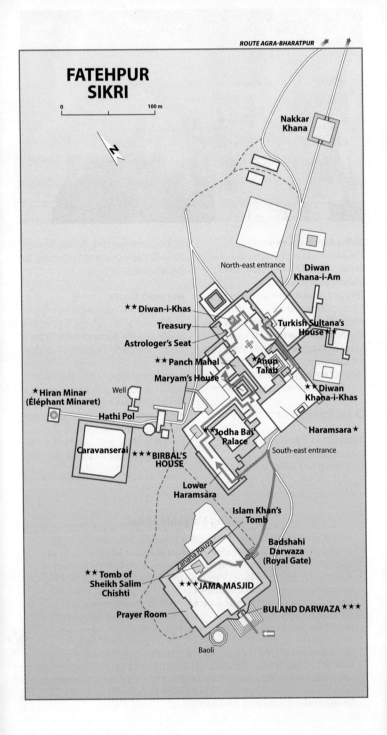

FATEHPUR SIKRI

0   100 m

N

Nakkar Khana

North-east entrance

Diwan Khana-i-Am

★★ Diwan-i-Khas

Treasury

Astrologer's Seat

Turkish Sultana's House ★★

★★ Panch Mahal

★ Anup Talab

Maryam's House

★ Hiran Minar (Éléphant Minaret)

Well

★★ Diwan Khana-i-Khas

Hathi Pol

Caravanserai

★★★ BIRBAL'S HOUSE

★★ 'Jodha Baï' Palace

Haramsara ★

South-east entrance

Lower Haramsàra

Islam Khan's Tomb

Badshahi Darwaza (Royal Gate)

Zenana Hauza

★★ Tomb of Sheikh Salim Chishti

★★★ JAMA MASJID

Prayer Room

BULAND DARWAZA ★★★

Baoli

Panch Mahal

© Julien Leblay/Fotolia.com

Panch Mahal★★
('Five-storey Palace')

Easily recognisable from afar with its high, triangular silhouette, this palace marks the boundary of the men's quarters. Its five hypostyle floors of decreasing size are stacked up like a house of cards. It is said that each of the 176 carved columns is different. The building must at some point in the past have been enclosed by jali screens that captured the breeze and made it an ideal place to sleep during the hot nights of summer.

Diwan-i-Khas★★
('Hall of Private Audiences')

Standing alone, north of the esplanade. The four *chhatris* (pavilions) rising from the corners of the roof terrace originally probably surrounded a larger central pavilion that has now been lost. The doors on each of the four sides lead to a room whose centre is marked by an extraordinary **column★★★**. It rises to meet an enormous capital made of a succession of brackets supporting a circular platform. Four walkways run to the central balcony, on which the emperor, the ruler of the four corners of the world, would sit enthroned. Seated here on a dais, he would receive visitors of note or preside over philosophical and religious debates.

As you leave, look out for the **stone rings** above on the façade; you will see similar features on many other buildings, which were used to attach marquees, awnings, tents and *vetiver* (sweet-smelling grass root) screens. They were slung between the buildings on posts, to provide protection from the sun or to mark out private spaces, creating portable architecture reminiscent of the way of life of the Turco-Mongols, Akbar's ancestors.

Treasury

West of the Diwan-i-Khas.

The state's gold was piled up in these three rooms, and legend has it that this pavilion was the location of riotous games of blind man's buff between the emperor and his courtesans, hence his nickname 'Ankh Michauli' ('eyes shut'). The pavilion nearby, known as the **'Astrologer's Seat'**, features delicately carved **arches** *(torana),* which were inspired by the work of Jain sculptors. Was this pavilion really the home of the court astrologer or was it used by the emperor himself, who from here could watch the movement of the pawns on the giant chessboard *(pachisi)* spread out in the shape of a cross on the flagstones at the centre of the esplanade? The chessboard was in fact a *chaupar,* a game resembling draughts or checkers; chroniclers record that naked slaves and prisoners of war were called upon to act as pieces.

▶ Head towards the centre of the esplanade.

Turkish Sultana's House★★
On your left.
This delightful L-shaped pavilion, styled like a wooden cabin, is surrounded by a veranda of exquisite workmanship. Within, there are bas-relief panels depicting lions and birds frolicking in lush vegetation. The square pool, **Anup Talab★**, divided into four sections like a reverse *char-bagh* (Mughal garden), holds a platform where musicians and dancers would take their places to beguile the emperor's evenings.

Diwan Khana-i-Khas★★
('Hall House of Private Audiences')
This day room looking out over the pool was used by the emperor as a place to work; seated on a high tribune that was covered with carpets, he would receive advisors, and from the window looking out onto the Archives courtyard to the south, he would present himself every morning to his subjects to offer them his *darshan* in assurance of his good health.

▶ Go back across the esplanade, heading north.

Diwan Khana-i-Am
('Hall House of Public Audiences')
Enter the hall house by the eastern portal to find a courtyard surrounded by porticos in which the emperor dispensed justice.
If you are not tired, head for the western side of the plateau *(accessible via a series of paths)*. The road leads through the **Hathi Pol** (Elephants' Gate), beside a **caravanserai,** and finally to Hiran Minar.

Hiran Minar★
The **Hiran Minar** ('Elephant Minaret'; named after Hiran, Akbar's favourite elephant, who lies buried beneath it), bristles with stone defences. Beyond, you will see the polo pitch.

ADDRESSES

🛏 STAY

If you wish to explore the site at first light, here are a few places to stay locally; you won't find the same value for money as in Bharatpur, 30min up the road. Avoid the hotels around the bus station (poor hygiene).

🛏 **Goverdhan Tourist Complex** – *Buland Darwaza Rd Crossing, 400m from the bus stop.* ☏ *05613-282643. www. hotelfatehpursikriviews.com.* ✕ 🍽. *15 rm. Rs.875/1,250.* 🍴 *Rs.250.* The rooms are arranged round a large, well-manicured lawn. This complex is the most comfortable place in town.

🛏 **Gulistan Tourist Complex (UPTDC)** – *First hotel as you arrive in Fatehpur, on the left after the Agra Gate, 1km from the bus stop.* ☏ *05613-282490.* ▦ ✕ 🍽 🍴. *24 rm. Rs.1,250/1,600* 🍴. A hotel run by the State of Uttar Pradesh and you can tell: scant attention has been paid to the finishing touches and maintenance is limited. The single-storey building arranged around a courtyard is damp; however, it wouldn't take much to make this a pleasant place to stop.

🍴 EAT

There are several low-budget places to eat around the Buland Darwaza. For a bit more comfort:

🍴 **Gulistan Tourist Complex (UPTDC)** – *The restaurant at the hotel.* 🍷🍴. *6am–10pm. Approx. Rs.300.* This is the only decent place to get a beer. Have it brought out to the courtyard garden, which is more pleasant than the large dining room, which is a bit like a canteen. If a group is passing through, there will be a buffet, otherwise the menu features classics such as chicken tikka, dal makhani, palak-paneer etc.

🍴🍴 **Joshi Resort** – *20km to the east, on the road to Agra (NH 11).* ☏ *9412259579. Rs.400/550.* Those with a car will prefer to dine here, under the parasols. Tandoori food and continental or Chinese dishes. Try the thali, which is made up of 12 different dishes.

EVENTS AND FESTIVALS

Urs de Sheikh Salim Chishti – During Ramadan. Qawwalis are sung non-stop in front of the saint's dargah (tomb).

Bharatpur★★

In the 18C, Bharatpur, a sizable agricultural town situated on a cultivated plain, was the capital of the only Jat kingdom of any significance in India. It retains the formidable fortifications of the period, but the city's principal attraction is its bird sanctuary, one of the richest in the world and declared a World Heritage Site by UNESCO. Occupying a wetland valley, the park is a natural paradise: some of the 365 species of birds can be found here, including the Sarus crane, but especially the critically endangered Siberian crane. Bharatpur also serves as a useful base for visiting the Deeg Palace, and possibly Fatehpur Sikri, too.

THE PARK AND TOWN

Many people come to Bharatpur to see the thousands of migratory birds that spend the winter in the national park. *The most interesting time to visit to see the birds is October to February.*

Keoladeo Ghana National Park★★

Bird Sanctuary Rd. www.rajasthan wildlife.com. Open daily sunrise–sunset. Closed May and Jun. Rs.400; video Rs.200. Car Rs.100 (access restricted to a zone up to approx. 1.5km from the entrance); after that, only pedestrians and cycle rickshaws are allowed. Guide (Rs.100/hr for 1 to 5 people), cycle rickshaws (Rs.70/hr/ person), binoculars (Rs.50/day) can be hired at the entrance. Allow at least 3hr. This national park was inscribed on the UNESCO World Heritage List in 1985 but has been in existence much longer. It dates from the mid-18C when it was a duck hunting reserve. Maharajah Suraj Mal ordered a dam to be built at the confluence of two rivers, creating a wet-land area suitable for ducks and other migratory birds, although the birds were ill-advised to come here: the Bharatpur archives record details of large hunting parties.

▸ **Population:** 263,000.

▯ **Info: Tourist Reception Centre** – At the far eastern end of Bird Sanctuary Rd, 4km south of the old town. Open daily 9.30am–5.30pm. Photos of resident and migratory species. Maps.

◐ **Location:** 56km from Agra, 174km from Jaipur, 251km from Delhi. Lohagarh Fort, surrounded by walls and moats, marks the centre of Bharatpur, a city of medium size. The train station is 3.5km north on the road to Mathura. The Main Bus Stand is located outside the town, to the west. The Keoladeo Ghana National Park (popularly known as the Bharatpur Bird Sanctuary) borders Bird Sanctuary Rd (the road to Jaipur), 5km south of the city centre. The tourist office and most of the guest houses are located approx. 700m east of the entrance to the park, near the crossroads at the Hotel Saras. The bus stop for the Agra–Jaipur route is also here.

▲▲ **Kids:** Cycle-rickshaw ride in the bird sanctuary.

◔ **Timing:** Allow at least a half-day (3hr for Keoladeo Ghana National Park and 45min for the town). Get up at dawn to be in the park when it opens. Bring a pair of binoculars. Avoid weekends, public holidays and school holidays as the noisy crowds scare the birds.

◉ **Don't Miss:** Keoladeo Ghana National Park (bird sanctuary).

GETTING THERE/LEAVING

BY TRAIN – Railway Station – 3.5km north of the town and 7km from the wildlife park. ✆ 139 (booking centre). There are 9 trains per day to Delhi (3hr to 4hr30min journey time), via Mathura (approx. 1hr) and 4 to 6 trains per day to Jaipur (approx. 3hr); frequent departures for Kota (3hr30min to 5hr), via Sawai Madhopur (2hr30min) as well as to Agra (1hr to 2hr).

BY BUS – Main Bus Stand – To the west, 4km from the wildlife park. ✆ 05644-260330. Express services stop every hour at Bharatpur, on the way to Jaipur (4hr) or Agra (1hr30min). Frequent departures to Delhi (4hr), 24hr; every 2 hours to Alwar (2hr) via Deeg (1hr15min). There are 2 or 3 buses per day to Ajmer (7hr) and Jodhpur (12hr) but it is better to change at Jaipur.

⊛ **Worth knowing** – Most buses go via the Hotel Saras (Saras Circle) crossroads, opposite the Tourist Reception Centre, near the hotels. Get off here and not at the bus station, 4km away.

TEMPO (motorised rickshaw) – This is the best way to get to Fatehpur Sikri. Tempos leave every 15 minutes from Saras Circle (20km, 30min drive).

GETTING AROUND

RICKSHAW – From the station to the wildlife park, expect to pay Rs.50–80 in an auto-rickshaw. Cycle rickshaws are used around the park (approx. Rs.50/hr), almost all driven by Sikhs. Those allowed to enter the reserve have a yellow plate.

TONGA – Two-wheeled carriage (approx. Rs.100/hr).

HIRING BICYCLES – From guest houses and at the entrance to the park (Rs.40/day). The most pleasant way to visit the reserve.

SAFETY

In the event of any dispute or scam:
Tourist Assistance Force, at the bus and train stations, near the City Palace and at Amer.
Police – ✆ 05644-222444..

Some 365 bird species from across Afghanistan, Turkmenistan, China and Siberia spend the winter here. The park spreads over 29 sq km of marshes rich in grasses and reeds, shaded by trees whose delicate foliage allows the light to pass through. Thanks to raised walkways, the sanctuary can still be explored even when it is submerged beneath the monsoon waters.

The main season for birdwatching is August and March, but there is something of interest to see each month. During the first rains (early Jul), the park is filled with birds nesting and breeding: herons, egrets, white ibis and grouse. During the winter (Oct–Feb), the reserve is at its busiest, with Greylag geese, Indian storks, ibis, darters, marabous, raptors, Sarus cranes, and the star attraction, Siberian cranes, an endangered species. The park has its permanent residents, including several varieties of duck, as well as many deer, otters, mongooses and monkeys.

Visitor Centre

On the edge of the vehicle zone, at the 2nd checkpoint.

Pictures of various bird markings help visitors to identify the different species. There is information on the threats to the birds: some have shunned the reserve in recent years due to recurrent water shortages (insufficient monsoon rainfall, the creation in 2003 of a dam upstream restricting the flow of water).

Lohagarh Fort

North of Bharatpur Bazaar. Allow 45min; hire a cycle rickshaw and ask it to wait 20min while you visit the museum.

Lohagarh means 'Iron Fort', and it is a building that fully deserves its name. Built in the early 18C, it has withstood any number of attacks from the Mughals

Sarus cranes, Keoladeo Ghana National Park
© Ramanan Padmanabhan/MICHELIN

and the British, although it was eventually captured by the latter in 1826. The fort is entered across a moat and through a door in the great **walls★**, one of two doors that Rajah Jawahar Singh brought to the fort as a trophy following the sack of Delhi in 1764. The door in the north wall had already suffered a similar fate, having been torn from the walls of Chittaurgarh and taken to Delhi in 1303. Inside the fort there are three palaces, all in poor condition.

Government Museum

🕐 *Open Tue–Sun 10am–5pm.* 👓 *Rs.10.*
The museum occupies two wings of the palace in the centre of the fort. An interesting collection of **sculptures** date from the 10C to the 18C. A pretty **hammam★** is at the back of the right wing, but all have been poorly looked after. There are fine views of Bharatpur and its ancient palaces from the terrace.

GOVARDHAN★

16km east of Deeg on road to Mathura.
The **royal cenotaphs** (19C) of two maharajahs of Bharatpur are found in the countryside on the edge of a lake. They are located near the town of Govardhan, a centre of pilgrimage for Krishna. Crowned by pavilions and Bengali roofs with gilded pinnacles, they lie opposite a 16C temple of Hari (another name for Vishnu). The cenotaph commemorating **Ranjit Singh** (*closed to the public*) is the most lavish.

EXCURSION TO DEEG

Half-day trip from Bharatpur or Mathura, or spend the night at Fort Kesroli. Buses run 7am–8pm, every 30–45min to and from Bharatpur (1hr, 32km) and Mathura (1hr, 35km), and every hour for Alwar (2hr30min, 70km).
It is hard to believe that this small agricultural town, with a population of 45,000, was the summer capital of a powerful **Jat principality** in the 18C. United under **Badan Singh** of Bharatpur, the Jats carved out a kingdom stretching from Delhi to Agra. Forced to recognise this new power, the Mughal emperor granted Singh the title of rajah in 1752. The subsequent rajahs, Suraj Mal and Jawahar Singh, became even more daring, looting Delhi and Agra in the 1760s, and bringing back booty that they used to decorated and enriched their two capitals, Bharatpur and Deeg. Faced with both Maratha and

Wanton Destruction

In British India, duck hunting at Bharatpur was a major event. A fleet of Rolls-Royces (a passion of the maharajahs of Bharatpur) would deposit prestigious guests in the park, who, once let loose, would shoot great numbers of birds. In 1914, Lord Hardinge, Viceroy of India, killed 4,082 birds in a single day; similar slaughters took place in 1921 and in 1938.

Deeg's Colorful Fountains

Deeg's chief attraction is its coloured fountains. Surprisingly, all 2000 of them are in working condition! Instead of different lights being projected on plain water fountains, in this case the water itself was coloured. The colourful fountains are put into action twice a year: 4 February and 8 days after Janmashtami, in the last week of August.

British invaders, Jat power waned, and in 1818 the rajah of Bharatpur was the first ruler of Rajasthan to sign a treaty with the British.

Deeg Palace★

200m from the bus station. ⏰ *Open Sat–Thu 9.30am–5.30pm.* 👁 *Rs.100. Allow at least 1hr for your visit.*

After travelling on a bumpy and dusty road on the flat plain, you see the palace appear before you like a mirage.

The ruler of Bharatpur, **Badan Singh**, began to build a palace at Deeg in 1730. It was enlarged and embellished regularly by successive 18C rajahs.

Two pavilions, with Bengali roofs jutting out over a pool of water in which they are reflected, flank the striking pink façade. Follow the main path to enter the **Mughal garden★**. Divided into four equal sections by canals, according to a classic char bagh plan, it contains

500 fountains (which only operate on Saturdays during August). Palaces and pavilions surround it on all sides, the most notable being the Gopal Bhawan, to the west.

ADDRESSES

🏠 STAY / 🍴 EAT

Guest houses are clustered east of the bird reserve, along the road to Jaipur. You can hire binoculars and books on ornithology from some. Given the lack of proper restaurants, the best place to dine is at one of these places.

🛏 **Birder's Inn** *Bird Sanctuary Rd.* 📞 *05644 227346, 222830. www.birdersinn. com. Rs.2,975. rm24. Wi-Fi, no wheelchair access,* 🛏. Great service, proximity to the park gate (200m) and a pool confirms why this is the No.1 perch for birders and photographers. Run by wildlife enthusiast Tirath Singh, the inn has attentive staff, clean spacious rooms, good food besides access to cycles, rickshaws and expert guides for park visits right at the doorstep. Has a small store with bird paintings and local handicrafts. Packed lunches are available for serious birders.

🛏 **Falcon Guest House** – *Next to the Jungle Lodge.* 📞 *05644-223815. www. falconguesthouse.com.* 🍽 ✂ 📶. *16 rm. Rs.600/1,000.* 🛏 *Rs.250.* A small place run by a friendly family. The bedrooms are spacious and well kept; some have a bath. There is also a garden.

🛏 **Jungle Lodge** – *In an alley east of Bird Sanctuary Rd, beyond the tourist office.* 📞 *05644-225622. www.junglelodge.dk.*

Keshav Bhawan, Deeg Palace

© Anurag Mallick, Priya Ganapathy/MICHELIN

🖼✕🍷🚬. *8 rm, including 4 with a cooler. Rs.600/1,200.* A nice family guest house with spacious bedrooms overlooking a small flowered lawn. The owner is a naturalist and can give information about the birds in the reserve.

😊😊 **Sunbird** *– Bird Sanctuary Rd.* 📞 *05644-225701. www.hotelsunbird.com.* 🖼✕🍷🚬. *10 rm. Rs.2,300/3,400 🛏. Rest. Rs.150/200.* A brick building in a garden, close to the reserve. Decent rooms, but ask for ones set back from the road, which is very busy. Picnic hampers are available for trips to the park.

😊😊 **Bharatpur Ashok Forest Lodge** *– 1.5km inside the park.* 📞 *05644-222722. www.bharatpurashok.com.* 🖼✕🍷. *17 rm. Rs.4,700.* This hotel's key attraction (it is run by the India Tourism Development Corporation) is its location among the trees and animals in the heart of Keoladeo National Park. The rooms themselves are fairly nondescript and the lodge surroundings somewhat neglected. Pleasant terrace restaurant.

😊😊😊 **Laxmi Vilas Palace (Heritage Hotels Assn)** *– On the old road to Agra, 2.5km from the park.* 📞 *05644-231199. www.laxmivilas.com.* 🖼✕🍷🛁. *Internet, exchange, massage. 30 rm. Rs.7,000/8,000. 🛏 Rs.300. Rest. Rs.750.* A small palace, pleasantly decorated in the late 19C Rajput style. Rooms and bathrooms have been renovated in the colonial style. Lots of character and a good restaurant and bar in a columned hall and courtyard. Excursions in the region available.

😊😊😊 **The Bagh Agra** *– Achnera Rd.* 📞 *05644-228333, 225415, www.thebagh.com. Rs.7,500-9,000. 23 rm. Wi-Fi, 🛏.* Vintage garden retreat spread over 12.5 acres with arched pavilions, fountains and marble wall inlays around an orchard of gooseberry, amaltas and rudraksha trees. Once owned by the Bharatpur rajas, it was designed as a *char-bagh* 200 years ago. The renovated rooms once housed their officers and horses, while the old well supplied water to the entire area. Feast on kebabs, Braj cuisine and regional delights such as papad ki sabzi, gatte ki sabzi and mirchi bada. Facilities include indoor and outdoor bars, a library, pool and vintage car ride to the bird sanctuary in a 1935 Ford Saloon Limousine or a WWII Ford Willy Jeep (Rs.4,000-5,000 for min 2 people). A new annexe with modern villas (15 rooms planned, 9 ready) has just been added.

😊😊😊😊 **Hotel Udai Vilas Palace** *NH-11, Fatehpur Sikri Road.* 📞 *05644-233161-2. www.udaivilaspalace.com Rs.4,400-14,000. 57 rm. Wi-Fi.* Not to be mistaken for its swanky namesake in Udaipur, this palace is a large modern hotel built on a sprawling 2-acre campus a short drive from the bird sanctuary. With villas, suites and deluxe rooms, it has all the trappings of urban luxury and comfort.

PEHARSAR

On the road to Jaipur, 23km west of Bharatpur, 1km north of the NH 11, after Luharu.

😊😊😊 **Chandra Mahal Haveli** *– B3. Off Jaipur-Agra Rd.* 📞 *91 8696919071, 011 25066241. www.amritara.co.in.* ✕🛁. *11 rm. Rs.8,500-10,500. Free Wi-Fi. 🛏.* The boutique heritage haveli built in 1850 and owned by Giri & Yoginder Singh of the Bharatpur royal family offers unexpected comfort in a nondescript village. Renovated by Amritara Hotels and reopened in Nov 2013, the haveli has a charming courtyard with elegant décor, swimming pool, a big lawn in the backyard and Bahist, a lounge bar. Besides 7 aesthetic deluxe rooms on ground level, narrow stairs lead to 4 terrace suites overlooking mustard fields. Village walks and camel cart rides to meet potters and weavers § enrich the holiday experience.

KARAULI

110km south of Bharatpur (104km north-east of Sawai Madhopur).

😊😊 **Bhanwar Vilas Palace (Heritage Hotels Association)** *– B3. www.karauli. com.* 📞 *09929773744.* 🖼✕🛁. *45 rm. Rs.4,400/5,000 🛏. Rest. Rs.500/600.* A palace built in 1930 by the grandfather of the present maharajah, chief of the Yaduvanshi, a Rajput clan. The rather inadequate lighting lends a touch of melancholy and nostalgia to this place, which has retained an atmosphere of yesteryear, with furniture, paintings and photographs from the period. There are eight beautiful suites, and the food is delicious. Horse riding is available.

EVENTS AND FESTIVALS

Braj Festival *– 3 days in Feb/Mar,* just before Holi. Bharatpur echoes with songs and dances celebrating the love of Krishna and Radha.

Gwalior★★

Set in the heart of Central India, the royal city of Gwalior is easily the tourism capital of Madhya Pradesh. Dynasties from the Guptas and Rajputs, to the Turks, and Mughals, as well as the British, have left an indelible imprint on the landscape and architecture, contributing to its evolution from a land of brave kings and fearless queens to a cultural centre par excellence. Under royal patronage, arts and crafts prospered as the Maratha weaving traditions of Chanderi, Maheshwari and Paithani saris thrived. The Gwalior fort dominates the skyline like a tiara atop the ancient sandstone hill. The city fans out at its base where people mill about in its dense web of markets and lanes. Today the busy city is sprinkled liberally with well-preserved monuments, palaces, statues and relics that lend Gwalior a timeless appeal.

In ancient times, Sanskrit texts mentioned Gwalior as Gopgiri or Gopadri, and the main hillock was called Gopachal. It belonged to the Nandas of Pataliputra in 600 BC and the Nagavanshis in 2C before they were overthrown by Samudra Gupta, the great. The Huns ousted the Guptas in 6C. The Rajputs ruled until 1196, after which invasions by Mohammad Ghori, Qutb-ud-din

> ▶ **Population:** 1,564,981.
> 🔲 **Info:** Regional Office 🖉0751 2234557. Tourist Office (Railway Station, Gwalior) 🖉 0751 4040777. www.mptourism.com.
> ▶ **Location:** 122km south of Agra.
> 🔖 **Guided Tours:** Gwalior Darshan 🖉 0751 2234557.

Aibak and the Slave Dynasty resulted in irreparable losses to the ruling Rajputs. Undaunted, the Rajputs reclaimed their position under the Tomars.

Around 14C during the reign of **Raja Man Singh** and his queen Mrignayani, an accomplished musician, Gwalior rose to its full glory with a dazzling Indian classical arts scene. The fort was eventually taken over by the Mughals after the Battle of Panipat; its palaces were transformed into grisly prisons under emperors Akbar and Aurangzeb. Thereafter, the fort fell into the hands of the British, followed by Tatiya Tope, and **Rani Laxmibai** of Jhansi, a warrior queen who fought the British during the Great Mutiny and died in Gwalior in 1858. With the rise of the Peshwas in Pune, Gwalior became the base of the Marathas, who reinstated Gwalior's former splendor.

SIGHTS
Gwalior Fort★★★

Nightly **Sound and Light Show** *at Man Mandir Palace.* 🎟 *Rs.250. Mar–Oct 7:30pm-8:15pm in Hindi language, 8:30pm-9:15pm in English (starts an hour earlier Nov–Feb). Man Mandir Palace.* 🎟 *Rs.100, Rs.25 video.*

Palace Complex – ⏰ *Open 5am–5pm.* 🎟 *Rs.250 to access Karn Palace, Vikram Temple, Jahangir Palace, Shahjahan palace, Bheem Singh Rana ki Chhatri, Johar Kund, Dhondapur Gate. Rs.25 Photos, Rs.100 video.*

A massive edifice built in sandstone with vestiges of blue and yellow tile cladding, the fort comprises medieval palaces, turrets and 80ft high impregnable walls.

Naming Gwalior

In 8C, Raja Suraj Sen, a Rajput chieftain of the Kachwaha Dynasty, lost his way on a hunting expedition and met a sage called Gwalipa in the forest. The sage directed him to a kund (pool) to quench his thirst. On sipping the water, Suraj Sen was cured of leprosy. As a token of appreciation, he built a tank (Surya Kund) and fort at the site and named the city Gwalior after the sage.

Its outer walls stretch for 3km around a mountain ridge with its vast eastern face extending up to 300ft. Road access from the southwest side via Urwai Road weaves past tall statues of **Jain collossi** carved into the rock on either side. The 57ft high statue of the 23rd Jain *tirthankara* Parswanath stands out amid the cluster of 21 rock cut temples.

A walking path from the northeast side of the fort base leads through seven gateways to **Hathi Pol**, the main entrance. **Man Singh Palace** or **Man Mandir Palace** is named after the celebrated king Raja Man Singh Tomar (1486-1516), who built it in 1508. Note the decorative frieze of ducks and elephants on the outer walls. The 4-storey palace has two subterranean levels and two open courtyards on the third floor with chambers like Jhula Gharand Phansi Ghar supported by decorated pillars and brackets. The stone carvings and lattices in the interior halls veiled the women's sections. The dark dungeons below echo the horrors faced by its inmates during Mughal rule. It is said that Emperor Aurangzeb executed his brother Murad here.

In a separate ticketed complex stand other palaces. Tomar ruler Kirti Singh (1480-86) also known as Karn Singh built **Karn Mahal**, a 2-storey palace with a large pillared hall that served as the royal *darbar* (reception hall). The ground floor had a hammam (bath) for women. Opposite is **Vikram Mahal**, built by Vikramaditya (1516-1523), the scion and successor of Man Singh. Measuring 65m in length, the palace has an inner open veranda with a central *baradari* (pavilion), where the king held his court. Sharing the premises are the palaces **Shahjahan Mahal** and **Jahangir Mahal**. **Bheem Singh Rana's Chhatri** is a three-level cenotaph capped by a dome, built in the memory of Jat King Bheem Singh Rana of Gohad. He was captured at the fort in 1754, and died here three years later.

Among the several temples within the fort complex, the ancient **Chaturbhuj Temple** carved on a rock face, allegedly boasts the oldest recorded use of the number '0'. This inscription of King Mihir Bhoj of the Pratihara Dynasty dates to 875-876. The 8C **Teli ka Mandir** dedicated to Lord Shiva is an architectural landmark with its unusual elements of style, ground plan and towering 35ft-high doorway. Built in 1093 by Kachwaha ruler Mahipal, the twin Vaishnava temples of Sahastrabahu became popular as the **Sas Bahu** temples. Several tanks to store and provide water to the fort were constructed, like the historic **Suraj Kund**.

Located west of the former jail opposite Hathi Pol, the **Archaeological Museum** (🕐 *open Sat–Thu 9am–5pm;* ✆ *Rs.2;* 📞 *0751 2481259*) has four galleries displaying antiques dating from 1C to 17C,

Gwalior Fort

excavated and recovered from historic sites around Gwalior.

Gujari Mahal and Museum

Lohamandi. 🕐 *Open Tue–Sun 10am–5pm.* 📷 *Rs.100. Rs.200 video, Rs.50 Camera.*

The 15C palace was built by Raja Man Singh Tomar for his Gujar queen Mrignayani. Fulfilling her demand of separate dwelling quarters with continuous water from the River Rai, the king built an aqueduct to channel water to the fort. The outer structure has endured for centuries, while the interior serves as an **archaeological museum** exhibiting priceless artefacts, some of which date back to 1C. The stone sculpture of the tree goddess Shalbhanjika from Gyaraspur is kept in the museum curator's office and can be seen on request.

Jiwaji Rao Scindia Museum

Jai Vilas Palace. 📞 *01751 2372390. www.jaivilasmuseum.org.* 🕐 *Open Tue–Sun 10am–5pm.* 📷 *Rs.350, Rs.70 Camera, Rs.120 Video.*

Commissioned by Maharaja Jayaji Rao Scindia in 1874, Jai Vilas Palace was built by prisoners from Gwalior Fort who also wove the exquisite wall-to-wall carpet over 12 years. Designed by Sir Michael Filose, the palace combines the best of European architecture across its three levels: Tuscan, Italian-Doric and Corinthian. The 100ft long by 50ft wide Durbar Hall soars to 41 ft and has two 4 tonne crystal chandeliers. Legend has it that six elephants were hung from the ceiling to check whether the roof could take the load! In 1964, one palace wing was opened to the public after being converted into a museum by Late Rajmata Shrimant Vijayaraje Scindia. The 35 rooms house dedicated galleries displaying a vast array of collectibles under themes such as Lineage, Textiles, Silver jewellery and others. Don't miss the opulent dining hall with a silver toy train whose monogrammed coaches carried after-dinner wines, decanters and cigars during royal feasts.

Tombs of Mohammad Ghaus/Tansen

Tansen Rd, Ghauspura. 🕐 *Open daily 8am–6pm.*

The tomb of 16C Sufi saint Mohammad Ghaus Shattari is set in a Mughal-style garden. Devotees flock to the domed structure with latticed pavilions to pay tribute to the saint. He was also the music teacher of **Mian Tansen**, a titan in the world of classical music who helped define Hindustani Classical Music as it is known today. Tansen is buried beside his master in the same complex. Under the shade of a tamarind tree stands a *makbara*, a humble 16C tomb marking his resting place. Locals believe that eat-

Durbar, Jiwaji Rao Scindia Museum

ing the tamarind leaves will bless singers with a fine voice. The site is the venue for **Tansen Samaroh**, the annual music festival featuring classical musicians.

Vivaswan Sun Temple

Residency Rd. 🕐 *Open daily sunrise–sunset. Temple closed daily noon–1pm, open Sat–Sun until 6:30pm.*
Set in lush lawns, the brick red temple built in 1988 by industrialist GD Birla is dedicated to the sun. Positioned on a plinth, the structure is inspired by the sun temple of Konark in Orissa and constructed akin to a chariot led by seven horses with a marble statue of Lord Surya. Carvings of other deities decorate the exterior walls.

ADDRESSES

🛏 STAY

🍽 **Tansen Residency** – *6A Gandhi Rd.* 📞 *0751 2340370. www.mptourism.com. 36 rm. Breakfast not included. Rs. 2590.* The government-run hotel is a decent, no

frills, economy option located near the railway station. Friendly staff and good food with an MPSTDC tourist counter as well.

🍽🍽 **Deo Bagh** – *Opposite Janaktal, Agra-Mumbai Hwy, near Shende ki Chhawani Rd, Bahodapur.* 📞 *0751 2820357. www.neemranahotels.com. 12 rm & 3 suites.* 🛏 *Rs.4,000-6,000. Lunch Rs.500 & Dinner Rs.600. Free Wi-Fi.* ♿. Spread across 5 wings are 15 rooms named after luminaries of the Jadhav family of Gwalior. The rooms face a Nau Bagh, a chequered garden divided into nine parts. Two 17C-18C Maratha temples, two cenotaphs and one pavilion with 36 arches are located within the property.
🍽🍽🍽🍽 **Taj Usha Kiran Palace** – *Jayendraganj, Lashkar.* 📞 *0751 244 4000. www.tajhotels.com. 40 rm. Breakfast not included. Wi-Fi available.* ♿. *Rs 8,500-15,500.* Set on 9acres of landscaped gardens dotted with fountains, the 120-year-old historic palace continues its tradition of royal-style hospitality as a heritage hotel. Luxuriate in the artistic splendor of its rooms and 8 suites, or be pampered at Jiva Spa.

Nandgaon

For 5,000 years, Brajbhoomi, a region encompassing the districts of Mathura, Bharatpur and Palwal in the Golden Triangle, has been regarded as the hallowed domain of Lord Krishna. The sacred land of Nandgaon, or Nandnagri, is linked irrevocably to the legendary stories of the God. It is believed to be the home of his foster father, NandRai Maharaj, who brought him up as his own son; hence Krishna is also known as Nandgopal and Nandlala. During Holi (*February and March*), Brajbhoomi is drenched with colours and echoes with performances of the lively Raas Leela (dance performances about the life and times of Krishna). His birth is celebrated here on Janmashtami (*July to September*).

▶ **Population:** 88,112.
🛈 **Info:** Directorate of Tourism, UP, Rajarshi Purshottam Das Tandon Paryatan Bhavan, C-13, Vipin Khand, Gomti Nagar. 📞+91 941 5609453.
◗ **Location:** 8.5 km north of Barsana on the road toward Mathura (56km away).
🗣 **Guided Tours:** Local guides near the temples charge a nominal fee to take you around.

TEMPLES AND SHRINES

Several holy texts record details of the Braj hills and their spiritual significance. Nandgaon is a hillock that was once dotted with numerous temples and 56 *kunds* (sacred tanks), many of which have disappeared. However, the crowning glory is **Nanda Bhavan** and the hilltop shrine of NandaRai. Look for the black marble statues of Krishna and Balrama with identical faces, which allude to Yashoda's impartial love for both siblings. Flanked by golden statues of Nanda, Yashoda, Rohini and Radha, the sanctum is embellished with art portraying events from Krishna's life.

The **Nandishwar Mahadev** shrine within the complex, established by Nanda for the protection of the children, is noteworthy. Maharaja Roop Singh, a Jat ruler, granted generous sums of money towards the construction of this ancient temple.

Nandgaon parikrama (circumambulation) starts and ends with the Shiva shrine, taking devotees past several temples on the hill: **Nitai Gaur, Raasbihari** (with a unique idol of Krishna and Radha in one form), **Radha Madanmohan, Yashoda Mata, Shri Govardhan-dharan** and **Mansa Devi. Chhanch Kund** marks the spot where all the excess buttermilk from Nanda Rai's home used to be collected.

Nearby is **Paavan Sarovar**, a lake that provided water for people of Nandgaon in earlier times; Krishna, the divine cowherd, would lead his cows down the *ghats* to quench their thirst here.

To the southwest are the temples of **Mohini Kund** and **Yashoda Kund. Udhoji ka Kyar** and **Kadamba khandi;** sacred groves of Krishna's favourite trees lie close by, rustling with stories of his dalliances with the *gopis*.

Chambal

Situated at the junction of Rajasthan, Uttar Pradesh and Madhya Pradesh, Chambal was the haunt of notorious dacoits for decades. The labyrinthine ravines of this *beehad* (wilderness) echoed with the exploits of Daku Man Singh, Paan Singh Tomar, Phoolan Devi and Nirbhay Gujjar. The rugged terrain, carved out by a 425 km stretch of the Chambal River (with 2km to 6 km wide swathes of ravines on either side), served as ideal hiding places for bandits. After the area was declared a wildlife sanctuary in 1978, attention moved to the wildlife of the riverine habitat. Weathered over centuries by flood and rain, this incredible maze of mud cliffs and scrub forest today resembles giant anthills. Explore the National Chambal Sanctuary by camel safari, a jeep ride through remote hamlets or a river cruise. Dholpur or Bah make for a great base from which you can visit historic sites such as Bateshwar and Ater Fort.

▶ **Population:** Dholpur 126,142, Bah 14,587.

▯ **Info:** DCF National Chambal Sanctuary, Mau Rd., Agra, UP ✆ +91 0562 2530091. DFO Morena, MP, ✆ 0753 2234742, CCF Gwalior ✆ 0751 2340050.

◐ **Location:** The sanctuary begins downstream of the Kota barrage in Rajasthan with its lower boundary near Panchnada, 5km after the confluence of the Chambal and Yamuna rivers at Bhareh. Access points are Bah (71km from Agra via Fatehabad) and Dholpur (57km from Agra/Gwalior, 287km from Delhi via NH3).

🐫 **Guided Tours:** Chambal Safari Lodge (✆ +91 9997066002) organises guided tours such as 3hr boat trips, jeep safaris and camel rides (Rs.2,500/ person/activity).

NATIONAL CHAMBAL SANCTUARY★★

Part of a large 5,400 sq km reserve that is co-administered by Rajasthan, Madhya Pradesh and Uttar Pradesh, the National Chambal Sanctuary is among the last surviving habitats of the Gangetic River dolphin. It harbours nearly 1,200 gharials, 300 marsh crocodiles, eight species of turtles as well as smooth-coated otters.

Autumn and winter are ideal for bird-watching, when altitude migrants from the upper Himalayas and the Arctic congregate here. It is the best place to see large populations of the Indian skimmer besides black-bellied tern, thickknee, pratincole and nearly 330 bird species. There are two bases for exploring Chambal: Raj Niwas Palace at Dholpur in Rajasthan *(4km from the boating site)* and Chambal Safari Lodge (🕯see STAY) near Bah in Agra district.

The boat jetty is located at Nadgavan Ghat, 25km from the lodge via Jarar, Badagaon and Jaitpur.

ADDRESSES

🍽 STAY

🛏🛏🛏 **Chambal Safari Lodge**§ – *Mela Kothi, Village Jarar, Tehsil Bah, Uttar Pradesh. ✆ +91-9997066002. www.chambalsafari.com. 12 rm. Closed May–Sept. breakfast not included (Rs.400). Meals Rs.900. Limited Internet. ♿. Rs.6,000-9,500.* Run by an environmental scientist and his wife, this eco-lodge won a Heritage Tourism Award in 2012. Set on 120 acres of woodland and farmland, the lodge prides itself in its carbon footprint offsetting, with 70% revenue plowed back to the local economy. The camel rides, jeep safaris and river cruises involve the **local community** of camel herders, woodcutters and local boatmen with livelihood projects around recycled handmade paper. Spot 180 birds around the lodge, which is the perfect base to explore Bateshwar *(9km)* and Holipura with stunning havelis of the Chaturvedi clan.

🛏🛏🛏 **Dholpur Palace** – *Raj Niwas Palace, Dholpur Rajasthan. ✆ +91 7665002151/3. www.dholpurpalace.com. 8 rm plus 18 villas. Free Internet in business centre. Rs. 6,500-10,500.* Built to welcome HRH Albert Edward for his royal visit in 1876, Raj Niwas Palace is an Indian royal home with European touches such as Victorian baths, Dutch ceramics, Chinese tiles, Persian carpets and mosaics transported from West Asia by camel caravans. Set in 13 acres of garden, with a restaurant overlooking manicured lawns, each room is a treasure house of artifacts. Poolside dinners and horse riding can be arranged..

Indian Skimmers, National Chambal Sanctuary

Jaipur and around

Highlights

Façade of Hawa Mahal
© Anurag Mallick, Priya Ganapathy/MICHELIN

Jaipur★★★

With its ubiquitous pink colour, whimsical crenellated ramparts, and Eastern-style architectural follies, Jaipur is one of the more attractive cities in India. Its name evokes images of grand palaces and perfumed bazaars full of precious stones and coloured silks. Although it has lost some of its splendour in recent decades as noise and pollution have encroached on the city, Jaipur remains a centre for highly skilled crafts, and its astronomical observatory, a UNESCO World Heritage Site, draws a large number of tourists. Spread out at the foot of the Aravalli Mountains, Jaipur was the capital of Dhundhar, the powerful kingdom ruled by the maharajahs of the Kachwaha Dynasty. The old walled town was laid out in the 18C in a grid formation resembling a giant chessboard. All the streets intersect at right angles, and the façades of the houses, built in the same style, are set in straight lines, creating a sense of unity. Today cars and motorbikes move about the streets, horns blowing, oblivious to the city's illustrious past. To escape the noise and bustle, head to the Amer Fort or Galta temples, which lie hidden in the hills less than 10 kilometres away, and spend an evening in one of the many hotels that have been established in ancient palaces or havelis (former homes of weathly merchants or nobles). There you can enjoy a taste of the princely life while you savour a cup of tea or a meal.

PINK CITY★★★

Map, see inside back cover.
◐ *Tour* 1 *marked in green on map, departing from Hawa Mahal on Sireh Deorhi Bazaar. Allow 3hr.*
Jaipur is the capital of the State of Rajasthan. Despite the expansion of the capital, the 'Pink City' remains its nerve centre. Its original layout, designed in the 1720s by order of Maharajah **Jai Singh II**, the founder of Jaipur, remains unchanged today, the only ancient Hindu urban plan to make it to the modern era. The original plans were destroyed when a successor of Jai Singh II sold off part of the palace library. In

1876, the whole city was painted pink for a visit by the Prince of Wales.

City Palace Complex★★★

Created under Jai Singh II, this vast palace complex includes, in addition to Rajasthan government buildings, the main attractions of the city: Hawa Mahal, Jantar Mantar and the City Palace itself, a part of which has been converted to a museum. The entire complex is surrounded by an 18C wall that backs onto shops, private homes and small temples.

Hawa Mahal★★

The façade overlooks Sireh Deorhi Bazar. To see inside, go to Tripolia Bazar and take the first door on the right. ◷ *Open 9am–4.30pm (last admission).* ▨ *Rs.50, photo and video rights included. Audio guide in English, Rs.110.*

⊚ **Worth knowing** – Visit early morning to see the façade in the best light.

Hawa Mahal ('Palace of the Winds') is situated within the walled precincts of the palace complex, but its amazing five-storey **façade★★★** can be clearly seen even from the street. It consists entirely of bays and screened openings: 61 *jharokhas* (windows; literally, 'sight') enclosed by fine jali that catch the breeze on three sides and allow the onlooker to look out in three directions. To watch and observe, this was the purpose of the palace: to see without being seen! In fact, the Hawa Mahal is now virtually nothing but a façade. Built in 1799, it is a gigantic screen from behind which the women of the palace could enjoy watching life in the street, cooled by the fresh air blowing through the lattice-work windows, while at the same time observing the strict rules of *purdah* that forced them to remain hidden from the eyes of strangers. Underground passages connect the royal *zenana* (where the royal women were secluded) to the Palace of the Winds. From the top floor a **panorama** of the palace, city itself and hills unfolds.

▶ **Population:** 3.1 million.

◐ **Location:** 273km south-west of Delhi, 238km west of Agra. The modern city spreads out around two main arterial roads: **Station Road** and **Mirza Ismail (M.I.) Road**. On the latter, you can orient yourself via Niros, to the east (C3 *on map*), and the **Ganpati Plaza** office complex to the west (B2). The walls form the boundary of the **'Pink City'**, the historic heart of Jaipur, to the north.

👫 **Kids:** The gigantic structures of Jantar Mantar, a folk dance and music show at Chokhi Dhani, a ride up to the Amer Fort on the back of an elephant.

⊚ **Don't Miss:** The façade of the Hawa Mahal in the morning, a half-day of shopping, Amer Fort.

◷ **Timing:** Allow three days for your visit including trips in the surrounding area. Stroll through the Pink City early in the morning when there is less traffic. Wait until the end of your stay in Jaipur to do your shopping.

🐾 **Guided Tours:** The tourism office (☎ 0141 2315714; www.rtdc.in) organises bus tours of the city (Rs.250 excluding guide and entrance fees), a full day tour (Rs.300), and a Pink City by night excursion with vegetarian dinner at the Nahargarh Fort (Rs.375). All these tours include a visit to Amer but only pass by the Hawa Mahal and Gaitor.

Jantar Mantar

© Anurag Mallick, Priya Ganapathy/MICHELIN

▶ Leave Hawa Mahal, return to Tripolia Bazar, turn right and enter the City Palace Complex via the first door on the right.

Beyond is **Tripolia Gate**, the 'triple gate', formerly reserved for the ruler alone. It is high enough to allow an elephant carrying a *howdah* (or seat) to pass through it. It leads to Chandni Chowk ('Moonlight Square'), on which stand the Jantar Mantar and the City Palace.

Jantar Mantar★★

🕐 *Open 9am–4.30pm.* 🎟 *Rs.200, photo and video rights included. Audio guide in English, Rs.250. Guides on entry. Allow 30min for visit. Sound and light show in English 6.30pm, 50min.*
👥 The strange geometric structures that compose the **observatory** are not giant abstract sculptures but huge astronomical instruments that Jai Singh II had built 1728–1733. UNESCO listed it among its World Heritage Sites in 2010.

The enlightened ruler intended to use these constructions to make careful observations and calculations of the movement of the stars, in order to revise the Hindu and Islamic calendars for astrological purposes. A few years earlier, he had built similar (but fewer) instruments in Delhi, at the request of the emperor. The maharajah had read the writings of all the experts—Hindu, Greek, Arab, Persian and European—and had brought astronomers to his court.

The 17 instruments, built in stone and covered in painted yellow stucco, are devoid of decoration, emphasising their extraordinary geometric shapes.

To the left of the entrance, the **Laghu Samrat Yantra** ('small sundial') determines the exact solar time in Jaipur, which is some 10 to 41 minutes different from the official time in India. Nearby, two hemispherical structures form the **Nari Valaya Yantra,** representing the northern and southern hemispheres, and can be used to calculate the time in different parts of the world. The large metal disc nearby, is the **Yantra Raj**. The hole in the centre is the polar star, while the line 27° above it corresponds to the latitude of Jaipur. The instrument helps to calculate the position of the various constellations.

Near the 'small sundial', the **Jai Prakash Yantra** – consisting of two sunken hemispherical cavities – was invented by the maharajah to check the calculations performed with the other instruments. The **Rashi Valaya Yantra**, 12 small trapezoid structures, occupy one side of the site, each designed to measure the appearance of a zodiac sign above the horizon. The **Ram Yantra** astrolabe, consisting of 2 cylindrical-shaped structures made up of 12 columns each, is designed to calculate the altitude and azimuth of the stars. In the park, the huge calibrated sundial, the **Brihat Samrat Yantra**, is used to determine local time via the shadow cast by its 27m-long 'needle' *(gnomon)*.

GETTING THERE/LEAVING

BY PLANE– Sanganer International Airport – 15km south of Jaipur. On arrival, pre-paid taxi service and Tourist Information Bureau. ℘ 0141 2550222. **JetKonnect** (www.jetkonnect.com), **Jet Airways** (www.jetairways.com), **SpiceJet** (www.spicejet.com) and **Air India** (www.airindia.com) provide daily flights to Delhi (50min flight time).

BY TRAIN – Jaipur Railway Station – *A2*. To the west of the town. Info ℘ 139 (booking centre). www.indianrail.gov.in. Tourism office, platform 1. ℘ 0141 2315714. The fastest train to Delhi, the Shatabdi (4hr30min journey time), leaves daily at 5.50pm and goes through Alwar (2hr). Around 15 trains daily for Delhi (5hr30min Superfast trains) via Alwar (2hr30min). The Jaipur Passenger serves the Shekhawati region 3 times per day (4hr30min to Churu stopping at Sikar, Lakshmangarh, Fathepur, Ramgarh, Mahansar and Bissau). There are 7 trains daily for Agra (approx. 4hr), 6 trains daily for Kota (3hr30min) via Sawai Madhopur (2hr), and approx. 15 for Ajmer (2hr on the Shatabdi or Superfast). 4 trains daily, including 1 Superfast, for Chittaurgarh (4hr), 3 for Udaipur (7hr30min), 8 for Jodhpur (5hr30min) and 4 for Bikaner (7hr30min by sleeper train).

BY BUS – Central Bus Stand – *B2*. Sindhi Camp, Station Rd. Info for Silver Line buses, platform 3; for the Express buses, platform 1. ℘ 0141 2205790. www.rsrtc.rajasthan.gov.in. Left luggage 24hr. Approx. 30 Express and a dozen air-conditioned buses leave daily for Delhi between 6.30am and midnight (5hr30min journey time). Frequent buses for Agra (5hr) and Mathura (5hr), some via Bharatpur; 7 for Kota (5hr) via Bundi, 20 for Chittaurgarh (6hr) and Udaipur (8hr45min), 1 for Mount Abu (11hr), 10 for Jodhpur (6hr30min), 4 for Ajmer (2hr30min) including 3 stopping in Pushkar, 3 for Jaisalmer (13hr). For Alwar, departures every 30min (4hr), via Sariska (3hr15min). The tourist centres of Shekhawati (Nawalgarh and Jhunjhunu) are served by the Express services (2hr30min to 4hr30min). For Sawai Madhopur, the train is more convenient. Private buses also leave from the Central Bus Stand.

GETTING AROUND

ON FOOT – Even if pollution, motorbikes and chaotic crowds make touring the Pink City tiring, don't miss the chance to explore its bazaars and discover its many temples on foot.

METRO – Two lines are expected to come into service in 2014. The **Green** Line, beginning at Badi Chaupar (*D2*), serves Civil Lines (*A3*) via Chandpole and the railway station. The **Orange** Line passes through the Ajmeri Gate before heading back to the airport. They intersect at the **Sindhi Camp** Bus Station (*B2*).

LOCAL BUS SERVICES – Buses are always completely packed and stop along major arterial roads and at major junctions. Bus no. 2 links the railway station (*A2*), the City Palace and Jantar Mantar (*D1–2*). For **Amer Fort** (*off map, E1*), bus no. 5 leaves the station every 10 to 20 minutes and stops at the Hawa Mahal, at New Gate and at the M.I. Rd/Railway Rd intersection. It also leaves the station for **Sisodya Palace**, via Ajmeri Gate.

RICKSHAWS – Auto-rickshaw drivers rarely use their meters. Always negotiate the price before starting the journey (Rs.20 for 2km or Rs.60/hr, for 10km maximum). A cycle-rickshaw costs 30% less. Booking offices for pre-paid rickshaws in front of the station and the Central Bus Stand.

TAXI – Ranks at the station (*A2*) and on M.I. Rd (*CD3*), between Ajmeri Gate and Sanganeri Gate. Book via an agency or your hotel to get a better price. Budget Rs.800 for 4hr (40km maximum).

Meri Car – ℘ 0141 4188888. www.mericar.in. Provides intercity

connections (Delhi Airport, Agra, Ajmer/Pushkar, etc.).
CAR HIRE – Ask your hotel or a travel agency. Allow at least Rs.2,500 per day (car plus driver, 250km maximum).

EMERGENCY/HEALTH
Ambulances – ℘ 102.
Modern pharmacies – Several on Station Rd, near Chandpole (*B2*), as well as on the corner of Sawai Ram Singh and Hospital Rd (*C3*).
Ayurvedic pharmacies – in Kishanpole Bazaar (*C2*).
Santokba Durlabhji Memorial (SDM) Hospital – *C4*. Bhawani Singh Rd. ℘ 0141 2566251. Private clinic.

SAFETY
In the event of any dispute or scam:
Tourist Assistance Force, at the bus and train stations, near the City Palace and at Amer.
Police – ℘ 100.

SIGHTSEEING.
Jaipur Tours – The Jaipur **Virasat Foundation**§, which has a particular interest in the traditional music of Rajasthan, organises **walking tours** of the Pink City on historical and cultural topics. Also **bicycle tours**. ℘ 0141 2369723. www.jaipurvirasatfoundation.org.

City Palace★★ (Maharaja Sawai Man Singh II Museum)
http://msmsmuseum.com. ⏲ *Open 9am–5.45pm (last admission 5pm).* ☞ *Rs.300 including photo rights; video Rs.200. Audio guide in English Rs.80. Best to visit at opening time and on a weekday. Allow 1hr30min.*
This part of the palace complex belongs to the royal family, who still live in the central building.

In the centre of the first courtyard stands the **Mubarak Mahal** ('Welcome Palace') (*photography prohibited inside*), a marble building surrounded by a loggia with slender columns. Maharajah Madho Singh II (reigned 1880–1922) had it built in 1899 to accommodate distinguished guests. It features a **royal robes★** section consisting of rich silk saris, with fabrics lavishly embroidered or printed by Sanganer craftsmen and beautiful shawls from Kashmir made of goat's wool (*pashmina*) or antelope hair (*shahtush*). Tradition states that the best are so fine that they could pass through the ring of a princess.

Note the Benares silk **robe of Madho Singh I** (reigned 1750–68); its gigantic measurements are on account of the maharajah's size: he was more than 2m tall and weighed 200kg.

Behind this building, the **Friends of the Museum** building includes restored objects that once adorned the Diwan-i-Am: a beautiful collection of **musical instruments** used for concerts held in the courtyard; sumptuous **howdahs** and palanquins, as well as a silver swing, and 17C carpets from Herat, Lahore and Agra; a valuable series of Mughal and Rajput **manuscripts and miniatures**, including a surprising representation of the Holy Family (Deccan school, 1627), painted from a European work: Mary is portrayed with the gentle face of an Indian princess, with a tika on her forehead and jet-black hair. There is also the superb **Razm Namah** in Persian, produced for Akbar in the 1580s, and a lavishly illustrated copy of the *Gita Govinda* about the life of Krishna, a copy of the *Bhagavad Gita* in minuscule, and works on astronomy that belonged to Jai Singh II, some of which are his own writings.

The **Singh Pol★** ('Lion's Gate') in white marble is guarded by two elephant statues and two palace servants dressed in white trousers, white or black achkans depending on the season, and red turbans.

Before going through it, go up to the first floor of **Maharani Palace** (*to the left of the Singh Pol*). Its access gallery displays miniatures at various stages of completion, providing an interesting insight into the production process. In

Peacock Gate, Pritam Niwas Chowk, City Palace

a suite of 18C rooms, beneath lavishly decorated **ceilings★★**, is an exhibit of a fine **collection** of Hindu and Mughal **weapons★** *(photography prohibited)*. Among the huge mass of ironwork, note the delicate Damascene arabesques inlaid on the steel blades, and the handles of the Mughal daggers *(khanjar)*, inlaid with jade, rubies and emeralds set in gold. Some *katar* (daggers with impressive blades) are accompanied by two small pistols. Note also the small cannon *(rekhla)* from Amer, one of the first pieces of Rajput artillery, and the sword of Maharajah Ram Singh II, its handle decorated with rubies, a gift from Queen Victoria.

On returning to the courtyard go, through the Singh Pol. It opens onto a second courtyard, enclosed by three floors of galleries behind jali. In the centre stands a pavilion with a flat Mughal-style roof, the **Diwan-i-Khas★** ('Hall of Private Audiences'). Salmon pink is the dominant colour, occasionally interspersed with white marble columns and a few ornamental arabesques. The whole effect is a superb synthesis of 18C Rajput and Mughal styles. In this courtyard, the maharajah annually participates in a religious ritual *(puja)* conducted with all the prescribed splendour, including fly swatters and elephants.

Inside the Diwan-i-Khas, the arches, painted pink with floral arabesques, are hung with Lalique crystal chandeliers. The new maharajah is anointed here; the latest, Prince Padmanabh Singh underwent the ceremony in 2011 at the age of 12.

On the left side of the courtyard with your back to the Singh Pol, a door leads to the **Pritam Niwas Chowk**, a small courtyard with four decorated **doors★**. They are covered with wrought copper plates surrounded by a shimmering painted porch depicting peacocks spreading their tails. The bright colours of the bird of immortality evoke memories of the dancing that once took place in this courtyard.

The **Chandra Mahal** ('Palace of the Moon'), overlooking the courtyard, has a pale yellow façade surrounded by six levels of galleries, which form a kind of gazebo with a view of the entire city.

The palace contains the **private apartments** of the maharajah and his family. Its finest rooms may be visited separately *(Rs.2,500, including a guide or audio guide in English; purchase tickets at the Singh Pol; tour lasts 1hr)*. During a visit you will see the **Chandra Mandir**, decorated with Mughal floral motifs dating from the time of Jai Singh II; the **Sukh Niwas**, a huge dining room with silver

furniture and Lalique chandeliers; the **Sobha Niwas**, a sumptuously decorated reception room reserved for important occasions; the blue and white paintings of the **Chhavi Niwas**; and the dazzling **Sri Niwas**, with its gleaming mirrors.
Go back to the Diwan-i-Khas courtyard and head to the wing opposite the Pritam Niwas Chowk.
On the walls of the **Sabha Niwas** are photographs of 19C Jaipur that Ram Singh II (1835–1880) took and developed himself. The corridor leads to the **Diwan-i-Am★★** ('Hall of Public Audiences') *(photography prohibited)*, where maharajahs gathered their *durbars* (assembly of nobles) and received guests. The crystal chandeliers from Bohemia, along with the delicate arabesques and floral motifs painted in bright shades inspired by Mughal designs, make this a fine example of an 18C reception room.

▶ On leaving the palace, take the passage on the left leading to Jaleb Chowk.

The vast courtyard of **Jaleb Chowk** is lined with the former houses of palace servants, which have now become the administrative offices of the State of Rajasthan. In the past it was a parade ground; nowadays an endless morass of mingling officials, animals of all kinds, cars and carts assemble here.

▶ Leave Jaleb Chowk through the Sireh Deorhi Darwaza (gate on the right) and turn left into Sireh Deorhi Bazaar. At the end, an alley leads to the Govind Dev Ji Temple.

Govind Dev Ji Temple
🕐 *Open all day.* 🚫 *No charge.*
Backed onto by the Jai Udthan Niwas garden, this former hunting lodge was transformed by Jai Singh II into a temple in the 1730s, during the construction of Jaipur, in order to install a statue of Govinda, the god **Krishna** in the form of a young herdsman. This sacred image was once worshiped in Vrindavan, where Krishna spent his childhood. Jai

Singh II rescued it from destruction by Aurangzeb's troops, and made him the patron deity of the maharajahs of Jaipur. The temple is a single hall in front of the shrine where the god resides.

🙂 **Worth knowing** – Try to time your visit to coincide with the *darshan* , which takes place seven times a day *(times vary per the lunar months; check the sign at the entrance).*

The *darshan* celebrated at nightfall is particularly popular. The faithful gather in the hall and wait for the priests to open the curtains shielding the altar. When the statue of the divine herdsman appears, accompanied by Radha and a cow, the crowd burst out with enthusiastic shouts and *bhajan* (religious hymns). This moment of fervour contrasts starkly with the commercial atmosphere of the city.

▶ Retrace your steps, passing in front of the façade of the Hawa Mahal to rejoin Badi Chaupar.

The Bazaars★★
The walk begins on Badi Chaupar.
🕐 *Most stores are open Mon–Sat 10am–8pm.*
A walk through the noisy and colourful old bazaars of Jaipur gives a visitor a real sense of this bustling city with all its crafts and commerce. The bazaars still specialise in individual trades and have barely changed since the 18C.
The place is renowned for its jewellery and enamel work, printed fabrics, blue pottery and marble. The city's relatively wide streets, which are laid out like a chessboard, are less exotic than the maze of winding alleys in other cities like Jodhpur and Bikaner. And the sound of motorcycle horns being tooted loudly in the narrowest streets forces pedestrians to remain constantly on their guard. To escape the brunt of the traffic and touts trying to lure you into shops, head away from the main thoroughfares, enter the bazaars and explore their nooks and crannies. The city is teeming with secrets.

Purohit ji ka Katla

© Anurag Mallick, Priya Ganapathy/MICHELIN

The following are some highlights:

Johari Bazar

North of **Badi Chaupar** (D2) lies the Palace of the Winds, Hawa Mahal , which is located next to the Rajasthan Legislative Assembly. Towards the east, the **Ramganj Bazaar** is home to cobblers and the shoe market.

To the south is **Johari Bazar**, the jewellers' market, one of the busiest trading centres in Jaipur. Like the other avenues that divide the Pink City into *mohallas* (districts), Johari Bazar is 35m wide and is lined with houses that have first-floor terraces that act as roofs for the stalls at street level below. It is mainly textile shops that are found here, with jewellers occupying the surrounding streets, where they rub shoulders with confectioners. Craftsmen are adept at all the various techniques of making enamel ware and polishing stones, and tinsmiths also produce vark (a silver foil used to decorate sweets).

If you walk through Johari Bazar on the right-hand side, pop into **Purohit ji ka Katla** in the first alley, where they sell all the costumes required for a Hindu wedding. Red dominates, of course (this is the colour in which women get married), as well as gold – the colour of the braid that decorates the ceremonial clothes.

▶ Carry on down Johari Bazar and take the next street on the right, Gopal ji ka Katla.

Gopal ji ka Katla

Further down the street you will pass the two elephants guarding the **Gopal ji ka Mandir** (*temple;* 🕐 *open mornings and late afternoons, ceremonies at 6pm and 9pm*) before you come to the Jain temple of **Shriji Amer** on your left (*open all day, ceremonies at 7am and 6.30pm, remove your shoes and socks*). Notice the amazing contraption at the entrance with mechanical drums and gongs to appeal to the gods. The sanctuary is home to dozens of statuettes of ferry boatmen made of crystal, bronze, white marble and semi-precious stones.

▶ Return to Badi Chaupar using the alley parallel to Johari Bazar, where wedding invitation cards are sold.

Choti Chaupar

Once back on Badi Chaupar, follow **Tripolia Bazar**—the go-to place for kitchen utensils and copper objects—as far as **Choti Chaupar**, at the southwest corner of the palace complex. Rickety buses make their way among the rickshaws and motorbikes, accompanied by a cacophony of horns, while a few camel- and horse-drawn carriages gradually make headway through the great chaos.

The road heading north at Choti Chaupar—Gangauri Bazar—passes through a less commercial mohalla.

Saras Sadan Haveli

Continue along Gangauri Bazar until you reach **Saras Sadan Haveli** (ask for the Vidhya Vihar School), where the ground floor is home to a school. This family residence, built by Maharajah Ram Singh in the 19C, was once a school for courtesans. The first floor contains a magnificent reception room, where valuable **frescoes★★** in red and gold decorate the walls; it now serves as the showroom for a jeweller's shop.

▶ Return to Choti Chaupar.

Ishwari Minar Swarga Sal★

🕐 *Open 9am–4pm.* 📷 *Rs.10. Photo Rs.10.*

You will see this minaret (35m tall), also known as **Isarlaat**, on the left. Climb the spiral ramp to the top from where there is a panoramic view of the city. The tallest building in the old town, it was erected inside the royal palace by the Maharajah Ishwari Singh, the successor to Jai Singh II. Less courageous than his predecessor, Ishwari Singh committed suicide rather than face a hostile Maratha army. His 21 wives were immolated on his funeral pyre, becoming *sati*.

▶ From Choti Chaupar continue due west on Chandpole Bazar, an extension of Tripolia Bazar.

Chandpole Bazar

On the divider of this main arterial road, one of four that criss-cross the city, the lamp posts are decorated with representations of the sun, recalling the solar origin of the Kachwaha Dynasty (Rajputs, the warrior clan to which all rulers of Rajasthan, including the Kachwahas, belonged, believed that they were either descendants of the sun, hence Suryavanshi, or of the moon, hence Chandravanshi, or had arisen from fire, hence Agnivanshi).

Farther to the left, **Khazane Walon ka Rasta** (C2) is a street traditionally occupied by stonemasons and sculptors from the Adi Gauds community, who were regarded as equivalent to Brahmins, because of their work creating sacred images in accordance with religious precepts. Their descendants, who mostly continue to work in stone, still live in this mohalla.

The main street leads beyond the crenellated walls, by **Chandpole★** ('Gate of the Moon') (C2), to the west—one of the gates that were still being locked every night at the beginning of the 20C. The area around it, close to the markets, comes alive with a myriad of activities early in the morning, including a produce market selling fish, poultry, and fruit and vegetables.

THE NEW TOWN

Map, see inside back cover.

▶ *Start from the New Gate. Allow 3hr in a rickshaw (around Rs.200).*

In the 19C the maharajahs of Jaipur embarked on construction and development projects. Ram Singh II gave the city a department of public works of interest, a postal service, gas lighting, colleges and institutes. The walls of the old town became too small to contain all the activities of the capital, which began to expand southwards.

Albert Hall

Ram Niwas Garden. www.alberthall jaipur.gov.in. 🕐 *Open daily 9am–5pm. Closed on public holidays.* 📷 *Rs.150. Photography and video prohibited.*

Located in the Ram Niwas Garden, this imposing building, with its hybrid style and pyramid structure, was designed by Colonel Jacob for Maharajah Ram Singh II, who wanted to build the Jaipur equivalent of the Victoria and Albert Museum in London. The first stone was laid in 1876 by the future Edward VII of the United Kingdom.

On the ground floor, there are interesting showcases displaying various traditional Rajasthani costumes and an overview of folk art. The collections on the first floor are diverse, with miniatures sitting alongside mineralogy samples or an Egyptian mummy.

Rambagh Palace★

Madho Singh II, who was very religious, transformed this former hunting palace in the early 20C, with the help of Colonel Jacob. The last reigning maharajah, Man Singh II, spent his youth here and made it his main residence in 1931, furnishing it in keeping with the taste of the period – Art Deco. After independence, he was unable to maintain his lifestyle, so in 1957 he had the idea of converting his palace into a luxury hotel, the first in India (🛏️ see STAY).

The place retains a hint of the aura of an easy and luxurious lifestyle. The sober and elegant white building, enhanced by a touch of red sandstone, sits amid huge lawns extended by a polo field. The place is particularly impressive during the monsoon season, when peacocks flock there for courtship.

Birla Mandir Off map.

Follow Jawaharlal Nehru Avenue south for approx. 2km. At the foot of the hill topped by the small Moti Dungri Fort (⊶ property of the royal family, no entry) stands the **Lakshmi Narayan Temple**. Built in the early 20C by the Birla family of industrialists, who originally came from Shekhawati, the sanctuary, in white marble, is dedicated to Narayan (another name for Vishnu) and his consort Lakshmi, the goddess of prosperity, a favourite among members of the merchant caste. Some superb windows represent Hindu gods, while the outer walls are decorated with **paintings** including, among others, Christ, Zoroaster, Moses, Socrates and St. Anthony: a perfect illustration of Hindu syncretism!

ALSO SEE

Map, see inside back cover.

Gaitor Cenotaphs★

The cenotaphs (🕐 open 9am–4.30pm; Rs.30) are located just outside the ramparts to the north of the old town, dominated by the Nahargarh Fort. The road there passes through traditional neighbourhoods with quiet streets.

Among the trees and bushes, 20 domed cenotaphs (chhatri) of various sizes, in white marble or ochre sandstone, stand on the site where the maharajahs and princes of the Kachwaha Dynasty were cremated (the chhatri of the women are further away, beside Lake Mansagar). The oldest is the **cenotaph of Jai Singh II**, in white marble, its dome decorated with sculptures representing 18 apsaras (nymphs) and gandharvas (heavenly musicians). Pause also at the **cenotaph of Madho Singh II**, which is the one before the cenotaph for his children.

🐦 To the right of the entrance, a long flight of stairs ascends the hill. Climb up for a view overlooking all the cenotaphs.

Nahargarh Fort★

🕐 Open 10am–5.30pm. 🎟️ Rs.50.
By car, the fort is reached via the same route as the Jaigarh Fort but, at the fork in the road, turn left. The splendid ridge ends at Nahargarh Fort (approx. 5km).

🐦 To walk up from Jaipur, ask to be dropped off by a rickshaw 'Nahargarh Qile ke nitche' ('at the bottom of Nahargarh') and allow for a pleasant 20min walk up the hill.

Jai Singh II had this 'Tiger Fort' built in 1734 to protect his new capital. Legend has it that this building work offended the spirit of Prince Nahar Singh Rathore, who had died a heroic death here and whose cenotaph Jai Singh had destroyed. Every morning, the work carried out the day before was mysteriously destroyed. A ceremony calmed the spirit and allowed the work to progress as planned.

The courtyard has a baori (stepwell). The **Madhavendra Bhawan** (palace), the most interesting building, was constructed in the 19C for the wives of Ram Singh II. Its façade, which is decorated with pavilions, can be seen from Jaipur. The interior, which has no furniture, has retained some murals. A maze of corridors, patios and rooms, some with stained-glass windows, surrounds the courtyard. The upper terrace offers a beautiful view of the Pink City.

EXCURSIONS *Off Map*
Allow half a day for each of these two nature walks in the hills.

While the forts of Amer, Jaigarh and Nahargarh evoke the glory days of the rulers of the Kachwaha Dynasty, a trip to the Galta Mandir (temple), hidden against the backdrop of a wild valley, will whisk you away from the noisy and polluted avenues of Jaipur for a few hours. Take the opportunity of your stay in the region to experience the princely lifestyle in Jaipur: the ancient kingdom of Dhundhar is full of palaces and castles that have been converted to luxury or boutique hotels.

Eastern Hills
8km east of Jaipur. This excursion is by car or auto-rickshaw (☜ Rs.250 for approx. 4hr), heading out of Jaipur via the road to Agra.

☜ This walk is approx. 5km. Allow at least 4hr. You will be dropped off at the Vidyadhar gardens and come back via the east gate of Jaipur, Galta Gate.

This walk, in wooded hills of acacias inhabited by goats and monkeys, offers a pleasant natural break and the opportunity to discover beautiful architecture and frescoes in a wilderness setting. After 7km, the Agra road suddenly passes through two rows of buildings topped by *chhatri*: these are **ancient shops** built near the original fortifications and are now the subject of an extensive restoration campaign. On the right, an esplanade overlooks the **Vidyadhar Gardens** (*Vidyadhar ji ka Bagh*, ☜ *no charge*), established in honour of the architect who re-designed the layout of Jaipur and decorated it with pavilions and ornamental lakes. The gardens have also benefited from a recent renovation (2011) and have now regained all their former glory.

Sisodya Rani Palace★
Approx. 200m after the Vidyadhar Gardens, take the small road on the left. The palace is located immediately on the right. 🕐 *Open 8am–6pm.* ☜ *Rs.10; photography and video – in the evening (8pm–9pm Rs.20) there are fountains and illuminations.*

This palace was built in 1710 for a wife of Jai Singh II, a princess of the Sisodya Dynasty, the rulers of Mewar. The alliance between the two families stated that the eldest son born of this union should become king and take precedence over the children of the other wives of Jai Singh II. This stipulation aroused much jealousy. To escape the intrigues of the court, the princess had this small palace built and raised her son there, the future Madho Singh I.

The restored **murals** depict court and hunting scenes, as well as various gods of the Vishnu pantheon. Within this charming pavilion with its multi-lobed arches, the reception hall and the somewhat dusty upper gallery, with its 1950s furniture, can be visited. The terraced **garden**, well maintained and decorated with pavilions and pools, is a pleasant place for a stroll. In front of the palace, on the other side of the road, stands a **temple to Shiva** built in 1745.

◗ Go behind the palace to take the road that winds through the hills, surrounded by groves of acacia trees and bougainvillia. After 1.5km, at the fork in the road, follow the sign pointing to the Vipasana Centre (on the left).

Approximately 300m further on is a temple dedicated to **Hanuman**, which is particularly busy during Tuesday and Saturday prayers, days dedicated to the monkey god. Its façade, adorned with *chhatris* and *jharokas*, gives it the air of a palace. The interior is modest, but has a few beautiful murals depicting Krishna, and an altar dedicated to Shiva.

Galta Mandir★★
3km from the Sisodya Rani palace via a scenic road in the hills. ☜ *Photos Rs.30, video Rs.50. The same family has looked after this place for 7 generations and is raising the alarm in a bid to save the site from the growing build-up of waste.*

Monkeys in a temple, Galta

© milosk50/Fotolia.com

A dozen 18C temples blend into the wild setting of a narrow picturesque gorge populated by hordes of monkeys. 😊 Watch out when leaving your shoes at the entrance to the temples! A miraculous spring flows from a rock shaped like a cow's muzzle *(gomukh)*. The water never seems to dry up and the peaceful valley is (almost) always green. It was the home of a pious ascetic, **Galtav**, at the start of the Christian era.

These huge religious buildings combine a sense of refinement with an advanced state of disrepair. Several temples and a *dharamsala* (a hostel for pilgrims), their walls decorated with **frescoes**, line the central driveway. Note the wall covered with paintings representing the army of Hanuman monkeys.

The driveway leads to tiered **pools**, built into the rock at the narrowest point of the pass, where the holy water flows. The lower one is for women, the top one for men. Bathing here with devotion releases one from the cycle of reincarnation. Some pilgrims jump in from a wall several metres high.

🐾 A paved path winds through the rocks from the upper pool. If you follow this for 20 minutes, you can reach a ridge overlooking Jaipur. Before reaching the hill, you will come across two tiny **shrines** dedicated to Rama and Hanuman, visited by scantily-clad *sadhus* (holy men) with a rather casual demeanour. A path *(left when you reach the hill)* leads to the small **Temple of Surya**, built in the 18C in honour of the Sun, the ancestor of the Kachwahas. From its terrace, there is a view of the forts of Amer, Jaigarh and Nahargarh.

▶ From the terrace, a path goes back down to Galta Gate (800m), where rickshaws are parked. The City Palace is approx. 3km away.

AMER *Off map.*

▶ *8km north of Jaipur, on the road to Delhi reached by taxi or minibus (take the crowded no. 5 from in front of the Hawa Mahal). By car, this trip can be combined with trips to Gaitor, Jaigarh and Nahargarh .*

Lake Mansagar

From Jaipur, the road to Amer runs along Lake Mansagar where, in the 19C, the maharajahs hunted ducks. The **Jal Mahal** (🔒 *cannot be visited*) appears to float serenely in the centre of the lake. Built in the 18C, it has been carefully restored in recent years. There are plans to convert the building into a luxury hotel. Cleaned and now free from the water hyacinths that were choking it, Lake Mansagar is once again attracting wading birds, to the great delight of birdwatchers.

Further on *(on the right)*, at the far end of the lake, the Mughal garden **Kanak Vrindavan** (🕘 *9am–6pm;* 🎫 *Rs.10*) was designed in the early 18C. Redeveloped by the Birla family in the 1990s, its fountains have been restored and its lawns are popular with Indian visitors, who love coming here to be photographed. The road rises and makes its way into a narrow gorge. After passing across a line of fortified walls, it opens into a steep valley of rugged beauty. Then the immense, impressive Amer Fort looms, anchored to the hillside. It is overlooked by the Jaigarh Fort, surrounded by hills across which run further protective walls. At its foot lies a small artificial lake, **Maota Sagar**, which is often dry in winter.

Amer Fort★★★

🕐 *Open 8am–5.30pm (last admission 5pm). ▧ Rs.200. Allow at least 1hr30min for this vast site. Avoid weekends. Sound and light show in English at 6.30pm. Rs.200. Book on 🖉 0141-2530844.*

👁 **Worth Knowing** – Morning is the best time to take photos of Amer, with the Jaigarh Fort in the background.

🚶♟ **Access ramp** – A long **ramp** provides access to the fortress. Climb it on foot *(10min)* or on the back of an elephant *(Rs.900 for 2 people)*. Noisy families dressed in their Sunday best and crowds of tourists in shorts and sun hats pose, as 'professional' photographers capture the moment in exchange for a few dozen rupees.

▷ Soon after the start of the ramp, take the path that bears left.

Dilaram Bagh★★ – This charming Mughal garden was laid out in 1588 on an artificial island to provide a fitting welcome for the Emperor Akbar. The garden is formed of star-shaped flower beds over three terraces crossed by a central channel through which water runs down to Maota Sagar. There is a good view of the whole garden from inside the palace.

▷ The ramp passes under several gates before reaching the palace.

Jaleb Chowk – The ticket office is at the bottom of Jaleb Chowk. The austere military façades are bare and smooth, with no windows, the design lightened by just a few turrets. The last gate, **Suraj Pol** ('Gate of the Sun'), opens onto Jaleb Chowk, the main courtyard enclosed by buildings that once housed stables, a guardhouse and servants' quarters. A ramp at the bottom left leads to the **Shila Devi Mandir** (temple dedicated to a reincarnation of Goddess Kali, Devi in her fearsome aspect); offerings of alcohol are made to this godess daily by devotees. Until the mid-20C a goat would be sacrificed here every day to the image of Shila Devi, brought from Jessore (in Bengal) by Man Singh I. The nearby stairs lead to a monumental gate.

Ganesh Pol★ – The first gate gives access to a terrace on which stands the **Diwan-i-Am★** ('Hall of Public Audiences'), a Mughal-style pavilion with a flat roof dating from the early 17C, which

---

Amer, Strategically Located

The city of Amer, which controls the road from Delhi to Rajasthan, was founded by the indigenous **Meenas,** but in the 12C it came under the control of Kachwaha prince **Duleh Rai** when he seized Amer and made it the capital of his nascent kingdom, Dhundhar. It is not known whether the name Amer is derived from the goddess Amba Mata (Durga), revered by the Meenas, or from Ambikeshvara (Shiva), the patron deity of the Kachwahas. The current Amer Fort dates back to the reign of **Man Singh I** (late 16C) and was enlarged in the 17C by **Jai Singh I** (1621–67). Jai Singh II lived there for some time, before abandoning it around 1733 and moving to Jaipur, the city he had just founded on the plain. Amer lost its role as capital but retained its strategic importance. The fort now belongs to the State of Rajasthan.

Jaipur Heritage Walks

Take one or all of the self-guided walks below, or contact **Virasat Experiences**§, a community tourism initiative, to arrange a guided tour *(2.5hr;* ⊛ *Rs.1,500, includes snacks and a copy of 'Jaipur: Six Walks to Discover the Old City";* ☏ *+91 9828 220140; www.virasatexperiences.com).*

Walk 1: Mandirs and Havelis
▶ Begin at Choti Chaupar (Police Station).

Around **Choti Chaupar** (small square), named after the ancient board game *chaupar*, are several temples that are well-worth a visit. Start with the twin *haveli* temples of **Sri Chaturbhuj** and **Roop Chaturbhuj** built by twin merchants. Flanked by stone elephants, the temples have paintings on the walls, ceilings and pillars. A local technique called *arishe*, wherein seven layers of limestone are applied on the surface and the last wet layer is rubbed with coconut husk, was used to keep the walls smooth.

Two centuries old, **Jharlaye walon ki mandir**, with four *pradakshinas* (circumambulations) across four levels, has an unusual image of Lord Krishna, surrounded by his eleven *sakis* (female friends).

▶ Turn onto Nahargarh Rd.

Atal Bihari, or **Laal Hathi**, **temple** is named after the two elephant sculptures guarding the entrance. **Kothari House**, built in 1839, sports an elaborate exterior.

The restored **Somani Haveli** features rooms with painted floral borders. The terrace in the central courtyard offers a **view** of the city as well as of Nahargarh and Jaigarh. Nearby, a rare **Tantra Temple** has a duo of sinister guards for Rudra Mahadev, the main deity. The private temple holds old pictures of Jaipur and a tiny complex of 11 Shiva *lingas* used in tantric rituals. Visit **Shri Gopinath Ji Krishna Temple** and then head for a breakfast of *aloo, puri* and sweets at **Bagru Ki Haveli**, home of a Rajput family that organises workshops for visitors on hand printing with wooden blocks on tablecloth and saris. A gold painting of the City Palace and eye-catching frescos adorn the ancient **Ramchandra Temple**.

Walk 2: Cuisine and Crafts
▶ Begin at Hawa Mahal (Badi Chaupar)

In the evening, the city's most popular street food vendors dish out their signature treats – from *laddus* at **Nathulal Mahaveer Prashad** to the legendary *rabdi* of **Ramchandra Kulfi Bhandar**.

Pass by **Purohit ji ka katla** and the **Swayambhu Hanuman Temple** and head toward **Hanuman Ka Rasta**, an alley bustling with bookbinders, paper-sellers, manufacturers of coloured envelopes for the local diamond trade. In **Gopalji ka Rasta's** workshops.,watch local artisans at **Ghat Darwaza** and **Vishveshwar ji** —jewellers, silversmiths, *kundan* artists and *gota* (gold and silver thread) embroiderers—at work. Sip tea at the 200-year-old *haveli* of **Pyare Miyan** appointed with rich tapestries, chandeliers,period furniture and rare art.

▶ Turn onto Ghee Walon ka Rasta.

Walk down **Ghee Walon ka Rasta** to see wholesalers of food displaying their wares. Walk past *paneer* (cottage cheese) *batasa*, *misri* and *dalmoth* (fried yellow lentils)) in glass containers at the *namkeen bhandars*. **Karodiya Dukan** (Shop no.150) specialises in *hing ki kachori* (deep-fried savoury pastry filled with a savoury). Brijmohan's **Ramdev Restaurant** serves sweets like *rajbhog*. Head down the 80-year-old **Kailash Pan Bhandar** toward the bazaars of **Tripolia Gate** for a *makhaniya* lassi near the famous sweet shop, Laxmi Mishthan Bhandar (LMB) in **Johri Bazaar**.

Walk 3: Modikhana Quarter
▷ Begin at Golcha Cinema (New Gate).

Jaipur's 18C quarter of **Chowkri Modikhana** is named after the **Modis**, a trading community whose buildings, museums and craft shops embody the city's living heritage. The **Kalyanji temple's** frescos depict incarnations of Lord Vishnu. **Sanghi Juta Ram Jain temple** is studded with *kundan* wall decorations, and the temples of **Sita Ramji** and **Tarkeshwar** are older than Jaipur itself. Browse in the **Fine Art Palace**, an antique store run by generations of an Afghan family, whose forefathers were brought by the kings to teach archery and the art of tie-dye. Note the hand-drawn family tree, and visitors' booklogs with 18C entries.

▷ Turn onto Nataniyon ka Rasta.

Walk through **Sankri gali** (narrow lane), whose crumbing *havelis* were renovated by the Jaipur **Virasat Foundation** with help from the Prince Charles royal fund. Pass along a lane for brass-smiths, an alley for *lac* bangle makers and a street called **Thatheron ka rasta** for ironsmiths. End at the **Rajasthan School of Arts**, the former residence of the Prime Minister of Maharaja Ram Singh II converted into a school in 1866.

Walk 4: Amer Walk
▷ Begin at Chand pol Gate, behind Amer Fort

Built by the Kachwaha Rajputs on the site of the former Meena citadel, this fort was probably named after the mother goddess Amba, worshipped as Gatta Rani or Queen of the Pass, or perhaps, after the ancient **Ambikeshwar Temple**, in Amer town, where the Shiva linga sinks deeper into the mud with each passing year. Stop at the 16C **Jagat Shiromani Temple**. Built in 1601 in South Indian style with local stone and white marble, it has frescos of mythological figures. **Parik Haveli**, once the largest mansion in town, is today a crumbling edifice but still inhabited.

▷ Turn north-west towards Kheri Gate.

The restored 16 stepwell, **Panna Miah ka Kund**, next to the **Ambikeshwar Temple,** remains cool down below; its geometric maze of criss-crossing stairs, octagonal gazebos and recessed doorways delight photographers. End at the **Anokhi Museum of Hand Printing** (🕯*see p203*), housed in a restored 16C mansion. Watch block-printing demonstrations or have a go yourself.

This walk can be combined with gentle hikes in the surrounding **Aravalli hills** to visit a ruined fort and hidden shrines and to meet the local **Meena community**. (*Approx 1.5 hours—also offered by Virasat*).

is remarkable for its **marble columns** with tapered shafts. The vast, symmetrical **Ganesh Pol**, dating from 1639, simply exudes power. Its façade, covered in painted decoration (1727), combines Mughal motifs inspired purely by the figure of the elephant god, Ganesh, which stands in the centre of the *iwan* (vaulted space) under a cross ribbed vault. Behind this lie the **private apartments** of the maharajahs, largely built under Jai Singh I.

Mardana★ ('men's quarters') – These are arranged around a small central garden. In the **Sukh Mahal** (Palace of Wonders) *(on the right)*, you will notice an ingenious cooling system: scented water from a tank on the roof runs down a small sloping channel that passes through the jali at the back of the room, cooling the air as it passes through. On the wall, a door made of sandalwood with inlaid ivory is evidence of a luxury that has been partly erased over time.

Jai Mandir★★★ – On the other side of the garden stands the **Jai Mandir**, a set of three magnificent rooms surrounding a veranda. Small slivers of convex mirror, embedded in plaster, are eve-rywhere, forming mirror mosaics. The **Sheesh Mahal** (Palace of Mirrors) is star-studded. In the **Diwan-i-Khas** ('Hall of Private Audiences'), in the centre and on the ceiling of the portico, the decoration combines multi-coloured glass mosaics with painted arabesques, their forms carved in plaster and inlaid with coloured glass. These various decorative techniques illustrate the entire range of iconography borrowed by the Mughals from Iran: bottles and jars, cups of fruit and bowls with lids, cypress and bouquets. Note also the white marble plinth, carved with bouquets and inlaid with black stone. The north side of the garden is bounded by a forbidding wall, with dark corridors that you can explore.

Upper Floor – Enter the sloping corridor (large enough to ride a horse through). Its walls feel soft and cool to the touch – they are covered with *arayish*, a mixture of marble powder, yoghurt and other ingredients, with which walls and sometimes even floors were coated.
Upstairs, the **Jas Mahal★** displays the same sophisticated and ornate style of decoration as the Jai Mandir, located just below. The room overlooks the valley and offers beautiful views over Maota Sagar and the Dilaram gardens. The jali enclosing the upper floor of the Ganesh Pol has a hexagonal pattern on the lattice through which the ladies of the court could discreetly follow the receptions taking place in the Diwan-i-Am. *Return to the ground floor.*

Zenana ('women's quarters') – *Access via a small open gate in the middle of the southern wall.* After the luxury of the royal apartments, the *zenana* seems very simple, even dull. A room to the right of the entrance still has a few badly-damaged paintings. If you walk through these dark galleries and tiny rooms, without windows or decorations, it becomes clear that the life of wives and concubines was not very pleasant. Each wife had her own apartment, which formed an independent unit, with a small courtyard and hammam, all arranged on two levels around a vast

© Anurag Mallick, Priya Ganapathy/MICHELIN

Sheesh Mahal, Jai Mandir

courtyard enclosed by high walls. The effect is more like a prison than the palace of a queen. The arrows indicate the way back to the main courtyard via the cafeteria and numerous souvenir shops. When you get back to Jaleb Chowk, head for the **terrace** (on the left), where there is a view of the fortifications and the nearby hill, topped by the fortress of Jaigarh, with the ancient city of Amer underneath.

🐾 You can access the Jaigarh Fort on foot from Chowk Jaleb by heading out via Chandpole (opposite the main entrance). At the foot of the hill, the road passes between a madrasa and a former royal residence before finally reaching the temple of Jagat Shirimani, the 'jewel of the world'. Allow half an hour for the walk.

Anokhi Museum of Hand Printing★§

Chanwar Palkiwalon ki Haveli, Sagar Rd (Kheri Gate), northern end of Amer behind Bihariji temple. ℘ 0141-2530226 or 2531267. www.anokhi.com. ○ Open Tue–Sat 10.30am–5pm, Sun 11am–4.30pm. Closed May–mid-Jul. ✏ Rs.30.

Housed in a restored haveli, a 20-minute walk (1.5km) from Amer fortress, the museum displays an array of traditional Rajasthani textiles, coloured with natural dyes, and decorated with block printing, and gives visitors an overview of the entire process of hand-printed cloth. The museum shop is worth a stop.

Jaigarh Fort★ Off map. E1

7km north-east of Amer Fort on a signposted road (30min walk). By car, drive back towards Jaipur, and when opposite Lake Mansagar, take the small road that heads (right) to Jaigarh and Ramgarh; after approx 1.5km, take the right fork (1km). ○ Open daily 9am–4.30pm. ✏ Rs.85; photo Rs.50; video Rs.200.

Although less interesting than Amer, Jaigarh Fort nonetheless provides spectacular evidence of the military power of the Rajputs under the Kachwaha

Dynasty. It was established in the 12C, when the Kachwahas took the Aravalli hills from the Meenas and made them the guardians of their treasure. Built to protect Man Singh I's Amer Palace, Jaigarh Fort was also a designated water reservoir, armoury and treasury. The current buildings date back to the 18C, but several changes were made in the years after.

Jaigarh is a tranquil contrast to the bustling tourist atmosphere of Amer. The Awami Gate opens onto a set of courtyards, buildings and temples, many of which are closed to the public. A tall watchtower, **Diva Burj**, dominates the imposing walls.

On the right, just past the entrance, is the old **cannon foundry** which was, in its time, one of the largest in India. It dates from the 18C and much of the equipment used to make the cannon is still virtually intact, including the blast furnace and the moulding system. The main charm of this part of the fort lies in its **scenic views** overlooking Amer and the surrounding hills.

Return to the fort's entrance. The path bearing to the left leads to the main buildings.

The first courtyard on the right, **Subhat Niwas**, served as an assembly hall for soldiers. It houses an miscellaneous collection of palanquins and chests displayed behind glass screens and metal bars.

At the far end of the **main courtyard** are two small 12C temples. One is dedicated to **Kali Bhairava** (the 'terrible' forms of Devi and Shiva), the other (rebuilt in the 20C) to **Hari-Hara**, a combined deity consisting half of Vishnu holding a disc, and the other half of Shiva, armed with his trident.

In the **weapons collection** in the next room, note in particular the guns, including a small one decorated with a tiger's head. The buildings opposite contain various objects that belonged to the royal family.

At the opposite end of the courtyard lie the fort's **water reservoirs**. Legend has it that it was under one of these that Jai Singh II buried the Kachwaha treasure.

Dreaming of Progress

Dhundhar, Ally of the Mughals

Jaipur was founded in 1727 by the Rajput Maharajah **Jai Singh II** (1699–1743), a member of the Kachwaha Dynasty. The dynasty ruled **Dhundhar** from their capital Amer, hidden in the hills 8km away, from the 12C onwards.

For some 400 years, Dhundhar remained a relatively small kingdom, but it was catapulted into prominence in the 16C, when Maharajah **Bhar Mal** (1548–74) formed an alliance with the Mughal Emperor Humayun. Bhar Mal placed himself under the sovereignty of Humayun, put his son in the service of the empire and, in an unprecedented move for a Hindu, gave his daughter in marriage to the son of the emperor, the future Akbar. In return, Humayun gave **Bhar Mal** command of an army and appointed him governor of the provinces he conquered on behalf of the empire.

This type of exchange would become traditional between the Mughals and Kachwahas and was soon imitated by other Rajput rulers. As for the Mughals, they had an interest in maintaining the alliance with Amer as it occupied a strategic position on the road between Delhi and Ajmer, an important centre of Islamic pilgrimage and capital of a Mughal province. Dhundhar's power flourished under **Man Singh I** (1589–1614) and **Jai Singh I** (1621–67), exceptional soldiers who won decisive victories on behalf of the Mughals.

A New Capital

The reign of **Jai Singh II** (1699–1743) marked another high point in Kachwaha power. A great soldier and brilliant statesman, he was also a scholar with an insatiable intellectual curiosity and a renowned astronomer who designed and built five innovative observatories. A visionary builder, it was Jai Singh II who gave Dhundhar its new capital, Jaipur.

On the death of Emperor Aurangzeb (1707), Jai Singh II united the Rajput kingdoms in a defensive alliance designed to liberate them from the waning Mughal power. By forming an alliance with the Sisodyas of Udaipur (longstanding enemies) and the Rathors of Jodhpur, he gained triumphant victories over the Mughals, with whom a peace treaty was signed in 1710. The city of Amer, perched awkwardly in a rocky mountain location, had become too small for such a powerful kingdom and in 1727 Jai Singh II decided to build a new capital on the plain. It would be a perfectly designed city, which he called 'Jaipur', meaning 'City of Jai', but also 'City of Victory'.

Urban Policy Dictated by Astronomy

Jai Singh II entrusted the construction of his new capital to Bengali priest and architect **Vidyadhar Bhattacharya**, who was also a mathematician. Bhattacharya planned the city on a grid layout, adopting the traditional diagrammatic form prescribed by the Vastu Vidya, an esoteric treatise on architecture: a square divided into nine equal sections (ten if you count the extension to the south-east) by four broad avenues intersecting at right angles. In fact, the symmetry is disturbed by the City Palace, which interrupts one of the two east–west arteries, and also to the north where the layout becomes irregular thanks to the general lie of the land and the failure of Jai Singh's successors to respect the original plan. The nine districts (mohalla) defined as a result, in parallel to the nine planets of Hindu astrology, were also divided according to caste, in other words by trade, with the two central districts being given over to the ruler for his state buildings and palaces. Descendants of the 18C stonecutters and jewellers still live in the neighbourhoods originally assigned to their ancestors. Each mohalla is crossed by streets and lanes parallel to the main thoroughfares. To create a sense of unity, all buildings were built in the same style and had the same number of floors. Attracted by Dhundhar's air of tranquillity, traders, moneylenders, jewellers and craftsmen, including many Jains, flocked to the new city, while the local nobility built havelis there.

Pink for the British

Until the early 19C, Dhundhar remained a haven of peace, security and prosperity, while unrest prevailed elsewhere – Sikhs paralysed trade routes through the Punjab, and the aggression of Jats and Marathas weakened the other Rajput states, which were also plagued by a series of succession disputes. However, in 1818, like other Rajput rulers, the Kachwahas eventually signed a separate treaty of defensive alliance with the British that guaranteed the security of their borders in exchange for some loss of independence. A British representative took up residence in Jaipur and the maharajah took advantage of the Pax Britannica to embark on public works to modernise the city. In 1876, Maharajah Ram Singh II (1835–80) painted the whole city pink to welcome the Prince of Wales (the future Edward VII), a tradition that continues to this day, with the local authorities ensuring that the old town is regularly repainted in his favourite colour.

Man Singh II, the Last Ruling Maharajah

In 1922 **Man Singh II**, originally the son of a local nobleman who had then been adopted by the previous maharajah who had no heirs, ascended the throne as a young boy. A handsome man, his ability on the polo field and his fashionable cosmopolitan lifestyle brought him fame and admiration. With his third wife, Gayatri Devi, whom Vogue ranked as one of the 10 most beautiful women in the world, they were the image of a modern and romantic couple, receiving the celebrities of the day at Rambagh Palace. In 1962, Maharani Gayatri Devi was elected to the Indian Parliament with a record majority according to the Guinness Book of Records. Maharajah Man Singh II died in 1970 after an accident while playing polo in Cirencester, England. His sons were businessmen and industrialists:the eldest, **Sawai Bhavani Singh**, was a supporter of the Indian National Congress party. When he died in April 2011 without a male heir, he was succeeded by **Sawai Padmanabh Singh**, aged 12, the son of his sister, as titular Maharajah of Jaipur.

A Great Modern Indian City

Man Singh II decided to establish his kingdom in the newly formed State of Rajasthan in 1949, two years after Indian Independence. Jaipur became the capital and its maharajah, governor of the new state. As contemporary India evolved, the harmonious, geometrical 18C layout so desired for the city by Jai Singh II, was totally forgotten as new districts emerged, extending beyond the city walls to the south and west. But it should be remembered that the population of Jaipur has quadrupled in just 50 years, a difficult situation, even for the most conscientious town planners.

Now head to the southernmost part of the fort, near its surrounding wall, to see the famous **Jaivan** cannon ('the Arrow of Jai'), reputed to be the largest cannon on wheels in the world, cast at Jaigarh in 1720. It is supposed to have fired just one cannonball.

Sanganer

Located 15km south of Jaipur.
Bus every 30mins from the bus station or Ajmeri Gate.

The town of Sanganer is principally of interest to textile enthusiasts (*see Shopping in Jaipur*). It takes its name from the 17C Kachwaha prince **Sangaji**, and is renowned for its block printing **textile workshops§**. The industry boomed in the 18C under the patronage of Jaipur's royal family. Now Sanganer seems a mundane and sleepy place, despite the many fabric shops that line its dusty streets.

A 16C Jain temple, **Shri Digambara Jain Mandir**, stands in the main bazaar, next to the Tripolia Gate. Dedicated to Adinatha, the first *tirthankara* (ascetic inspiration of the Jain religion), it contains beautiful sculptures, in striking contrast to the town's general state of decay.

On the banks of the *nala* (drainage channel), north of the city, miles of colourful fabrics are hung out to dry.

👥 Chokhi Dhani

25km south of Jaipur. Bus from Ajmeri Gate. www.chokhidhani.com. ☞ Rs.500, including meal. If you go in the evening, pre-book your taxi home.

This is a 'typical' Rajasthan village recreated as a theme park. It is popular with Indians and tourists alike. In addition to a small museum, it has a few craft shops and a whole series of restaurants and offers evening entertainment with traditional dances, songs and puppet shows, and for a few dozen extra rupees you can ride a camel. It is constantly busy at weekends.

ADDRESSES

🛏 STAY

It is advisable to book in advance in the high season (Nov–Mar), as this coincides with the wedding season.

STATION & SANSAR CHANDRA RDS

☞ **Sunder Palace Guest House** – *B2. Sanjay Marg. ☎ 0141-2360178. www.sunderpalace.com.* 🖥 ✕ 🗺. *Wi-Fi, English newspapers. 20 rm. Rs.950/1,550.* 🍽 *Rs.90. Rest. Rs.150/250.* Spacious and impeccable rooms, plus a lovely rooftop restaurant (with excellent thalis). Meticulous attention to detail. Friendly staff ready to provide detailed information about the city and the region. A pleasant garden and an excellent location.

☞ **Pearl Palace** – *B3. Hari Kishan Somani Marg. ☎ 0141-2373700. www. hotelpearlpalace.com.* 🖥 ✕. *25 rm. Rs.1,250/1,350.* Pearl Palace has a flashy pink façade but pleasant well-decorated rooms. It is often full, as it is popular with young British and American travellers. Book at least a month in advance.

☞ **Teej (RTDC)** – *A2. Sawai Jai Singh Highway. ☎ 0141-2205482. www.rtdc.in.* 🖥 ✕ 🍽 🗺. *47 rm. Rs.1,200/2,900* 🚗. A clean, rather quaint and peaceful place, halfway between the train and bus stations. This is one of the four RTDC hotels in Jaipur. Some rooms are not airconditioned.

☞ **Chirmi Palace (Heritage Hotels Association)** – *B3. Dhuleshwar Garden, Sardar Patel Rd. ☎ 0141-2365063. www.chirmi.com.* 🖥 ✕ 🍷 🛁. *24 rm. Rs.1,450/2,600.* 🍽 *Rs.200. Rest. Rs.400.* This 18C residence is set in a quiet and spacious neighbourhood, 8 minutes' walk from M.I. Rd. It is a pleasant place to stay and the rooms are large and comfortable, if a little dark. There's a beautiful dining room decorated with frescoes.

☞ **Arya Niwas** – *B2. Set back from Sansar Chandra Rd. ☎ 0141-4073456. www.aryaniwas.com.* 🖥 ✕. *Shop, bookshop, Internet, Wi-Fi. 94 rm. Rs.1,900/3,100* 🚗. *Rest. Rs.250.* A perfectly comfortable and friendly hotel, with plain but very large rooms, especially the 13 deluxe rooms with flatscreen TVs and safes. There's a garden and pleasant terrace for eating meals. Excellent value for money; good travel agency.

Bissau Palace (Heritage Hotels Association) – C1. Chandpole. ☏ 0141-2304371. www.bissaupalace.com. ✗ � �. Internet, travel agency. 51 rm. Rs.3,600/5,000. In a district north of Chandpole, this beautiful property was built in 1919 for the rawa of Bissau, whose descendants still live in the area. Choose a room in the old building but have a look at several of them, as they are all different. You can tour the town in an old 1931 convertible.

Mansingh Hotel and Mansingh Towers (Mansingh Group) – B2. Set back from Sansar Chandra Rd. ☏ 0141-2378771. www.mansinghhotels.com/jaipur.aspx. ✗ � �. Spa, beauty salon. 159 rm. Rs.4,600/7,600 ☎. Rest. Rs.1,000. An international hotel with all mod cons (flatscreen TV, wi-fi, safe). Beautiful bay windows make the rooms very light. The newest building, Mansingh Towers, was designed especially for business people.

Alsisar Haveli (Heritage Hotels Association) – B2. Sansar Chandra Rd. ☏ 01412368290. www.alsisarhaveli.com. ✗ � �. Internet. 45 rm. Rs.6,600/8,300. ☎ Rs.350. Rest. Rs.750. This tastefully restored haveli is shielded from the street by a garden and has a large pleasant terrace, charming inner courtyards, a lovely lounge and dining room. The rooms are clean, tastefully decorated, and all have a bath. There is a TV in some of them.

Rajputana Palace Sheraton (ITC Group) – A2. Palace Rd. ☏ 0141-5100100. www.itchotels.in. ✗ � �. Shops, beauty salon, Internet, wi-fi, spa. 218 rm. Rs.9,000/12,000 ☎. A luxury hotel in a huge brick building with wings that spread out onto beautiful lawns. Endless corridors lead to the bedrooms and bathrooms, with neat green marble floors and designer furniture. All very comfortable, but lacking in warmth.

Sarovar Portico – Jaipur Plot No. 90, Bhan Nagar B, Prince Road, Queens Road, Vaishali Nagar. ☏ 0141-5157777. www.sarovarhotels.com. Rs.8,000-12,000. r82 �, Wi-Fi, ☎. A modern elegant city hotel, 14km away from airport and 5km from the Railway station. Unwind at Sunset Bar or dine at The Pavilion, a 24/7 restaurant with Indian and international cusine or Jaipur Grill, a lovely rooftop restaurant sizzling with scrumptious grills.

BANI PARK DISTRICT

This chic and quiet residential district extends approx. 2.5km west of the old town. The only downside is that the only local restaurants are those in hotels.

Jaipur Inn – B2. B-17 Shiv Marg, Bani Park. ☏ 0141-2201121. www.jaipurinn.com. ✗ �. Wi-Fi. 25 rm. Rs.1,500/2,000. ☎ Rs.150. Rest. Rs.300 (buffet, including vegetarian option; book before 5pm). This is a hospitable, well-run hotel with a friendly atmosphere and a full range of services (including a book exchange and table tennis). Jaipur blue pottery adorns the public areas. The rooms, which are spacious and bright, are decorated in traditional cotton fabric and overlook beautiful wooded terraces. There's a nice rooftop restaurant, open to non-residents.

Umaid Bhawan Guest House – A2. Behari Marg, Bani Park. ☏ 0141-2316184. www.umaidbhawan.com. ✗ �. Internet, lift. 32 rm. Rs.2,200/3,300 ☎. A large house rich in Mughal architectural features, where lavishly decorated hallways, bedrooms and patios are filled with traditional furniture and regional handicrafts. The whole place is very well kept. The hotel offers a pick-up service on arrival in the city.

Raj Mahal Palace – A4. Sardar Patel Marg. ☏ 0141-4143000. www.rajmahalpalacejaipur.com. ✗ � �. Library for guests, Wi-Fi. Rs.5,000/7,000. This elegant palace, built in the early 18C by Jai Singh II, the founder of Jaipur, was the residence of the British representative in the 19C. It then became a royal residence in the 1960s. Its conversion into a hotel has not changed its structure or diminished its intimate and refined atmosphere. The superior suites are all very different sizes for the same price; one of them consists of four separate rooms.

Jai Mahal Palace (Taj Group) – A3. Jacob Rd, Civil Lines. ☏ 0141-6601111. www.tajhotels.com. ✗ � �. Wi-Fi, shops, beauty salon, spa, miniature golf course. 100 rm starting from Rs.22,000 ☎. This Indo-Muslim style palace, where the Resident Surgeon, Colonel Thomas Holbein Hendley lived in the late 19C, became the official residence of the prime ministers of Jaipur. He opted for a contemporary décor: with a monochrome aesthetic in the 'turquoise' or 'red' rooms, all very stylishly designed.

OLD TOWN

L.M.B. Hotel – *D2. Johari Bazar.* *0141-2565844. www.hotellmb.com.* *Lift. 33 rm. Rs.3,200/5,500.* You might wish to cast a blind eye on the corridors, which are rather creepy, as the rooms, despite extremely simple décor, are bright, spacious and very reasonable. The hotel has a great location in the heart of the old town and is above the restaurant of the same name.

Giri Sadan – *08, Devi Niketan Compound, Sardar Patel Marg.* *0141-2371385, 2364191. www.girisadanhomestay.com. Rs.2,900. r11. Wi-Fi,* . With spacious rooms and balconies, this popular homestay, located 3.5km from Hawa Mahal, is known for its proprietor Capt. S.K. Singh's warm hospitality, friendly staff and home-cooked meals (veg Rs.350, non-veg Rs.450).

SOUTH OF OLD TOWN

Nana ki Haveli – *D3. Fateh Tiba, Moti Dungri Rd.* *0141-2615502. www.nanakihaveli.com.* *Internet. 15 rm. Rs.2,500/3,600.* Situated in a neighbourhood of artisans, 700m from the old town, this late 19C residence is inhabited by a charming Rajput family. Clean and bright rooms, simply, but carefully decorated with beautiful fabrics and dhurries.

Diggi Palace (Heritage Hotels Association) – *C3. Diggi House, Shivaji Rd, 1km from the old town.* *0141-2366120. www.hoteldiggipalace.com.* *Internet. 60 rm. Rs.5,000/6,000* . The zenana of the palace of the Thakur of Diggi (early 18C) offers functional rooms but nothing more. You will probably prefer those of the haveli in the garden, which are spacious and bright. There's a nice courtyard and terraces extending to a large peaceful garden that gives the impression of being in the countryside. The owner, a polo fan, also organises literary and musical events, the most popular of which is the Jaipur Literature Festival (21-25 Jan in 2015).

Narain Niwas Palace (Heritage Hotels Association) – *C4. Kanota Bagh, Narain Singh Rd, 2.5km from the old town.* *0141-2561291. www.hotelnarainniwas.com.* *Billiards room, Internet. 37 rm. Rs.7,700/10,000* . *Rest. Rs.1,000.* This patrician house is of mixed architectural style and has a large garden. It was built in 1881 by Narain Singh of Kanota and extended around 1930 by the diplomat and general Amar Singh. The Kanota family itself manages this boutique hotel, which is chic but a bit outdated. You could spend hours on the porch and in the living room where the late 19C furniture and family mementos have remained in place. The spacious but dark rooms could do with a lick of paint.

Rambagh Palace (Taj Group) – *C4. Bhawani Singh Rd, 3km from the old town.* *0141-2211919. www.tajhotels.com.* *Wi-Fi, shops, spa. 79 rm, starting from Rs.30,000* . A former hunting lodge enlarged in 1905 by Sir Swinton Jacob and decorated in Art Deco style for Man Singh II, who made it his principal residence before transforming it into a hotel in 1957, thereby opening the first palace hotel in India. A garden sits alongside, with two U-shaped sections around a lawn, forming a kind of marble salon. It is a great place to take tea. The enormous rooms have lavishly fitted bathrooms, with the countless little extra touches that make all the difference.

ROAD TO AMER

Holiday Inn – *E1. Amer Rd, 500m from Zorawar Gate.* *0141-2672000. www.holidayinnjaipur.com.* *Wi-Fi, shops, gym. 84 rm. Rs.4,100/5,900* . An excellent hotel, built around a courtyard in the haveli style and offering every possible comfort. However, somewhat lacking in atmosphere.

The Trident (The Oberoi) – *E1. Amer Fort Rd, Jal Mahal.* *0141-2670101. www.tridenthotels.com.* *132 rm approx. Rs.16,000* . Facing the Jal Mahal posed like a mirage overlooking the lake, this luxury hotel has impersonal décor but a lively and friendly atmosphere. Ask for a room overlooking the lake.

Samode Haveli – *E1. Gangapole.* *0141-2632407. www.samode.com.* *Wi-Fi, spa, travel agency. 39 rm. Rs.17,000/19,000* . In a quiet corner of the walled city, on the road to Amer, this beautiful 18C haveli belonging to the thakur of Samode is one of the finest places in Jaipur. The reception rooms and dining room have retained their outstanding original frescoes, and the rooms are decorated in traditional style, but with great taste. Huge pool in a large garden. The entire place is delightful.

The Raj Palace – *E1. Chomu Haveli, Zorawar Singh Gate, Amer Rd.*

📞 0141-2634077. www.rajpalace.com.
🖥 ✗ 🍷 🗑. Wi-Fi, spa. 40 rm. Rs.30,000/
46,000. 🛏 Rs.1,750. Rest. Rs.4,000/5,000.
This impressive five-storey pale yellow
haveli, built in 1728 for the Lord of
Chomu, is among the oldest in Jaipur.
The quality of its architecture, arayish
(plastering) and marble floors cannot be
denied, although in the bedrooms, the
décor leaves something to be desired.
The service is rather disorganised.

AROUND JAIPUR

🛏🛏 **Lebua Lodge, Amer** – *Kunda,
NH-8, Tehsil Amer.* 📞 *0141-3057211. www.
lebua.com/lebua-lodge-amer. Rs.11,000. 40
tents. Wi-Fi.* ♿, 🛏. Follow the meandering
Amer fort wall past an ancient gateway.
Located in a geometric garden against
a backdrop of rocky hills, Lebua's cuboid
canvas tents are interspaced with
sculpted landscape. Each tent comes
with hill views, light-filtering curtains, a
private pavilion and an attached bath
with garden area. Toran restaurant serves
Indian dishes and the spa by L'Occitane
offers Indian and Mediterranean
treatments.

🛏🛏🛏🛏 **Lebua Resort** – *Jamdoli, Agra
Road, Tehsil Ballupura.* 📞 *0141-3050211.
www.lebua.com/lebua-resort-jaipur.
Rs.13,143-18,776. 60 rooms & villas. Wi-Fi.*
🛏. Themed after the navratnas (nine
precious gems) with interiors inspired
by Jantar Mantar and Jaipur's legendary
gem craft, this boutique red sandstone
hotel (earlier Devi Ratn) is flamboyance
personified. It has louvered walkways, a
filigreed lobby, a dining space that seems
to float and crescent shaped streets at
varying heights, so that each suite has
an uninterrupted view of the Aravallis.
Located 10km from town, the Vajra
restaurant and Chakra bar ensure you
don't need to step out.

🛏🛏🛏🛏 **Fairmont Jaipur** – *2, Riico
Kukas.* 📞 *0142-6420000, +91 8772891012.
www.fairmont.com. Rs.8,887-22,218.
r199. Wi-Fi.* 🛏. Built with the sensibil-
ity of a Mughal palace with traditional
Rajasthani ethos, Fairmont is located
20km from the city, both a boon and
a bother. Equipped with a pool, it has
eight dining options including Zoya, an
all-day dining restaurant, specialty teas
at Anjum and Aza the library bar.

🛏🛏🛏🛏 **Tree of Life Resort & Spa** –
Kacherawala, Kookas. 📞 *+91 9602091000,
9602092000. www.treeofliferesorts.com.*
*Rs.10,500-21,000 (plus taxes). 13 villas.
free Wi-Fi available.* ♿, 🛏, pets allowed.
Spread over 7 acres, with distinctive
villas, Tree of Life is special. The spacious
garden or pool villas have a backyard
with an outdoor bathtub for a dip under
the stars. Meditate in the Ganesh pavilion
or Navagraha platform with luxurious
spa treatments, a personalised menu
with five-course organic meals and an
infinity pool inspired by the step-wells
of Rajasthan. Activities like Teach A While
(in the nearby school that the resort
supports); Dinner With Your Elephant and
The Chef In You where you go grocery
shopping with the chef who guides you
to cook your own meal!

🛏🛏🛏🛏 **Chomu Palace Hotel** –
33km from Jaipur, Chomu District. 📞 *01423-
300300. www.chomupalacehotel.com.
Rs.12,000-75,000. r58. no Wi-Fi.* 🛏, ♿.
The 300-year-old palace changed several
hands and was used as a rice mill and
storehouse before being renovated by
the Dangayach Group into a striking
luxury hotel. Its vast compound, majestic
rooms, antique furniture, fine wall frescos
and lush gardens reverberate with Old
World lavishness. The fort palace hotel
fuses European gabled roofs with Indian
and Mughal architectural elements.
Relax in the opulent Sheesh Mahal, a
lounge bar or drop by at Sansha Spa.

PACHAR

*Via NH 11, 85km north-west of Jaipur. At
Chomu, turn left towards Kishangarh, where
you then turn right.* Pachar has a beautiful
Jain temple.

🛏🛏 **Golden Castle Resort (Heritage
Hotels Association)** – *A3. Book in Jaipur.*
📞 *0141-2226920. www.castlepachar.com.*
✗ 📠. *15 rm. Rs.4,200* 🛏. Cooler supplied
on request – booking essential. Situated
between some sand dunes and a lake,
this beautiful old castle is full of character;
it has been restored but without altering
the structure or décor. Jeep and camel
tours, and visits to Shekhawati are
available.

BHANDAREJ

*On the road to Bharatpur and Agra (NH 11),
approx. 65km east of Jaipur. 9km after
Dausa, turn right.* Interesting baori in a
pretty village.

🛏🛏 **Bhadrawati Palace (Heritage
Hotels Association)** – *B3. Bhandarej.*
📞 *01427-283351. Book in Jaipur.* 📞 *0141-
2363262. www.hotelbhadrawatipalace.com.*

🛏✕🍷🛋. *35 rm. Rs.3,500/4,500* 🚗. Booking recommended. A large 16C palace, with flower gardens and interior courtyards. Although they vary in size, the rooms are comfortable with modern bathrooms. Meals are served in the beautiful durbar hall, a combination of white marble and turquoise plastering. Horseback excursions are available.

PACHEWAR
On the road to Ajmer and Pushkar (NH 8), 90km south-west of Jaipur. At Dudu, take the road on the right to Malpura.

🛏🛏**Pachewar Garh (Heritage Hotels Association)** – *A3.* ✆ *09413340169. Book in Jaipur.* ✆ *0141-2601007. www. pachewargarhfort.com.* ✕🛋🛁. *10 rm. Rs.5,500* ♿. Booking recommended. A charming small 17C fort. The rooms are fairly comfortable, although there are frequent power cuts and the service is rather disorganised, but overall the hotel has character and a friendly welcome.

KANOTA
On the road to Bharatpur and Agra (NH 11), 15km east of Jaipur.

🛏🛏🛏**Royal Castle Kanota (Heritage Hotels Association)** – *A3. Kanota, right at the edge of town.* ✆ *0141-2561291. www. hotelnarainniwas.com.* ✕🍷. *15 rm. Rs.10,000* 🚗. *Rest. Rs.1,000.* Booking essential at the Narain Niwas Palace Hotel in Jaipur. A beautiful 19C building in the grounds of a medieval fort. The architecture and the garden are charming, and the rooms have kept their old-fashioned, albeit slightly worn, look. Excursions on horseback.

SAMODE
40km north of Jaipur on the NH 11. At Chomu, take the small road on the right (8km).

🛏🛏🛏**Samode Bagh (Heritage Hotels Association)** – *A3. Fatehpura, 3km from Samode.* ✆ *0141-2632370. www.samode.com or book at the Samode Haveli Hotel in Jaipur.* 🛏✕🍷🛋. *44 rm. Rs.10,000* 🚗. A lovely Mughal garden with canals, ponds, fountains and marble pavilions aligned with the row of 44 luxurious tents, each with a marble-floored bathroom. Meals are cooked in the kitchens at Samode Palace (see opposite) and are reheated on site.

🛏🛏🛏🛏**Samode Palace (Heritage Hotels Association)** – *A3. Samode.* ✆ *0141-2632370. www.samode.com.* 🛏✕🍷🛋. *43 rm including 18 suites. Rs.21,000* 🚗. Book well in advance on the Internet or at the Samode Haveli Hotel in Jaipur. Situated in the foothills of the mountains, this imposing palace has fortified Rajput architecture and elegant decoration, making it one of the finest in Rajasthan. To see the lavish room where the rawals (rulers) of Samode held their durbar (courts), you will need to pay Rs.500 or have dinner at the hotel (approx. Rs.1,500).

JAMWA RAMGARH
22km north-east of Jaipur. Head out on the Amer Road and turn right 1.5km after the Zorawar Singh Gate. Access to the hotel is by the dam on the left side of the road.

🛏🛏🛏🛏**Ramgarh Lodge** – *A3. Ramgarh Lake, Jamwa Ramgarh.* ✆ *0142-6214027. www.thegatewayhotels.com.* 🛏✕🍷🛋. *Billiards room, tennis court. 14 rm. Rs.14,000/18,000* 🚗. Half-board only. Also known as Gateway Hotel Ramgarh, this royal hunting lodge nestling between the hills and the lake was built in 1931 in the Art Deco style. Nothing has changed since then, it seems. A lawn slopes gently, almost serenely, down from the verandah to the lake. Hunting trophies decorate the wooden staircase and lounge. The rooms are large and elegant, and the best have views over the lake.

🍽 EAT

AROUND STATION RD AND SANSAR CHANDRA RD

🛏**Rawat** – *B2. Station Rd.* ✆ *0141-2363593.* 🚗. *Open daily 10am–10pm. Rs.170/250.* This group of tall, red buildings is very popular for its kachori (deep-fried and stuffed savoury pastry) and Bengali sweets which can be enjoyed on the terrace set back from the street. Pay when you order. Quick service.

🛏🛏🛏**Peshawri** – *A2. Rest. at the Rajputana Palace Sheraton Hotel.* 🍷. *Open daily 12.30pm–2.45pm, 7.30pm–11.30pm. Approx. Rs.1,200.* This is the sister establishment of the famous Bukhara restaurant in Delhi. It has the same décor, like an inn in the mountains of Afghanistan, and serves cuisine from the former North-West Frontier Province, consisting mainly of delicious kebabs.

OLD TOWN

🛏**Lakshmi Mishtan Bhandar (L.M.B.)** – *D2. Rest. at the hotel of the same name.* ✆ *0141-2578845. www.hotellmb.com. Open daily 8am–11pm. Rs.350/450.* An institution! No Indian comes to Jaipur without having at least one meal in the great hall of L.M.B. with its velvet and white tableclothes. The menu, which is completely vegetarian, is full of northern Indian and Rajasthan dishes, with special emphasis on thalis. Sattvic cuisine, prepared according to the principles set out by Krishna in the Bhagavad Gita. Finish your meal with sweets, their speciality.

ON MIRZA ISMAIL RD

A 2km stretch of this street contains the well-regarded restaurants in Jaipur as well as a large number of popular establishments.

Pizza Hut – *B2. Ganpati Plaza.* 0141-4008628. www.pizzahut.co.in. *Open daily 11am–11pm. Rs.200/500.* An anodyne setting but the best pizzas in town.

Surya Mahal – *C3. M.I. Rd, near Niros.* 0141-2362811. www.suryamahal.com. *Open daily 8am–11pm. Rs.300/450.* Two bustling dining rooms which serve vegetarian cuisine from North and South India, continental and Chinese dishes, pizzas and ice cream.

Natraj – *C3. M.I. Rd. Not to be confused with the Natraj Hotel, also on M.I. Rd.* 0141-2375804. *Open daily 9.30am–11pm. Rs.350/450.* A comfortable but windowless restaurant which serves classical vegetarian food from North and South India. Its speciality is the vegetable kofta (dumplings of chopped vegetables, cooked in a spicy sauce). You choose your dessert from a showcase of Bengali sweets.

Geetanjali – *B2. Rest. at the Maharani Palace Hotel, Station Rd.* 0141-2204378. *Open daily 1.30pm–3pm, 7.30pm–11pm. Rs.400/550.* Large, comfortable air-conditioned room with frescoes and wooden panelling. The maharani thali gives you the chance to try several Rajasthani specialities. Ghazals from 8pm. Bar adjacent.

Handi – *B3. M.I. Rd, opposite the GPO.* 0141-2364839. www.handi restaurant.com. *Open daily 12.30pm–3.30pm, 6.30pm–11pm. Approx. Rs.500.* Good Mughlai and tandoori cuisine, but the portions could be more generous. Specialities include handi, meat simmered in a clay pot, and roomali roti, a thin bread like a handkerchief. The place is expensive for what it is and is sometimes very smoky.

Hightz – *B2. Rest. at the Mansingh Hotel. Open daily 7pm–10.30pm. Approx.*

Rs.550. Bar adjacent. A cosy room in the basement where you will be served the best Mughlai cuisine in Jaipur. Try the specialities, pudina paneer masala (cheese and spinach cooked in mint) and tarkari papad rolls (crispy lentil flour pancakes stuffed with potato, herbs, raisins and cashew nuts). There is ghazal singing here Sunday to Friday from 7.30pm, while on Saturdays there is a disco.

Moti Mahal Delux – *C3. M.I. Rd.* 0141-4017733. g. *Open daily 11am–11pm. Rs.450/600.* Chicken, mutton and fish cooked in the tandoor or in curries are served in an air-conditioned room on two levels. It is not particularly charming, but is popular with a local clientele.

Niros – *C3. M.I. Rd. t 0141-2218520.* www.nirosindia.com. g. *Open daily 10am–11pm. Rs.600/1,000.* This is one of the major landmarks of the city. It has an extensive menu offering both fish and meat dishes. A lively atmosphere with the large mirrors on the walls compensating for the lack of natural light. Good Indian, tandoori and continental cuisine.

Indiana – *C3. J2-34 Mahaveer Rd.* 0141-2362061. www.indianajaipur.com. *Open daily noon–3pm, 7pm–10pm. Rs.800/1,000.* Wicker chairs and tables are scattered on a lawn and inside two buildings with earthen walls. Try the Indiana chicken, cooked in the tandoor and finished in a tomato and cream sauce scented with herbs. There's a folk show from 7pm to 10pm. Inflated prices.

CIVIL LINES DISTRICT

Marble Arch – *A3. Rest. at the Jai Mahal Palace Hotel.* *Open daily 6.30am–11.30pm. Approx. Rs.1,500.* One of the best restaurants in Jaipur. The menu offers a range of continental, Chinese, Indian and Rajasthani dishes, including the famous lahsuni murg tikka, a garlic chicken tikka.

SOUTH OF OLD TOWN

Flow – *C3. Rest. at the Diggi Palace Hotel.* *Open Wed–Mon 1.30pm–10pm. Rs.350/500.* Some tables beside the swimming pool are ideal for a quiet lunch. The limited menu offers carefully selected modern Mediterranean and Asian dishes with organic vegetables.

Narain Niwas Palace – *C4. Rest. at the hotel of the same name.* *Open daily 7am–11pm. Approx. Rs.1,000.* Many people in Jaipur think this is one of the best restaurants in town. You can enjoy tandoori, continental and Chinese dishes in a lovely room with columns, or in the orchard when the weather permits. Alcohol is served in the adjoining lounge and veranda.

🍷🍷🍷 **Rajput Room** – *C4. Rest. at the Rambagh Palace Hotel.* 🍷 *Open daily 6am–midnight. Approx. Rs.2,000.* Marble and chandeliers beneath large arches make for a refined ambience. In terms of the dishes available, you can enjoy caviar, coquilles Saint-Jacques à la tapenade, risotto and other sophisticated and luxurious recipes from a wide variety of cuisines. Delightful food in an exceptional setting.

🍷🍷🍷 **Suvarnal Mahal** – *C4. Rest. at the Rambagh Palace Hotel.* 🍷 *Open daily noon–3pm, 7pm–midnight. Approx. Rs.3,500.* One of the three restaurants in the finest hotel in the city has a menu containing the favourite dishes of the royal families of four regions of India. Everything is a speciality here! A superb (but expensive) wine list.

TAKING A BREAK

Bake Hut – *C3. Arvind St, near the Surya Mahal restaurant.* A good place for its fresh baked cookies and pastries that are packed in pretty boxes.

Lassiwala – *C3. Opposite the Natraj restaurant.* Try the most famous lassi in the city at one of three tiny adjacent stalls with the same name. They also serve samosas, mirchi pakoda (chilli fritters) and kachori in their back room.

Lakshmi Mishtan Bhandar (L.M.B.) – *D2. Johari Bazar.* 📞 *0141-2565846. Open daily 8am–11pm.* To eat in or take away, sweets and tempting namkeen fill the windows. Other sweets include rasmalai, balls of semolina and condensed milk, flavoured with lemon and cardamom, served in a pistachio cream.

BARS

Indian Coffee House – *C2–3. M.I. Rd, in the same building as Lacoste, at the back of the courtyard. Open daily 8am–9pm.* In these three small rooms, you will find intellectuals commenting on the news in a warm atmosphere that combines coffee and business. Enjoy a real coffee and snacks for a few dozen rupees.

Bouncer Bar – *C2–3. M.I. Rd, east of Niros.* 🍷 *Open daily 11am–11pm.* A proper Indian bar, long and dark, decorated with false bricks and cheap wood. You can savour a few snacks with your beer.

Mansagar – *off map, D1. Bar at The Trident Hotel.* 🍷 *Open daily 11am–11pm.* A very pleasant place to stop when you come back from Amer. A covered terrace overlooks the lake and the Jal Mahal.

Polo Bar – *C4. Bar at the Rambagh Palace Hotel. Noon–midnight.* This is the only room in the palace that has not been altered by the creation of the hotel. Armchairs and sofas surround a blue faience pool. On the walls, mallets, photographs and prints reflect the passion of Maharajah Man Singh II for polo. Wine is sold by the glass, along with a wide range of cocktails and Cuban cigars.

SHOPPING

BAZAARS

The following is a list of the specialities of each mohalla of the Pink City – worth bearing in mind for souvenir shopping or photographs.

Silver – Hawa Mahal (*D2*), Kishanole Bazaar (*C2*) and, outside the city walls, Chameli Market (*B3*)

Wicker chairs – Choti Chaupar (*C2*)

Shoes – Ramganj Bazaar (*D2*)

Leather – Hawa Mahal (*D2*), Bapu Market (9 km from Johari Bazar)

Copper and bronze – Thateron ka Rasta (near Chaura Rasta) (*D2*)

Gold and silver leaf – around Johari Bazar (*D2*)

Lacquer – Maniharon ka Rasta (*C2*)

Pickles – Chandpole (*C2*)

Semi-precious stones – Gopal ji ka Rasta (*D2*)

Pottery – Kumharon ki Nadi (near Ramganj Bazaar) (*D2*)

Suits and namkeens – Chaura Rasta (*D2*)

Marble cutters – Kalyan ji ka Rasta (*C2*)

Block printing – Purani Basti (all the streets to the north of Chandole Bazaar) (*C1–2*)

Fabrics – Johari Bazar (*D2*)

Turbans – Badi Chaupar (*D2*)

The most modern and reputable shops are along **M.I. Rd** and they also offer many brands of ready-to-wear Western clothing. Modernised stalls in **Bapu Bazar** (*D3*) and **Nehru Bazar** (*C2*), inside the walls, mark the transition between M.I. Rd and the traditional bazaars of the old town, where you have to haggle hard. Most are closed on Sundays, with the exception of shops in the Nehru Bazar, which are closed on Tuesdays.

Worth knowing – Compare items and shops to the bazaars; make your purchases at the end of your stay, once you are more aware of the prices.

MARKETS

The busiest are outside **Chandpole** (C2), as well as on **Choti Chaupar** (C2) and to the south of **Johari Bazar** (D2–3). Notice the heavy sticks the sellers carry – look up to the treetops and rooftops for monkeys waiting for the right moment to dash down to steal fruit and vegetables.

CRAFTS

As you wander through the bazaars, you will find plenty of opportunities to buy small items of craftwork and amazing jewellery.

Rajasthali – C3. M.I. Rd, beside Ajmeri Gate. www.rajasthali.gov.in. Open Mon–Sat 11am–7.30pm. This state store offers a good range of regional crafts, but at excessive prices.

SOUVENIRS

Tour buses make their way along Amer Road, which is lined with shops (open daily), especially around **Zorawar Singh Gate** (DE1). They sell jewellery, textiles, carpets, paintings… The prices are higher than elsewhere, because the commission paid to the driver by the shopkeepers is recouped via the selling price. It is best not to shop here; there are other souvenir shops around the City Palace and opposite the Hawa Mahal, where prices are much lower and negotiable.

FABRICS

A speciality of the Jaipur region, the cotton fabrics from Sanganer and Bagru, block-printed and dyed with natural or synthetic pigments, are sold by the metre or made up into tablecloths, scarves or clothes. Another speciality is cotton or silk decorated with chevrons (lahariya) or small white circles on a coloured background (bandhani), produced by using tie-and-dye techniques. These are also sold not only by the metre but made up into saris, dupattas (long scarves) and turbans.

Rajasthan Handloom House – C3. M.I. Rd, next to Rajasthali. Hand-woven fabrics, sold by the metre. Prices are marked and haggling is not possible.

Textorium – C3. M.I. Rd, between the Indian Coffee House and Ajmeri Gate. www.textorium.com. Open Mon–Sat, 10am–8.30pm. A good place to buy silk fabrics by the metre, saris, dupattas and scarves. Some fine woollen shawls. A little expensive.

At Sanganer – You can see dyers and block printers at work here and buy their products, too. **J.K. Arts** – Main Rd. Open daily 10am–7pm. Exports mainly to Japan. The factory stands on the banks of the nala (drainage channel). **Shilpi Handicrafts** – On a narrow alley parallel to the nala. www.shilpihandicraft.com. Open Mon–Sat 8am–7.30pm. Specialist in silks block-printed with natural dyes.

CLOTHES, HOUSEHOLD LINEN

The enduring interest in 'ethnic' fashion and the arrival of stylists and designers who have revived the use of traditional Rajasthani motifs, means that Jaipur's textile production is now some of the most creative and dynamic in India. There are several places where you can buy good-quality clothes, accessories or home and table linen, such as the famous razais (quilts), which are light as a feather.

Anokhi – B3. Prithviraj Rd. www.anokhi.com. Open daily 9.30am–8pm. Involved in the collection and preservation of Rajasthan's crafts and craftwork environment, Anokhi has contributed to the revival of traditional textiles. Also at Amer in the Anokhi Museum of Hand Printing.

Soma – A3. Jamnalal Bajaj Rd. www.somashop.com. Open Mon–Sat 10am–8pm, Sun 10am–6pm. Block-printed household linen, accessories and ready-to-wear clothes.

Sodhi's – off map, E1. Amer Rd, near the Trident Hotel. Premium fabrics, but watch out for bright colours that fade when washed. High prices.

CARPETS

The textile warehouses along **Amer Road**, north of Zorawar Singh Gate (E1), offer a wide selection of new carpets and rugs (dhurries), in knotted wool and woven cotton. You can also see the various stages of carpet manufacture. The tourist buses all stop here but it's as well to make it clear that you are not part of one of these tours to be offered lower prices.

Carpet Mahal – E1. Amer Rd, on the left after Zorawar Singh Gate. www.carpetmahal.com. Specialises in woollen carpets.

Arihant Arts – E1. Amer Rd, on the right after Zorawar Singh Gate, in an alley which runs alongside the Raj Palace Hotel. A small family business, generally overlooked by tourists, which only sells dhurries.

HANDMADE PAPER

Salim's Paper – *In Sanganer. Gramodyog Rd (perpendicular to Main Rd). www. handmadepaper.com.* An export-oriented family business. Before entering the store itself, you will be able to see the various stages of the manufacturing process, demonstrating how paper is made from scraps of cloth and how it is decorated with flower petals, herbs or leaves.

BLUE POTTERY

This beautiful, predominantly blue pottery, with details picked out in white, yellow or green, has been made in Jaipur since the 19C. Vases, small boxes, tiles, etc. are decorated with flowers or geometric patterns.

Kripal Khumb – *B2.* Shiv Rd, Bani Park. www.kripalkumbh.com.

Neerja International – *A3.* Anand Bhawan, Jacob Road, Civil Lines. www.neerjainternational.com. Open Mon–Sat 9.30am–6pm. A wide range of pottery is sold here.

Blue Pottery Art Centre – *off map, E1.* Amer Rd, near the Holiday Inn. Jewellery and ceramics.

In Sanganer – **Jaipur India Blue Art Pottery** – Basement of Sakshi textile store, Main Rd.

SHOES

Ramganj Bazaar – *D2.* Jutti (footwear) in sheepskin, camel skin or goatskin leather, embroidered with colourful stitching or covered with velvet embroidered in gold.

JEWELLERY

Gold jewellery is a speciality of the region, including cabochon (kundankari), polished on one side and with enamel work (minakari) on the reverse. All the jewellers also sell antique jewellery, only displayed on request.

🕮 **Worth knowing** – Make the most of your stay in the Rajasthani capital to shop for jewellery. You can find some excellent bargains, but only buy from reputable outlets. If you have any doubts, have the stones tested at the **GemTesting Laboratory** – *D3, set back from M.I. Rd, near New Gate.* 📞 *0141-2568221. Open Mon–Fri 10am–5.30pm.* The results will be provided the next day at 4pm.

Never buy stones in bulk or agree to export them on behalf of a jeweller: scams like this are common in Jaipur and Agra.

Gem Palace – *C3. M.I. Rd. www.gem palacejaipur.com. Open daily 10.30am–6.30pm.* This place is a real institution. In the jewellery trade since 1852, the Kasliwal family supply the royal family of Jaipur. Many jewellers in the Place Vendôme in Paris rely on them for precious stones. There is an antique car collection in the courtyard.

Jaipur Emporium – *C3.* M.I. Rd, beside the Gem Palace. Open Mon–Sat 11am–7.30pm.

Gem Plaza – *C3.* M.I. Rd. Gyan Chand Dhaddha will show his personal hookah collection to those interested.

Royal Gems & Arts – *C1. Saras Sadan Haveli, Gangauri Bazaar (entrance next to a primary school). www.royalgemsandarts. com. Open Mon–Sat 10am–8pm.* The shop is located upstairs in a room covered with stunning frescoes. An upmarket company that sells several collections of jewellery and works of art.

ETHNIC JEWELLERY

Tholia's Kuber – *C3. M.I. Rd, opposite Niros. Open Mon–Sat 10am–7.30pm.* Original pieces of jewellery or good-quality copies.

Amrapali – *C3. Panch Batti Circle. www.amrapalijewels.com. Open daily 11am–9pm.* Antique jewellery and pieces inspired by traditional themes.

Johari Bazar (the 'jewellers' market') and the adjacent streets (especially Gopal ji ka Rasta and Haldiyon ka Rasta) (*D2*) contain a large number of jewellers' shops. Go to the shops just mentioned, unless you come across a genuine dealer for small purchases (they generally speak good English and are paid a commission).

SILVER JEWELLERY AND BANGLES

Traditional stalls selling silver jewellery line the south-east corner of **Badi Chaupar** and the start of **Ramganj Bazaar** (*D2*). If you are looking for glass bangles or bracelets, try the north-west corner of **Badi Chaupar** (*D2*), or **Maniharon ka Rasta** (*C2*) for brightly coloured lacquer bracelets.

CULINARY SPECIALITIES

If you are a fan of *mithayan* (confectionery) and *namkeen* (spicy or sweet and sour appetisers) make sure you visit **L.M.B.** (🕮 *see TAKING A BREAK, p208*). In the streets running north and south of here, you'll be able to see how mithayan and paneer (curd cheese) are made. Or stroll along **Acharwallon ki Galli**, the 'street of the achar sellers' to see the wide array of achar or pickles (vegetables and fruit preserved in oil, vinegar or lemon juice and spices) on sale.

BEAUTY CARE

Shahnaz Husain Herbal – *D4. C-70, Raman Marg, Tilak Nagar.* Herbal products and beauty treatments. Manicure, facial massage, henna applications.

Biotique – *C3. M.I. Rd, east of Niros.* Facial massage; more expensive than Shahnaz Husain.

BOOKSHOPS

Books Corner – *C3. M.I. Rd, next to Niros. Open daily 10am–10pm.* Newspapers and magazines, novels, art books. Also in the **Rajputana Palace Sheraton (Bookwise), Arya Niwas** (illustrated books) and **Rambagh Palace Hotel** (including antiquarian books).

🕮 **Worth knowing** – If you are planning to visit Shekhawati, invest in a copy of the guide by Ilay Cooper, The Painted Towns of Shekhawati (updated 2008), from one of the bookshops.

SHOPPING CENTRES

Shopping complexes and malls such as **Crystal Palm**, Sadar Patel Rd (*A4*), **Metropolitan Mall**, opposite (*A4*), or **Gaurav Towers**, on Jawaharlal Nehru Rd (*C4*), sell both Indian and European branded products.

SPORTS AND ACTIVITIES

CINEMA

Raj Mandir – *C3. Bhagwan Das Rd, Panch Batti Circle.* ☏ *0141-2379372.* Screenings (approx. Rs.110, lasting almost 3hr) at 12.30pm, 3.30pm, 6.30pm and 9.30pm. Opulent and luxurious, an amazing venue – the perfect place to watch Bollywood films. Not to be missed.

SPORTS

🏊 Swimming pools – Several hotels have swimming pools open to non-residents: Umaid Bhawan Guest House, Raj Mahal Palace, Narain Niwas Palace. Budget for approx. Rs.150–200.

Horse riding and polo – **Rajasthan Polo Club** – *B4. Near the Rambagh Palace and the Polo Ground.* ☏ *0141-2385380. www.indianpolo.com.* During the polo season, tournaments are held between December and January and in March, but some matches take place as early as October. They are usually held between 3pm and 5pm. The owner of the Diggi Palace Hotel is happy to provide anyone interested with the details.

MEDITATION AND YOGA

Free yoga sessions are held in **Central Park** (*BC4*) 6.30am– 7.30am and 6pm–7pm daily.

Dhamma Thali Vipassana Meditation Centre – *off map, E2. Road to Galta.* ☏ *0141-2680220. www.thali.dhamma.org.* Sessions are held in the open air; 10-day meditation courses follow the teaching of S.N. Goenka. Donations.

EXCURSIONS

TRAVEL AGENCIES

Rajasthan Tourism Development Corporation (RTDC) – *B3. Transport Unit, Old Govt. Hostel Campus, M.I. Rd, on the corner of Ajmer Rd.* ☏ *0141-2375466. Open daily 8am–8pm.* Daily tours of the city. Car hire (minimum 60km Rs.1,600; maximum 120km, 12hr for approx.

Arya Niwas – *B2. Arya Niwas Hotel, Sansar Chandra Rd.* ☏ *0141-2372456. www.tours2rajasthan.com.* A small, well-run agency that organises trips to Shekhawati, Pushkar, Agra, etc. Car hire at reasonable prices. Excursions to Amer and Sanganer.

Athens Tours – *C1. Kinnra Guest House, opposite the Bissau Palace Hotel.* ☏ *0141-2300324. www.athenstours.in.* Treks by camel or horse, day trips to Pushkar, Ranthambore, Sariska and Shekhawati. Car hire at reasonable prices.

EVENTS AND FESTIVALS

Makar Sankranti – 14–15 Jan. A festival that marks the entry of the sun into the sign of Capricorn with a flurry of kite flying.

Festival of elephants – *See Calendar of Events.*

Gangaur – 3rd and 4th day after the new moon in Mar–Apr (22–23 Mar 2015, 10–11 Apr 2016, 30–31 Mar 2017). In honour of spring and the goddess Gauri (Parvati), a procession with elephants and camels makes its way from the City Palace to Tal Katora, leading Shiva and Parvati to their home as newlyweds. The festivities last for 18 days.

Teej – 3rd and 4th day after the new moon of Jul–Aug. A procession takes place similar to the one for Gangaur to celebrate the arrival of the monsoon and the marriage of Teej (Parvati) with Shiva. Swings are decorated with leaves from the ashoka tree.

Ranthambore National Park★★

Imagine a dry forest of dhak and banyan trees with, in their centre, a rocky outcrop crowned with an imposing fort in ruins. The scene is set and ready for the leading actor: Shere Khan, the lord tiger of the jungle. The region of Ranthambore is one of the homes of the last living specimens of the breed, in danger of extinction. With luck, you can catch a glimpse of him on the trail of a gazelle or bathing in a lake. If he fails to favour you with an appearance, the sight of stags, nilgai and wild boar may perhaps console you. There is also the possibility of exploring the ruined fort, now partially over-run by the jungle, and the highly revered shrine of the elephant-head god.

Most of the area's hotels are located out in the countryside, along the road from Sawai Madhopur to the park. From dusk to dawn, visitors are plunged into this unspoilt wilderness, which is undeniably one of the attractions of a visit. If given the opportunity, don't miss a trip to the **outlying villages** to see their white-washed paintings; the local women decorate the outer walls of their mud-built dwellings with peacocks and elephants symbolising the goddess of prosperity, Lakshmi, as well as parrots, suns and, of course, tigers.

▷ **Location:** The railway station of Sawai Madhopur, the town near which the park is situated, will be your main point of reference. North-west of the station lie the few streets of Sawai Madhopur where you will find a bank and post office. There are several small restaurants around Bazriya Market or on Main Bazaar, the main commercial thoroughfare. Ranthambore Road leads to the park; it is just south of the railway tracks and it is along this road that the hotels are located.

🕐 **Timing:** Wherever you are coming from, it is best to travel to Sawai Madhopur by train, as this transportation is much quicker than the buses in this region. Once in Sawai Madhopur, book your safari the day before (at the latest) or book online, and allow a half-day. From July to September, during the heaviest rains, do not bother stopping here, as the park is closed. For a quieter atmosphere, which will increase your chances of seeing animals, avoid weekends and Indian holiday periods.

Site of the First Jauhar

Ranthambore Fort, founded in the 10C by the **Chauhan** Rajputs, is claimed to be the oldest stronghold in Rajasthan still standing, after that of Chittaurgarh. It was also the scene of the first *jauhar* (collective immolation) in 1301, when the sultan of Delhi, Ala uddin Khilji, treacherously captured the fort after a year-long siege. All the Rajput women threw themselves into the flames, preferring death to being captured alive by the Muslims. Recaptured by the Rao Chauhans of Bundi, the stronghold was surrendered to Emperor Akbar in 1569 almost without a struggle—the last major Rajput fort to give in to the Mughals. In the late 17C, the region fell under the control of the maharajahs of Jaipur, and it became one of their favourite big-game hunting grounds.

GETTING THERE AND AROUND

BY TRAIN – Take the train rather than the bus, which is much slower, to **Sawai Madhopur**. The train station is located south-east of Sawai Madhopur, between the city and the entrance to Ranthambore park, approx. 10km away. ✆131 and 07462 220222. www.irctc.co.in. For Jaipur, take the morning Superfast train (2hr journey time). Every day, 5 Express trains leave for Delhi (5–6hr journey time) via Bharatpur (2hr 30min) and Mathura (3hr 45min).

BY BUS – For Jaipur, avoid local buses that leave from **Dausa–Jaipur Bus Stand**, a simple hut on a street perpendicular to Bazriya Market; instead take the 3 Express services (5hr via Tonk), which depart from the **Tonk Bus Stand**, at the west end of Bazriya Market, or better still, take the train. For Delhi (10hrs) and Ajmer (6–8hr), change in Jaipur.

TOURIST INFO

Info: Tourist Reception Centre (RTDC) – Ranthambore Rd, 1.5km from Sawai Madhopur Train Station, and opposite Anurag Resort Hotel. ✆ 07462 220808. www.rtdc.in. For the park, visit www.ranthambore nathionalpark.com..

Tiger Project Reception Centre – 2km before entrance to park, on Ranthambore Rd, set back from the road. ✆ 07462 220223. www.project tiger.nic.in/ranthambhore.htm.

🕙 **Worth knowing –** Purchase **tickets** and book **vehicles** for the park the day before. Your hotel will arrange these for a small commission. Please note that, as the reserve does not admit more than 280 visitors per day, it is strongly advised to book on the website www.rajasthanwildlife.in, which has a larger number of places. Do not leave it too late: jeep seats are sometimes difficult to book.

TIGER TRAIL SAFARI

12 km from Sawai Madhopur. Park 🕙*closed Jul–Sept* 🎟 *Entrance charge Rs200, video Rs200. The park can be visited only in groups and in Tiger Project vehicles (Rs403/person in one of the 10 jeeps that carry 6 people or Rs310/person in one of the 4 canters—trucks with 20 places). Both daily tours start at Tiger Project Centre (those staying in a hotel in Ranthambore Rd can join en route) between 6am and 7am, depending on time of year, and between 2pm and 3.30pm.*

Allow a half-day: 30min drive to the entrance, 3hr in the reserve and 30min for return. Carry binoculars.

In April, when dhak *(Butea monosperma* or 'flames of the forest'*)* flowers, the vast forest is covered in red scarlet patches. Then the torrid heat of May and June burns the dead leaves brown. This pre-monsoon period is the time when the **sightings of tigers** are most frequent: the drought makes the undergrowth less dense and forces the animals to drink at water holes created by park staff in the park's 1,330sq km.

🕙 **Worth knowing –** May and June find the fewest tourists in the park.

The rest of the year visitors are likely to meet more humans than wild beasts, but the local tigers have have been known to appear in front of lorries packed with enthusiastic, noisy tourists. Other local inhabitants you might see include panthers (cheetahs or leopards) or wild cats. Cervidae (sambar, chital) and antelopes (chinkara gazelles) are numerous and regularly sighted. In addition, the park's lakes abound in **crocodiles** (introduced by park staff) and are also home to diverse species of waterfowl.

In the heart of the park lies the 13C **fort** (🕙*open sunrise-sunset; access from car park near inner gate at departure point for the safaris; fort is not included in safaris; rent a jeep or ask to be dropped off after the morning safari, but make sure you hire*

Man or Tiger?

Safeguarding the survival of the tiger (and the forest) or protecting the lives of the villagers? That is the dilemma Indian environmentalists face since the man-tiger balance was overturned in the 1950s–60s. The creation of national parks, followed by the ban on tiger hunting (1970) and the launch in 1973 of the **Tiger Project** (see Sariska) have greatly helped to protect the endangered feline, but to the detriment of the villagers living around the park lands. At Ranthambore more than 1,000 Meena peasants were expelled from their lands in order to extend the forest and the tigers' territory. Nothing was done to re-house the villagers. The people living around the park's edges turned to the forest to find grazing for their cattle, wood for fires and water when their wells ran dry. The **Ranthambore Foundation** was set up in 1988 with the goal of promoting good relations between the villagers and the park. It has implemented various development projects (see p 7), such as one aimed at replacing outdoor grazing stock with barn-fed cattle and at developing alternative revenue sources such as local crafts. Incorporated into the Tiger Project in 1973 and declared a national park in 1980, the park had 15 tigers when first created; now the number is about 50.

a guide). The steep path up to it passes four successive gates. The impressive ramparts and bastions can still be seen, but they are only ruins, half-hidden under brambles and gigantic trees of the jungle. Paving stones have been forced upwards and dislodged by the vigorous underground root systems. A walk through the ruins will lead to a small **temple** to Ganesha, which is particularly popular at the time of Ganesh Chaturthi, the god's birthday *(Aug–Sept)*. Ranthambore's Ganesha is also quite sought-after by engaged couples, and he always receives the first invitation to their wedding since he is thought to bring luck to any enterprise.

ADDRESSES

STAY

RANTHAMBORE RD:

Vinayak (RTDC) – *6km from train station.* ✆ 07462221169. www.rtdc.in. 14 rm. Rs.600/2,200. A pleasant, well-run hotel, situated, on the edge of the 'buffer zone' around the park. Rather expensive, but the price is explained by the setting. Simple, somewhat repetitive, but decent food.

Castle Jhoomar Baori (RTDC) – *1km from Ranthambore Rd and 6.5km from train station.* ✆ 07462 220495. www.rtdc.in. 12 rm. Rs.2,750/4, 600. Built against a hillside, hidden within the trees on the edge of the park's 'buffer

Sambars, Ranthambore National Park

© Anurag Mallick, Priya Ganapathy/MICHELIN

zone', this modest mid-19C hunting lodge of the maharajah of Jaipur has spacious rooms and smaller rooms, most of which still have their original *arayish* (traditional wall coverings). Hardly in the luxury bracket, the hotel offers the usual laid-back service found in an RTDC establishment. Its excellent location means that it is often fully booked, particularly at the weekend.

Dining Room, Nahargarh Ranthambore

© Anurag Mallick, Priya Ganapathy/MICHELIN

Ranthambore Bagh – 07462 221728, 91 8239166777, www.ranthambhore.com. *23 rm & tents. Wi-Fi. pets allowed. Room Rs.3300, Tent Rs.3780.* Run by a wildlife conservationist and photographer, this small wildlife lodge attracts photographers, filming crews, and birders who can vouch for the unparalleled jungle experience offered here. Safaris with expert wildlife guides and naturalists and visits to craft centres arranged. Relax in the homey ambience of your room or tent, relish fresh meals in the dining room and music by folk singers.

Dev Vilas – *Village Khilchipur.* 07462 252168/94. www.devvilas.com. *28 rm. All meals included. Wi-Fi. Rs.12,500, Foreigners $240.* Set on 3.5 acres close to the park entrance, this jungle lodge harks to bygone times. Each of its 21 suites and 7 tented villas is built and designed differently, using local material and crafts. Fateh's, the bar named after legendary tiger conservationist Fateh Singh Rathore, has tiger paintings from the Ranthambore School of Art. Dine at the Audubon Room adorned with limited edition lithographs by Audubon himself. Enjoy al fresco dining by the pool or savour the sunset from the terrace overlooking the magnificent Aravalli ridges. Park safaris can be arranged.

Nahargarh Ranthambore – *Village Khilchipur.* 07462 252281/82. www.nahargarh.com. *69 rm. All meals included. Wi-Fi. Rs.12,400–Rs.16,300.* Built from scratch in 2002 by the royal family of Alsisar, the colossal fortress edifice is surrounded by grass and scrubland and evokes the grandeur of blue-blood ancestry. Plush rooms fitted with divans in bay windows, large garden compounds and courtyards and a generous pool. The spa has soft-lit niched walls with mirror motifs. Fairytale dining in a setting with hand-painted walls, while the staff caters to your culinary needs. **The Annexe**

(Haveli), a smaller palace nearby, offers 21 rooms. *Rs.11,000.*

Oberoi Vanyavilas – *Ranthambore Rd, Sawai Madhopur.* 07462 223999. www.oberoihotels.com. *Wi-Fi. 25 tents. Rs.56,000.* India's premiere wildlife resort, Oberoi offers luxury tents with king-size four-posters, wooden flooring, luxe bathrooms and private decks overlooking a watercourse. Dine on Indian, Thai or Western cuisine in a restaurant decorated with hand-painted nature frescoes, relax by the poolside bar and try innovative therapies like the Indian Spice Wrap at the spa.

Sawai Madhopur Lodge – *(Taj Group) 2.5 km from train station.* 07462 220247. www.tajhotels.com. *Billard, Internet. 36rm. 133/173€.* The public areas of the hotel are in a bungalow built in the 1930s by the maharajah of Jaipur: a round Art Deco living room leads onto a veranda and a wood-panelled restaurant. Guests travel by golf buggy to small, somewhat nondescript rooms situated in cottages in an attractive park.

Treehouse Anuraga – +91 9871034969, 8805881439, www.treehousehotels.in. *44 rm. Wi-Fi. Rs.12,000-Rs.30,000. Deluxe, premium rooms and suites.* This classic luxury resort spells Rajasthani splendour in marble and stone with pillared passageways, floral designs and sprawling rooms. Established in 1987 by one of the oldest families in Sawai Madhopur, the place offers memorable experiences such as visits to farms, craft centres and pottery villages.

Sariska National Park★

These wild rambling hills, covered in acacia trees and scattered with rocks, shelter one of Rajasthan's two tiger reserves (the other is at Ranthambore). The site was formerly a favourite hunting ground of Alwar's maharajahs. The capricious Jai Singh, who used to spear-hunt boar and tiger here, also had a palace built in 1902 (now the Sariska Palace Hotel), whose grandiose turrets and façade contrast with the forest's wild beauty.

TIGER RESERVE TOUR

Created in the 1950s, the reserve was incorporated into the **Tiger Project** (*see sidebar below*). The reserve became a national park in 1982. More than a third of its 866sq km of land is still occupied by villagers. Decimated by poaching, tigers were reintroduced in the park in 2009. But the chance of your sighting one of the two tigers is slim. You are more likely to see leopards and panthers. Those who want to increase their chances of seeing a tiger have to brave the stifling heat of April through June; the dry weather of the pre-monsoon periods makes the animals dependent on the artificial water holes dug by park authorities near the trails. Animals you will see might include the chital and sambar, antelopes, both the large nilgai, the four-horned chousingha, Arabian gazelles (chinkara), wild boars, peacocks and langurs.

Info: Tiger Project Reception Centre – 300m from park entrance. 0144 2841333. Open Oct–Mar 7am–3.30pm, Apr–Sept 6am–4pm. Buy park tickets and make jeep reservations at the centre.

Location: 35km south-west of Alwar.

Timing: Buses from Alwar (45min) and Jaipur (3hr) stop at park entrance every 30min. Park open sunrise–sunset. Day fee: Rs.200/person, Rs.125/vehicle; Rs.200 for video. www.sariskanationalpark.com.

Safety – Exploring the park on foot is not permitted as wild cats are present. Visitors must take a guide (Rs.150).

About 20km into the park's interior, the ruins of the 17C **Kankwari Fort** rise from the water's edge. Here Emperor Aurangzeb is said to have imprisoned his brother, the rightful heir to the throne. The **Pandu Pol** ('the Gate of Pandava'), dates back to the mythical era of the *Mahabharata*, when the five Pandava brothers and Draupadi, the wife they shared among them, were exiled in the region. One of the brothers, Bhim, of legendary strength, is said to have shattered a rock with his sword, creating a waterfall that provides drinking water for the thirsty animals even today.

Tiger Project: Boon or Bane?

The tiger protection program, with a total of some 20 reserves throughout India, was started jointly in 1973 by the Indian and State governments. Despite a promising start, it was soon undermined by negligence and corruption. Hunting parties organised for wealthy city dwellers and other irregularities transformed the project into a disaster, to the extent that, in the early 1990s, the number of tigers had dropped below the counts of 10 years earlier. The poaching scandal ended the presence of tigers in the park altogether, until 2009 when the Ranthambore National Park gave two of its tigers to Sariska. The terms of delivery—that the reserve ban private cars and limit the number of visitors—have not yet been enacted.

Alwar★

This small town, languorously sprawled at the foot of a circle of rocky hills, constitutes the meeting point between the rectilinear plain of Delhi and the first eastern foothills of the Aravalli Range. The north-eastern flat, monotonous terrain stops dead at Alwar, replaced there by rocky outcrops that paint the countryside a colourful blend of pinks. With its majestic natural setting, Alwar, the historic gateway to Rajasthan and the district capital, is a quiet provincial town. Few vehicles are found in the narrow lanes around the palace, and few tourists venture this far. This city is one of the last remaining in Rajasthan where provincial life can be observed unchanged while enjoying a cup of tea at a corner cafe.

▰▰ WALKING TOUR

To absorb the city's atmosphere, stroll along the Sarafa Bazaar, a commercial street of jewellers and bakeries sitting side-by-side.

▶ If coming from the bus station, follow the main avenue that forks left for about 200m, then turn right in front of the Ashok Theater. Begin the tour at the Tripolia Gate. Allow 2hr.

▶ **Population:** 313,000.
▯ **Info: Tourist Reception Centre (RTDC)** – This welcoming centre has a map of the city.
▷ **Location:** 143km north-east of Jaipur, 163km south-west of Delhi.

CITY PALACE★

The monumental **Tripolia Gate★** (Third gate), impressive but dilapidated, houses a small temple devoted to Shiva. Off to the left, a little lane leads to a square frequented during office hours by public writers and civil servants. The district's administrative centre is installed in the royal palace, the façade of which, adorned with Bengali-roofed balconies, can be seen to the right of the square. The local authority's numer-ous employees take frequent tea breaks here, nibbling on snacks presented on leaves, fastened together by an acacia thorn to make small bowls *(dona)*. The empty bowl is much appreciated by foraging pigs and cows, and the acacia thorns can frequently be found 'stapled' to official administrative documents. The **royal palace** (or Vinay Vilas) was built at the turn of the 18C by Pratap Singh and his successor Vinay Singh. The entrance to the **main courtyard** reveals an attractive multi-coloured

Baby of the Rajput Kingdom

The city of Alwar was founded around the end of the first millennium AD. Soon its value as a strategic observation point made it a much coveted prize. It passed from hand to hand: from the Rajputs to the Mughals, the Pathans, and then to the Jats of Bharatpur. Finally in 1771, the Rajput **Pratap Singh** (related to the Kachwahas of Jaipur) conquered Alwar, and founded one of Rajasthan's most recent independent kingdoms. A subtle blend of astute diplomacy enabled the new dynasty to withstand the neighbouring Rajput and Jat kingdoms and the military might of the Maratha chiefs. In 1803 Bakhtawar Singh formed an alliance with the British, thus ensuring his kingdom's continued peace. Freed of their military duties, the town's sovereigns, turned maharajahs, became active patrons of the arts, investing generously, even extravagantly, as in the case of Jai Singh, maharajah from 1857 to 1933.

Deposed for Cruelty to Animals

Jai Singh considered himself to be an incarnation of Ram. He went so far as to have a copy of the god's crown made, which he wore in place of the traditional Rajput turban. A great car enthusiast, particularly of Hispano-Suizas, Jai Singh bought them three at a time, painted blue (Alwar's colour) or gold-plated, and had them buried when he felt they were past their prime. Lavish and sophisticated, he was a keen hunter, and his reputation as a cruel sadist was legendary. He was finally deposed by the British (for cruelty to animals, having had his horse burnt alive), and ended his days in Paris, dying in 1937.

marble floor. A ceremonial staircase, complete with Bengali-roofed loggia and flanked by two elegant *chhatris* (pavilions), leads to the **durbar** (reception hall), which is now empty, but whose white and gold walls have kept their pristine appearance.

Government Museum★

Access by the staircase in the wing that opens onto the square. ○ *Open Tue–Sun 10am–4.30pm.* ○ *Rs.10. Photography is not permitted.*

The museum occupies the top floor of the palace. Its collections are presented in an old-fashioned manner that suits the antiquated appearance of the building. Some of the timeworn, dusty wooden display cases house pleasant surprises, but most of the explanations are in Hindi and so not easy to comprehend. The **first room** depicts life at court, with royal costumes, trinkets, ivory sandals and **musical instruments**, among which are two magnificent peacock-shaped *dilrubas* (stringed instruments). In the section devoted to **manuscripts and miniature paintings★★**, note the exquisitely illustrated 18C *Bhagavad Gita* and *Ramayana* manuscripts, together with those of the *Babur Nameh* (Emperor Babur memoirs) and the *Gulistan* ('The Rose Garden'), the work of a 13C Persian poet, Saadi. Among the various Rajput schools are works by the Alwar kalam (Alwar's school of painting), notable for their vividly coloured borders. The **weapons** section is well supplied with sabres, daggers and katar, including swords and armour worn by Muhammad of Ghor, and emperors Akbar and Aurangzeb. The **terrace** provides fine views of Alwar, the surrounding hills and the old fort.

▷ Back on the square, walk past the palace to the right, to an open staircase that leads to a platform on which the cenotaph stands.

City Palace

© Anurag Mallick, Priya Ganapathy/MICHELIN

CENOTAPH OF MAHARAJAH BAKHTAWAR SINGH★★

Erected in 1815 by Singh's son, the cenotaph is also called **Rani Mausi ki Chhatri** in honour of the sovereign's widow, who died on her husband's funeral pyre.

The red sandstone of the lower storey, dotted with kiosks, contrasts pleasantly with the white marble of the upper storey *(shoes must be removed)*. Around the base of the elegant **ribbed dome** can still be seen a few damaged paintings (a frieze of horsemen and camels and geometric blue and gold motifs) and fine **carving** (musicians, divinities and camel and elephant processions) . Relief footprints on the white tiled floor commemorate the sacrifice of the queen. Admirers of the devoted widow regularly bring flowers here. Surrounded by *ghats* that punctuate slender *chhatri*, the pool would be romantic if it were not covered by a crust of greenish foam.

☺ **Worth knowing –** The rear of the palace is especially photogenic in late afternoon, when the sun shines on it. Dominating the whole area is the rocky peak crowned by **Bala Qila Fort**, one of Rajasthan's oldest strongholds *(now a radio station that can be visited; check with the palace office).*

ADDRESSES

🛏 STAY / 🍴 EAT

🍽🍽🍽🍽 **Amanbagh** – *Ajabgarh.* 𝄢 *01465 223333, 91 9828 166737. www.amanresorts.com.* ♿. *40 rm. Wi-Fi. 🖵 only in packages. Rs.24,000-Rs.42,000.* Surrounded by vestiges of a lost kingdom, this swish resort at Ajabgarh bears the signature style of Aman Resorts. Located on the erstwhile hunting grounds of the Maharaja of Alwar, it echoes Mughal-era glory with immaculate *haveli* suites, marble bathtubs, lush lawns and candlelit dinners under *chhatris*. Pamper yourself with a spa treatment and a choice of courtyard suites, garden suites, terrace suites or pool pavilions, each with private pool.

Guided walks and short excursions via camel or jeep, wildlife trips to Sariska and historical trails to fort ruins, ancient temples, *chhatris* and the haunted city of Bhangarh *(15km away)* can be arranged for you by the resort.

🍽🍽🍽🍽 **Tijara Fort§** – *Village Tijara, 60km from Alwar, Off NH 8 (Delhi-Jaipur Highway).* 𝄢 *(011) 46661666, www.neemranahotels.com. 20 rm. Wi-Fi. 🖵 Rs.12,000-plus.* Resuscitating a king's incomplete dream project conceived in 1835, this magnificent fort-palace hotel hugs a bare hill with seven-tiered hanging gardens. As Rajasthan's first tourism initiative under Public-Private Partnership, it is a celebration of art and architecture. Don't miss the sunken pool, underground spa, quirky camel-column pergola, giant handwoven magic lantern and Rani Mahal's 20 rooms honouring India's famous women artists. High in windy Hawa Mahal, guests enjoy splendid countryside views and delicious cuisine.

🍽🍽🍽 **Dadhikar Fort** – *Village Dadhikar, 6km from Alwar.* 𝄢 *+91 9950449900, www.dadhikar.com, 17 rm+3 tents. 🖵. Rs.4700-Rs.10,000. Lunch buffet Rs.500, Dinner buffet Rs.600. Entry for non-resident guests Rs.200.* Set on a hillock in the Aravallis, this hidden 10C fort served as a royal camp *(dera)* for King Chand's family, and was earlier known as Derakar. After the family moved to Nikumbh Mahal at Bala Qila in Alwar, it became a military base for making artillery. The secluded fort-palace hotel offers a choice of unusual heritage rooms or a tented stay. Traditional vegetarian fare is served, and activities include cooking lessons, camel rides and treks to ancient caves with pre-historic rock art.

🍽🍽 **Hill Fort Kesroli** – *Village Kesroli, near MIA Post Office-Bahala.* 𝄢 *011 46661666, 9414050053. www.neemranahotels.com, 21 rm, Wi-Fi. 🖵 Rs.3000-7000. Lunch Rs.500, Dinner Rs.600.* Neemrana's tiny medieval fort occupying a rustic setting ranks among India's oldest hotels. The historic fort was built 700 years ago and still captures Old World warmth with creeper-clung walls, narrow stairways and terraces overlooking swathes of mustard fields. Quiet garden spaces, starlit evenings of folk music and good food make it an unforgettable stay.

Pushkar★★

One of the holiest cities of Hinduism, Pushkar is quite popular among young Westerners visiting India, some of whom stay for months at a time. The local population has adapted to this clientele and opened terrace restaurants (all strictly vegetarian), inexpensive guest houses and large numbers of stalls selling poor-quality arts and crafts at high prices. This charming little town nestling at the foot of the Aravallis, with its picturesque lake surrounded by hills and its pedestrian-only lanes and streets is an ideal spot to stop and rest for a few days. Hindus hold Pushkar Lake to be the most sacred in India and a purifying dip in its waters is considered to be particularly beneficial at certain dates, primarily during the full moon of October–November, when the incredible camel fair takes place. The fair, extolled by travel agents all over the world, now attracts vast numbers of tourists who come especially to India to attend. This fame has left Pushkar with a somewhat artificial atmosphere. Nonetheless, it is well worth taking the time to enjoy the sound of the bells ringing in the ceremonies held in the town's numerous temples, or taking a walk out of the town's bustling centre up into the quiet peace of the surrounding hills, animated only by the chirping of crickets.

●ⱳ WALKING TOUR

Allow 3hr, or 4hr if you include a visit to the temple of Savitri.

On the main street, which provides regular glimpses of the *ghats*, the atmosphere is more markedly commercial, given the long tourist tradition there. Local monkeys are always on the lookout for something to snatch *(so hold onto your bags)*

PUSHKAR LAKE★

Shoes must be removed on the ghats and before entering the temples. Photos of worshippers on the ghats are not allowed.

The lake at Pushkar is said to have appeared when a lotus petal, falling from the hands of Brahma, dropped to the ground here. The northern and western banks of the lake are lined with *ghats* (wide staircases leading down to the water guarded and used by a specific category of Brahmins).

The lake makes the town feel like a miniature white-washed Benares. Early risers will see pious Hindus taking their ritual bath in the lake's waters and will avoid the 'offerers of offerings' who will certainly beg for offerings from you. They stand, facing the rising sun and dip their hands in the water, reciting the

ℹ Info: Tourist Reception Centre (RTDC) – Next to Hotel Sarovar. Open 10am–5pm. General information about the city (small map) and its surroundings. You won't be told anything that you don't already know.

🕐 Timing: To fully appreciate the tranquillity of the city, do not visit in November, during the camel fair. However, if you do want to come for this fair, book your hotel months in advance. Allow 3hr for walking round on foot, 4 hr if you include a trip to the temple of Savitri. Allow an additional half-day for a trip to Ajmer.

🐾 Don't Miss: The lake and ghats (steps) at dawn or at dusk, the hour of prayer; a trip to Ajmer.

following verses: 'I take this bath to wash away the sins of my body, my mind, my words and my touch.' Then they plunge twice under the lake's surface, before pouring water on their heads while

☺ **Touring Tip** ☺

Do not accept any offering (flower petals or other things) to throw into the lake: it is a scam, although many people still allow themselves to be taken in.

Daily Devotions

In this holy city, faith and worship are omnipresent, with all the activities and rituals associated with them. Vendors installed at the entrance to the temples sell mountains of **marigolds** and coloured **powder** that pilgrims use as offerings.

The devout ring the bells hanging at the entrance to the temples to attract the attention of the divinity and, at the same time, to scare away the demons. They set down their **offerings** (including money) at the feet of the divinity, following a ritual of gestures that seem almost automatic, as if observing the ritual is sufficient to please the gods. The latter serves to recharge the worshippers' batteries by the vision *(darshan)* of pious images.

At dusk crowds flock to the shrines to take part in **aarti**. The officiating priest *(pujari)* pays homage to the god by waving a lamp in front of his statue, to the sound of cymbals, bells and tambourines. Monkeys, often present in droves, love to grab the offerings left for the gods.

praying to have the strength to remain pure. They will then recite mantras, sometimes up to 108 times, including the famous *Gayatri Mantra*: 'Brahma is the sun'. The same prayer is repeated at midday and at dusk.

TEMPLES★

Most temples are open sunrise–8.30pm.
Access to the main sanctuary is forbidden to non-Hindus.
Remove shoes before entering.

For Hindus, no more sacred city than Pushkar can be found in Rajasthan. Unfortunately all the old temples of this major pilgrimage centre were razed by Emperor Aurangzeb in the 17C. Pushkar's current shrines, rebuilt in the 18C and 19C, are thus of limited architectural interest, but the atmosphere there represents a unique experience, a complete immersion in the most fervent popular Hinduism. Given their numbers (the city has more than 400 temples), it is pointless to try to visit them all.

Described below are some of the most interesting.

Pushkar Lake

© Anurag Mallick, Priya Ganapathy/MICHELIN

Temple of Brahma

© Jose Fuste Raga/age fotostock

Temple of Brahma

West of the lake. Leave cameras and bags at the entrance.

The most famous temple in the holy city, this is the only temple devoted to Brahma in the world. The 'creative principle' god of the Hindu trinity *(trimurti)* is worshipped as the 'great ancestor' without whom (like the sun) there would be no life on earth.

The entrance stands at the top of a marble staircase. In the courtyard, commemorative plaques show how popular the temple is. Inside the crudely painted blue hall, notice the shrine that houses a four-headed **statue of Brahma**. The four heads symbolise the four *Vedas*. When Brahma fell in love with Goddess Saraswati, he was unable to take his eyes away from her, so he grew three new heads to follow her every movement. Saraswati, embarrassed by such adoration, attempted to flee to the sky, but a fifth head appeared on Brahma's skull. This fifth head was later cut off by Shiva. .

Temple of Savitri

Walk round Brahma temple to the right and take the path on the left. The path drops into peaceful countryside, before leading to the top of the hill *(allow 1hr)*, where this small temple stands, offering superb views of Pushkar, particularly towards the end of the afternoon.

Temple of Radha and Krishna

From Brahma temple, return to the lake. Take first road on the left towards the Paramount Hotel. The family that lives here allows visitors to enter for a small donation. However, they do not want too many tourists, so please be discreet.

Located in a late 19C *haveli,* the temple has a **façade★** covered in **frescoes** depicting musicians, elephants, oxcarts and, reflecting a fascination for European novelties, even cars and an aeroplane. Situated in the left-hand wing of the courtyard, it is decorated with murals evoking the life of the blue-skinned cowherd god.

Temple of Purani Rangji

North of the lake.

The portal of this temple was formerly decorated with frescoes that are almost all covered in whitewash today.

The temple opens onto a courtyard. The façade of the sanctuary, which stands in the middle, has retained its paintings and bas-reliefs depicting mainly Vishnu (to whom the temple is dedicated) lying on Ananta, the snake of eternity. An architectural element typical of the temples of South India, the **gopuram** or doors surmounted by a pyramid with hundreds of carved gods, sit alongside Bengali roofs and locally made multi-lobed arches.

EXCURSION TO AJMER★

Travellers, usually in a hurry to reach Pushkar, see only the bus station in Ajmer. That's a shame because this city of nearly half a million residents may at first appear noisy and polluted, but its old quarters merit a look. In Ajmer, skull-caps and the call of the muezzin replace turbans and temple bells: year-round the faithful come from all over the country to India's most venerated Muslim shrine, the *dargah* (tomb) of the Sufi saint Khwaja Moinuddin Chishti. Urs, the festival that commemorates the saint's death in 1236, draws massive crowds.

AJMER SIGHTS
Dargah Bazaar

The way in to the old town is through the **Delhi Gate**. Walk down the historic centre's narrow streets, lined with popular restaurants and colourful shops. Stroll along the **Dargah Bazaar**, the main street leading to the *dargah* (tomb). Shops selling basic necessities alternate with those offering pious works in Urdu, brightly coloured chadars to lay over the pir's tomb and flower petals for offerings. Wander through the peaceful, picturesque alleyways on the left before entering the *dargah*.

Moinuddin Chishti Dargah★★

Leave shoes at the entrance and cover your head. ☞ *Donations appreciated.*
The *dargah* (tomb) is entered via a garish, green and white **grand gate**, over which rise two minarets. The gate overlooks a courtyard paved with marble where there are stalls selling petals. Note the two gigantic **cauldrons** on either side of the gate, into which pilgrims throw rice and money. During **Urs**, these pots are used to cook large quantities of rice, the distribution of which prompts a joyous free-for-all among the pilgrims. The **mosque** on the right side of the courtyard was built by Akbar and repainted in the colours of Islam. In the second courtyard, the **tomb** of Khwaja Moinuddin Chishti stands out with its white marble dome; a group of *qawwali* singers sit opposite the door, ecstatically singing their love for Khuda (God) to the

Ajmer Info

- **Info:** Tourist Reception Centre (RTDC) – In Khadim Hotel. Open Mon–Fri 9.30am–6pm. List of lodgings and car hire. A small counter at the train station is open for the arrival of major trains.
- **Location:** 15km south-east of Pushkar. Allow 3hr for a visit.

music of *harmoniums* (portable, hand-pumped organs). The **door**, decorated with floral motifs and Quranic inscriptions, opens into the tomb, protected by a silver barrier.

The faithful, dressed in white and wearing traditional skull-caps, walk around the tomb, covering it in rose petals. Visitors may be asked for a donation. During Urs, it is almost impossible to get in, such is the press of the crowds.

Behind the tomb is the grave of the saint's daughter, **Bibi Hafez Jamal**, venerated for her saintliness, together with the tomb of Shah Jahan's daughter. At the rear of the *dargah*, admire the 11-arched façade of the **mosque**, built in white marble by Shah Jahan.

Dargah Bazaar

© Anurag Mallick, Priya Ganapathy/MICHELIN

Adhai-din ka Jhonpra★★

On leaving the dargah, take the road to the left, then turn left by the door and continue straight on for about 150m; take the stairs on the right leading to the mosque.

The enigmatic name of the **mosque**, 'the Hut of Two and a Half Days', appears to stem from the Urs festival, which used to be held here for two and a half days. Another version claims that this was the time it took Muhammed of Ghor and his lieutenant, **Qutb ud-Din**, to destroy, in 1198, all the Jain temples and build a mosque in their place. The early 13C façade was added by Sultan **Iltutmish**. From the road, look at the impressive staircase *(on the right)* that leads to the mosque's door. At the rear of the courtyard stands the superb **façade★★** of the prayer room, reminiscent of the Seljuk style with seven **ogee arches**. The screen made by these arches is covered in intricately sculptured arabesques and carved Quranic inscriptions.

Inside the **prayer room★**, the pillars are composed of three superimposed columns salvaged from the 12C Hindu and Jain temples destroyed by the Muslims. Note the **five domes**, the rosette and other floral motifs.

Back on the road, continue on towards the right. In about 1hr 30min, the ruins of **Taragarh Fort**, founded in 1100, appear. The fine **view** of Ajmer is worth the climb.

Jains

Jainism was founded by **Mahavira** ('the great hero'), a noble and a contemporary of Buddha, who revolted against Hindu ritualism. He advocated a new path in favour of asceticism and the sanctity of life (hence a rigid vegetarian diet). Jains revere 24 **jinas** ('conquerors') who definitively annihilated the karmas. The jinas are also known as **tirthankaras** ('finders of the path'). The white-robed svetambara sect are more numerous in Rajasthan than the more rigorous digambara sect, most of whom live in southern India.

Emperor Akbar's Fort

Walk back down along Dargah Bazaar, head north and then turn right. ○ *Open 10am–4.30pm.* ◎ *No charge.*

Built in 1570, the fort has limited interest. In the courtyard, the handsome private audience hall was the scene of the first meeting in 1616, between a Mughal emperor (Jahangir) and a representative of the British crown (Sir Thomas Roe). It resulted in an agreement whereby the East India Company was granted major trading rights in exchange for protection against Portuguese naval power, an agreement that helped to lay the foundations of British power in the subcontinent.

The **Government Museum** (○ *10am–4.30pm,* ◎*Rs.10*) houses sculptures from the 7C to the 14C.

Nasiyan Jain Temple

On the outskirts of the old town, about 100m north of the fort.
○ *Open 8.30am–5pm.* ◎ *Rs.5.*

Built in 1865, this temple (Soni Temple) hides a surprising **interior**. Resembling a showcase two floors high, the large room, the walls of which are covered in giltwork and mirrors, is filled entirely by a **gold-plated model★** depicting **Jain cosmogony**. A procession of dancers, musicians and elephants with palanquins encircles a gilded miniature palace. A flat circle represents the intermediate area in which mankind lives. The **life of Adinatha**, the first *tirthankara* (○*see sidebar*), is related in five episodes, from his miraculous conception by the God Indra to his 'liberation from earthly life'. The whole impression is one of a playroom for child prodigies rather than a place of worship. The prayer room *(ground floor;* ○*closed to non-Jains)* presents an ornate façade of murals depicting the life of the *tirthankara*.

End with a walk around **Anasagar Lake**, created in the 12C. In the 17C, Emperor Shah Jahan added a Mughal garden, the **Daulat Bagh** (today converted to a public garden, where families picnic on weekends), in which five handsome **marble pavilions** stand.

The Shekhawati★★★

Backed by the last hills of the Aravalli Range, this sand-coloured land spreads out over an arid steppe region, an extension of the Thar Desert to the east. On its long, winding roads, visitors are more likely to encounter camels or donkeys pulling carts than motor vehicles. Trees are few. Only crops such as millet, barley and lentils grow on the sandy terrain, protected by thorny hedges. The towns of the Shekhawati have little more than 50,000 inhabitants, hardly more than a village by normal Indian standards. Yet this apparently forbidding landscape has vast numbers of havelis (dwellings of wealthy merchants) sumptuously decorated with exuberantly naïve frescoes adorning their walls. The works comprise one of the world's largest concentrations of mural paintings.

🙂 *Visit The Shekhawati as soon as possible, as the murals are under threat by owners' negligence, the ignorance of villagers as to their historical value, and the greed of antique dealers who break apart the buildings on behalf of Western collectors.* On haveli walls, paintings of camels and horses mingle with symbols of modernity introduced by the British: trains, motor cars and sewing machines. Families will often let you visit your first courtyard, where there are a few pieces of mixed interest, in exchange for sums that vary considerably. Bear in mind that, when visiting the havelis, you are intruding on the personal living space of families, who are sometimes tired of such invasions of their privacy.

🚗 DRIVING TOUR

The cities on this tour are fairly close to each other (average of 20km apart), but within the cities themselves the streets are narrow and crowded, not suitable for vehicular traffic. To find your way to a haveli, ask at your hotel about the services

🛈 **Info:** At Jhunjhunu, Mandawa Circle, Churu By-pass Rd. ☏ 01592 232909. Open Mon–Sat (except 2nd Sat of month) 10am–1.30pm, 2pm–5pm. The tourist office is far from everything and of little help.

▶ **Location:** Nawalgarh: 145km north-west of Jaipur; Jhunjhunu: 245km south-west of Delhi.

🕑 **Timing:** In Jaipur, rent a jeep with a driver who is familiar with the villages and their havelis for a 2.5-day tour.

☏ **Guided Tours:** In the absence of an excursion organised by the tourist office, check with one of the hotels.

☺ **Don't Miss:** The painted façades of Nawalgarh and Mandawa; a guided tour of the Nadine Le Prince haveli in Fatehpur.

😊 Touring Tip 😊

For a detailed tour of the havelis, buy the guidebook by Ilay Cooper entitled *The Painted Towns of Shekhawati*, on sale at bookstores in Jaipur.

---

of a guide (☞ about Rs.350/day). If you are not pressed for time, explore the streets on your own; the villages are small, and you should not get lost if you ask the local people for directions. Allow 2.5 days.

NAWALGARH★★★

145km north-west of Jaipur.
Allow half a day on foot.
This pleasant town of 60,000 inhabitants, with its well-trodden sandy streets, is one of the best preserved of Shekhawati (it benefits from its stone, rather than

brick, foundations), and makes an ideal base for touring the region. Founded in 1737 by Nawal Singh, one of Rao Sardul Singh's five sons, Nawalgarh was the cradle of prosperous merchant families such as the **Goenka** and the **Poddar**.

Aath Haveli

Take a taxi or rickshaw to **Nansa Gate**, *a decrepit arch that used to provide access to what was once a fortified city.* The first lane on the left leads to a group of six havelis, the Aath Haveli; as *aath* means eight, it is probable that the former owners left the region before completing their building. Most structures are closed and only the paintings on the outer walls can still be admired.

West of the passage, the **Morarka Uattaraa Haveli**★ (🕐 *open 8am–6pm* 🎟 *Rs.50*), features carriages and elephants blessing a couple on either side of the door. Two courtyards are open to the public (note the carved teak doors and windows), but rooms on this floor are empty.

Close by, the **Jhunjhunuwala Haveli** has friezes representing traditional processions with elephants, trains, etc.

Further South

The **Ganga Mai temple** (second half of the 19C), devoted to the goddess Ganga, resembles a haveli with its elegant frescoes and mirrors.

The road that runs to the north, lined with painted houses and traditional shops, crosses a road that you take to the right for 300m to reach the **Parasurampura Haveli**, built at the beginning of the 20C and a rather pretentious construction covered in Europeanised statues and paintings. In the parallel

street, the **Dharni Dharka Haveli** (1930) provides a strange blend of mythological and political scenes: Nehru (in his car) and Mahatma Gandhi are easily recognisable.

Poddar Haveli

Dr Ramnath A. Poddar Haveli Museum.
🕐 *Open 9am–7pm (6pm in winter).*
🎟 *Rs.100 including guided tour. Photos Rs.30; video recording Rs.50.*
Built in 1902, the haveli was renovated in the 1980s. In the **first courtyard**, notice among the frescoes of dancers, warriors and Krishna and his adoring *gopi* (cowherd girls), the outline of an incongruous train. Local artists were just as excited as the rest of India by the appearance of the incredible machines from Europe. A wood and bronze door opens to the **second courtyard** (*reserved only for the family*), also decorated in frescoes. The rooms have been arranged in traditional Rajasthani style and house collections grouped by theme: wedding costumes, musical instruments, even polystyrene models of forts in the region.

Morarka Haveli

50m north. 🕐 *Open 9am–6pm.* 🎟 *Rs50.*
Another haveli owned by the Morarka family (🔆 *see Morarka Uattara Haveli above*), this one has been tastefully restored using original techniques. Note the stained-glass peacock's tail above the doors and in the women's courtyard, there is an unexpected portrait of Christ.

Bhagaton ki Choti Haveli★★

🕐 *Open 7am–6pm.* 🎟 *Rs20.*
This haveli has some well-preserved paintings on its **outer façade** and inner **courtyard**, including those of proces-

Organic Products§

Besides offering traditional games like satola, rounder balla, hardara and lunkyar, and folk art forms of mehndi (henna), mandana and bandhej(tie-dye), the last Shekhawati Festival *(mid-Feb)* also showcased the **Organic Food Bazaar**. Nearly 40 local families involved in organic farming, cooked and served traditional food to tourists. Morarka Organic's **Down to Earth** store (📞 *+91 9414 068505*) in Nawalgarh is a good place to pick up organic products.

sions, the God Krishna and his gopis and a steamboat. The upper-floor **rooms** have frescoes of stylised European scenes typical of the 1930s, including one showing a woman on the accordion and a man with a dog on his shoulders.

Sheesh Mahal★

🕐 Open 7am–6pm. ∞ Rs.20. Leave your shoes next to the family's own.
Going past **Poddar Gate** and along the narrow streets, you will reach the courtyard of a small military fort, **Bala Qila**, where there is a market, shops and tailors. On the left, at the back of the courtyard, a discreet staircase leads to the **Sheesh Mahal** (1737), the Queen's chamber, containing a mosaic of mirrors and fully painted Mughal miniatures.

Around Nawalgarh
Parasurampura★

N 20km south-east of Nawalgarh. Visit in late afternoon when the light is best.
Few visitors ever get as far as this hamlet. Nonetheless, it houses the **cenotaph★★ of Sardul Singh**, and the frescos on its **dome** are among Shekhawati's oldest. Set in a shady garden (offer the guardian in the small square a tip of Rs10), this chhatri was built in 1750 on the site where Rao Sardul Singh was cremated. Note the use of natural pigments. On the lower part of the dome

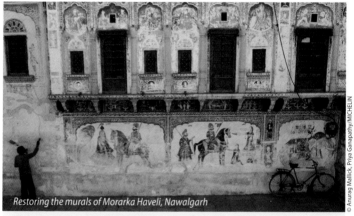

Restoring the murals of Morarka Haveli, Nawalgarh

© Anurag Mallick, Priya Ganapathy/MICHELIN

Case Study in Restoration§

Suffused with striking frescos that have withstood the vagaries of time, Nawalgarh's **Morarka Haveli Museum** occupies a *haveli* that was built in the late 18C, by the current owner's great-great-great-grandfather, who was a patron of the arts. After years of disuse, Kamal Morarka began its restoration in 2004 under the supervision of mural and conservation expert, Dr Basandani Hotchand. Some 700 frescoes and 160 sculpted doors and windows have been painstakingly renovated. The emphasis was on preserving the *haveli* by using traditional materials with minimum intervention in treating the frescoes. Instead of cement and limestone, *laal mitti* (red mud) and river sand were used to strengthen surfaces. Marble dust and slaked lime replaced synthetic resins to reinforce surface plaster. Care was taken to keep the original paintings intact and re-create the past with antique artefacts, old utensils and manuscripts. The museum guide will explain the *haveli*'s typical architectural plan with courtyards, public and private spaces, Marwari culture, and royal palaces versus homes of business tycoons. Today, the *haveli* wears its history in boldly coloured scenes that embody religious images, iconic themes and social commentary. *Painted Heritage Kamal Morarka Haveli Museum*, a fine coffee-table book by Mukesh Gupta, captures the remarkable story of restoring this gem of Nawalgarh.

are deities Rama and his wife Sita, the elephant god Ganesh, and the incarnations of Vishnu. Above are depicted scenes from Hindu Mythology. Note also Sardul Singh, flower in hand, sharing his kingdom among his five sons. The upper part is devoted to Krishna, the favourite divinity of the Rajput Shekhawats.

In 1742, shortly before his death, Sardul Singh had the **temple of Gopinathji** (Krishna) built (in the village), with pious paintings that were never finished. The façade of the **Saraf Haveli** (late 18C) was repainted white (probably for a marriage), but the **inner courtyard** still has its original frescoes.

DUNDLOD

7km north-west of Nawalgarh, on the road to Jhunjhunu. Allow 1hr for a visit.

Renowned for its 18C **fort** (🕐 *open 8am–6pm, ⊜ Rs.20*), now a hotel, the village of Dundlod is a bit disappointing. A branch of the wealthy Goenka family settled in Dundlod, building a large number of havelis before moving to Calcutta. They are now mostly closed and abandoned.

Go down the street 150m; on the left, on an esplanade, the **Seth Arjun Das Goenka Haveli Museum**★★ (🕐 *open 9.30am–6.30pm in winter, 8am–8pm in summer; ⊜ Rs.40*), the only one in town open to the public, has different rooms with mannequins illustrating daily life in times past. Both courtyards

feature frescoes restored in 2006. Leaving the museum to the right, stop by the **Jagathia Haveli**; on its east wall are a thousand and one small scenes that are worth a look.

Return to the square and cross the main road. Down the lane running perpendicular lies a **well** typical of Shekhawati, consisting of a raised platform, decorated with pavilions.

Nearby, the **cenotaph**, built in 1888 in memory of Ram Dutt Goenka, has a dome whose elegant paintings depict, among other things, episodes from the *Mahabharata*.

MANDAWA★★

18km north of Dundlod.
Allow 1hr30min for a visit.

About 1km before reaching Mandawa, stop at the large **water reservoir** *(johda) (right side of the road)* decorated with pavilions, where caravaners used to stop and bathe. A nearby reservoir used to provide drinking water for camels.

The main purpose of a stop in Mandawa is a stay in its **fort** (🕐 *see STAY*) in the centre of town; it belongs to the descendants of Rao Shekha. Its terraces provide an interesting **view** of the town and its spacious haveli, whose walls are unfortunately often black with damp.

Most of the village's havelis suffer from lack of maintenance – many have lost parts, which have been exported. Their concentration and ample frescoes justify

Seth Arjun Das Goenka Haveli Museum

© Anurag Mallick, Priya Ganapathy/MICHELIN

a walk in the streets. One of the most interesting is the **Goenka Double Haveli**, north-west of the town, both buildings of which are covered in faded elephants and horses.

South of the bus station, you will pass several houses with magnificent façades: the **Chokhani Double Haveli**, built in 1875, and the **Mohan Lal Saraf Haveli**, built in 1890, which has retained some of its paintings. Ask to see the **Gulab Rai Ladia Haveli** (behind the fort) as well. Its first courtyard is open to the public. On the outside, the west wall features painted scenes of rural life and of wells in use today.

JHUNJHUNU★★

25km north-east of Mandawa. Plan a half-day; the city should be seen on foot. With 127,000 inhabitants, Jhunjhunu is the second city of Shekhawati, after Sikar. One forgets the size of the city when strolling through its peaceful, historic centre, which is partially closed to traffic. As a result of 350 years of domination by the Qaimkhani Nawabs (1384–1730), the city retains a certain Muslim flavour. As well as a number of havelis, it has a revered dargah (tomb of a Muslim saint), a fort and temples.

Qamr ud-Din Shah Dargah

Accessed by the road from bus station. The *dargah* (tomb) stands on a hillside, removed from the bustle of the nearby bazaar. Qamr ud-Din (1784–1859) was a pir (Muslim saint) worshipped by the Hindu rulers. The latter granted him land on which to build a school, and upon his death, had this shrine built in his honour. Topped with a **white dome**, the tomb is decorated with **paintings** depicting gardens, a lake and floral motifs – out of respect for Islamic precepts that forbid any human or animal representation. Inside, the tomb is covered in a green chadar, the symbolic colour of Islam.

Nehru Bazar★★

Begin your visit on foot at Khatri Mahal, 400m from the dargah. Allow 1hr. In the morning fruit and vegetable sellers set up their stalls right next to the old houses. The narrow, twisting lanes house a number of havelis, several of which still have their original frescoes. Although devoid of its paintings, the **Khatri Mahal** palace, built in the late 18C, used to be one of the region's most impressive monuments, but its two storeys of ochre sandstone, embellished with chhatri and balconies, are now abandoned. Staircases have been removed and replaced by ramps that reach the terrace, where a view takes in the city. You can see the **Badal Fort** (fort of clouds), where, within its imposing walls, stands a statue of Sardul Singh, two uninspiring temples and a garden. In this mainly Muslim neighbourhood, barbers, and dyers specialising in tie-dye techniques, ply their trade outdoors.

Situated 200m from the Khatri Mahal, the **Modi Haveli** has a façade with paintings depicting Krishna as a child, horsemen, and a woman dressed in a sari listening to a gramophone.

In the nearby lane, the **Biharji Temple★** (1776) has fine old paintings, some of the earliest in Rajasthan.

Return to the bazaar's main street to find the **Kaniram Narsinghdar Tibrewal Haveli**, to admire its frescoes.

A little further along the main street, another **Modi Haveli★** (🕐 *open 7am–6pm, 🎫 Rs.50*) preserves fine original frescoes, featuring in particular Krishna and Lakshmi, the goddess of prosperity. Also note the Englishman with his colonial hat.

North of Town

Take a rickshaw to this part of the city: sights are further apart. Allow 1hr. About 1km north of the Nehru Bazaar, the **Rani Sati Temple** is a garish hodge-podge of buildings. It comprises a dharamsala (hostel for pilgrims), courtyards, halls and shrines, the gaudy colours of which are further exaggerated by a myriad of mirrors, silverwork and flashy statues. Built in the late 16C, the temple commemorates Rani Sati, the wife of a local merchant who committed sati by throwing herself on her husband's funeral pyre, thus becoming an object of worship by all staunch defenders of

© Anurag Mallick, Priya Ganapathy/MICHELIN

Detail, Sone ki Dukan

traditional values. Such traditionalists remain legion, for it appears that the shrine is second only to that of Tirupati (in Andhra Pradesh) in the amount of donations it receives. Considered to be an incarnation of Durga, Rani Sati is worshipped in the form of a trident, complete with skirt. Pause for a moment in the **principal hall** *(remove your shoes)*, and admire the walls and ceiling whose frescoes illustrate the saint's sacrifice. Some 800m to the west, a stepwell built in the late 18C, **Mertani Baori★**, presents striking arches, and stairs plunging some 30m underground.

North of town, the small artificial lake, **Ajit Sagar**, was created in the early 20C and adorned with **pavilions** decorated with paintings. On the way, note the **well of Badani Chand**, whose four high towers can be seen from a distance.

MAHANSAR
40km west of Jhunjhunu, on the road to Churu, then turn left towards Ramgarh.
Allow 45min to visit.
This peaceful village, far away from the main roads, produces a famous liqueur called **asha**, based on honey, orange, aniseed, ginger and cardamom.

Dustry lanes wind up to the ochre-coloured walls of this tumble-down **fort**, part of which has been transformed into a hotel. Nearby, in the main street of the hamlet, you'll find a haveli built in about 1850 by an opium and precious-metal merchant, a member of the Poddar family. The ground-floor contains one of the finest examples of a painted room: the **Sone ki Dukan★★**, or gold shop *(⊞ Rs.100 entry fee)*. The reception room is covered in mainly red and gold frescoes. The ceiling features reincarnations of Vishnu *(in the centre)* and episodes from the lives of two of his personifications, Krishna and Rama (in particular the terrible battle during which the Lord Rama, assisted by Hanuman and his army of monkeys, bravely confronted the many-headed demon Ravana, king of Lanka.

As you leave, 100m on the left, the **Tola Ramji ka Kamra** *(⊞ Rs.50)* contains a lavish reception hall (Diwan Khana), commonly known as the Dancing Hall. It has retained its glass chandeliers from Belgium and Austria under a large arch constructed in one piece.

RAMGARH★
6km south-west of Mahansar.
Allow 1hr 30min for a visit.
Founded in the late 18C by the Poddar family, Ramgarh experienced a period of intense commercial activity in the 19C. The Poddars built a number of haveli, the majority of which today are closed and have been dismantled by antique dealers. Even if you are not able to visit the haveli, you will enjoy the atmosphere of this small town, mostly ignored by tourists. It has a charming street bazaar, bordered almostly entirely by haveli, the first floors of which project over the stalls down below, and provide a lovely view. The constant comings and goings of pedestrians and villagers in carts pulled by tiny donkeys makes an enchanting picture.

On the west side, 200m from the street, stand the **Poddar★ cenotaphs** (second half of the 19C) whose domes and Bengali roofs have been blackened by the rains.

Several impressive buildings surround them, but do not be fooled into thinking they are havelis, despite their appearance: they are in fact temples dedicated to Ganesh and Hanuman.

Further on, you reach the 1872 **chhatri of Ram Gopal Poddar★**. Its dome is covered in frescoes, executed with natural pigments, which depict the final combat of the Ramayana: General Hanuman is shown opening the way for Rama's chariot, while the monkeys battle against the horned demons of Ravana, who has kidnapped the virtuous Sita.

End your visit at the **temple of Shani** (Saturn) *(west of the large gate over the main street)*, built in the 1840s, whose decoration combines paintings, a mosaic of mirrors and coloured tiles.

FATEHPUR★

19km south of Ramgarh, on the road to Jaipur. Allow 2hr to visit.

This dusty backwater was formerly the capital of the Muslim dynasty of the Qaimkhani Nawabs until 1731, when it fell under the control of the Hindu raos. It is endowed with large numbers of havelis, most in pitiful condition (several collapse each year), although some nevertheless have stunning frescoes. In streets littered with rubbish and open sewers, little value is given to these treasures.

Constructed in 1802 by a silk merchant, the **Nadine Le Prince Haveli★★★** (📞 0157 123 3024; 🕐 open 9am–6pm; 🎫 Rs.100) was acquired by a French painter who devoted 10 years to restoring it. Visiting here will help you to understand the other old houses, where you will find the same Indo-Mughal architectural structures: a courtyard for visitors, a lodge for musicians, and a richly decorated lounge for guests. Set at an angle to keep out prying eyes, a door leads into the women's courtyard and double kitchen, while upstairs, the master bedroom overlooks the two courtyards. At the rear there is a caravanserai for pack animals. You can continue by visiting the contemporary art galleries in the **Cultural Centre** *(www. cultural-centre.com)*, which exhibit paintings and sculptures by both Indian and foreign artists.

North of the village, the **Jagannath Singhania Haveli★** features intricate predominantly blue-coloured paintings: note Lakshmi surrounded by elephants. You can enter the first of three courtyards. The **Mahavir Prasad Goenka Haveli★★** *(often closed)* possesses magnificent paintings showing Indra and Shiva, elephants and horses, as well as Nehru holding the national flag. Nearby is an 18C well.

LAKSHMANGARH

20km south of Fatehpur. Allow 45min for a visit.

This important market town is largely unknown by tourists. Lakshmangarh was built at the beginning of the 19C by the sovereign of Sikar, and designed along the same lines as the grid layout of Jaipur. Narrow, poorly maintained streets plunge visitors into the depths of

Nadine Le Prince Haveli

rural Rajasthan, dominated by the outline of a **fort** *(visitors not allowed)*. Climb to the top of the ramp to see the gigantic **Char Chowk Haveli** (haveli with four courtyards). A few yards away are the blackened Bengali roofs of the **Murlimanohar Radha Temple** (dedicated to Radha and Krishna), which has retained a number of paintings. Wander round the town, especially around the Clock Tower, to see many painted houses, with frescoes echoing the themes popular in 19C and early 20C Shekhawati: elephants and horses, trains and cars.

ADDRESSES

☜ STAY / ☕ EAT

DUNDLOD

☜☜ **Dundlod Fort** – ☎0159 4252199. www.dundlod.com. 🛏 ✕ ☕ *22 rm. Rs.2,900/3,500* ☐ This 18C fort hotel is located in the heart of town. Portraits of maharajas atop their famous steeds adorn the durbar (reception hall). The hotel has simple rooms as well as an equestrian centre: the focus is clearly on horses rather than home décor.

FATEHPUR

☜ **Haveli Hotel (RTDC)** – *400 m after the state bus stop. Head in the direction of Jaipur.* ☎ 01571 230293.www.rtdc.in. 🛏 ✕ ⊠ *- 8 rm. Rs.1,100/1,650.* ☐. Far from the noise and dust of the city, this house offers bright but poorly kept rooms. The hotel is still a practical place to stay.

JHUNJHUNU

☜ **Shiv Shekhawati** – *Muni Ashram, on the outskirts of the city* ☎ 01592 512695. www.shivshekhawati.com - 🛏 ⊠ *10 rm. Rs.800/1,200.* This small hotel, which is clean but drab, is an acceptable place to stay. Do not expect fine decoration in the rooms. The owner, a former lawyer keen on the culture of Shekhawati, will advise you on interesting tours of the city's havelis.

☜ **Jamuna Resort** – *500m from the Shiv Shekhawati, of which it is part.* ☎01592 232871, http://hoteljamunaresort.com. 🛏 ✕ 🐴⊠ *4 rm. Rs.800/2,200.* The rooms, comfortable and clean, are arranged on either side of a small lawn. The resort has a peaceful, rustic feel. The most

expensive room is full of traditional frescoes depicting couples embracing in poses from the *Kama Sutra*. Classes in Rajasthani cuisine are offered.

MAHANSAR

☜ **Narayan Niwas Castle** – *Mahansar -* ☎ 0159 5264322. http://mehansarcastle.com. 🛏 ✕ ☕ ⊠ *14 rm. Rs.1,600/1,800* ☐ *Rs.150. Rest. Rs.250.* Located in the town centre, this massive 18C fort is a maze of terraces and stairs. With a warm and rustic family atmosphere, this place is ideal for experiencing the life of a desert *thakur* (lord). Rooms have lots of character (columns, ancient frescoes), but little comfort. From the terrace you can enjoy a splendid view over the region. Horseriding and camel trips.

MANDAWA

☜☜ **Mandawa Haveli** – *On the main street, near Sonthaliya Gate.-* ☎ 0159 2223088. www.hotelmandawa.free.fr. 🛏 ✕ ☕ *20 rm. Rs.1,900/3,200.* ☐ *Rs.250. Rest. Rs.300/400.* In this carefully restored haveli, the rooms, furnished with regional antiques, retain its former character. Frescoes, paintings, terraces and an inner courtyard all make this a charming place to stay. The hotel will find a guide for you.

☜☜ **The Desert Resort** – *1.5 km south, along the road to Nawalgarh.* ☎0159 2723151. 🛏 ✕ 🐴 *74 rm. Rs.2,800/3,500.* ☐. Overlooking the plain, these comfortable desert-style cottages, with mud walls and thatched roofs, host a variety of groups. The standard rooms in the main building are less pleasant. Guided tours, using jeeps, horses or camels, offered with the director, a Shekhawati art enthusiast.

☜☜ **Castle Mandawa (Heritage Hotels Association)** – *Town centre.* ☎0159 2223124. www.castlemandawa.com. 🛏 ✕ ☕ 🐴 *86 rm. Rs.4,200/7,000.* ☐. This important 18C Rajput fort is a maze of courtyards, stairs and terraces. Comfortable and furnished with great taste (in a mixture of Rajput and Colonial styles), it enjoys a magnificent setting. Ask for deluxe split-level rooms. Discreet yet friendly service. In the dining room, with dark frescoes, go for the buffet, which in the evening is served in the garden or in a patio surrounding a fire. Guided trips on camels and treks on horseback.

NAWALGARH

🛏 **Shekhawati Guesthouse** – *800m east of Poddar Gate.* ☎ *(01594) 22 46 58.* *www.shekhawatiguesthouse.com.* ✕ *10 rm. Rs.500/800.* ⛄ *Rs.130. rest. Rs.200/300.* Bedrooms in the main building (choose one overlooking the terrace, upstairs) and traditional desert cottages set further back, offer peace and quiet. Internet access, excursions, and an organic vegetable garden used for the preparation of meals, which the hostess will be happy to show you.

🛏 **Apani Dhani§ ((also called 'Eco Farm')** – *At the western edge of the village, on the Jaipur to Jhunjhunu road.* ☎ *01594 222239. www.apanidhani.com.* 📧 ✕ 📠 *9 rm. Rs.1,200/1,350.* ⛄ *Rs.150.* Nice 'ethnic' décor. Attention to detail and cleanliness in small mud and thatched cottages surrounding the central area. Environmentally friendly bathrooms, water heated by solar energy, milk from buffalo at the back of the cottages, and garden vegetables used for meals (vegetarian). Some may find the rules too restrictive *(no smoking and drinking)*.

🛏🛏 **Roop Niwas Kothi (Heritage Hotels Association)** – *1km east of Poddar Gate.* ☎ *01594 222008. www.roopniwaskothi.com.* 📧 ✕ ▼ 🐎 *26 rm. Rs.3,000/5,000.* ⛄ *Rs.200. rest. Rs.400.* A large pale yellow building, with shady lawns at the front and a veranda. The rooms are furnished in Anglo-Indian style but vary greatly, although they are all the same price: look at several. Excellent horseriding facilities – the stables at the rear of the garden have 70 Marwari horses.

🛏🛏 **Roop Vilas Palace** – *Just behind the Roop Niwas Khoti.* ☎ *01594 224321. www.roopvilas.com.* 📧 ✕ ▼ 📠 *Internet. 20 rm,*

3 tents. Rs.3,800/5,000. ⛄. On two floors around a courtyard, the rooms and bathrooms were completely renovated in 2008. The deluxe rooms, which are three times larger than the standard ones, are also much nicer. A large yet well-kept garden opens onto fields and is a great place to while away the time.

🛏🛏 **Koolwal Kothi (WelcomHeritage Hotels)** – *In the historic centre.* ☎ *01594 225817. www.koolwalkothi.com.* 📧 ✕ ▼ *10 rm. Rs.4,000/4,500.* ⛄. This magnificent mansion, built in 1934 in British style, is the only place to stay in the heart of the Nawalgarh havelis. Comfortable rooms in the newest boutique hotel in the area, opened in late 2008.

RAMGARH

🛏 **Ramgarh Fresco Hotel** – *0/19, Subhash Chowk.* ☎ *01571 240595, +91 9971133230. www.ramgarhfresco.com. 14 rm. Rs.2,400-2,950. Fixed menu buffet dinner Rs.400.* Formerly known as Khemka Haveli, the renovated boutique hotel is covered with frescos, from George V to ladies listening to gramophones. Enjoy Rajasthani cuisine and guided walks.

EXCURSIONS

BY CAMEL

Almost all hotels offer camel trips (🐪 *Rs.450/hr/person, Rs.1,800/day*). It is more interesting to go on the trip that starts at Mandawa than the one from Nawalgarh, where the time spent travelling by road is longer.

ON HORSEBACK

Two excellent equestrian centres: The **Shekhawati Brigade Horse Safari** – At the Roop Niwas Kothi Nawalgarh Hotel, www.royalridingholidays.com, and **Royal Equestrian and Polo Centre** – At the Fort Dundlod Hotel (Dundlod), www.dundlod.com. Both organise rides (🐪 *Rs.600–750/hr, Rs.3,000–6,000/ day, already included*) and treks in the Shekhawati (🐪 *Rs.2,000–8,000/day/person depending on the type of accommodation chosen*) or to Pushkar *(1 week)*, Bikaner and Jaisalmer. Possibility of excursions from Jodhpur to Udaipur and Chittaurgarh. Reservations essential. The Dundlod centre also offers polo —on bicycles!

ON FOOT

The **Roop Niwas Kothi**, at Nawalgarh, organises 4-day treks with accommodation, either camping or in the forts of Mahansar and Lohargal.

Roop Niwas Kothi

© Anurag Mallick, Priya Ganapathy/MICHELIN

Rural Stays in Shekhawati

Promoting organic farming, preserving havelis and organising a rural festival since 1996, the MR Morarka Foundation also arranges overnight stays§ in Shekhawati villages that often include organic food, village life experiences and rides on camel, horse and bullock carts. *Rates include breakfast and dinner. Contact Program Co-ordinator SS Shekhawat at Morarka Haveli Museum (☎ +91 9649 578317, 01594 224982) to fix your itinerary. Bookings for the Rural Tourism Initiative can be made at Sahaj Morarka Tourism (☎ 0141 4026094; www.naturetour.in).*

Jor ki Dhani Godham, Katrathal – *Katrathal-Hardyalpura Rd. 24km from Nawalgarh. Host: Kan Singh Nirvan.* ☎ +91-9875039977. *6 rm. Rs.750/person.* Set in a village that dates to 3000 BC, the 15-acre farm has rustic huts made of mud bricks with a wash of cow dung and walls of *aran*, a medicinal plant eaten by goats and camels. When sunlight and air hit the stems, they have a therapeutic effect, air-cooling the huts naturally. The focal point of this stay is the *desi gaay* (country cow). Due to the anti-bacterial properties of cow dung and urine and their immunity against natural diseases, the host uses them in *jivamrit* (organic nectar), spraying it on his plants. Seeds washed in *jivamrit* and mixed with local *chuna* (lime) sprout easily, are resistant to termites and require less water. As a result, crops of *jau* (barley) and *genhu* (wheat) remain free of disease. In the garden, rose bushes, papaya and *musambi* (sweet lemon) grow without being watered, deriving moisture from the atmosphere and not the roots. A small pit for organic waste and dry leaves is covered by dry brush to keep it moist. The host's genuine warmth is complemented by his efficient wife, Sushila Kunwar Rathore, and her delicious cooking. She even leads horse rides. Guests linger for weeks and go back home with deep gratitude. The village and famous Harsh Pahadi nearby, besides ruins of ancient Buddhist temples, can be explored.

Singh Haveli, Singhasan – *4 km from Katrathal. Host: Girwar Singh Shekhawat* ☎ +91-9001675282. *12rm. Rs.750/person.* Ask the host to recount the legend of the village of Singhasan. When it was a small *dhani* (settlement of huts) without a name, the villagers asked a *sanyasi* (sage) who lived in a *dhuni* (sacred place of penance) nearby what the village should be called. He named it after the *singhasan* (throne), where he enshrined the sacred *saligrama* stone, giving the place its unique name. Guests listen to fantastic folk tales and play royal board games like *chausar* during their stay in this 150-year-old haveli with a family that has traditionally served the Raja of Sikar. Though made of bricks, the building remains cool in peak summer.

Explore havelis, the local *garh* (fort) and temples of Thakurji, Satiji and Ramdas Baba and take excursions to Lohargal. Bullock cart rides, horse safaris, camel cart rides and camping in the dunes with stops at various *dhanis* en route can be arranged.

Neki Ram ki Dhani, Bidasar – *8km from Nawalgarh on the Laxmangarh Rd. Host: Neki Ram Godara.* ☎ +91-7577772823. *4 rm, common bath. Rs.650/person.* The host, a certified organic farmer, runs a 9.25ha farm that grows mustard, onion, wheat, cabbage and *bajra* for cattle. He uses only *gobar khad* (cow dung), *kechua khad* (vermi-compost) and organic products. Rustic huts are made of *pani*, a local plant that keeps the room cool in summer and warm in winter; beds (*khaats*) are equipped with mattresses and blankets. Guests can help with farm activities like planting onion saplings, harvesting and chopping wood. The leaves and stems of Khejri trees are used as fodder; logs serve as firewood. Feast on *genhu* (wheat) and *bajra, rotis, chhaas*, curd, *kadhi, rabdi, halwa, kheer*. Off the farm, visit the 300-year-old Dadu Panti Ashram with fine paintings, the Gogaji Mandir, and *teelas* (sand dunes) for camel safaris.

Hari Ram Meel ki Dhani – *3km from Nawalgarh from the Keshav Vatika turn near Rama ki Dhani. Host: Hari Ram Meel.* ☏ *+91- 9828652338. 6 rm, common bath. Rs.1200/person.* This pleasant farm near Nawalgarh grows wheat, barley and vegetables. The old *jhopdas* (huts) have been replaced by a *pakka* structure with clean rooms and toilets for guests. Those who stay here are treated as part of the family and given the same vegetarian fare that the family eats. You can work on the farm during the day and relax with cultural programs in the evening. Visit the Gopalana Johda and Bhadrana Johda, ancient rainwater-harvesting tanks maintained for the upkeep of cattle.

Jor ki Dhani Godham, Katrathal

Laxman ka Baas, Sikar – *7km from Sikar on the Sikar-Jhunjhunu hwy. Host: Ramkumar Kajla. 5 rm. Rs.750/person.* The farm stay in this scenic village offers hands-on rural activities such as cutting fodder, feeding cattle, milking cows, using quaint farm instruments and, relishing home-cooked food in a traditional family set up. Enjoy the simple pleasures of swinging in a *jhoola* (swing) hanging from trees. Explore the picturesque terrain at leisure on foot or in a local jeep.

Kurja Resort, Kalyanpura – *5km from Nawalgarh on the Sikar-Jhunjhunu hwy. Host: Ramovtar Bogalia.* ☏ *91 9414744837. 5 rm. Rs.750/person.* Blending rural hospitality with basic modern comforts, the well-equipped eco-farmhouse of this organic farmer offers a good break from city life. Ample farmland spreads across 3 *bighas (a little more than 1 acre)*, providing the setting for an ethnic lifestyle, sumptuous delicacies and night-time bonfires. Interact with local people and unearth stories of Kalyanpura, Beri and nearby areas. Traditional folk music performances and trips to Nawalgarh's painted havelis.

Village Crafts

Katrathal is counted among the oldest villages of Rajasthan. It is India's largest producer of **clay chillums**§ (earthen pipes for smoking). Katrathal is distinguished for its *karamaati mitti*, Shekhawati's 'magical mud'. Nearly 250 households are involved in the trade, passed down generations. Older craftsmen prefer the hand-turned wheel since the speed can be regulated. Products like *ghadas* and *matkas* (pots and vessels), *gullak* (piggy banks), *chillums* (Rs.5-100), and *diyas* or earthen lamps (Rs.5-10)

Making clay chillums in Katrathal

are available. At the nearby **Ghori market**, watch **bangle-makers**§ dexterously melt, roll, cut and transform *lac* into colourful ornaments. Thereafter, veiled women embellish them with beads and glass crystals. Several homes double up as bangle-making studios, with entire families involved in the process.

INDEX

INDEX

MAP LEGEND

	Sight	Seaside resort	Winter sports resort	Spa
Highly recommended	★★★	🏖🏖🏖	✵✵✵	‡‡‡
Recommended	★★	🏖🏖	✵✵	‡‡
Interesting	★	🏖	✵	‡

Selected monuments and sights

◉ ⇨	Tour - Departure point
⛪ ✝	Catholic church
⛪ ✝	Protestant church, other temple
✡ ☪	Synagogue - Mosque
▱	Building
■	Statue, small building
✝	Calvary, wayside cross
◎	Fountain
•—•—•►	Rampart - Tower - Gate
⋈	Château, castle, historic house
∴	Ruins
⌣	Dam
☼	Factory, power plant
☆	Fort
∩	Cave
▱	Troglodyte dwelling
⊓	Prehistoric site
▼	Viewing table
|/	Viewpoint
▲	Other place of interest
⚶	Hindu Temples

Sports and recreation

⌁	Racecourse
⅄	Skating rink
≋ ⊡	Outdoor, indoor swimming pool
🎬	Multiplex Cinema
⚓	Marina, sailing centre
⌂	Trail refuge hut
◻—■—■—◻	Cable cars, gondolas
◻—+—+—◻	Funicular, rack railway
▂🚂	Tourist train
◇	Recreation area, park
🎭	Theme, amusement park
⚕	Wildlife park, zoo
⊛	Gardens, park, arboretum
⊙	Bird sanctuary, aviary
🚶	Walking tour, footpath
☺	Of special interest to children

Abbreviations

G, POL	Police (Federale Politie)	**P**	Local government offices (Gouvernement provincial)
H	Town hall (Hôtel de ville ou maison communale)	**ℙ**	Provincial capital (Chef-lieu de provincial)
J	Law courts (Palais de justice)	**T**	Theatre (Théâtrè)
M	Museum (Musée)	**U**	University (Université)

Additional symbols

🅘	Tourist information	⊠	Post office
═ ═	Motorway or other primary route	☏	Telephone
❶ ❶	Junction: complete, limited	⊠	Covered market
⊏⊐ ═	Pedestrian street	⸭	Barracks
⊥═══⊥	Unsuitable for traffic, street subject to restrictions	△	Drawbridge
⸺ ----	Steps – Footpath	℧	Quarry
🚆 🚇	Train station – Auto-train station	✕	Mine
🚌 S.N.C.F.	Coach (bus) station	Ⓑ Ⓕ	Car ferry (river or lake)
⊷	Tram	⛴	Ferry service: cars and passengers
Ⓜ	Metro, underground	⛴	Foot passengers only
🅿	Park-and-Ride	③	Access route number common to Michelin maps and town plans
♿	Access for the disabled	Bert (R.)...	Main shopping street
		AZ B	Map co-ordinates

239

Michelin Travel Partner

Société par actions simplifiées au capital de 11 288 880 EUR
27 cours de l'Ile Seguin - 92100 Boulogne Billancourt (France)
R.C.S. Nanterre 433 677 721

© Michelin Travel Partner
ISBN 978-2-067195-02-8
Printed: March 2014
Printed and bound in France : Imprimerie C HIRAT, 42540 Saint-Just-la-Pendue - N° 201403.0221

Although the information in this guide was believed by the authors and publisher to be accurate
and current at the time of publication, they cannot accept responsibility for any inconvenience,
loss, or injury sustained by any person relying on information or advice contained in this guide.
Things change over time and travellers should take steps to verify and confirm information,
especially time-sensitive information related to prices, hours of operation, and availability.